Shojo Beat

ORESAMA TEACHER

Vol. 15

Story & Art by
Izumi Tsubaki

ORESAMA TEACHER

Volume 15
CONTENTS

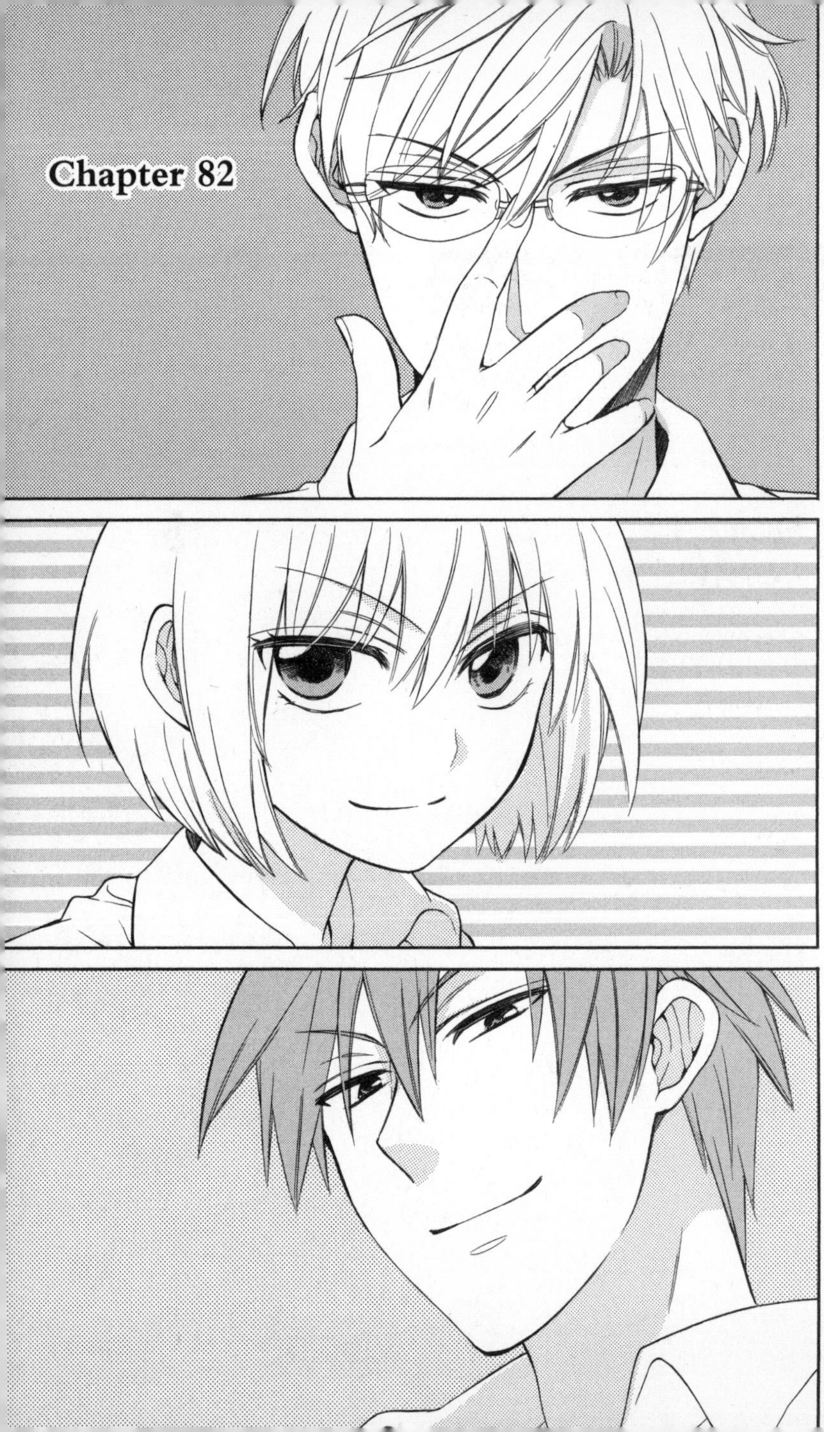
Chapter 82

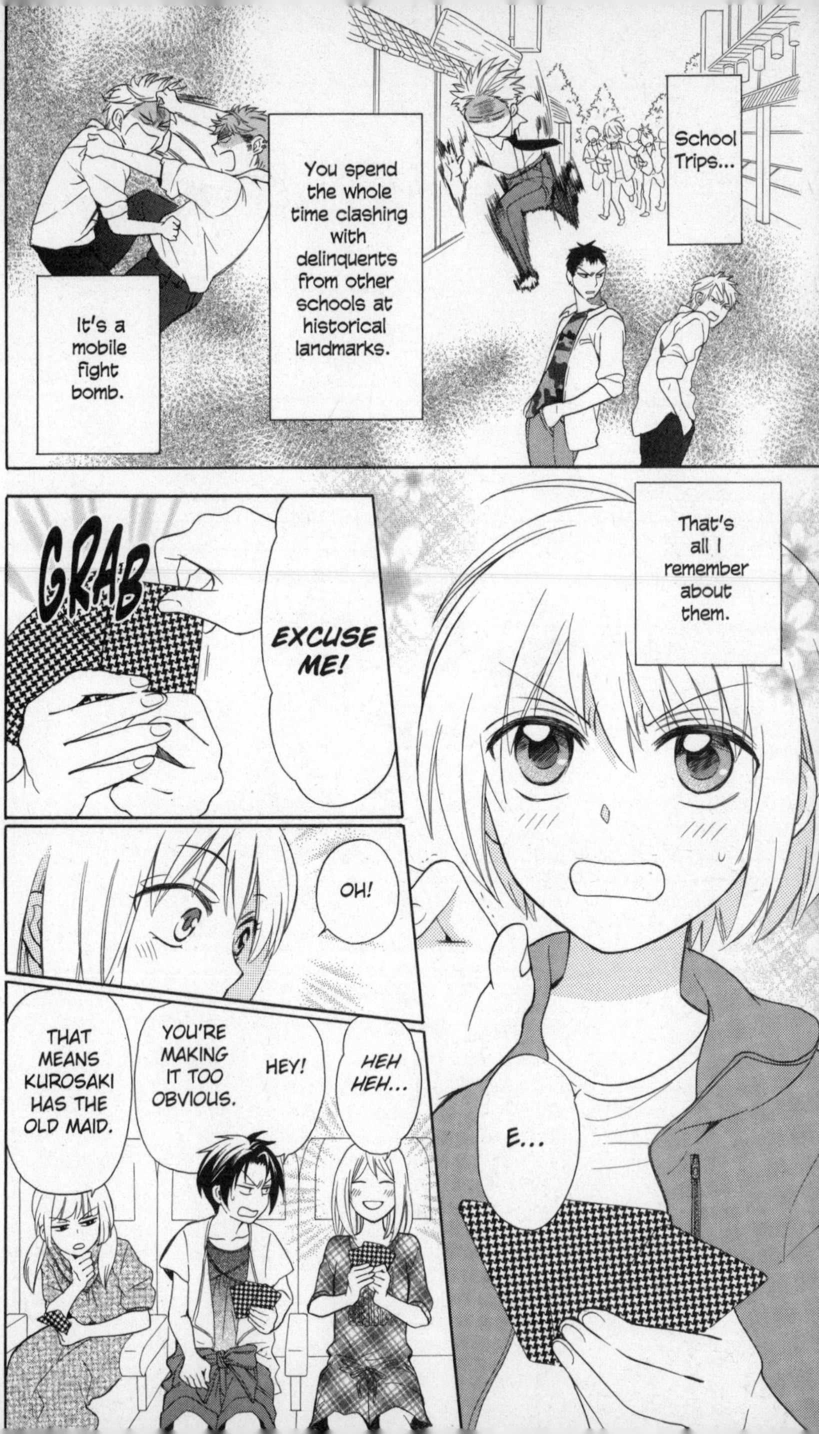
School Trips...
You spend the whole time clashing with delinquents from other schools at historical landmarks.
It's a mobile fight bomb.
That's all I remember about them.
E...
GRAB
EXCUSE ME!
OH!
HEH HEH...
HEY!
YOU'RE MAKING IT TOO OBVIOUS.
THAT MEANS KUROSAKI HAS THE OLD MAID.

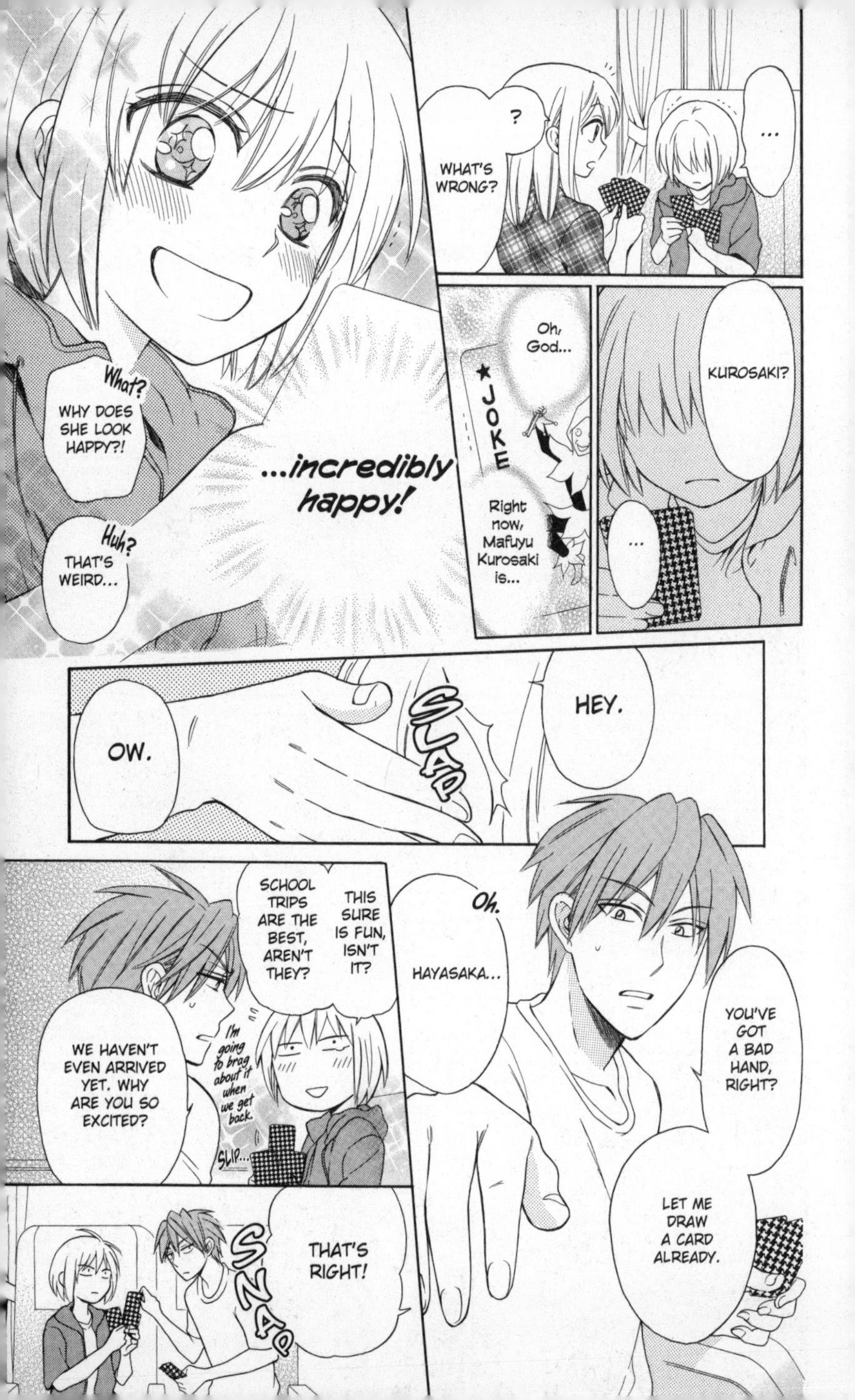
...
?
WHAT'S WRONG?
KUROSAKI?
...
Oh, God...
★JOKE
Right now, Mafuyu Kurosaki is...
...incredibly happy!
What? WHY DOES SHE LOOK HAPPY?!
Huh? THAT'S WEIRD...
HEY.
SLAP
OW.
YOU'VE GOT A BAD HAND, RIGHT?
LET ME DRAW A CARD ALREADY.
Oh.
HAYASAKA...
THIS SURE IS FUN, ISN'T IT?
SCHOOL TRIPS ARE THE BEST, AREN'T THEY?
I'm going to brag about it when we get back.
SLIP...
WE HAVEN'T EVEN ARRIVED YET. WHY ARE YOU SO EXCITED?
SNAP
THAT'S RIGHT!

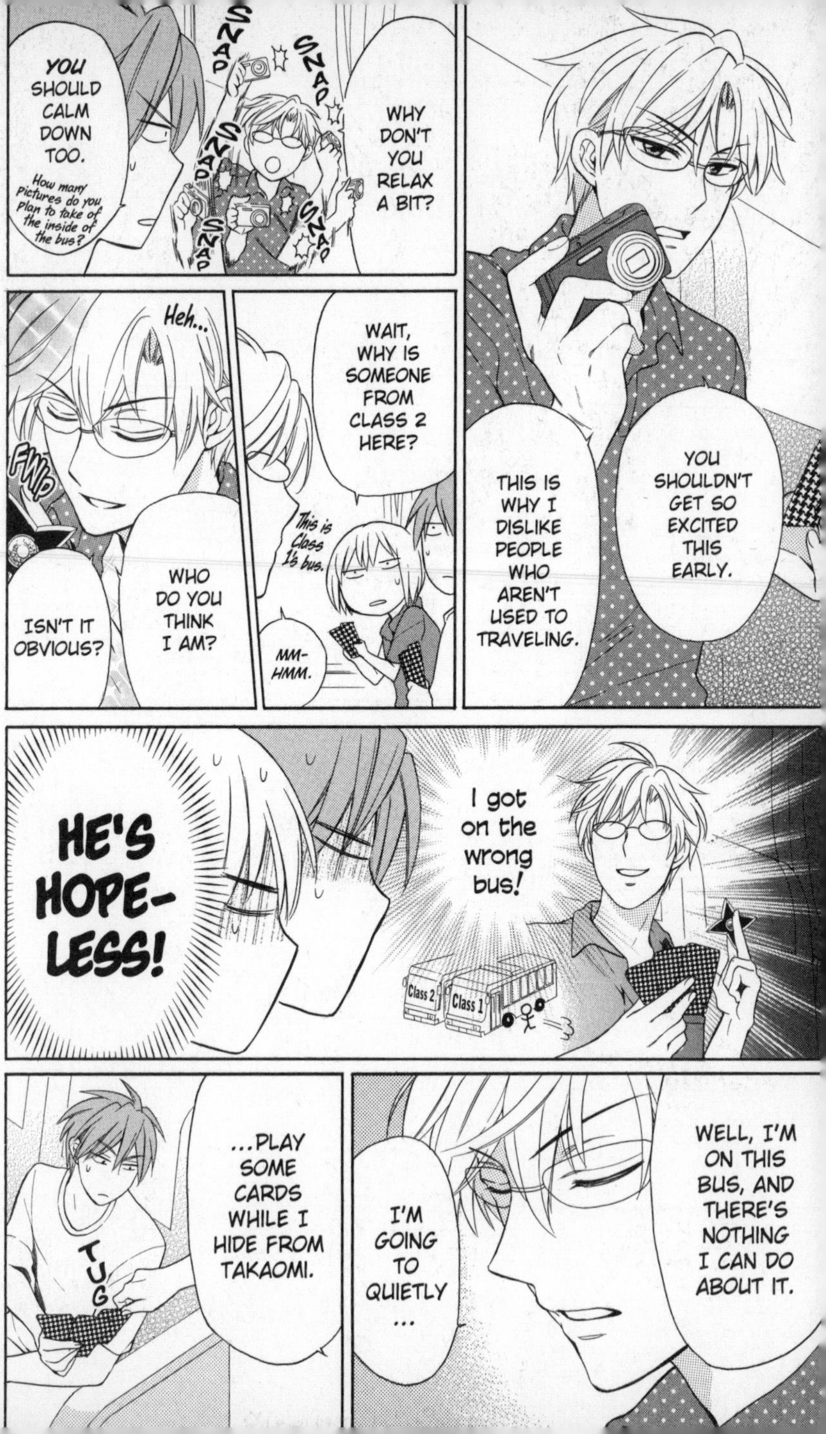
YOU SHOULDN'T GET SO EXCITED THIS EARLY.
THIS IS WHY I DISLIKE PEOPLE WHO AREN'T USED TO TRAVELING.
WHY DON'T YOU RELAX A BIT?
SNAP SNAP SNAP SNAP SNAP
YOU SHOULD CALM DOWN TOO.
How many pictures do you plan to take of the inside of the bus?
WAIT, WHY IS SOMEONE FROM CLASS 2 HERE?
This is Class 1's bus.
MM-HMM.
Heh...
FWIP
WHO DO YOU THINK I AM?
ISN'T IT OBVIOUS?
I got on the wrong bus!
Class 1
Class 2
HE'S HOPE-LESS!
WELL, I'M ON THIS BUS, AND THERE'S NOTHING I CAN DO ABOUT IT.
I'M GOING TO QUIETLY...
...PLAY SOME CARDS WHILE I HIDE FROM TAKAOMI.
TUG

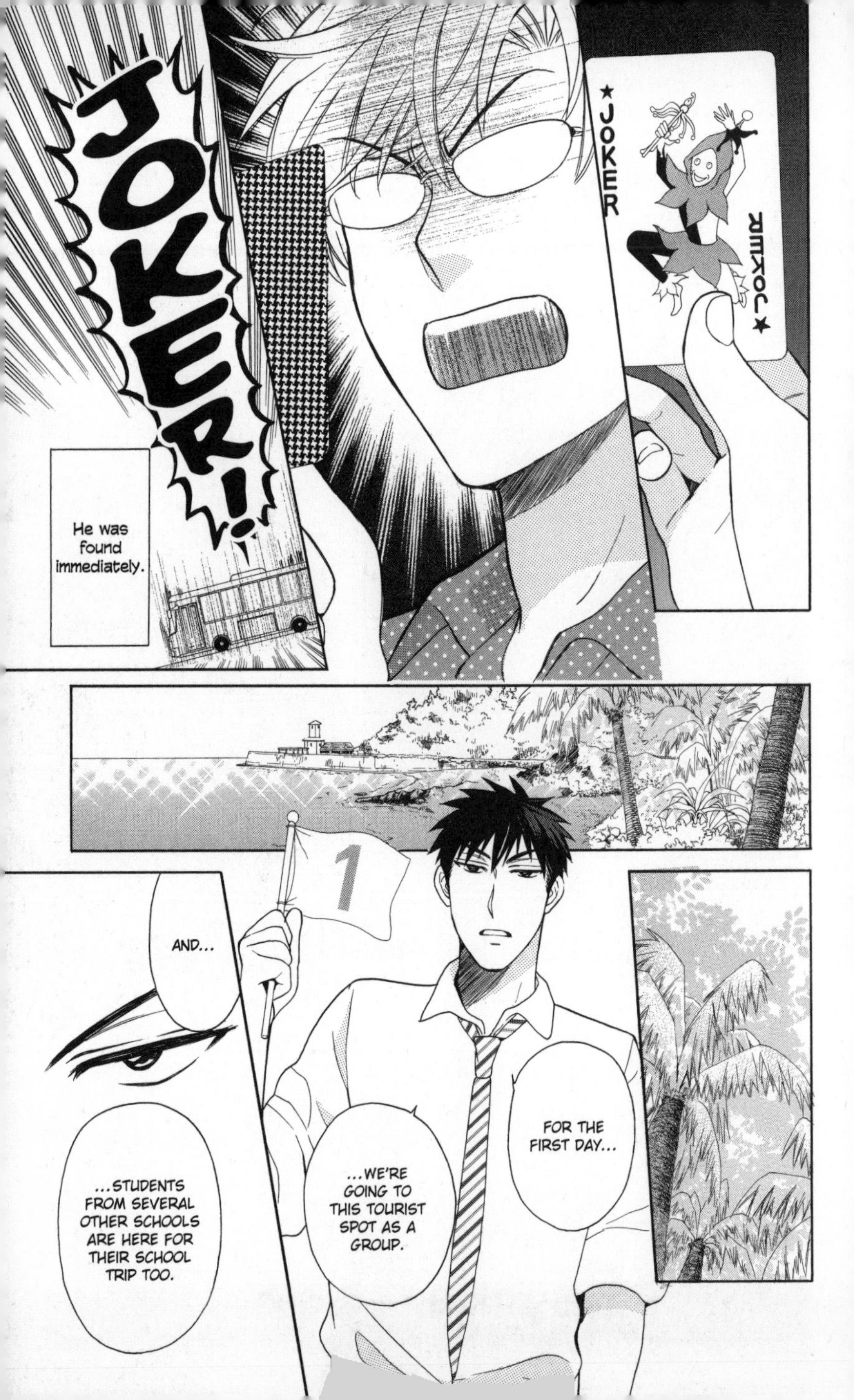
★JOKER
JOKER★
JOKER!
He was found immediately.
FOR THE FIRST DAY...
...WE'RE GOING TO THIS TOURIST SPOT AS A GROUP.
AND...
...STUDENTS FROM SEVERAL OTHER SCHOOLS ARE HERE FOR THEIR SCHOOL TRIP TOO.

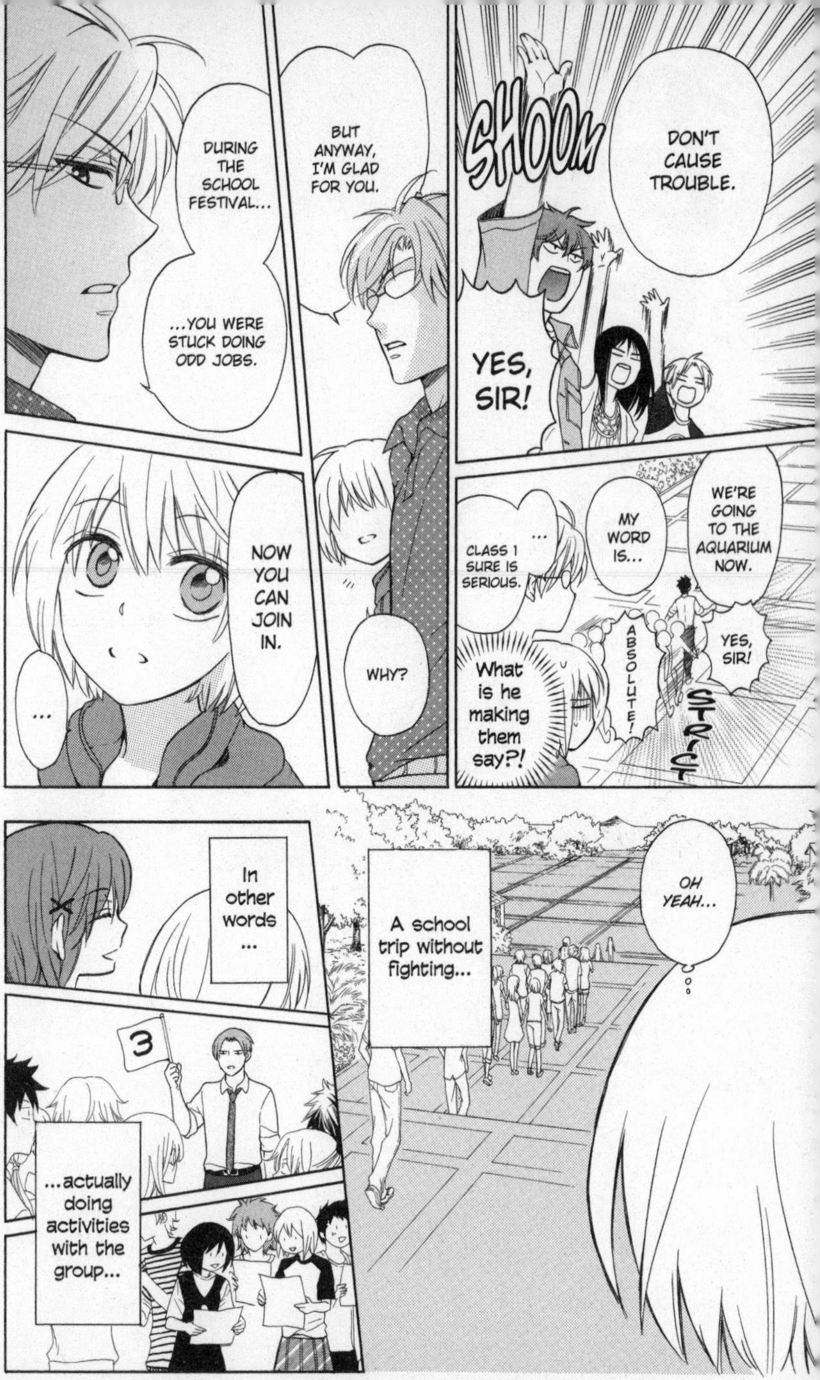
DON'T CAUSE TROUBLE.
SHOOM
YES, SIR!
BUT ANYWAY, I'M GLAD FOR YOU.
DURING THE SCHOOL FESTIVAL...
...YOU WERE STUCK DOING ODD JOBS.
WE'RE GOING TO THE AQUARIUM NOW.
MY WORD IS...
YES, SIR!
ABSOLUTE!
STRICT
...
CLASS 1 SURE IS SERIOUS.
What is he making them say?!
WHY?
NOW YOU CAN JOIN IN.
...
OH YEAH...
A school trip without fighting...
In other words...
...actually doing activities with the group...

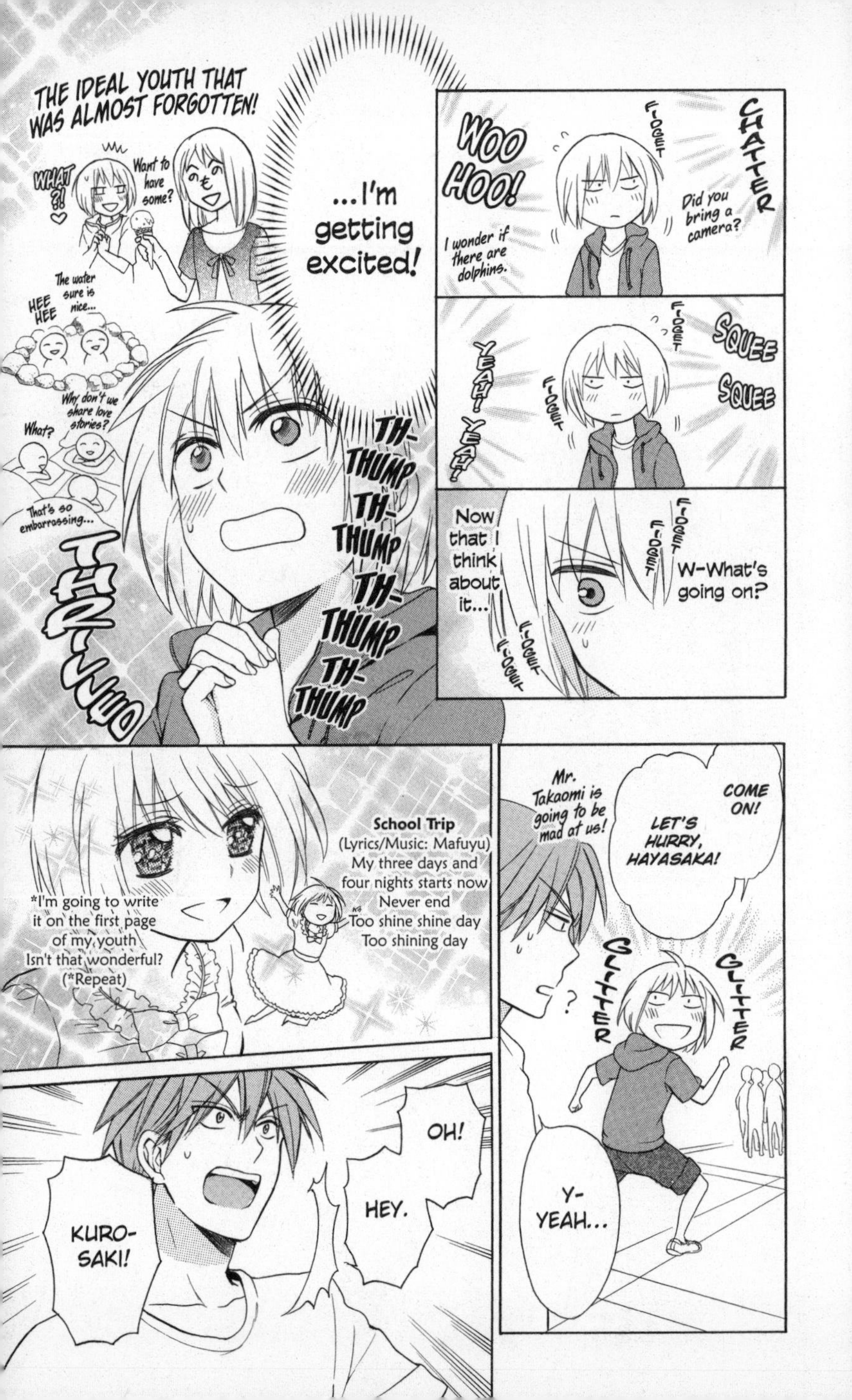
CHATTER
Did you bring a camera?
FIDGET
WOO HOO!
I wonder if there are dolphins.
SQUEE
SQUEE
FIDGET
FIDGET
YEAH! YEAH!
FIDGET
FIDGET
W-What's going on?
Now that I think about it...
FIDGET
FIDGET
...I'm getting excited!
THE IDEAL YOUTH THAT WAS ALMOST FORGOTTEN!
Want to have some?
WHAT?!
The water sure is nice...
HEE HEE
Why don't we share love stories?
What?
That's so embarrassing...
TH-THUMP TH-THUMP TH-THUMP TH-THUMP
THRO-UMP
COME ON!
LET'S HURRY, HAYASAKA!
Mr. Takaomi is going to be mad at us!
GLITTER
GLITTER
?
Y-YEAH...
School Trip
(Lyrics/Music: Mafuyu)
My three days and four nights starts now
Never end
Too shine shine day
Too shining day
*I'm going to write it on the first page of my youth
Isn't that wonderful?
(*Repeat)
OH!
HEY.
KURO-SAKI!

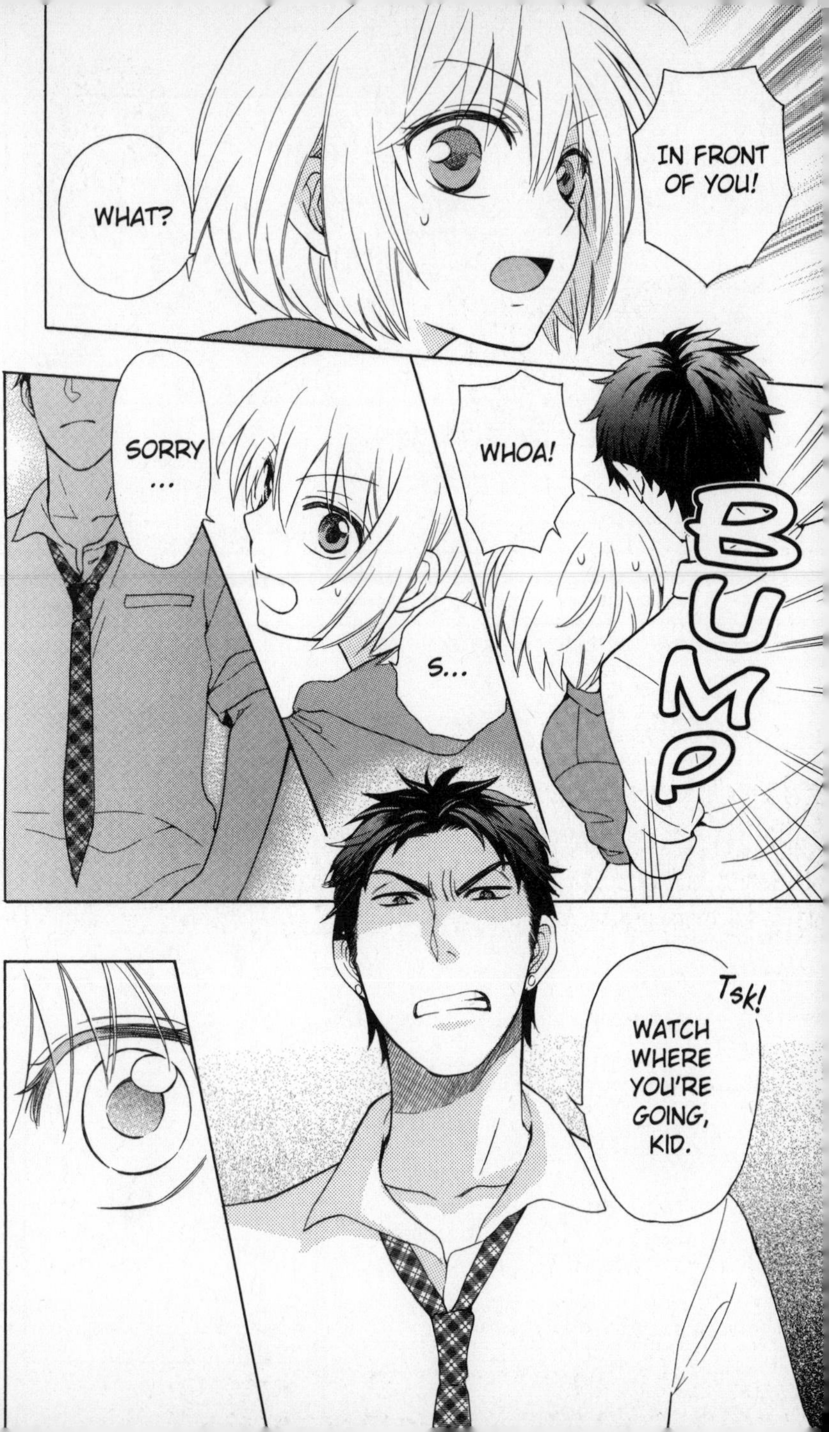
IN FRONT OF YOU!
WHAT?
WHOA!
BUMP
S...
SORRY ...
Tsk!
WATCH WHERE YOU'RE GOING, KID.

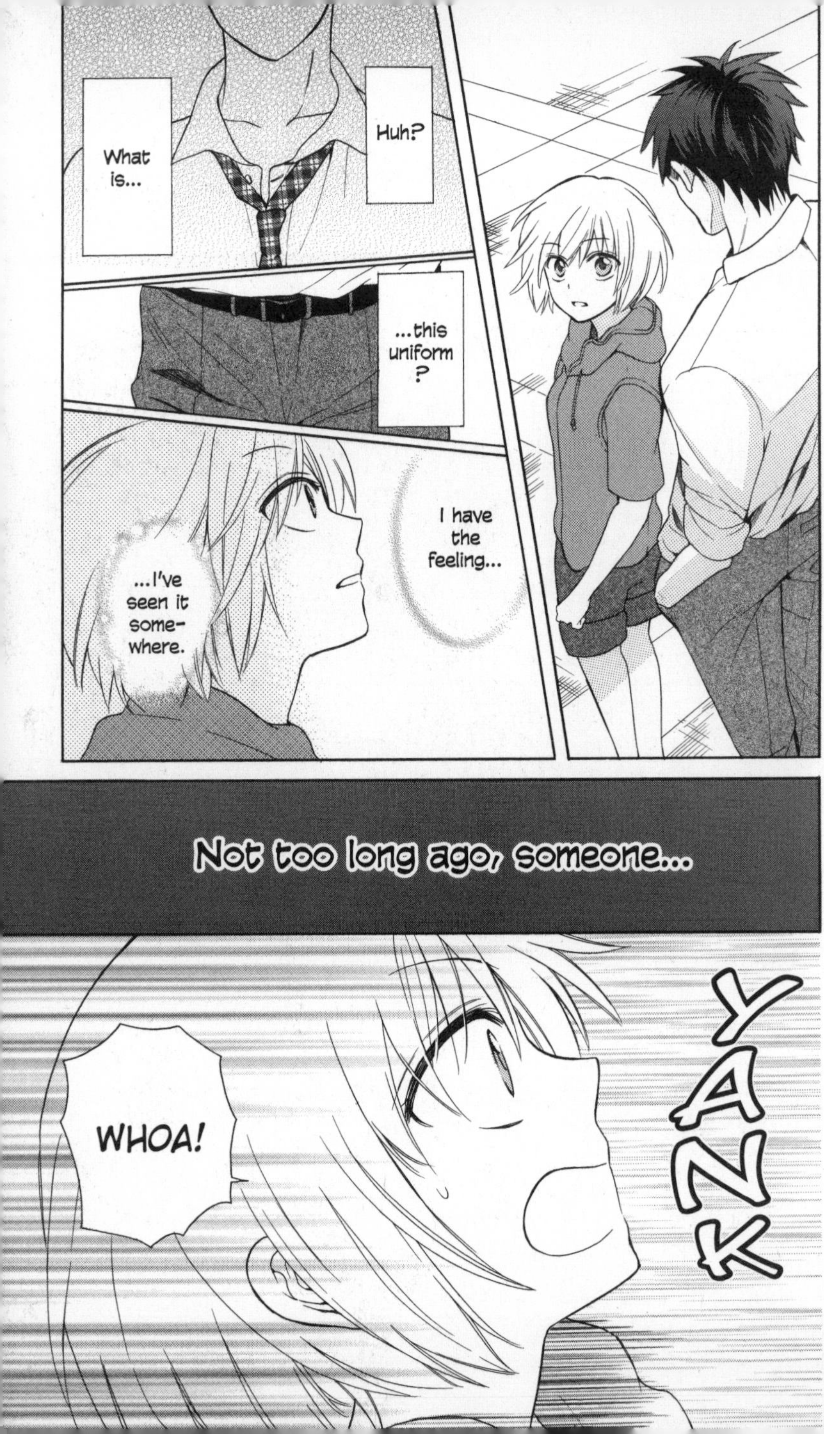
Huh?
What is...
...this uniform?
I have the feeling...
...I've seen it somewhere.
Not too long ago, someone...
YANK
WHOA!

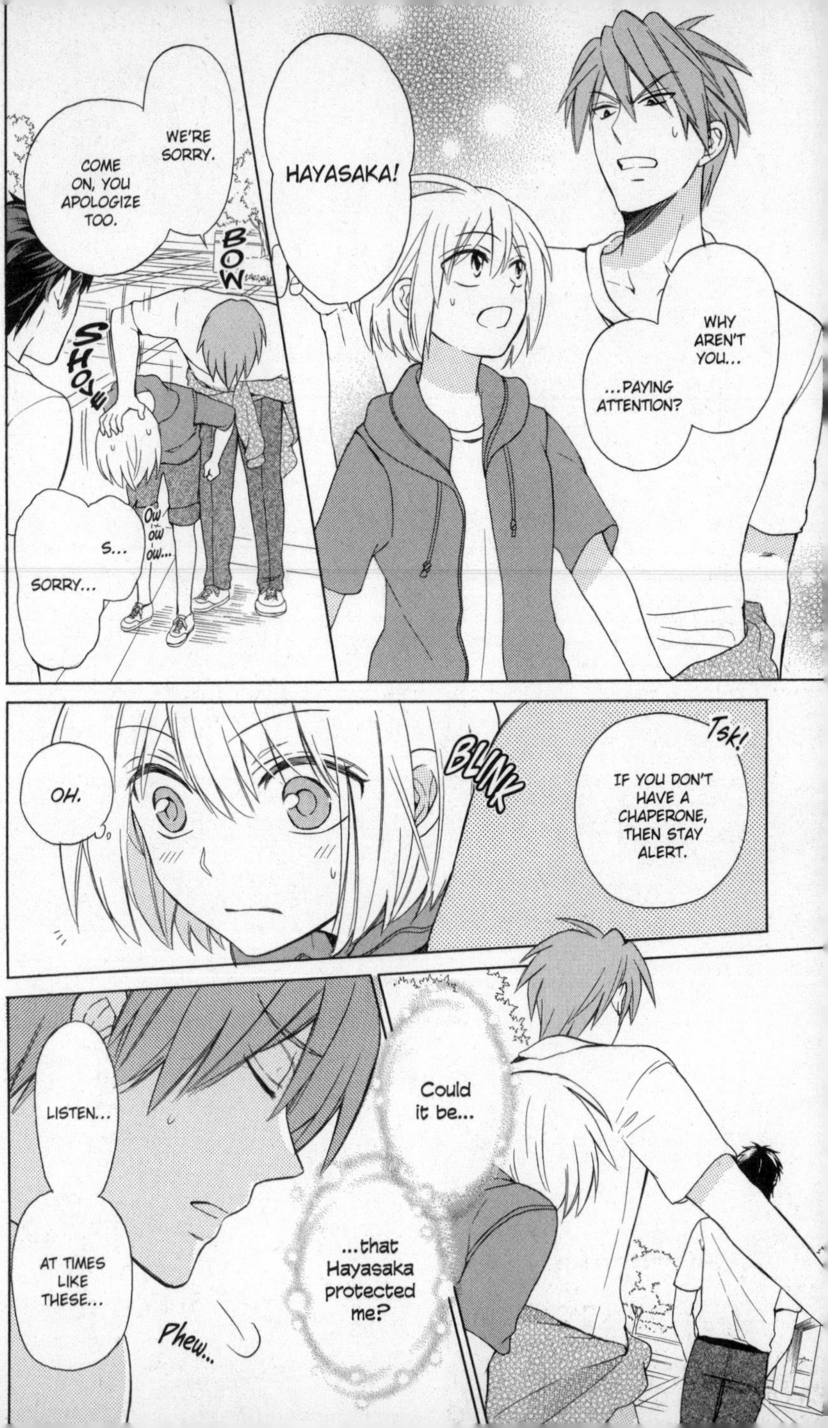
WHY AREN'T YOU...
...PAYING ATTENTION?
HAYASAKA!
WE'RE SORRY.
COME ON, YOU APOLOGIZE TOO.
BOW
SHOVE
OW OW OW...
S...
SORRY...
Tsk!
IF YOU DON'T HAVE A CHAPERONE, THEN STAY ALERT.
BLINK
OH.
Could it be...
...that Hayasaka protected me?
LISTEN...
AT TIMES LIKE THESE...
Phew...

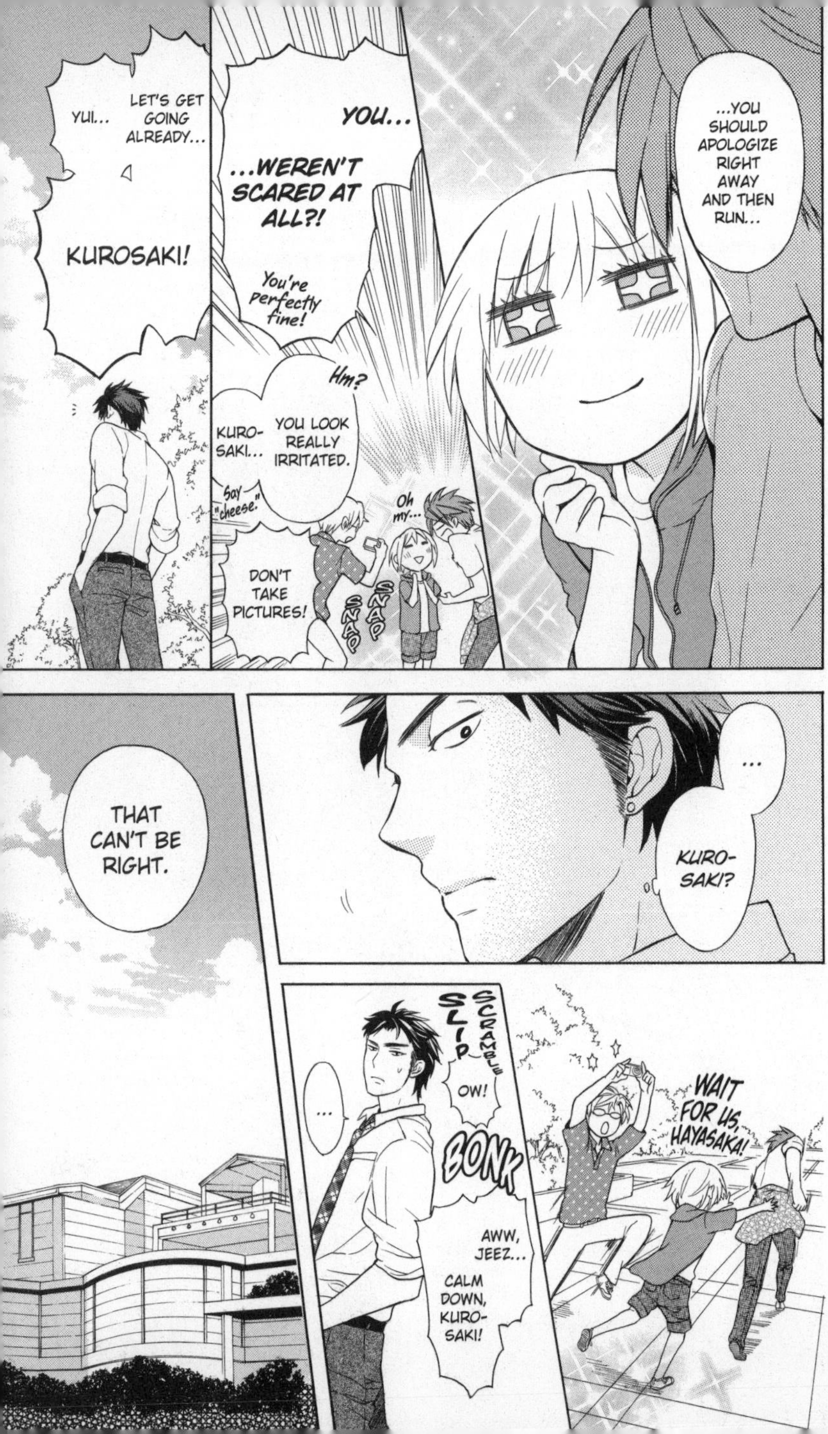
...YOU SHOULD APOLOGIZE RIGHT AWAY AND THEN RUN...
YOU...
...WEREN'T SCARED AT ALL?!
You're perfectly fine!
Hm?
Oh my...
SNAP SNAP
DON'T TAKE PICTURES!
YOU LOOK REALLY IRRITATED.
KURO-SAKI...
Say "cheese."
LET'S GET GOING ALREADY...
YUI...
KUROSAKI!
...
KURO-SAKI?
THAT CAN'T BE RIGHT.
WAIT FOR US, HAYASAKA!
SCRAMBLE
SLIP
OW!
BONK
AWW, JEEZ...
CALM DOWN, KURO-SAKI!
...

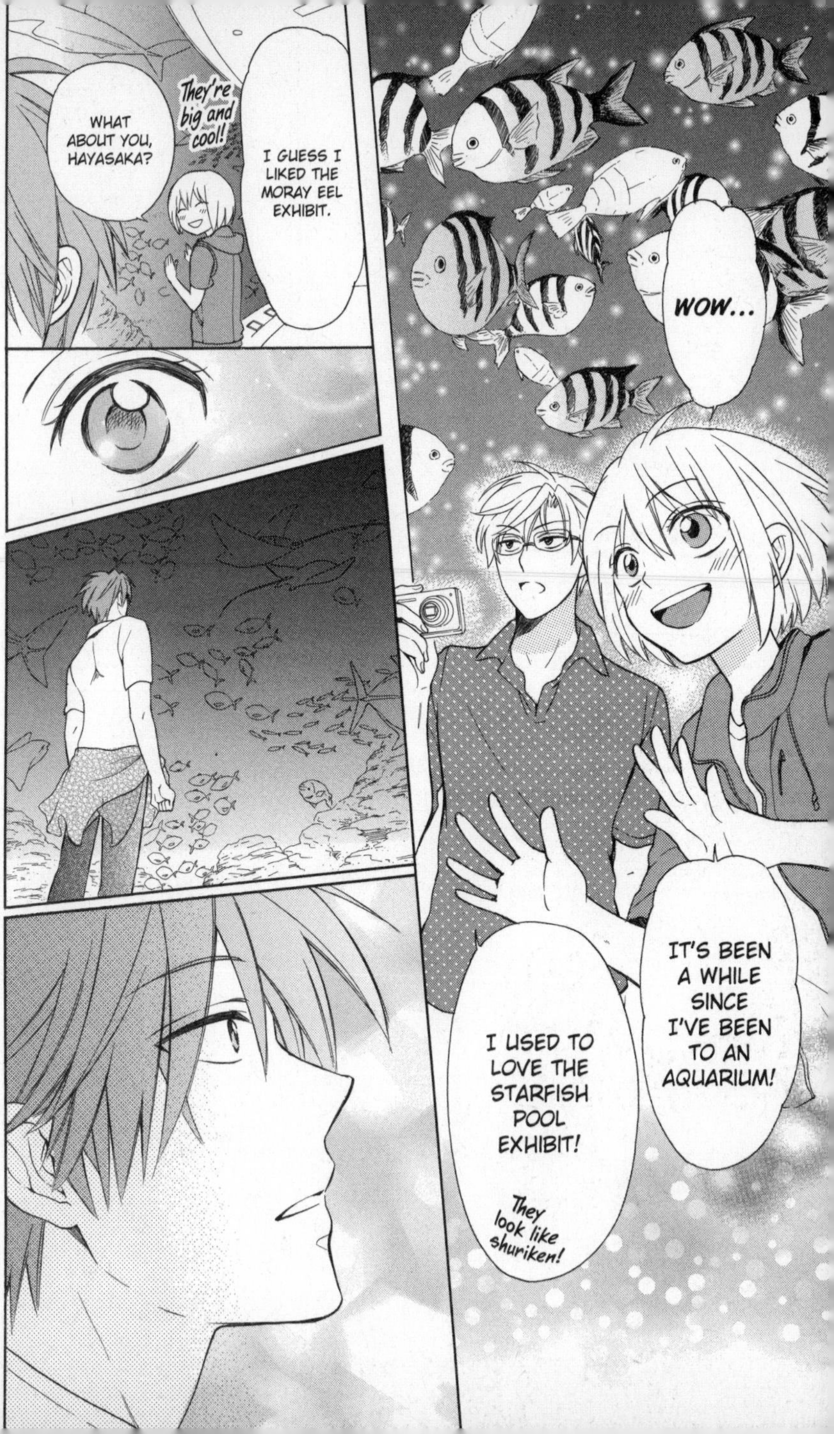
WOW...
IT'S BEEN A WHILE SINCE I'VE BEEN TO AN AQUARIUM!
I USED TO LOVE THE STARFISH POOL EXHIBIT!
They look like shuriken!
WHAT ABOUT YOU, HAYASAKA?
I GUESS I LIKED THE MORAY EEL EXHIBIT.
They're big and cool!

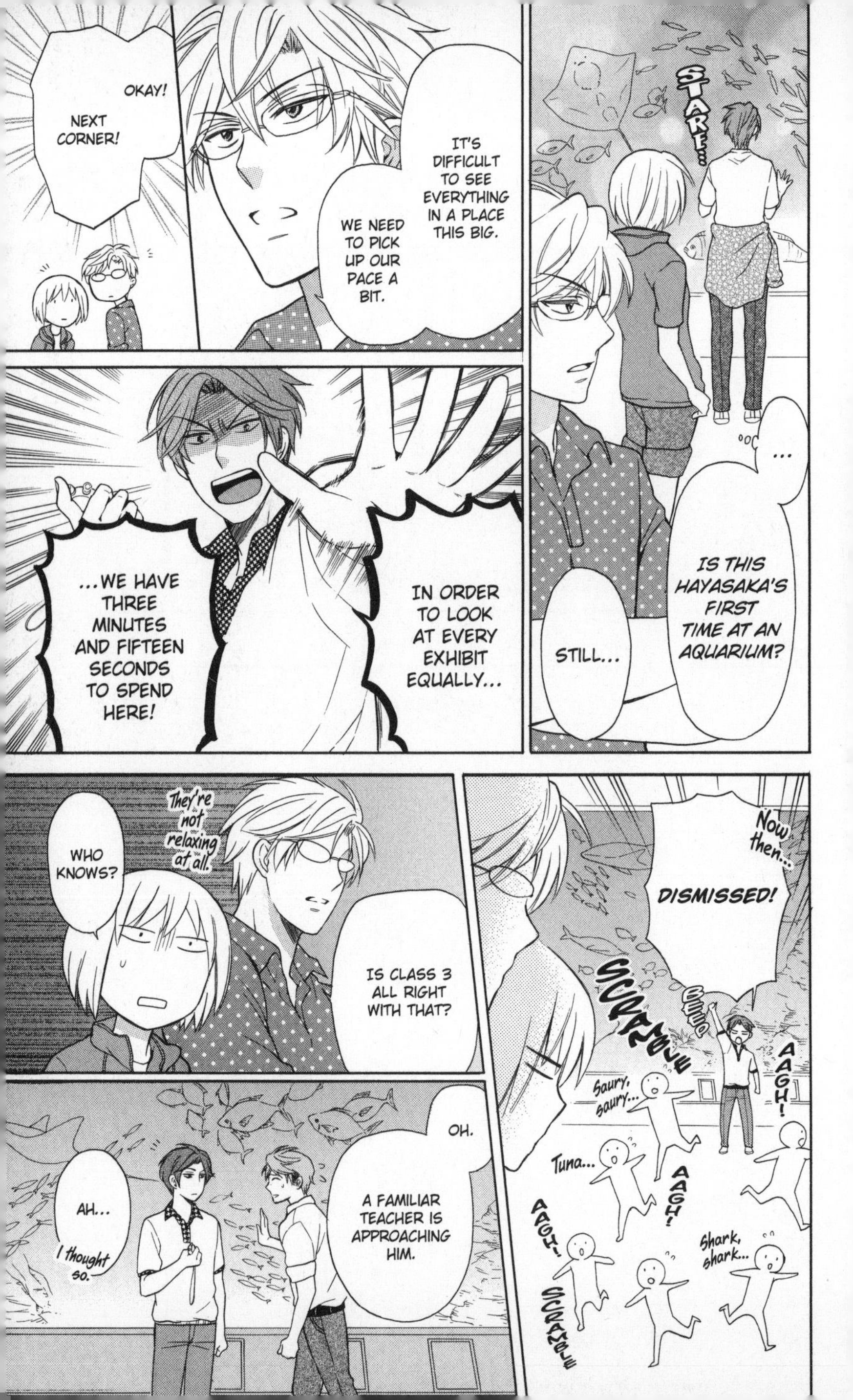
STARE...
...
IS THIS HAYASAKA'S FIRST TIME AT AN AQUARIUM?
STILL...
IT'S DIFFICULT TO SEE EVERYTHING IN A PLACE THIS BIG.
WE NEED TO PICK UP OUR PACE A BIT.
OKAY!
NEXT CORNER!
IN ORDER TO LOOK AT EVERY EXHIBIT EQUALLY...
...WE HAVE THREE MINUTES AND FIFTEEN SECONDS TO SPEND HERE!
Now then...
DISMISSED!
SCRAMBLE
AAGH!
Saury, saury...
Tuna...
AAGH!
AAGH!
Shark, shark...
SCRAMBLE
They're not relaxing at all.
WHO KNOWS?
IS CLASS 3 ALL RIGHT WITH THAT?
OH.
A FAMILIAR TEACHER IS APPROACHING HIM.
AH...
I thought so.

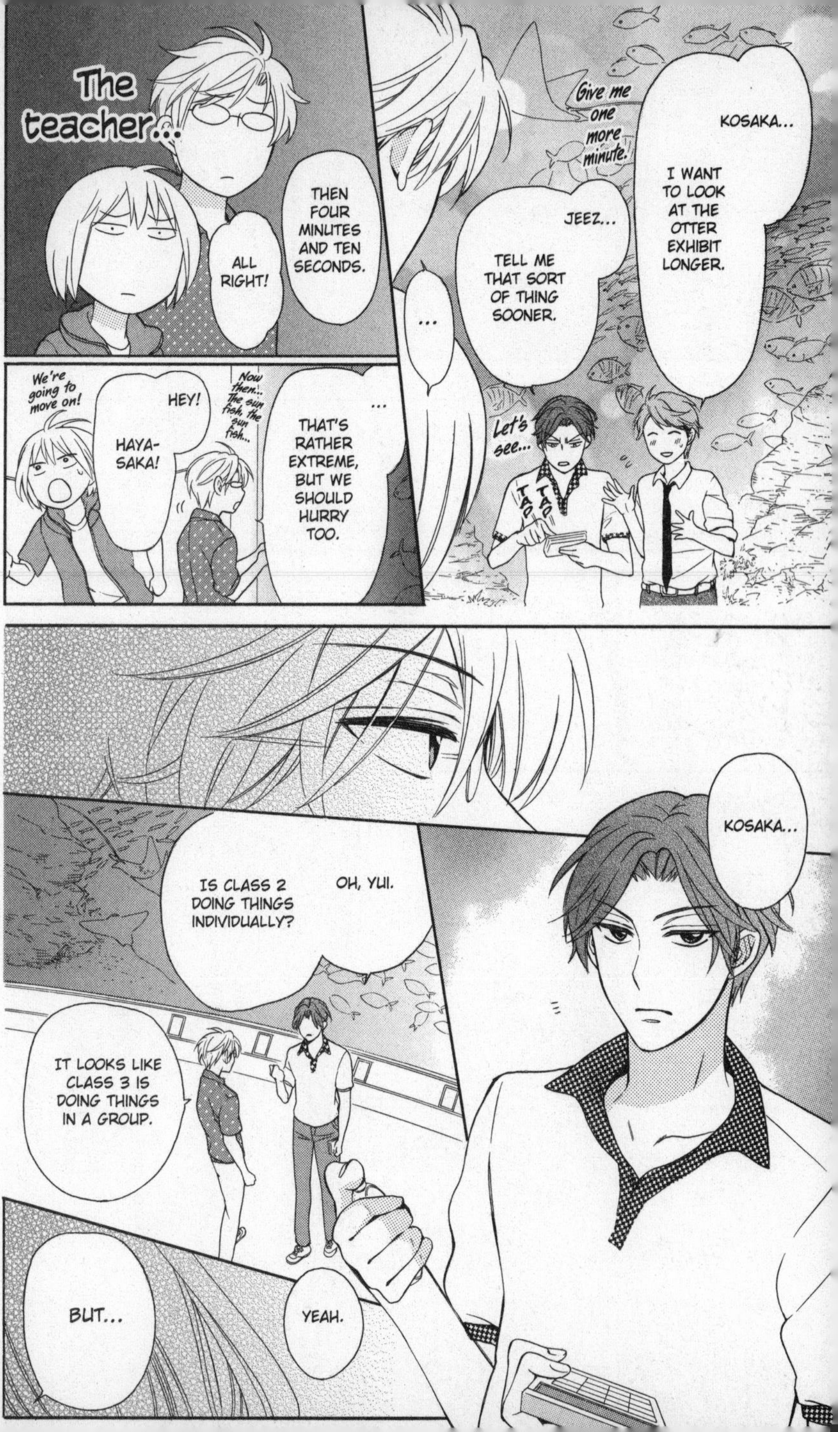
KOSAKA...
I WANT TO LOOK AT THE OTTER EXHIBIT LONGER.
Give me one more minute.
JEEZ...
TELL ME THAT SORT OF THING SOONER.
Let's see...
TAP TAP
...
The teacher...
THEN FOUR MINUTES AND TEN SECONDS.
ALL RIGHT!
...
THAT'S RATHER EXTREME, BUT WE SHOULD HURRY TOO.
Now then... The sun fish, the sun fish...
HEY!
HAYA-SAKA!
We're going to move on!
KOSAKA...
OH, YUI.
IS CLASS 2 DOING THINGS INDIVIDUALLY?
IT LOOKS LIKE CLASS 3 IS DOING THINGS IN A GROUP.
YEAH.
BUT...

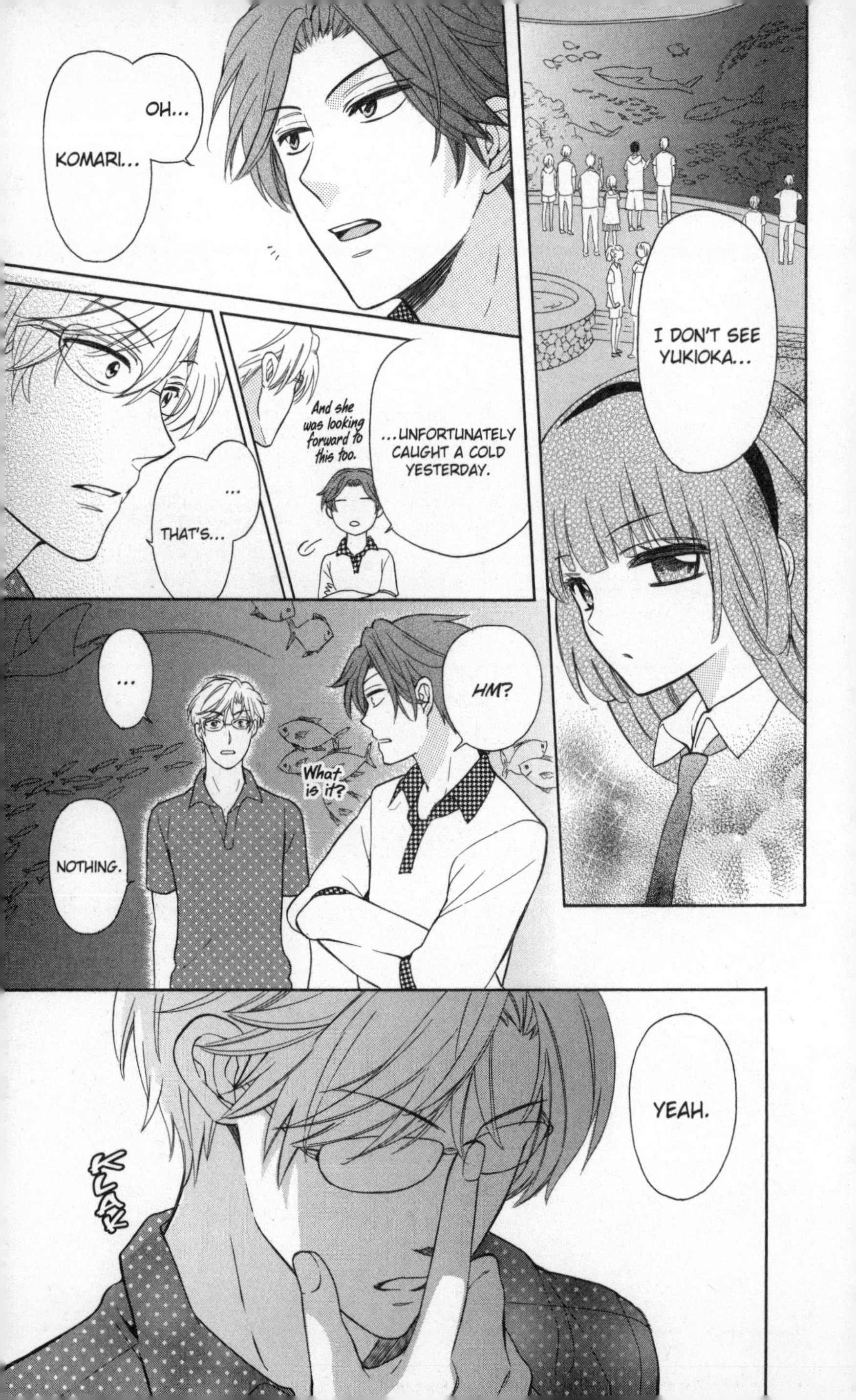
I DON'T SEE YUKIOKA...
OH... KOMARI...
...UNFORTUNATELY CAUGHT A COLD YESTERDAY.
And she was looking forward to this too.
... THAT'S...
HM?
What is it?
...
NOTHING.
YEAH.
KLAK

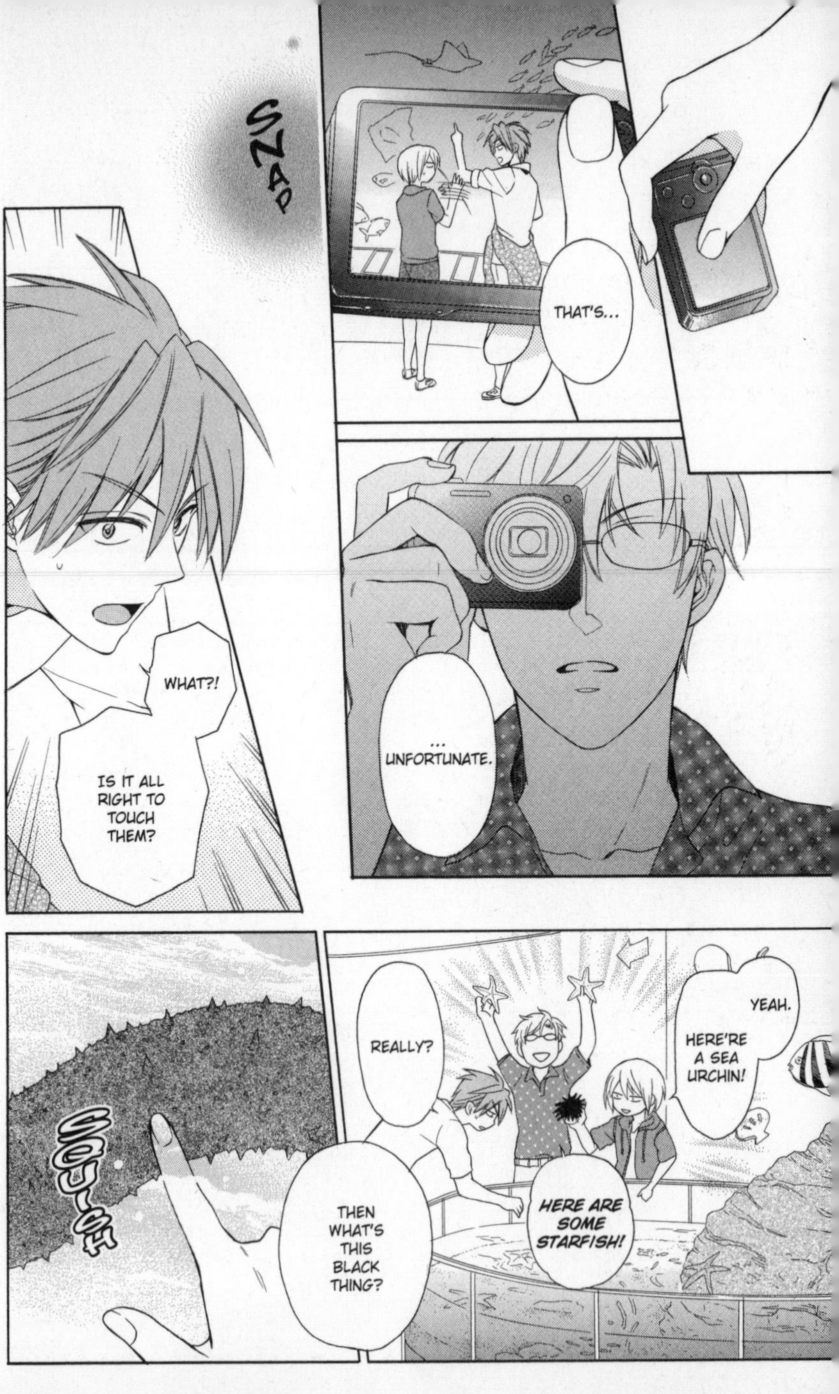
THAT'S...
SNAP
... UNFORTUNATE.
WHAT?!
IS IT ALL RIGHT TO TOUCH THEM?
YEAH.
HERE'RE A SEA URCHIN!
HERE ARE SOME STARFISH!
REALLY?
THEN WHAT'S THIS BLACK THING?
SQU-CH

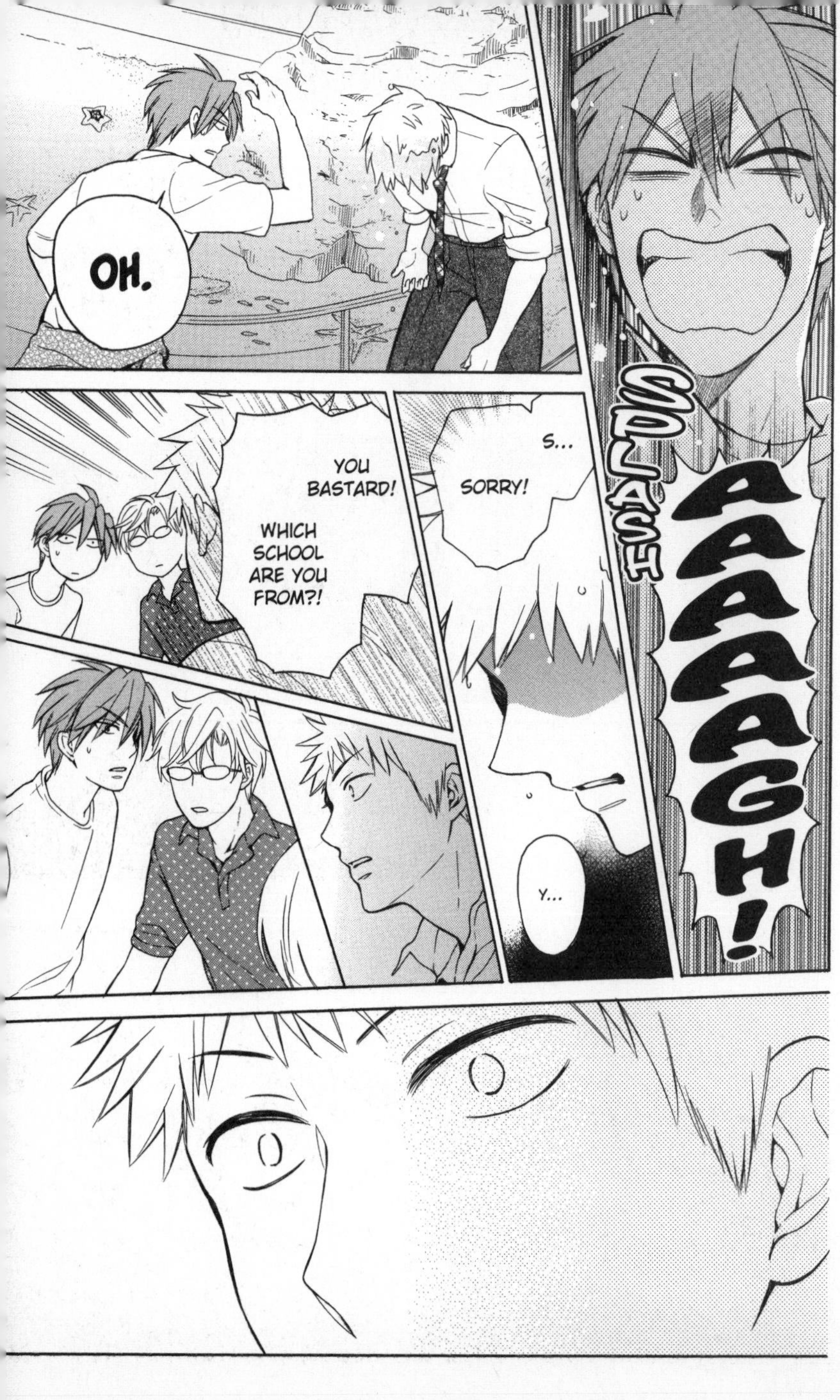
SPLASH
AAAAAGH!
OH.
S...
SORRY!
Y...
YOU BASTARD!
WHICH SCHOOL ARE YOU FROM?!

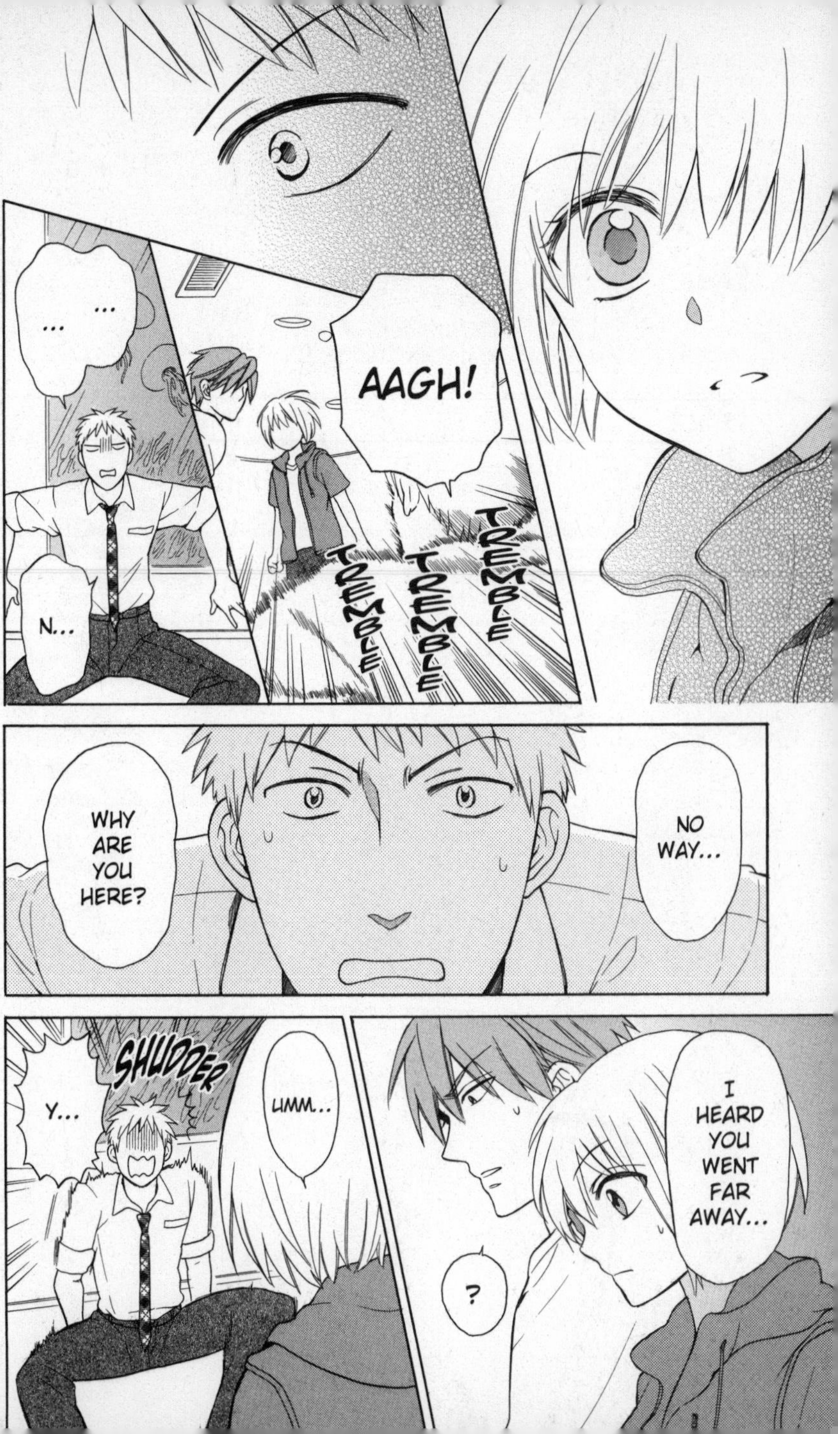
AAGH!
TREMBLE
TREMBLE
TREMBLE
... ...
N...
NO WAY...
WHY ARE YOU HERE?
I HEARD YOU WENT FAR AWAY...
?
UMM...
SHUDDER
Y...

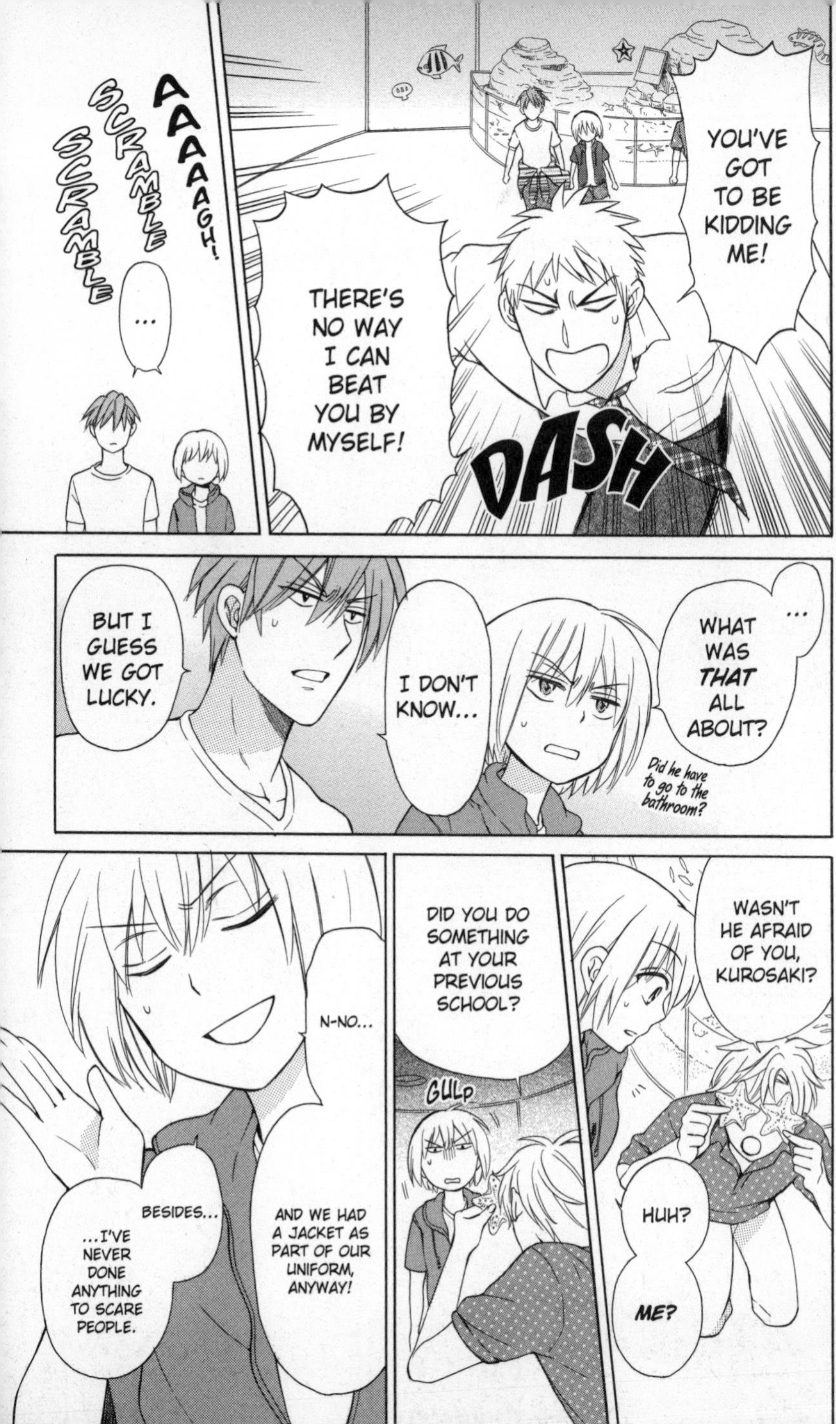
YOU'VE GOT TO BE KIDDING ME!
DASH
THERE'S NO WAY I CAN BEAT YOU BY MYSELF!
AAAAAAGH!
SCRAMBLE
SCRAMBLE
...
...
WHAT WAS THAT ALL ABOUT?
Did he have to go to the bathroom?
I DON'T KNOW...
BUT I GUESS WE GOT LUCKY.
WASN'T HE AFRAID OF YOU, KUROSAKI?
HUH?
ME?
DID YOU DO SOMETHING AT YOUR PREVIOUS SCHOOL?
GULP
N-NO...
AND WE HAD A JACKET AS PART OF OUR UNIFORM, ANYWAY!
BESIDES...
...I'VE NEVER DONE ANYTHING TO SCARE PEOPLE.

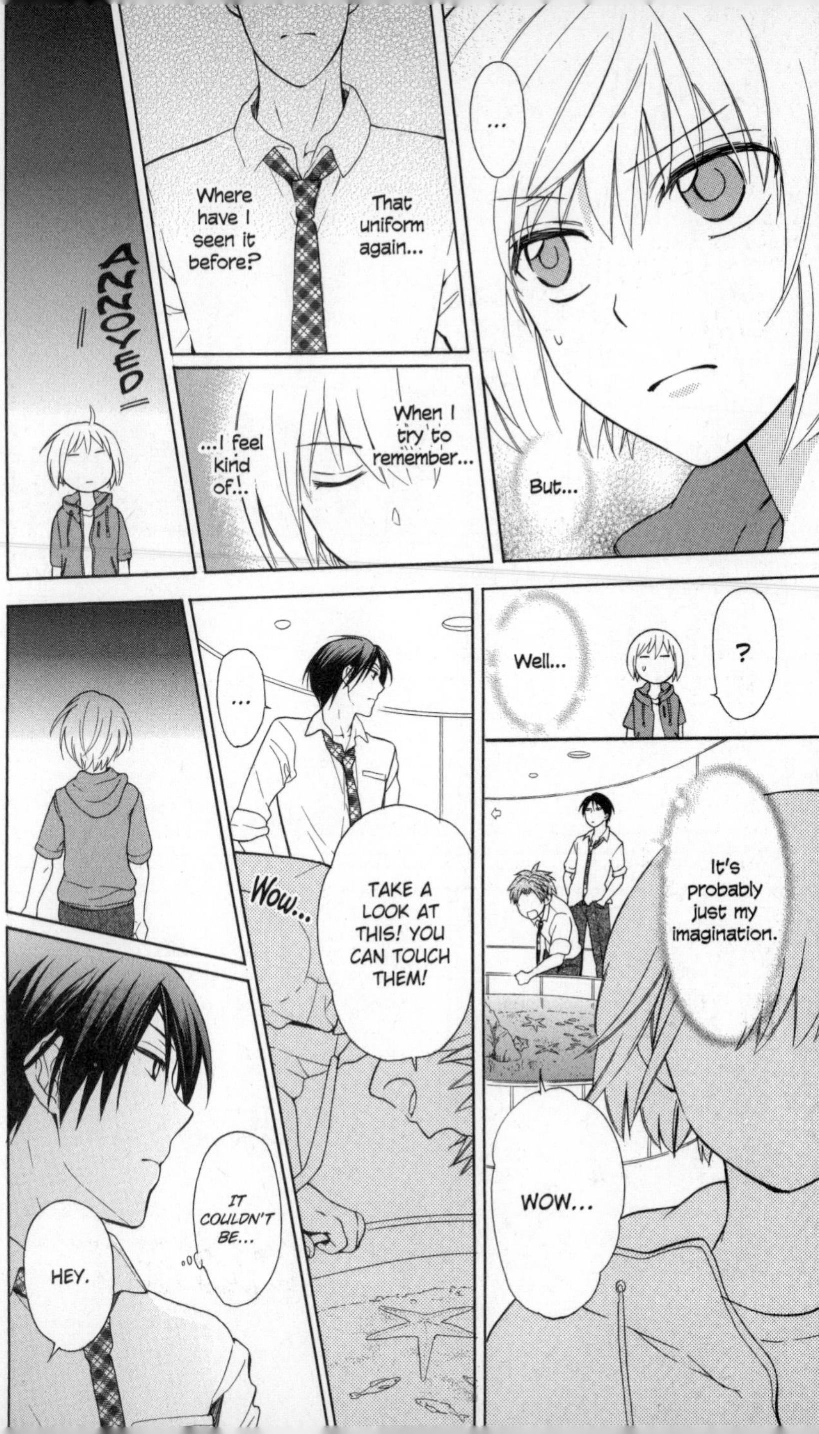
...
That uniform again...
Where have I seen it before?
ANNOYED
But...
When I try to remember...
...I feel kind of!..
?
Well...
...
It's probably just my imagination.
TAKE A LOOK AT THIS! YOU CAN TOUCH THEM!
Wow...
WOW...
IT COULDN'T BE...
HEY.

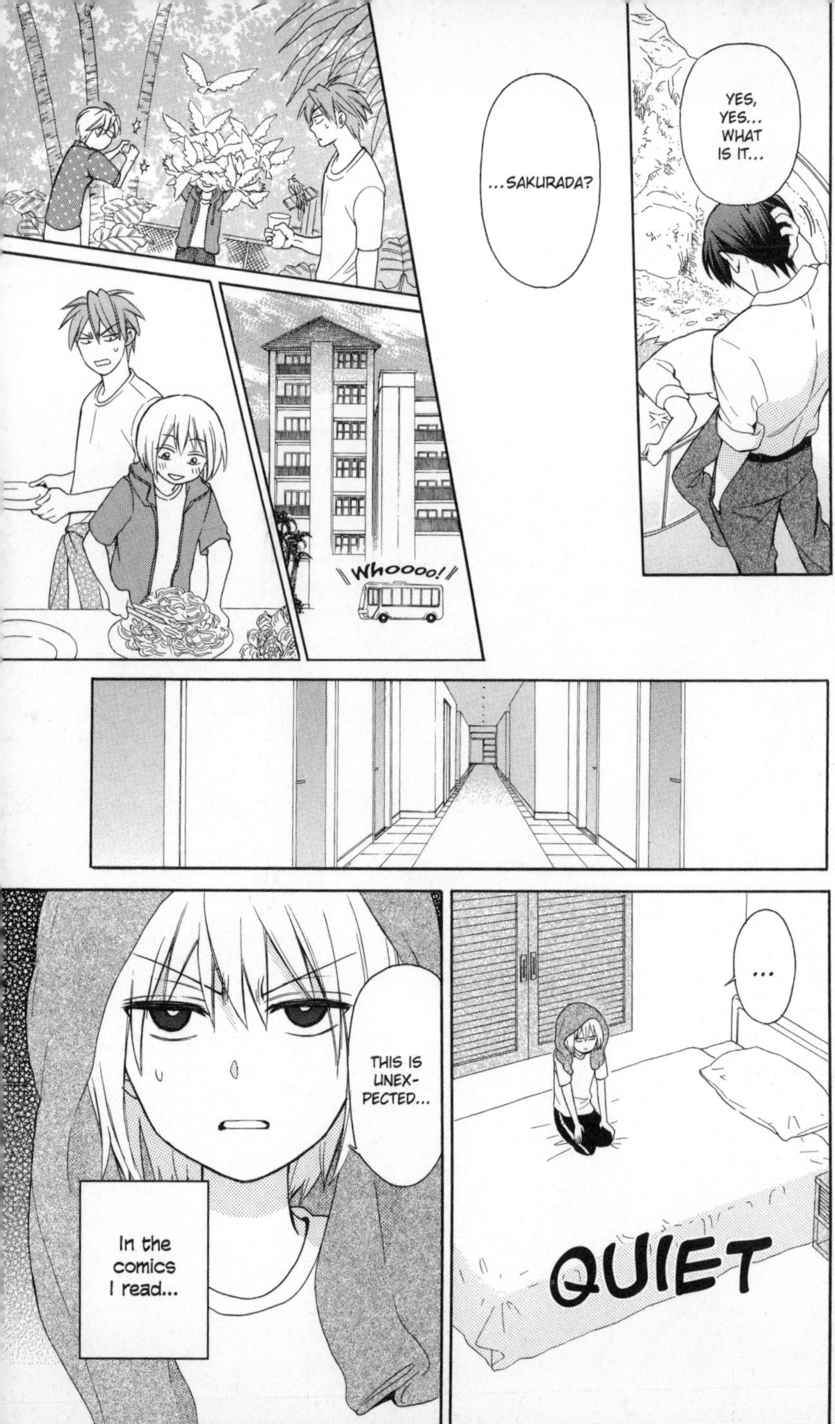
YES, YES... WHAT IS IT...
...SAKURADA?
Whoooo!
...
QUIET
THIS IS UNEX-PECTED...
In the comics I read...

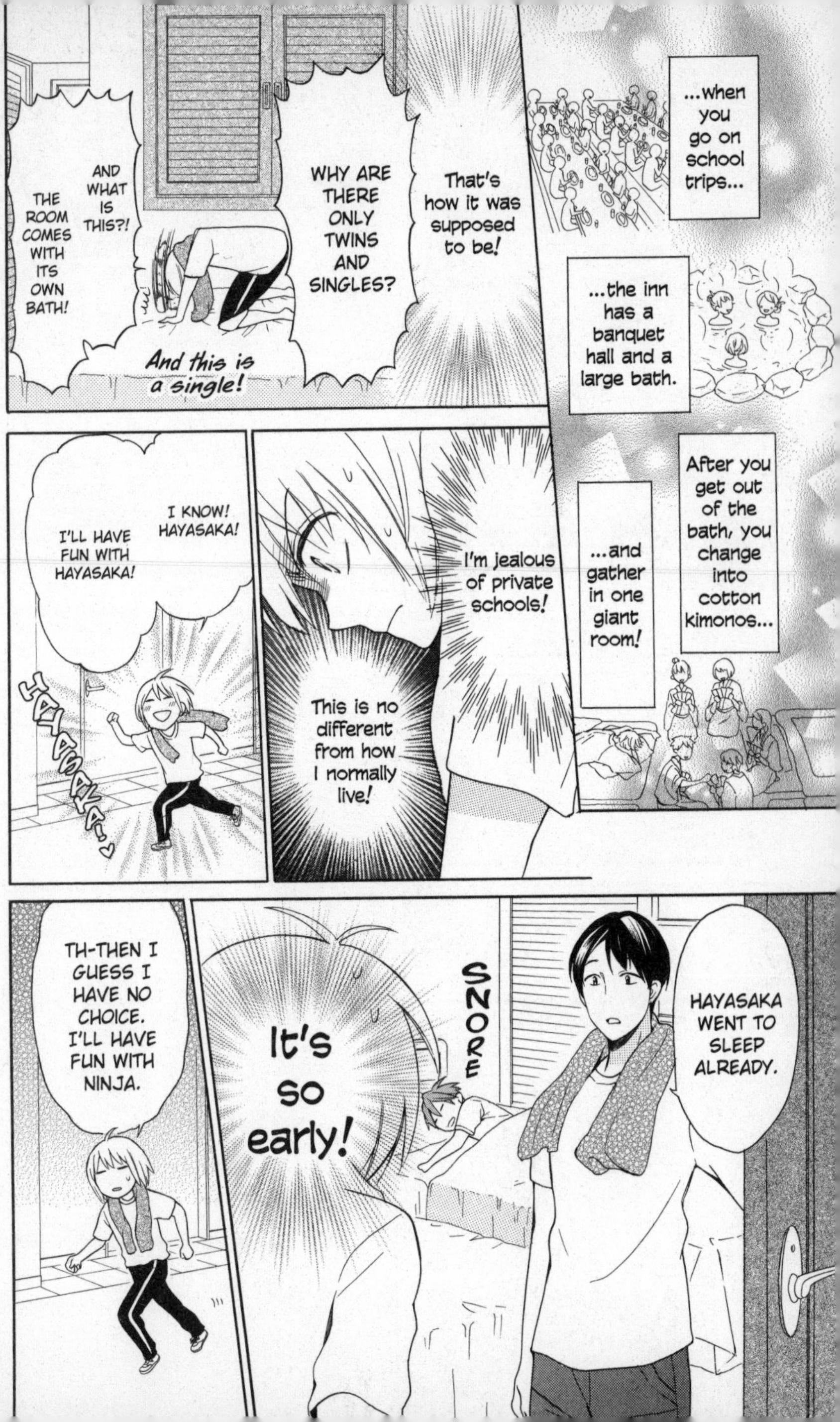
...when you go on school trips...
...the inn has a banquet hall and a large bath.
After you get out of the bath, you change into cotton kimonos...
...and gather in one giant room!
That's how it was supposed to be!
WHY ARE THERE ONLY TWINS AND SINGLES?
AND WHAT IS THIS?!
THE ROOM COMES WITH ITS OWN BATH!
And this is a single!
I'm jealous of private schools!
This is no different from how I normally live!
I KNOW! HAYASAKA!
I'LL HAVE FUN WITH HAYASAKA!
HAYASAKA~!
HAYASAKA WENT TO SLEEP ALREADY.
SNORE
It's so early!
TH-THEN I GUESS I HAVE NO CHOICE. I'LL HAVE FUN WITH NINJA.

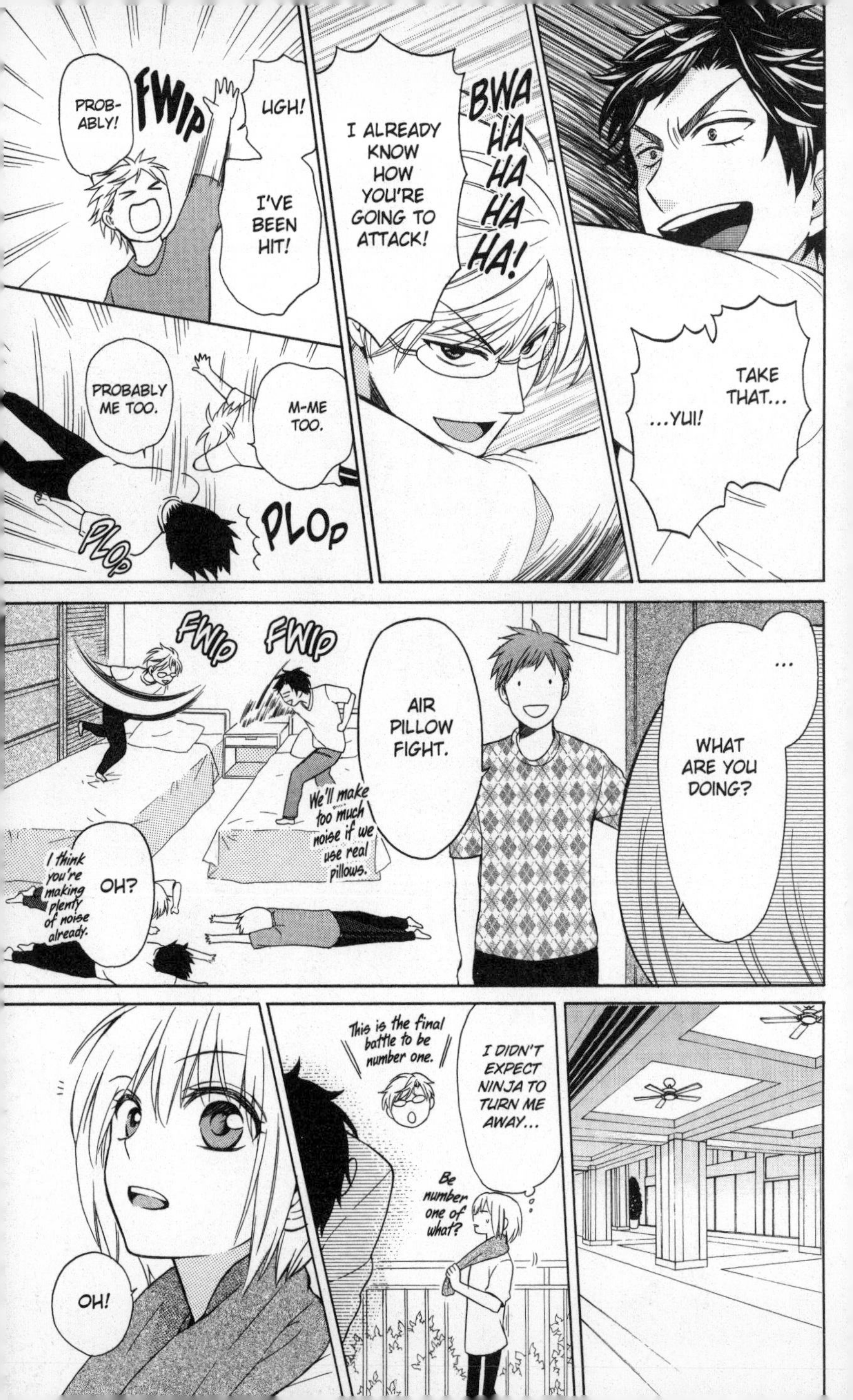
TAKE THAT...
...YUI!
BWA HA HA HA HA!
I ALREADY KNOW HOW YOU'RE GOING TO ATTACK!
UGH!
I'VE BEEN HIT!
FWIP
PROB-ABLY!
M-ME TOO.
PLOP
PROBABLY ME TOO.
PLOP
...
WHAT ARE YOU DOING?
AIR PILLOW FIGHT.
We'll make too much noise if we use real pillows.
FWIP
FWIP
OH?
I think you're making plenty of noise already.
I DIDN'T EXPECT NINJA TO TURN ME AWAY...
This is the final battle to be number one.
Be number one of what?
OH!

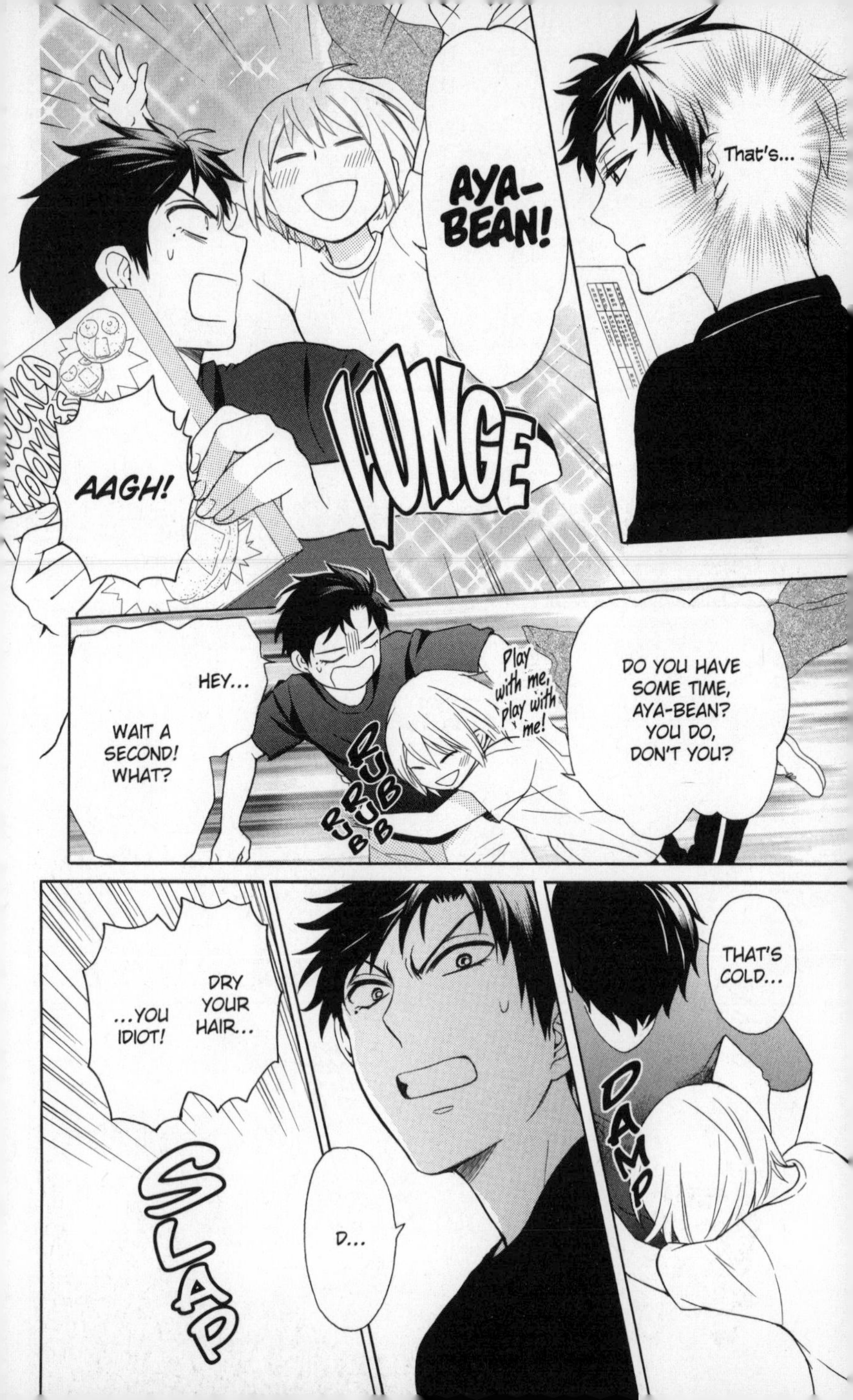
That's...
AYA-BEAN!
LUNGE
AAGH!
DO YOU HAVE SOME TIME, AYA-BEAN? YOU DO, DON'T YOU?
Play with me, play with me!
RUB RUB RUB
HEY...
WAIT A SECOND! WHAT?
THAT'S COLD...
DAMP
D...
DRY YOUR HAIR...
...YOU IDIOT!
SLAP

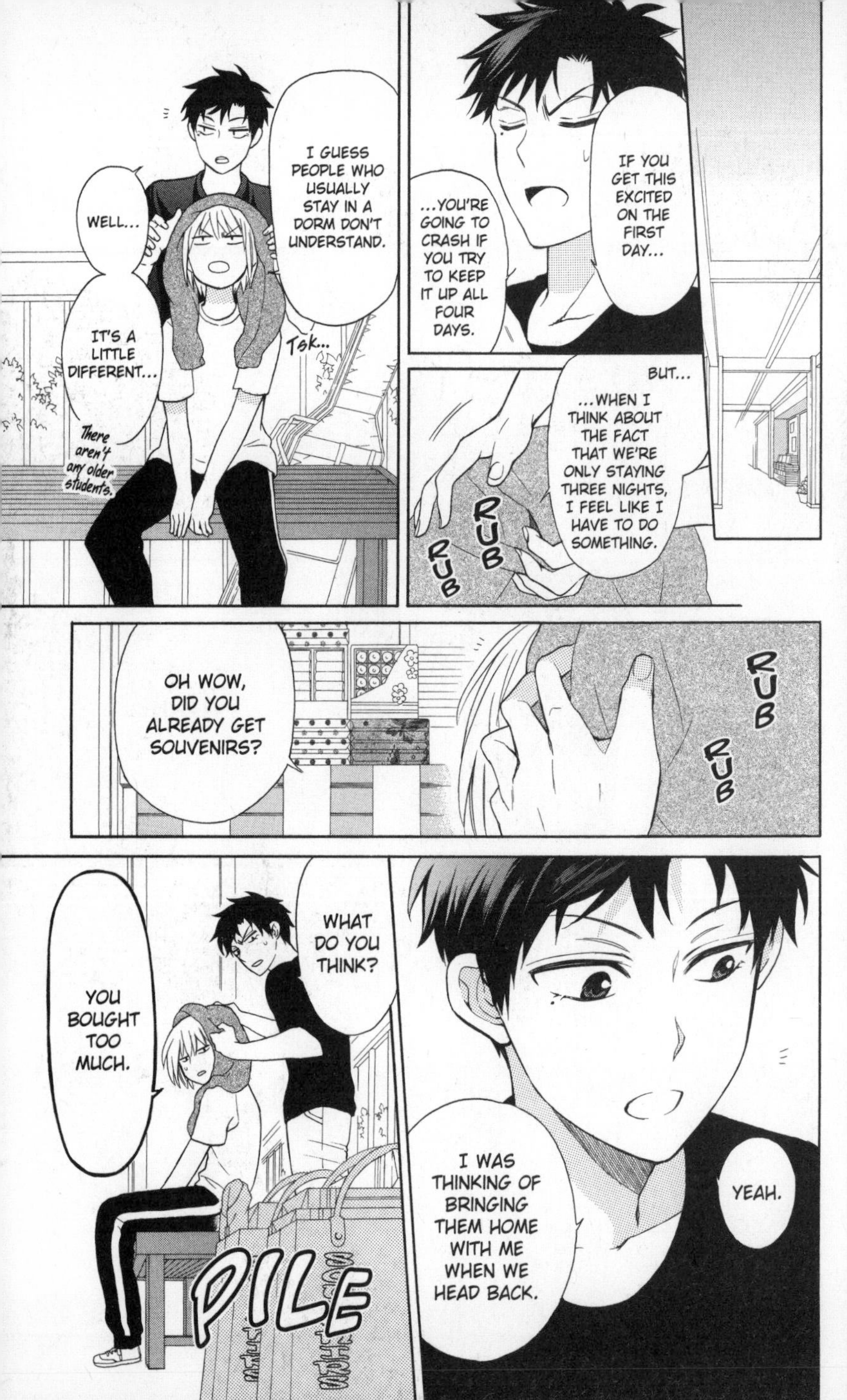
IF YOU GET THIS EXCITED ON THE FIRST DAY...
...YOU'RE GOING TO CRASH IF YOU TRY TO KEEP IT UP ALL FOUR DAYS.
I GUESS PEOPLE WHO USUALLY STAY IN A DORM DON'T UNDERSTAND.
WELL...
IT'S A LITTLE DIFFERENT...
There aren't any older students.
Tsk...
BUT...
...WHEN I THINK ABOUT THE FACT THAT WE'RE ONLY STAYING THREE NIGHTS, I FEEL LIKE I HAVE TO DO SOMETHING.
RUB
RUB
RUB
RUB
OH WOW, DID YOU ALREADY GET SOUVENIRS?
I WAS THINKING OF BRINGING THEM HOME WITH ME WHEN WE HEAD BACK.
YEAH.
WHAT DO YOU THINK?
YOU BOUGHT TOO MUCH.
PILE

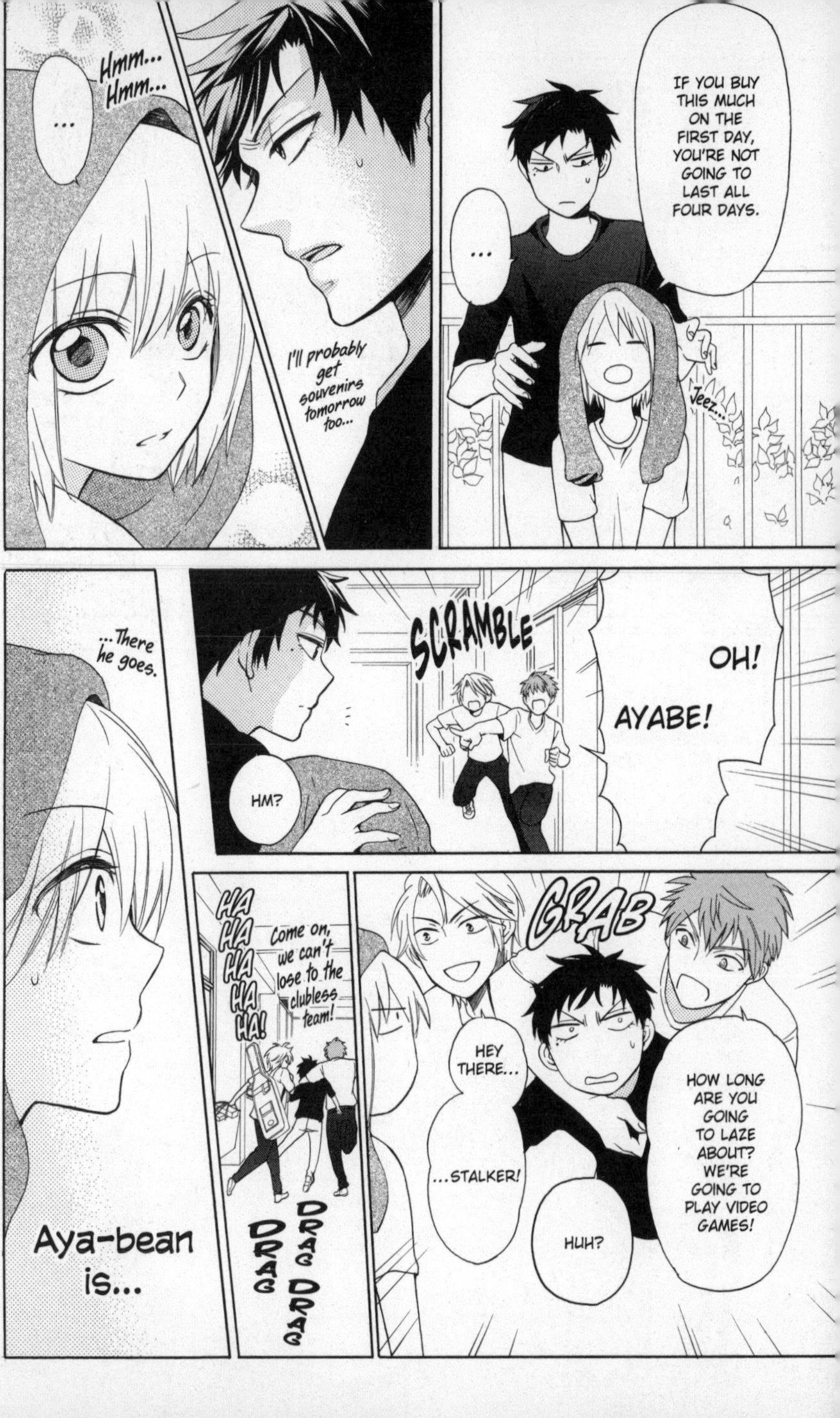
IF YOU BUY THIS MUCH ON THE FIRST DAY, YOU'RE NOT GOING TO LAST ALL FOUR DAYS.
...
Jeez...
I'll probably get souvenirs tomorrow too...
Hmm... Hmm...
...
OH!
AYABE!
SCRAMBLE
HM?
GRAB
HOW LONG ARE YOU GOING TO LAZE ABOUT? WE'RE GOING TO PLAY VIDEO GAMES!
HEY THERE...
...STALKER!
HUH?
HA HA HA HA HA!
Come on, we can't lose to the clubless team!
DRAG DRAG DRAG DRAG
...There he goes.
Aya-bean is...

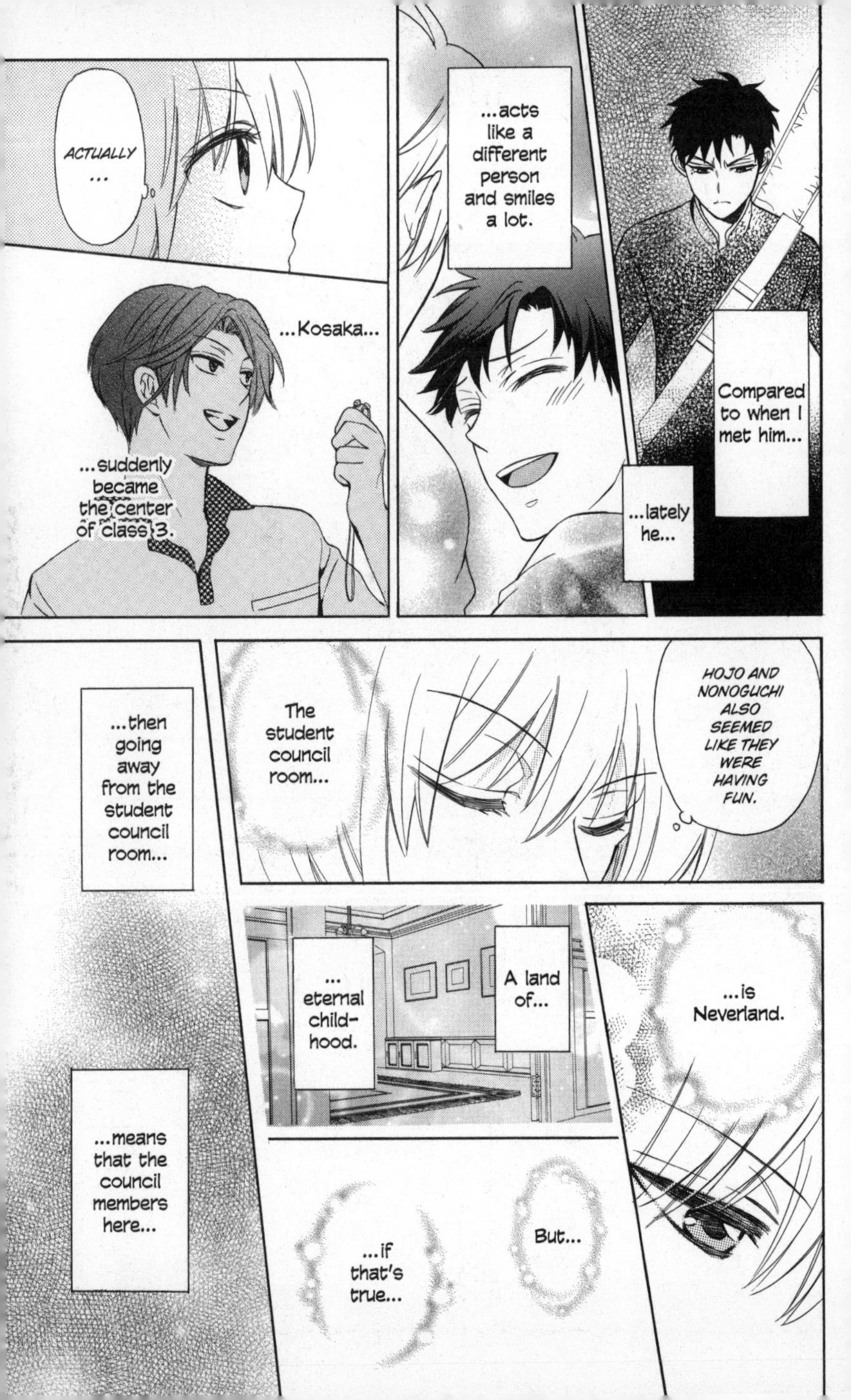
Compared to when I met him...
...lately he...
...acts like a different person and smiles a lot.
ACTUALLY ...
...Kosaka...
...suddenly became the center of class 3.
HOJO AND NONOGUCHI ALSO SEEMED LIKE THEY WERE HAVING FUN.
The student council room...
...then going away from the student council room...
...is Neverland.
A land of...
... eternal child-hood.
But...
...if that's true...
...means that the council members here...

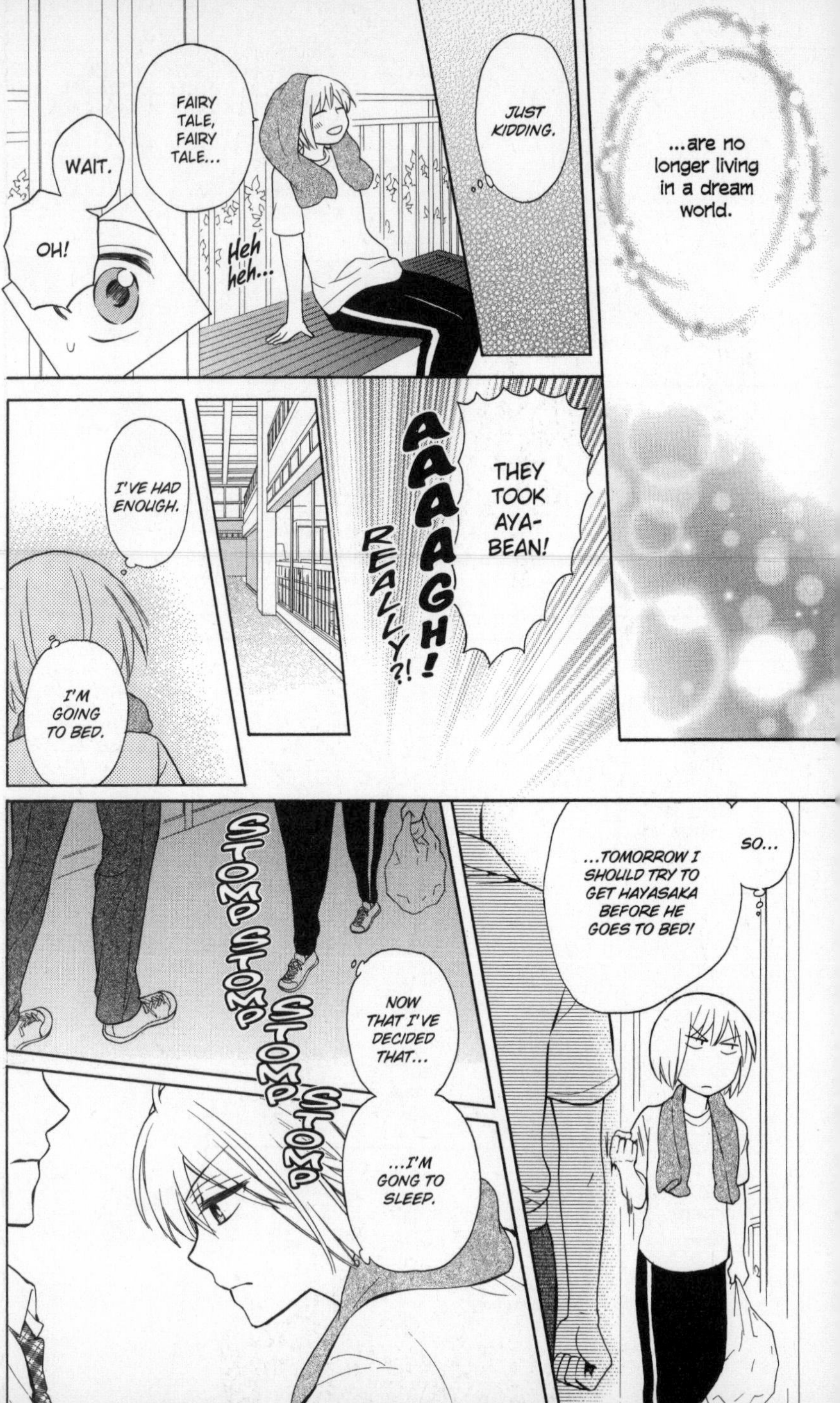
...are no longer living in a dream world.
JUST KIDDING.
FAIRY TALE, FAIRY TALE...
Heh heh...
WAIT.
OH!
THEY TOOK AYA-BEAN!
AAAAGH! REALLY?!
I'VE HAD ENOUGH.
I'M GOING TO BED.
SO...
...TOMORROW I SHOULD TRY TO GET HAYASAKA BEFORE HE GOES TO BED!
STOMP STOMP STOMP STOMP
NOW THAT I'VE DECIDED THAT...
...I'M GONG TO SLEEP.

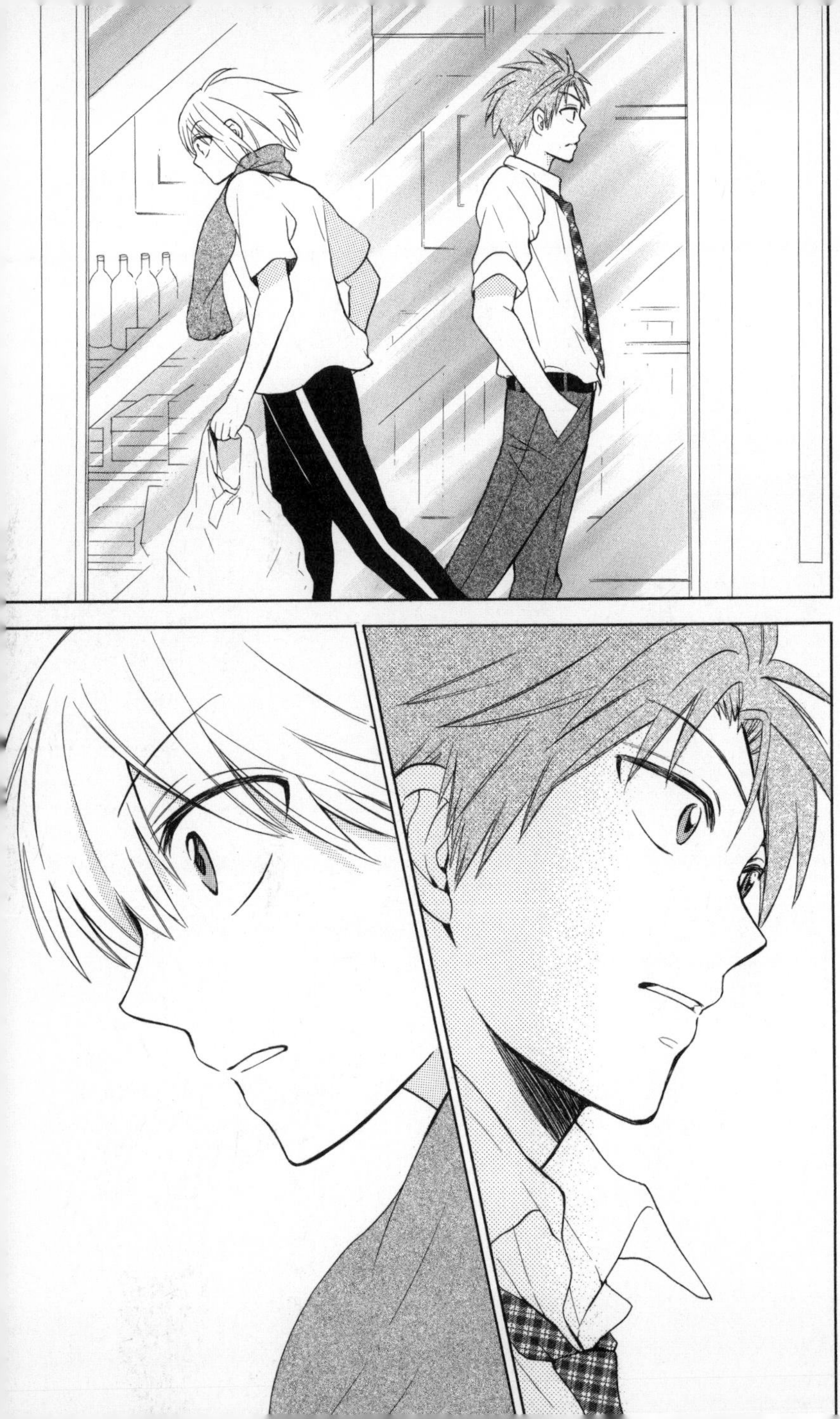

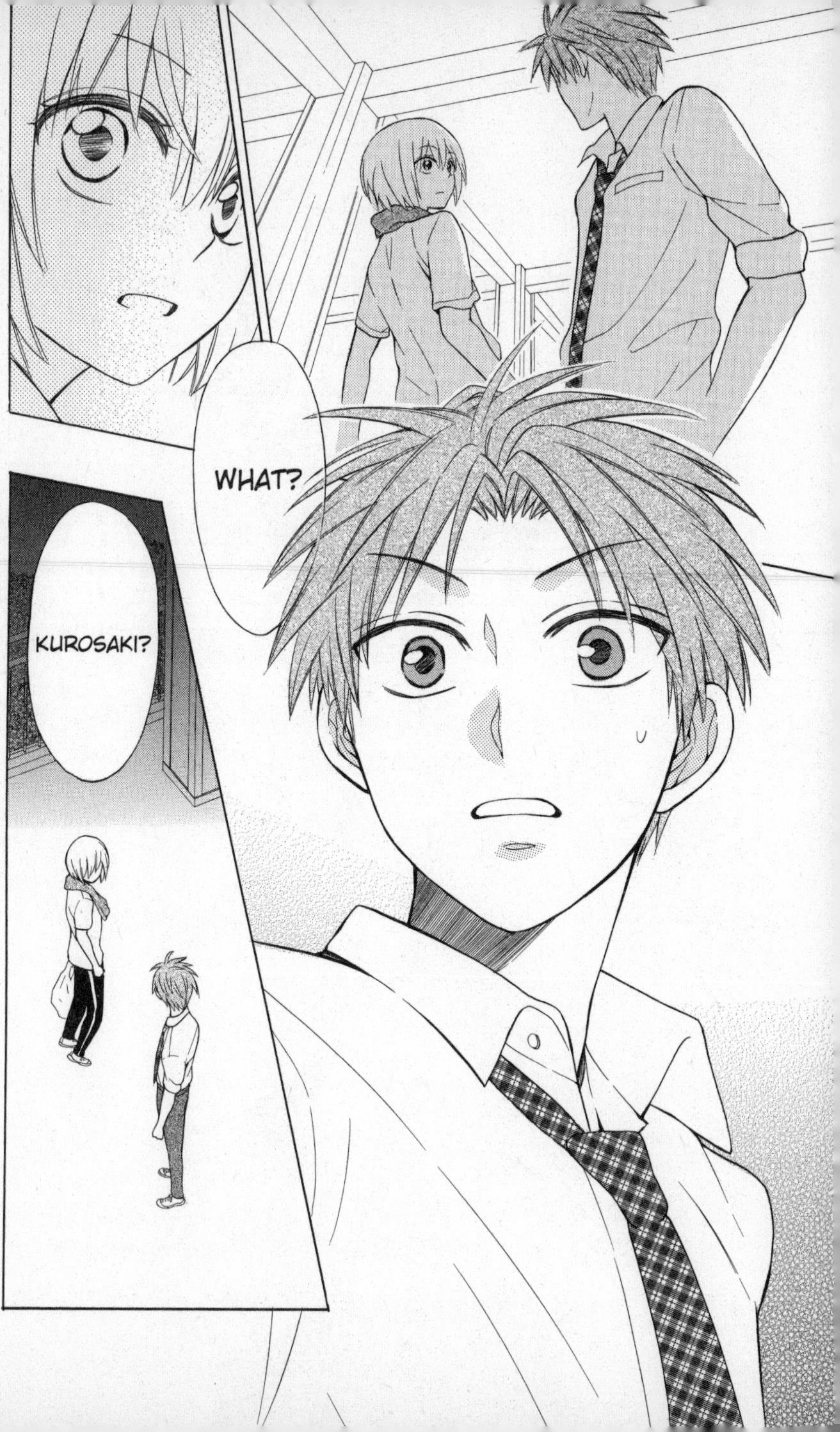
WHAT?
KUROSAKI?

AIR ________

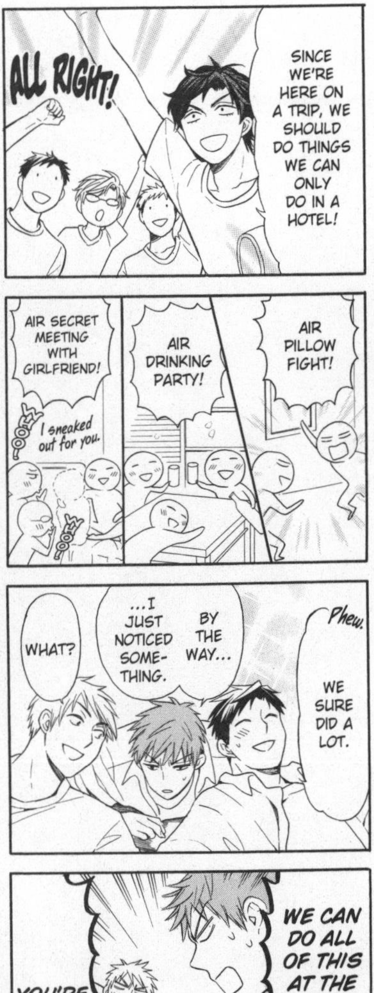

SINCE WE'RE HERE ON A TRIP, WE SHOULD DO THINGS WE CAN ONLY DO IN A HOTEL!
ALL RIGHT!
AIR PILLOW FIGHT!
AIR DRINKING PARTY!
AIR SECRET MEETING WITH GIRLFRIEND!
I sneaked out for you.
Phew.
WE SURE DID A LOT.
BY THE WAY...
...I JUST NOTICED SOME-THING.
WHAT?
WE CAN DO ALL OF THIS AT THE DORM!
YOU'RE RIGHT!
SHOOM

AN EXCITING GUEST 1

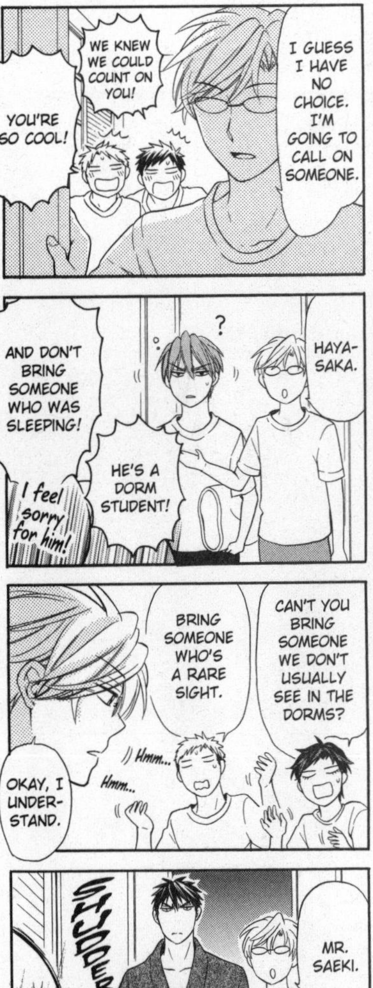

I GUESS I HAVE NO CHOICE. I'M GOING TO CALL ON SOMEONE.
WE KNEW WE COULD COUNT ON YOU!
YOU'RE SO COOL!
HAYA-SAKA.
?
AND DON'T BRING SOMEONE WHO WAS SLEEPING!
HE'S A DORM STUDENT!
I feel sorry for him!
CAN'T YOU BRING SOMEONE WE DON'T USUALLY SEE IN THE DORMS?
BRING SOMEONE WHO'S A RARE SIGHT.
Hmm...
Hmm...
OKAY, I UNDER-STAND.
MR. SAEKI.
SHUDDER
SHUDDER

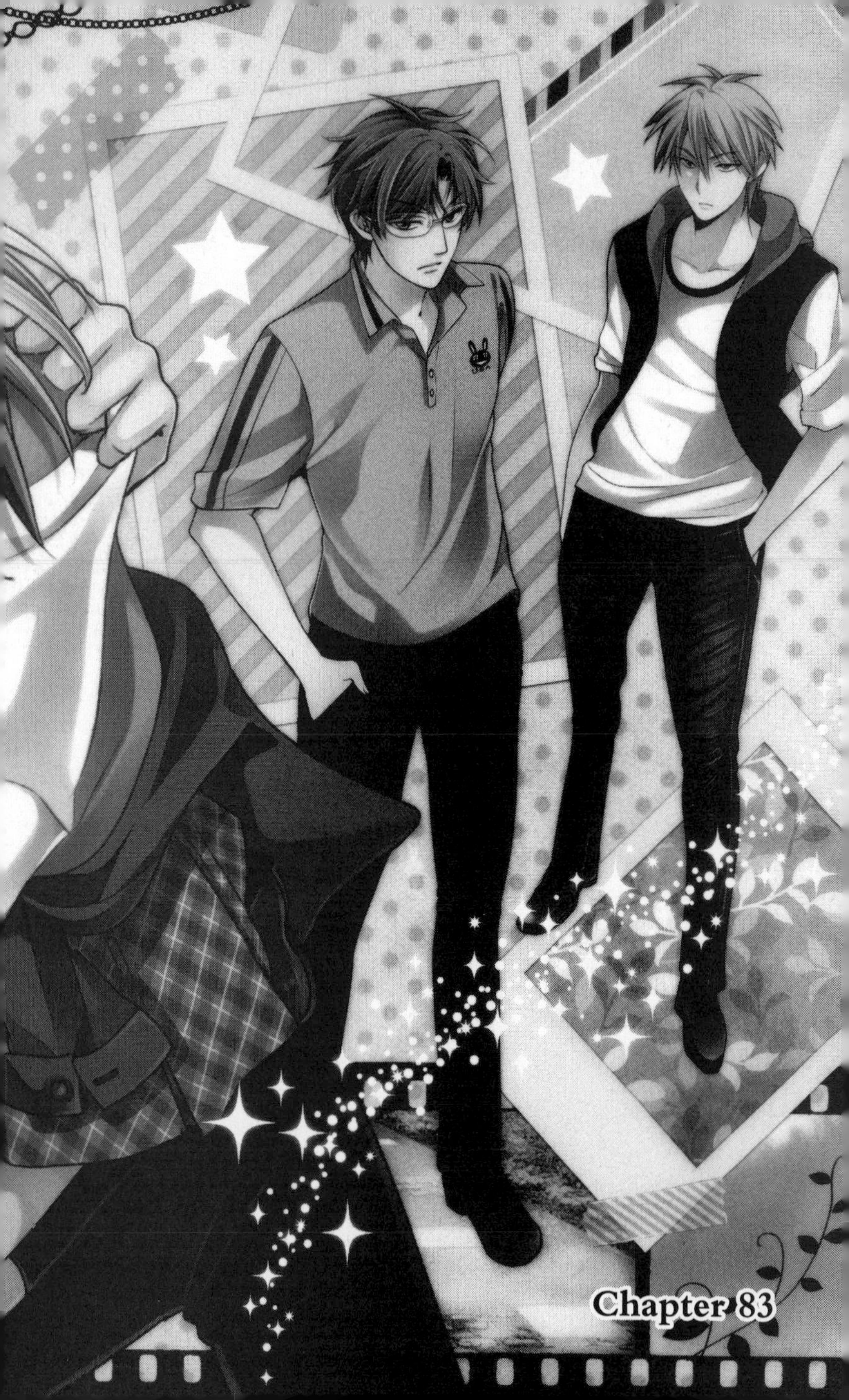
Chapter 83

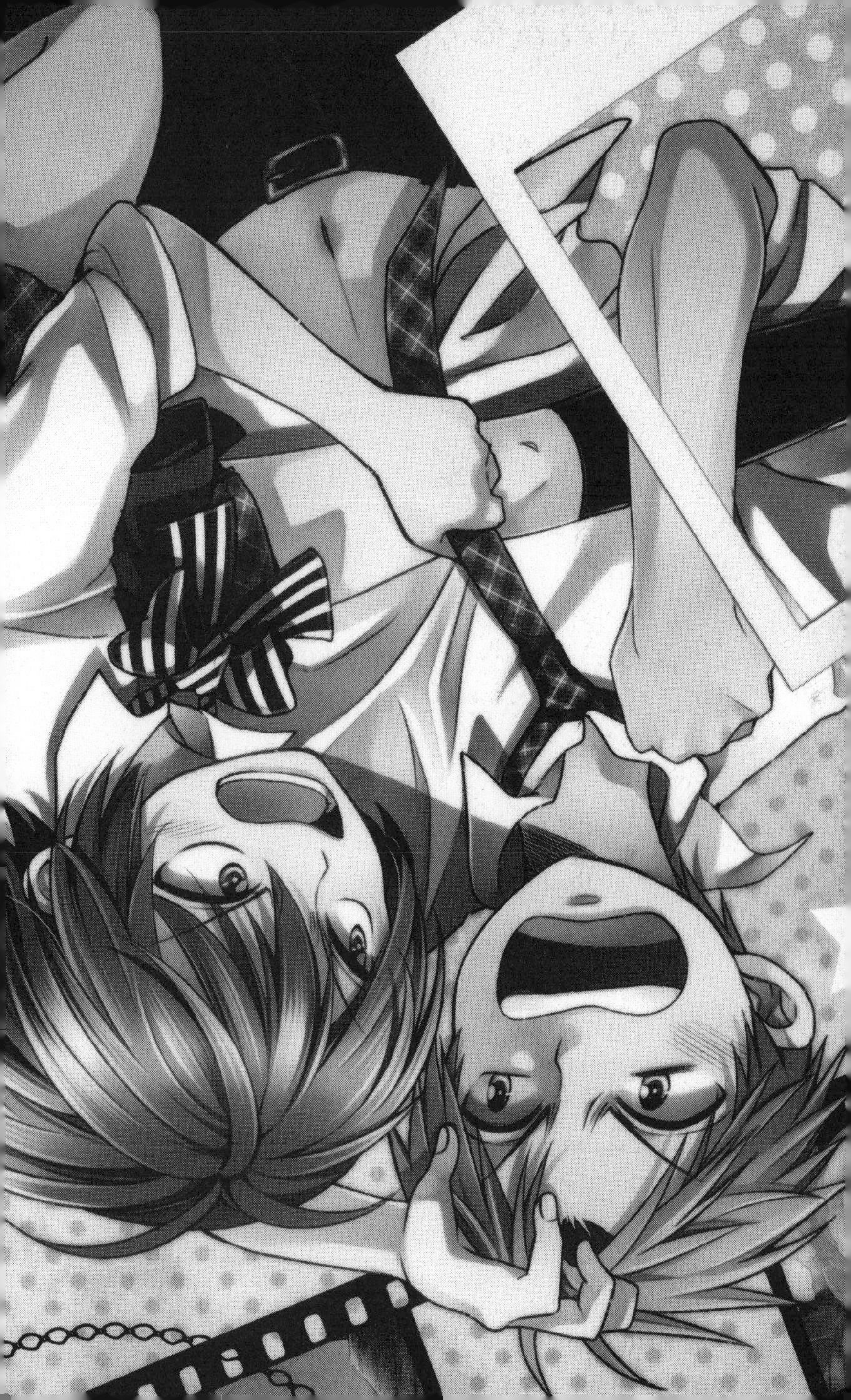

AN EXCITING GUEST 2

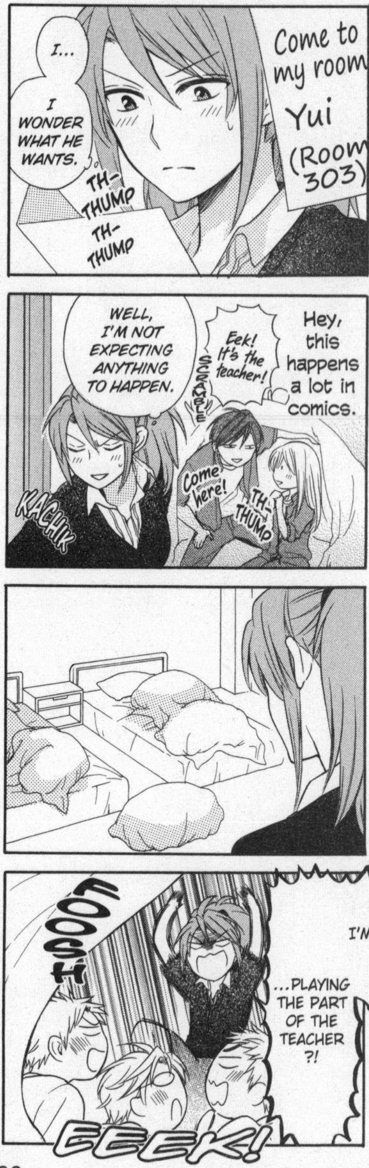
Come to my room Yui (Room 303)
I...
I WONDER WHAT HE WANTS.
TH-THUMP
TH-THUMP
Hey, this happens a lot in comics.
Eek! It's the teacher!
SCRAMBLE
WELL, I'M NOT EXPECTING ANYTHING TO HAPPEN.
Come here!
TH-THUMP
KACHIK
I'M...
...PLAYING THE PART OF THE TEACHER ?!
WOOSH
EEEK!

DIRECTION OF HER CONCERN

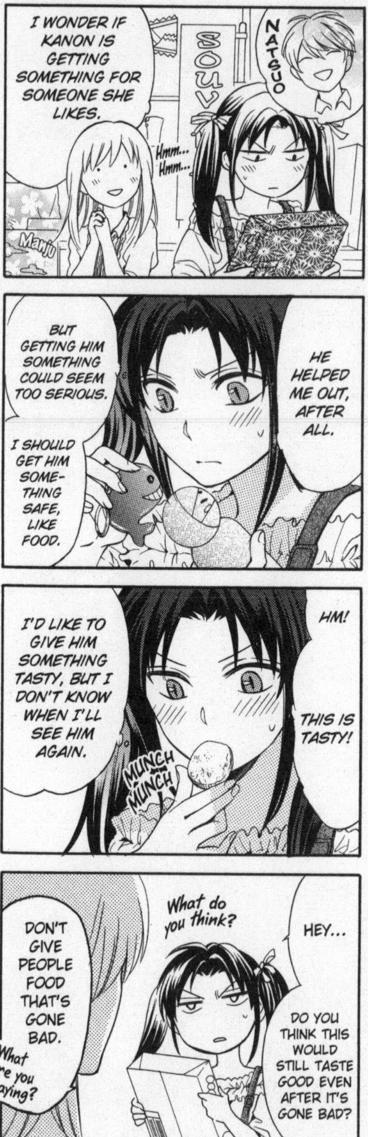
NATSUO
SOUV
I WONDER IF KANON IS GETTING SOMETHING FOR SOMEONE SHE LIKES.
Hmm... Hmm...
Manju
HE HELPED ME OUT, AFTER ALL.
BUT GETTING HIM SOMETHING COULD SEEM TOO SERIOUS.
I SHOULD GET HIM SOME-THING SAFE, LIKE FOOD.
HM!
THIS IS TASTY!
I'D LIKE TO GIVE HIM SOMETHING TASTY, BUT I DON'T KNOW WHEN I'LL SEE HIM AGAIN.
MUNCH MUNCH
HEY...
What do you think?
DO YOU THINK THIS WOULD STILL TASTE GOOD EVEN AFTER IT'S GONE BAD?
DON'T GIVE PEOPLE FOOD THAT'S GONE BAD.
What are you saying?

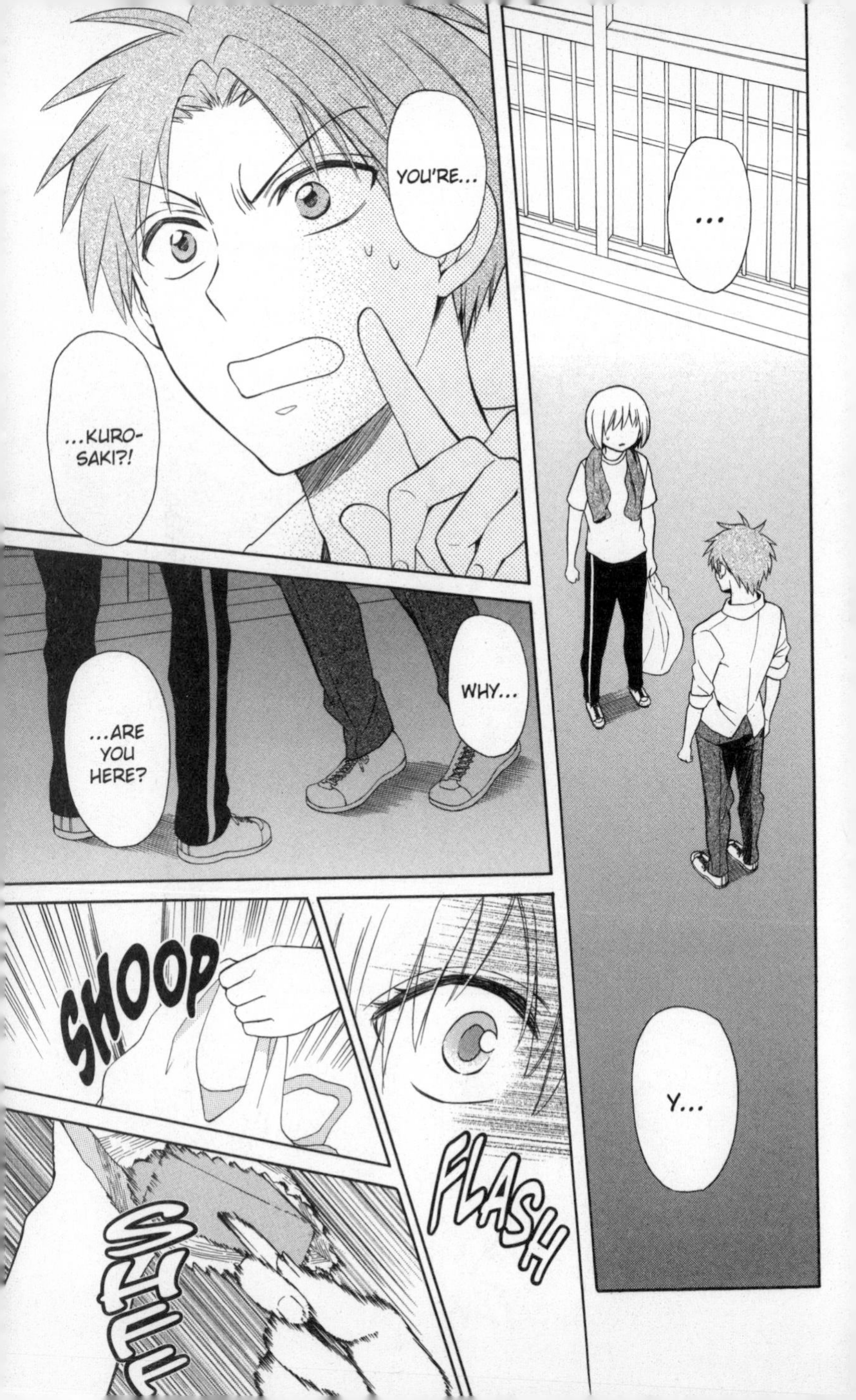
...
Y...
YOU'RE...
...KURO-SAKI?!
WHY...
...ARE YOU HERE?
FLASH
SHOOP
SHUFF

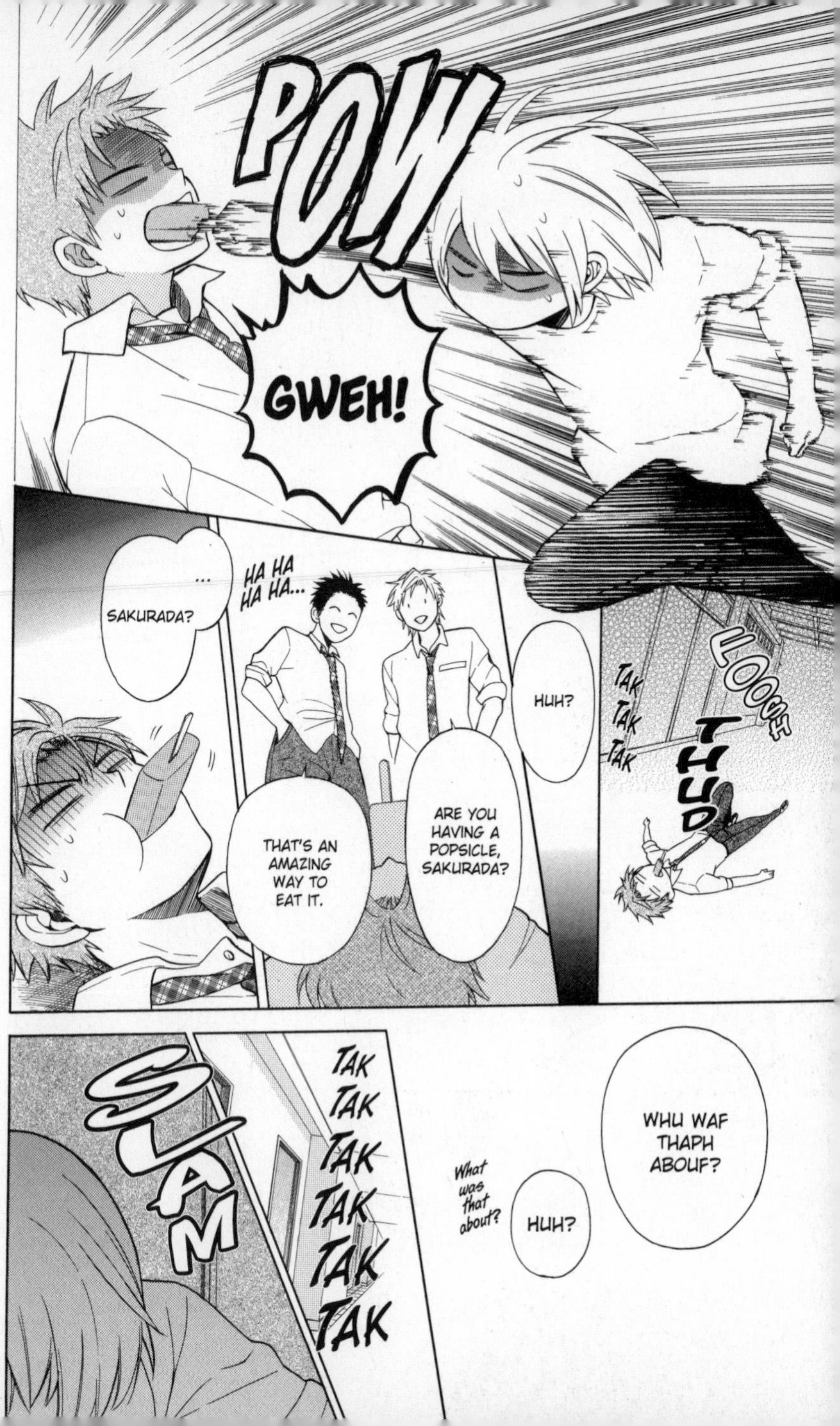
POW
GWEH!
THUD
TAK TAK TAK
HUH?
ARE YOU HAVING A POPSICLE, SAKURADA?
HA HA HA HA...
THAT'S AN AMAZING WAY TO EAT IT.
... SAKURADA?
WHU WAF THAPH ABOUF?
What was that about?
HUH?
SLAM
TAK TAK TAK TAK TAK TAK

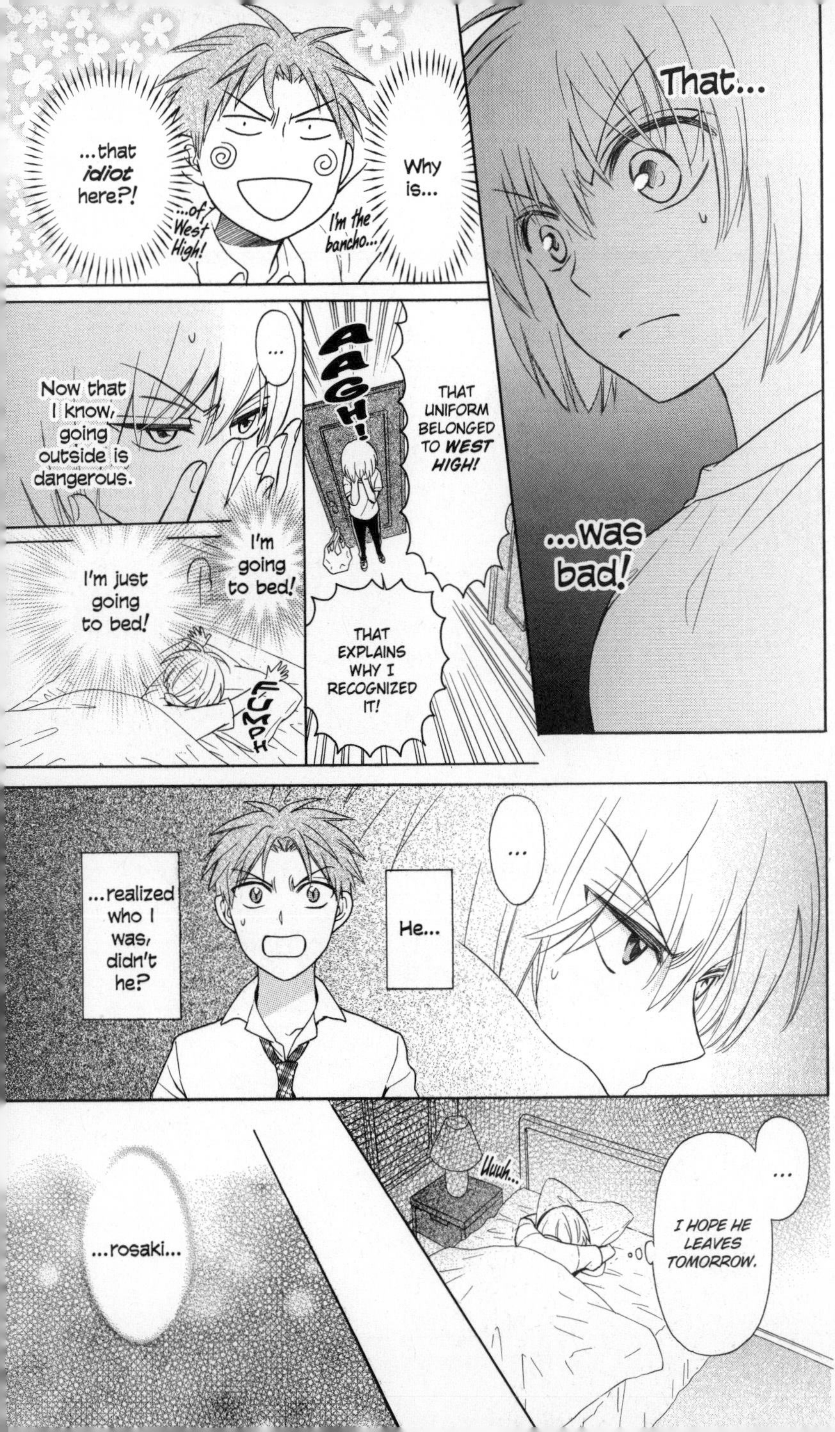
That...
...was bad!
Why is...
I'm the bancho...
...of West High!
...that *idiot* here?!
THAT UNIFORM BELONGED TO ***WEST HIGH!***
AAGH!
THAT EXPLAINS WHY I RECOGNIZED IT!
...
Now that I know, going outside is dangerous.
I'm going to bed!
I'm just going to bed!
FUMPH
...
He...
...realized who I was, didn't he?
...
I HOPE HE LEAVES TOMORROW.
Uuuh...
...rosaki...

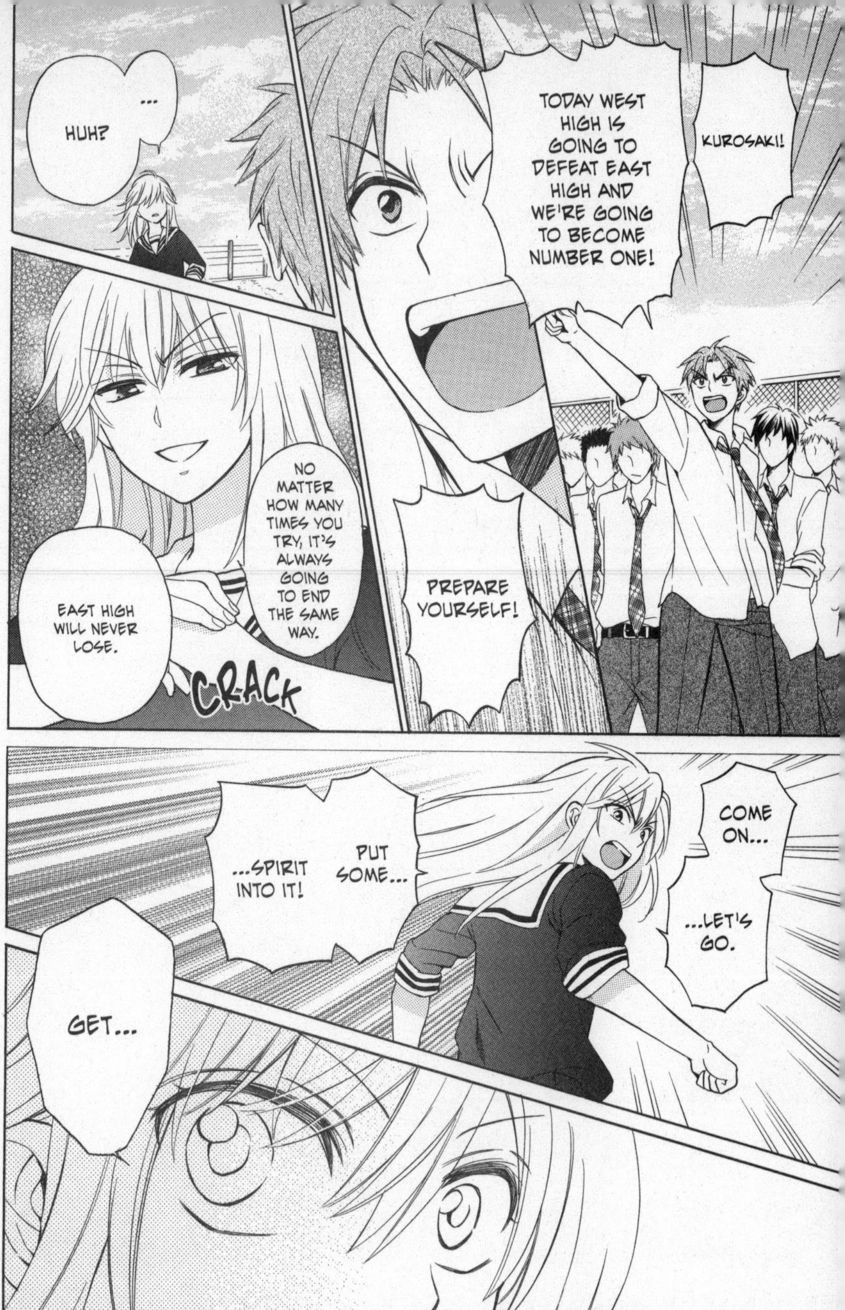
KUROSAKI!
TODAY WEST HIGH IS GOING TO DEFEAT EAST HIGH AND WE'RE GOING TO BECOME NUMBER ONE!
...
HUH?
PREPARE YOURSELF!
NO MATTER HOW MANY TIMES YOU TRY, IT'S ALWAYS GOING TO END THE SAME WAY.
EAST HIGH WILL NEVER LOSE.
CRACK
COME ON...
...LET'S GO.
PUT SOME...
...SPIRIT INTO IT!
GET...

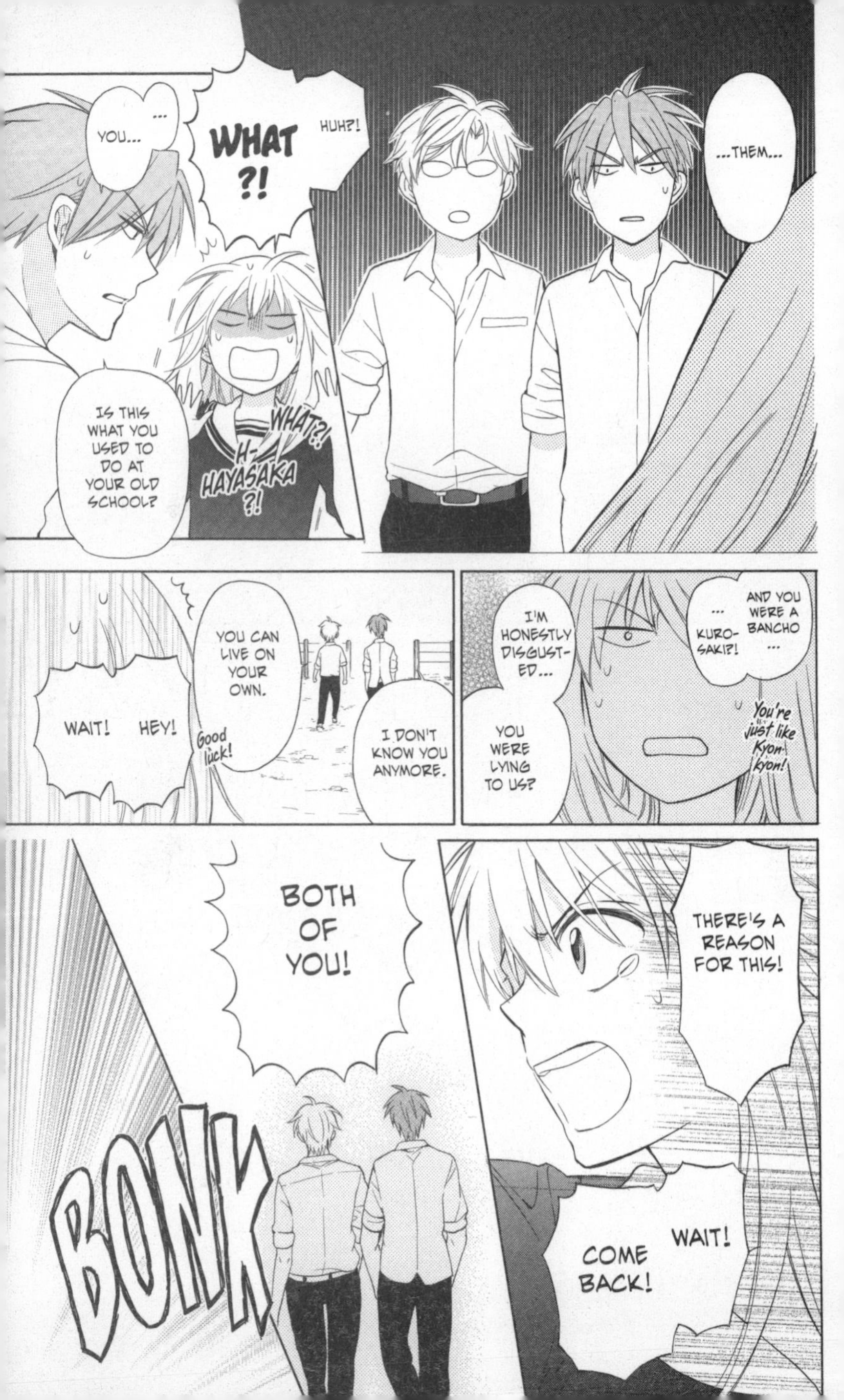
...THEM...
...
YOU...
WHAT ?!
HUH?!
IS THIS WHAT YOU USED TO DO AT YOUR OLD SCHOOL?
WHAT?!
H-HAYASAKA ?!
AND YOU WERE A BANCHO ...
... KURO-SAKI?!
You're just like Kyon-kyon!
I'M HONESTLY DISGUST-ED...
YOU WERE LYING TO US?
I DON'T KNOW YOU ANYMORE.
YOU CAN LIVE ON YOUR OWN.
Good luck!
WAIT! HEY!
THERE'S A REASON FOR THIS!
WAIT!
COME BACK!
BOTH OF YOU!
BONK

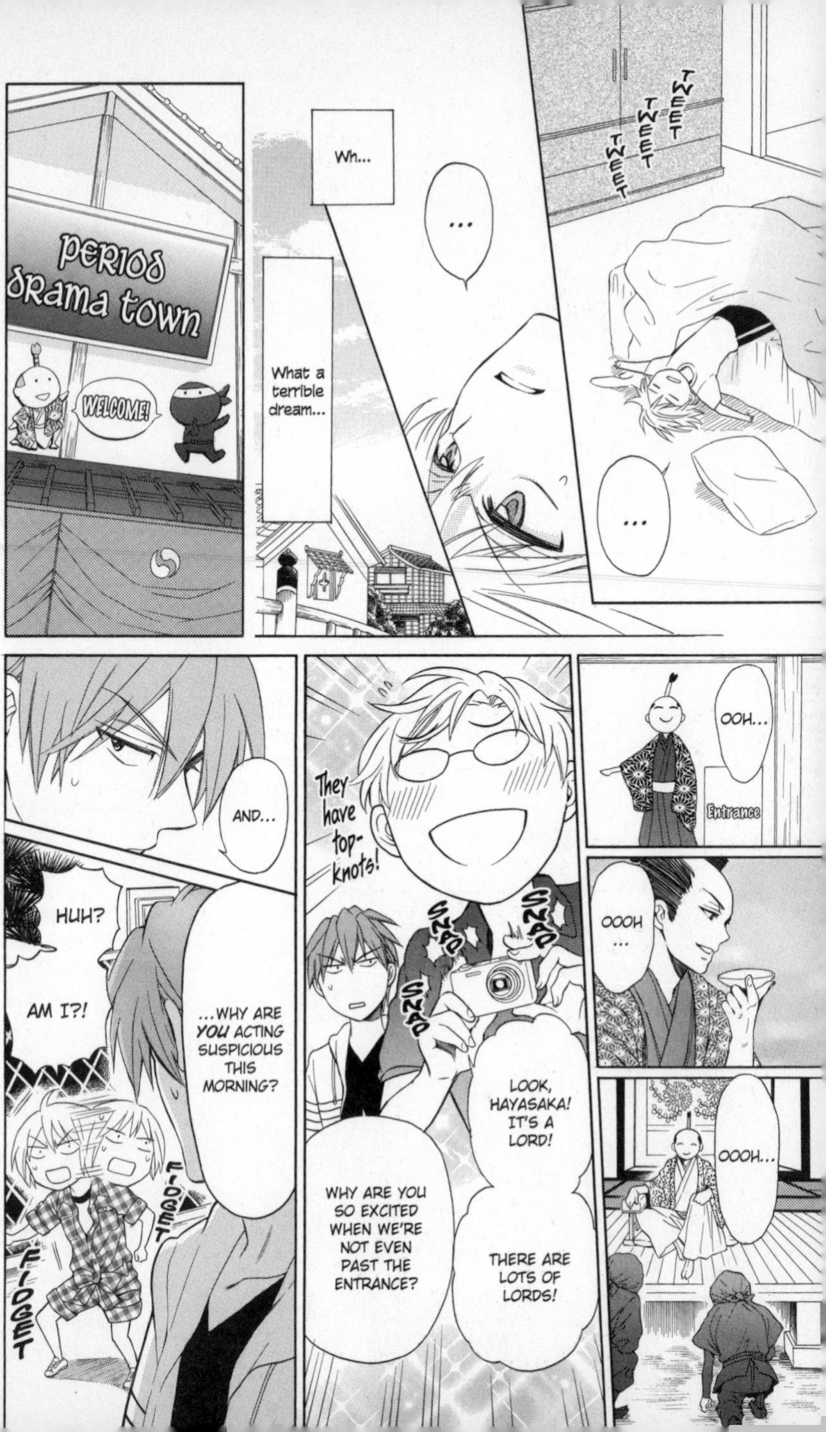
TWEET TWEET TWEET
...
Wh...
...
What a terrible dream...
PERIOD DRAMA TOWN
WELCOME!
OOH...
Entrance
OOOH...
OOOH...
LOOK, HAYASAKA! IT'S A LORD!
THERE ARE LOTS OF LORDS!
They have top-knots!
SNAP SNAP SNAP
WHY ARE YOU SO EXCITED WHEN WE'RE NOT EVEN PAST THE ENTRANCE?
AND...
...WHY ARE YOU ACTING SUSPICIOUS THIS MORNING?
HUH?
AM I?!
FIDGET FIDGET

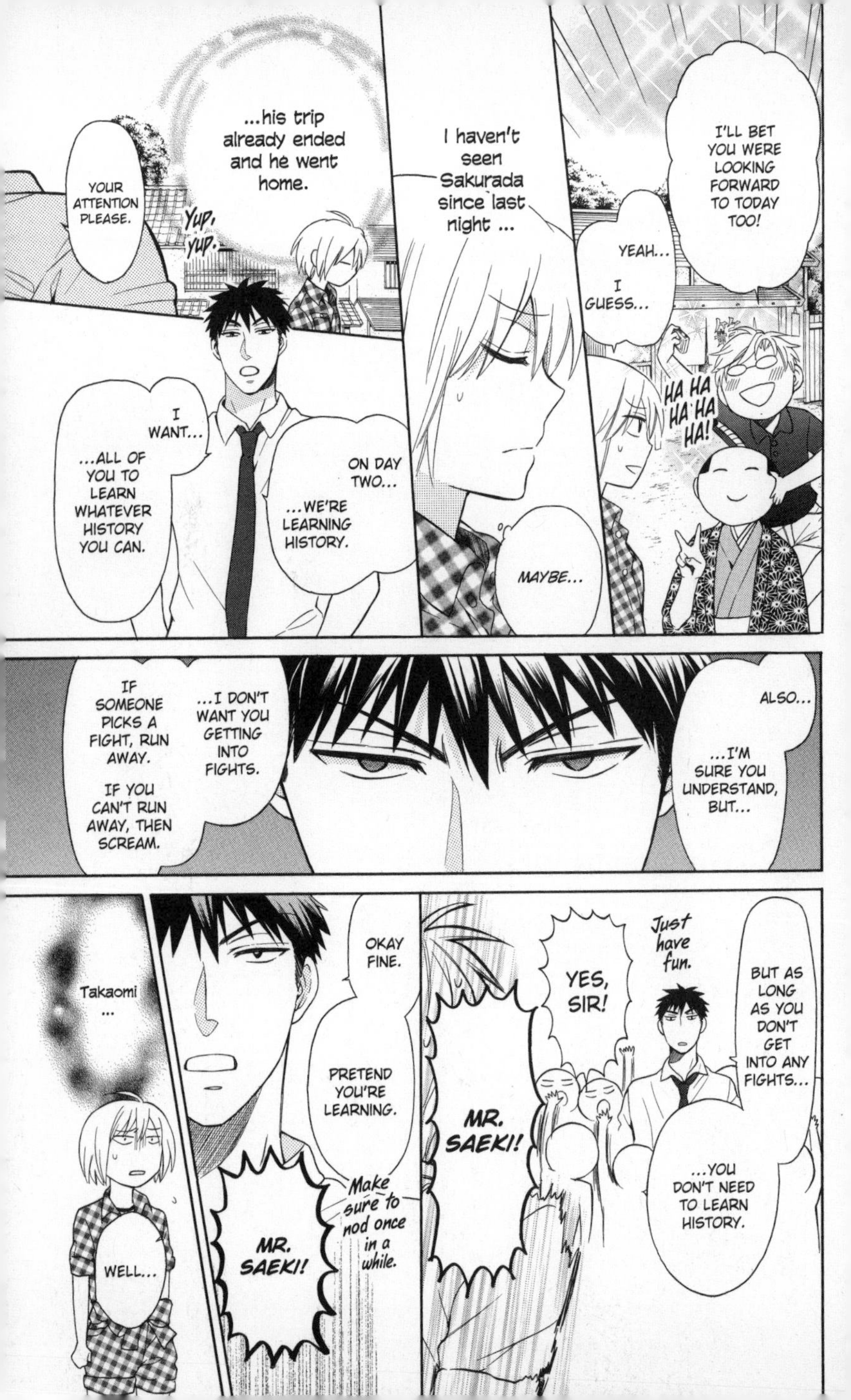
I'LL BET YOU WERE LOOKING FORWARD TO TODAY TOO!
YEAH...
I GUESS...
HA HA HA HA HA!
I haven't seen Sakurada since last night ...
MAYBE...
...his trip already ended and he went home.
Yup, yup.
YOUR ATTENTION PLEASE.
I WANT...
...ALL OF YOU TO LEARN WHATEVER HISTORY YOU CAN.
ON DAY TWO...
...WE'RE LEARNING HISTORY.
ALSO...
...I'M SURE YOU UNDERSTAND, BUT...
...I DON'T WANT YOU GETTING INTO FIGHTS.
IF SOMEONE PICKS A FIGHT, RUN AWAY.
IF YOU CAN'T RUN AWAY, THEN SCREAM.
BUT AS LONG AS YOU DON'T GET INTO ANY FIGHTS...
...YOU DON'T NEED TO LEARN HISTORY.
Just have fun.
YES, SIR!
MR. SAEKI!
OKAY FINE.
PRETEND YOU'RE LEARNING.
Make sure to nod once in a while.
MR. SAEKI!
Takaomi ...
WELL...

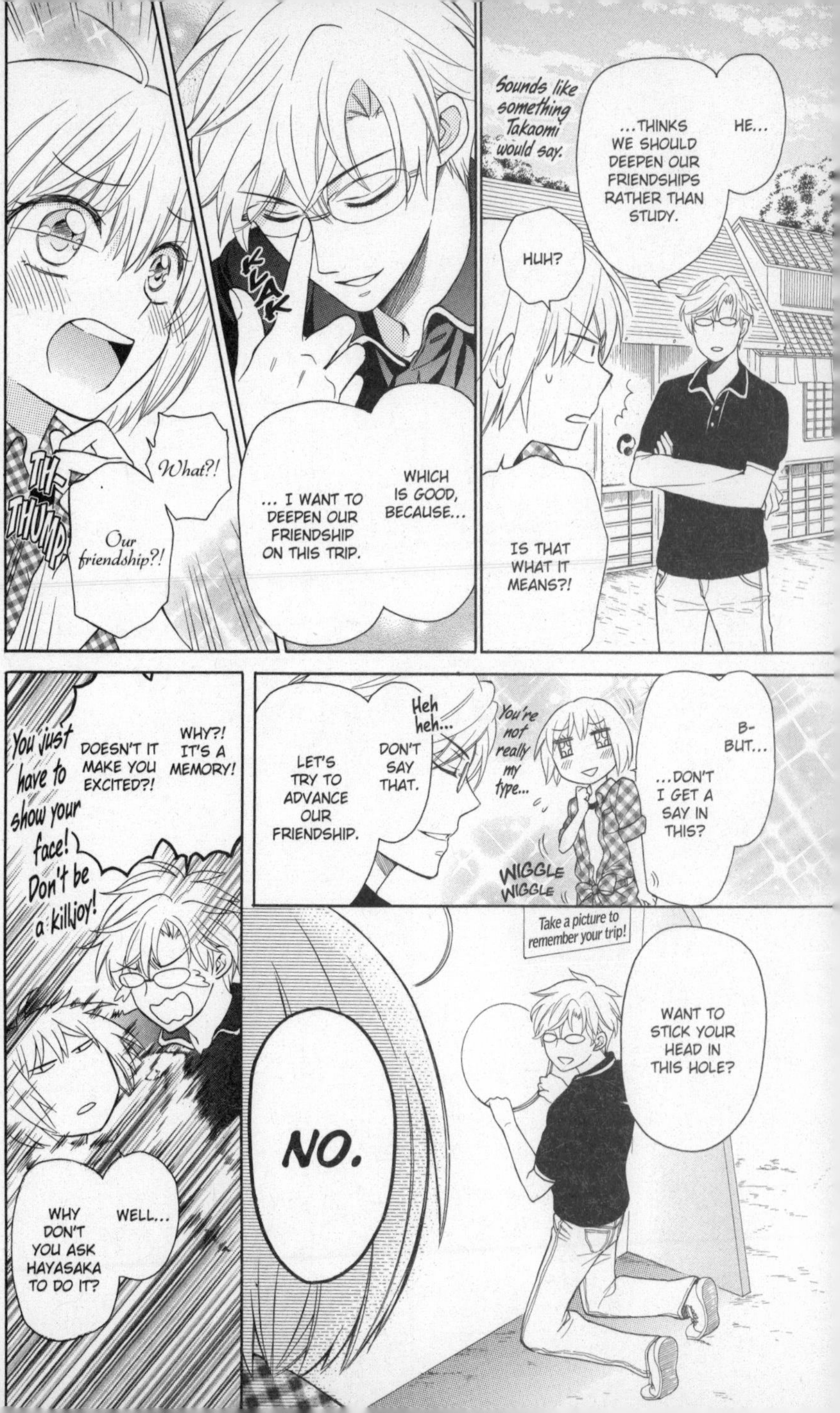
HE...
...THINKS WE SHOULD DEEPEN OUR FRIENDSHIPS RATHER THAN STUDY.
Sounds like something Takaomi would say.
HUH?
IS THAT WHAT IT MEANS?!
WHICH IS GOOD, BECAUSE...
... I WANT TO DEEPEN OUR FRIENDSHIP ON THIS TRIP.
KVAK
What?!
Our friendship?!
TH-THUMP
B-BUT...
...DON'T I GET A SAY IN THIS?
You're not really my type...
WIGGLE WIGGLE
Heh heh...
DON'T SAY THAT.
LET'S TRY TO ADVANCE OUR FRIENDSHIP.
Take a picture to remember your trip!
WANT TO STICK YOUR HEAD IN THIS HOLE?
NO.
WHY?! IT'S A MEMORY!
DOESN'T IT MAKE YOU EXCITED?!
You just have to show your face! Don't be a killjoy!
WELL...
WHY DON'T YOU ASK HAYASAKA TO DO IT?

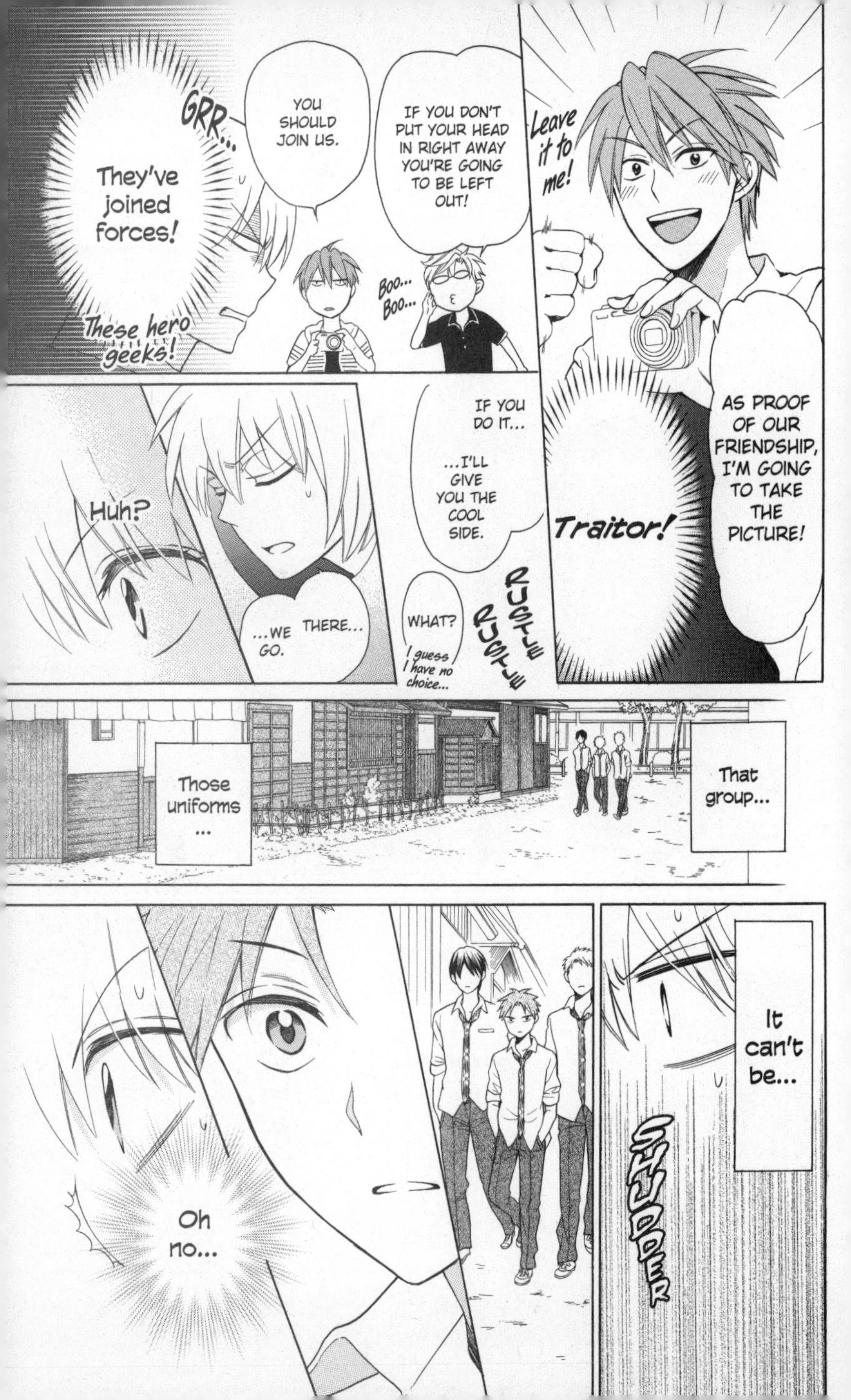
Leave it to me!
IF YOU DON'T PUT YOUR HEAD IN RIGHT AWAY YOU'RE GOING TO BE LEFT OUT!
YOU SHOULD JOIN US.
GRR...
They've joined forces!
Boo... Boo...
These hero geeks!
AS PROOF OF OUR FRIENDSHIP, I'M GOING TO TAKE THE PICTURE!
Traitor!
RUSTLE RUSTLE
IF YOU DO IT...
...I'LL GIVE YOU THE COOL SIDE.
WHAT?
I guess I have no choice...
THERE...
...WE GO.
Huh?
That group...
Those uniforms ...
It can't be...
SHUDDER
Oh no...

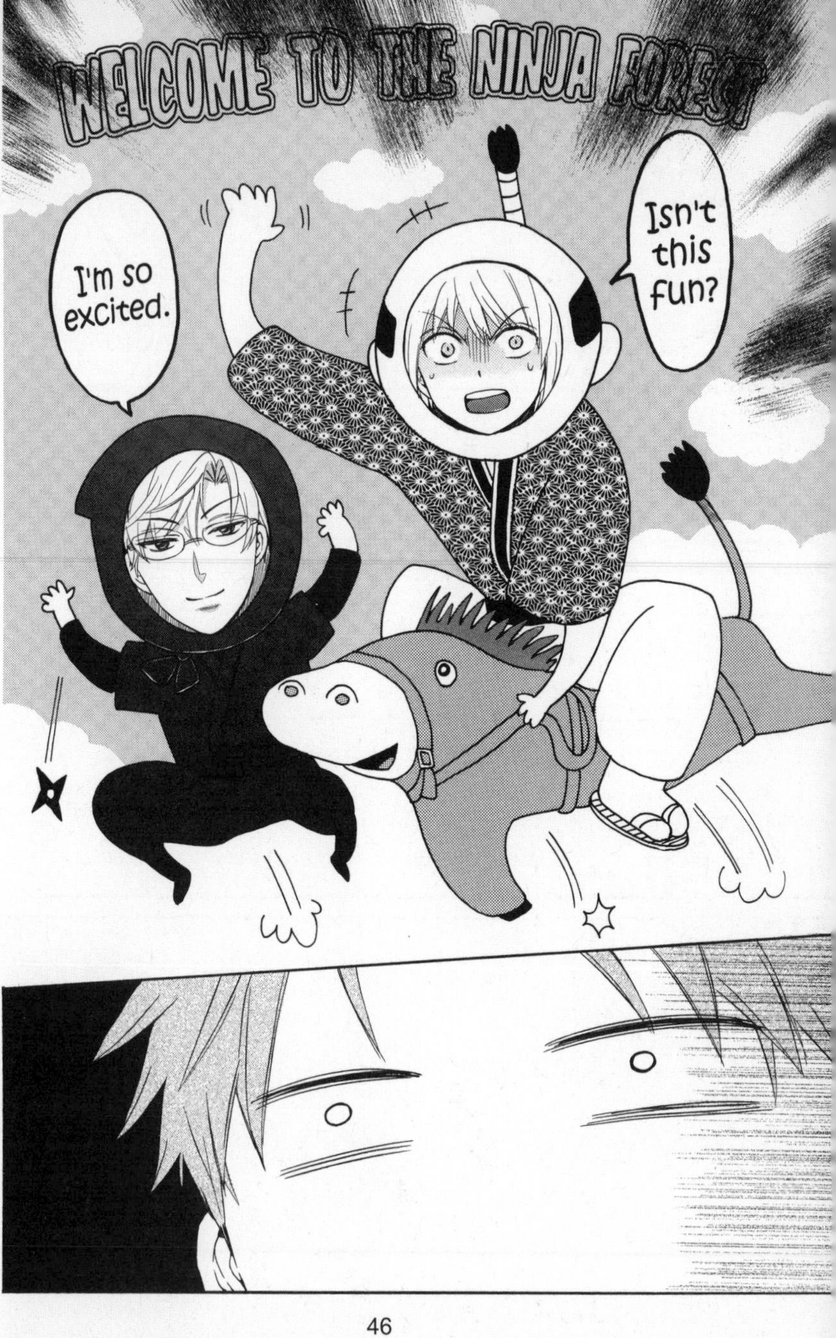
WELCOME TO THE NINJA FOREST
Isn't this fun?
I'm so excited.

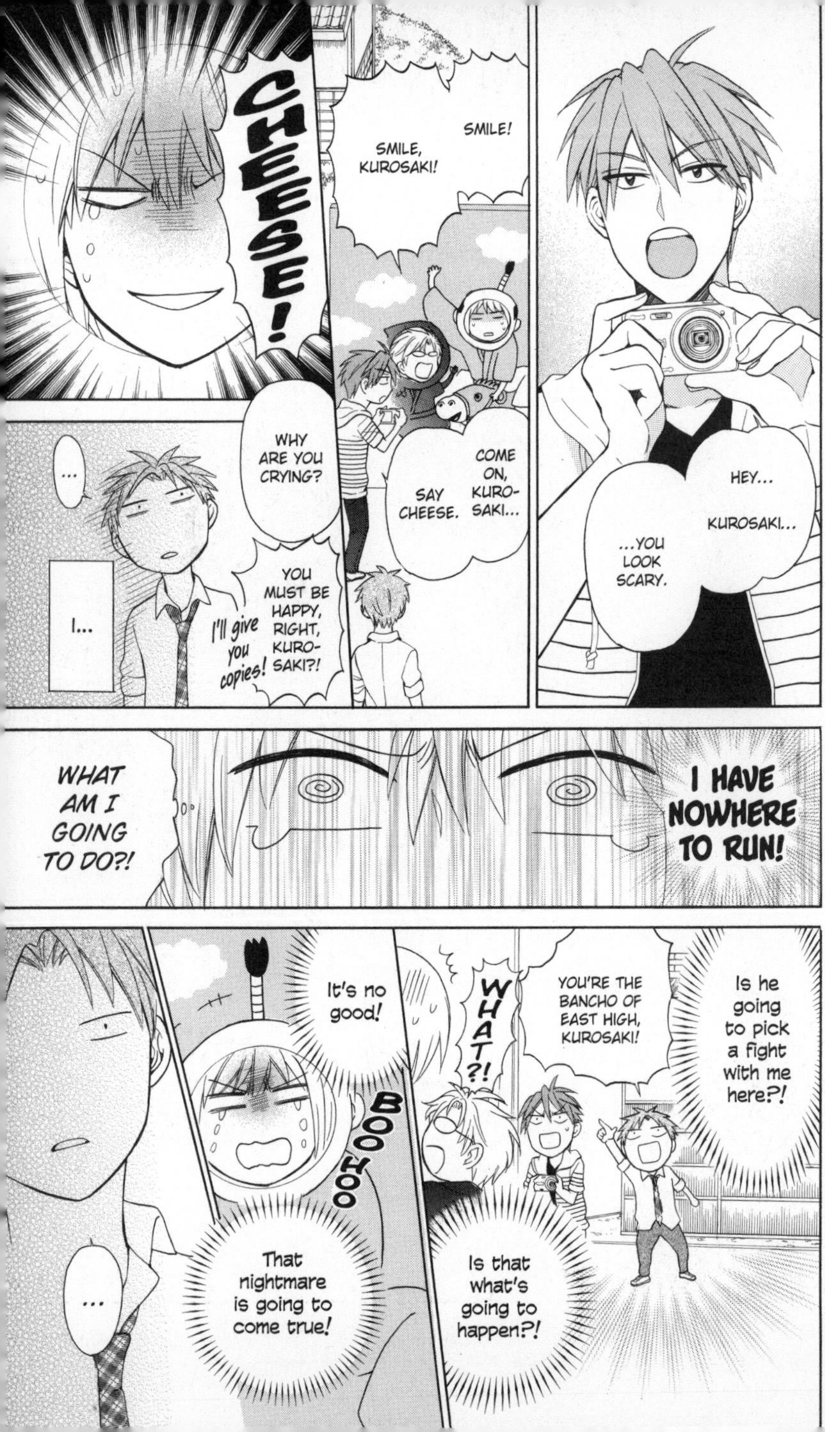
HEY...
KUROSAKI...
...YOU LOOK SCARY.
SMILE!
SMILE, KUROSAKI!
COME ON, KURO-SAKI...
SAY CHEESE.
CHEESE!
WHY ARE YOU CRYING?
YOU MUST BE HAPPY, RIGHT, KURO-SAKI?!
I'll give you copies!
...
I...
I HAVE NOWHERE TO RUN!
WHAT AM I GOING TO DO?!
Is he going to pick a fight with me here?!
YOU'RE THE BANCHO OF EAST HIGH, KUROSAKI!
WHAT?!
Is that what's going to happen?!
It's no good!
BOO HOO
That nightmare is going to come true!
...

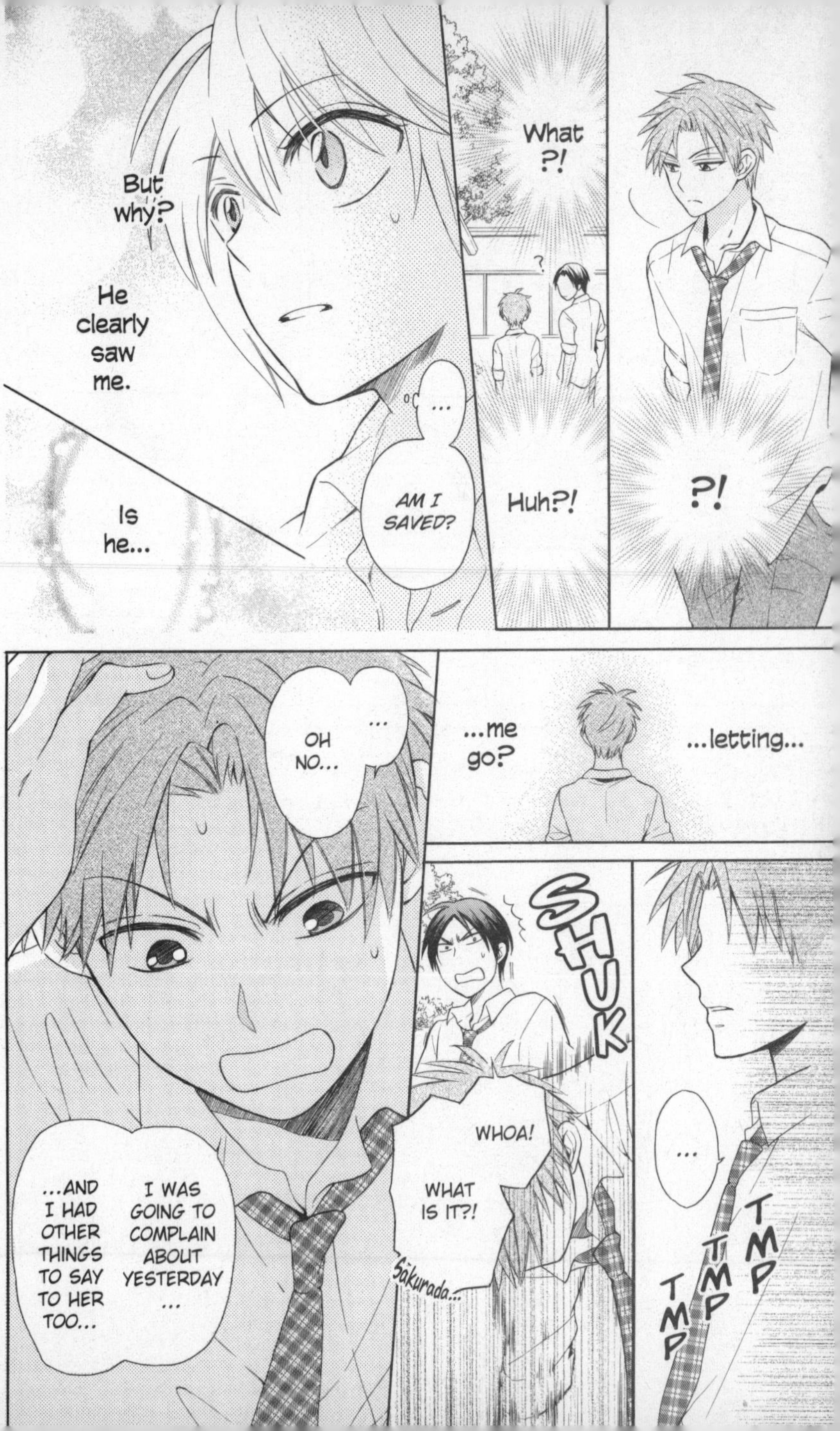
?!
What ?!
Huh?!
But why?
He clearly saw me.
...
AM I SAVED?
Is he...
...letting...
...me go?
TMP TMP TMP
...
SHUK
WHOA!
WHAT IS IT?!
Sakurada...
... OH NO...
I WAS GOING TO COMPLAIN ABOUT YESTERDAY ...
...AND I HAD OTHER THINGS TO SAY TO HER TOO...

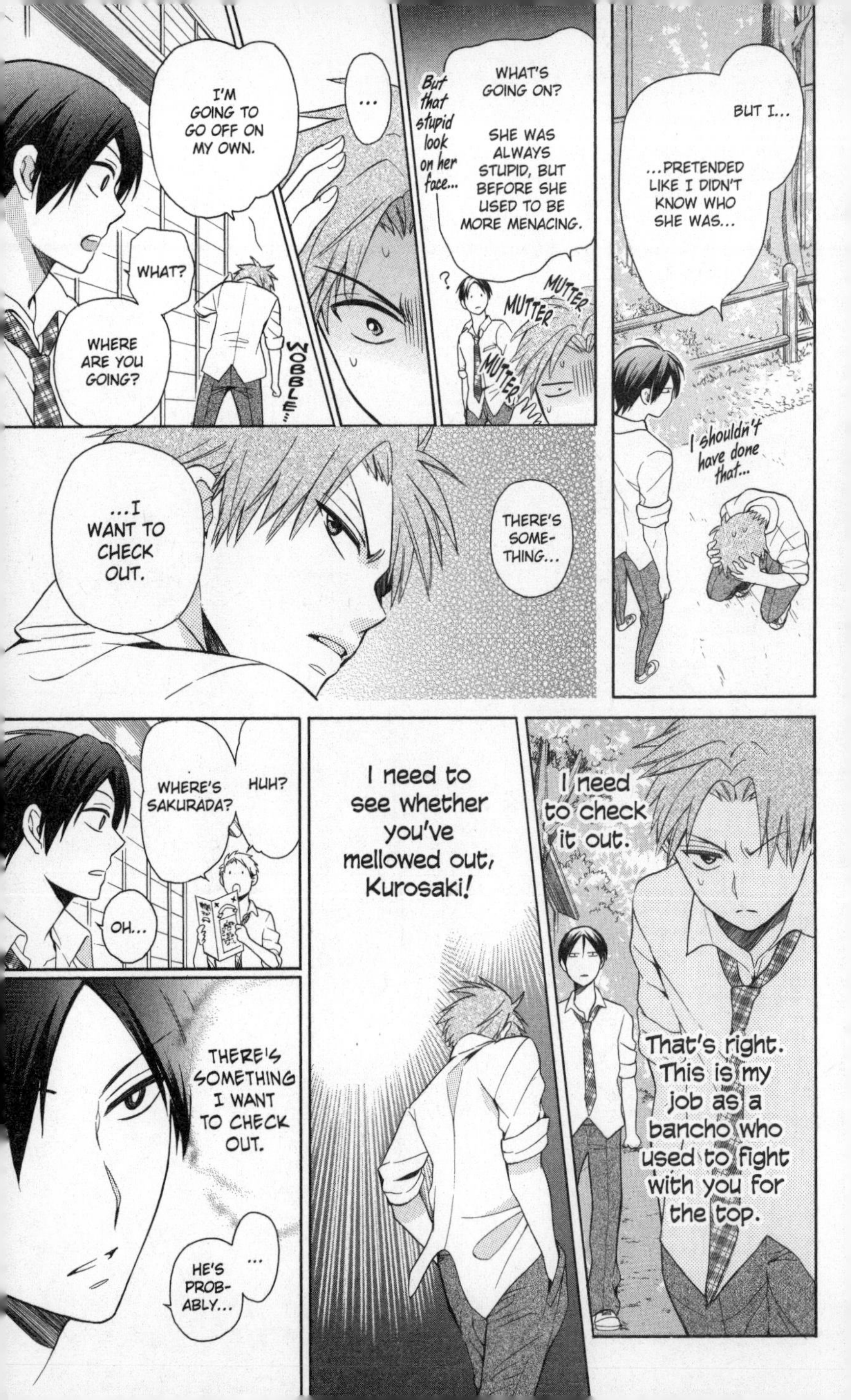
BUT I...
...PRETENDED LIKE I DIDN'T KNOW WHO SHE WAS...
I shouldn't have done that...
WHAT'S GOING ON?
SHE WAS ALWAYS STUPID, BUT BEFORE SHE USED TO BE MORE MENACING.
But that stupid look on her face...
MUTTER
MUTTER
MUTTER
...
I'M GOING TO GO OFF ON MY OWN.
WHAT?
WHERE ARE YOU GOING?
WOBBLE...
THERE'S SOME-THING...
...I WANT TO CHECK OUT.
I need to check it out.
That's right. This is my job as a bancho who used to fight with you for the top.
I need to see whether you've mellowed out, Kurosaki!
HUH?
WHERE'S SAKURADA?
OH...
THERE'S SOMETHING I WANT TO CHECK OUT.
...
HE'S PROB-ABLY...

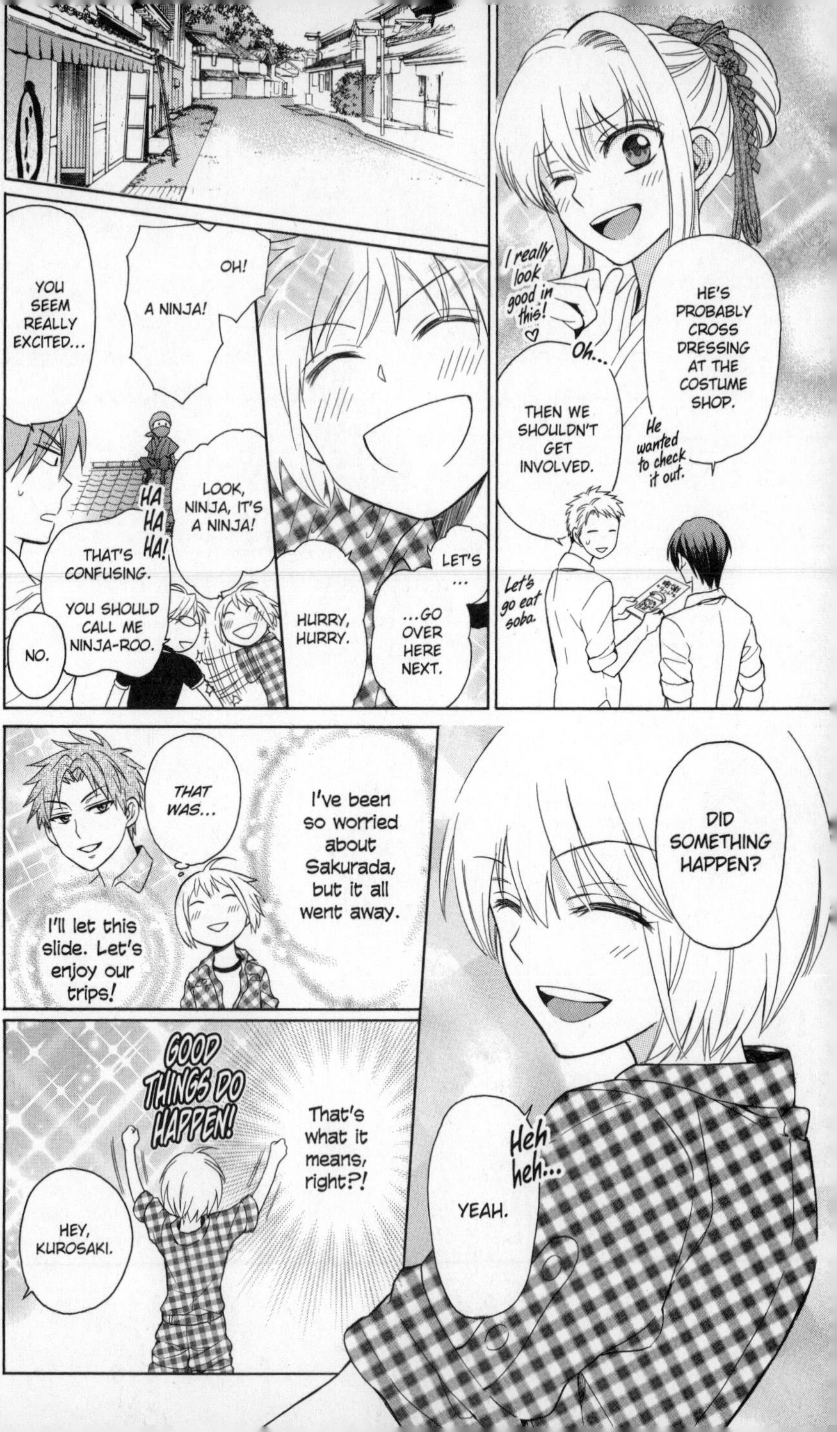
HE'S PROBABLY CROSS DRESSING AT THE COSTUME SHOP.
I really look good in this! ♡
He wanted to check it out.
Oh...
THEN WE SHOULDN'T GET INVOLVED.
Let's go eat soba.
OH!
A NINJA!
YOU SEEM REALLY EXCITED...
LET'S ...
...GO OVER HERE NEXT.
HURRY, HURRY.
LOOK, NINJA, IT'S A NINJA!
HA HA HA!
THAT'S CONFUSING.
YOU SHOULD CALL ME NINJA-ROO.
NO.
DID SOMETHING HAPPEN?
Heh heh...
YEAH.
I've been so worried about Sakurada, but it all went away.
THAT WAS...
I'll let this slide. Let's enjoy our trips!
GOOD THINGS DO HAPPEN!
That's what it means, right?!
HEY, KUROSAKI.

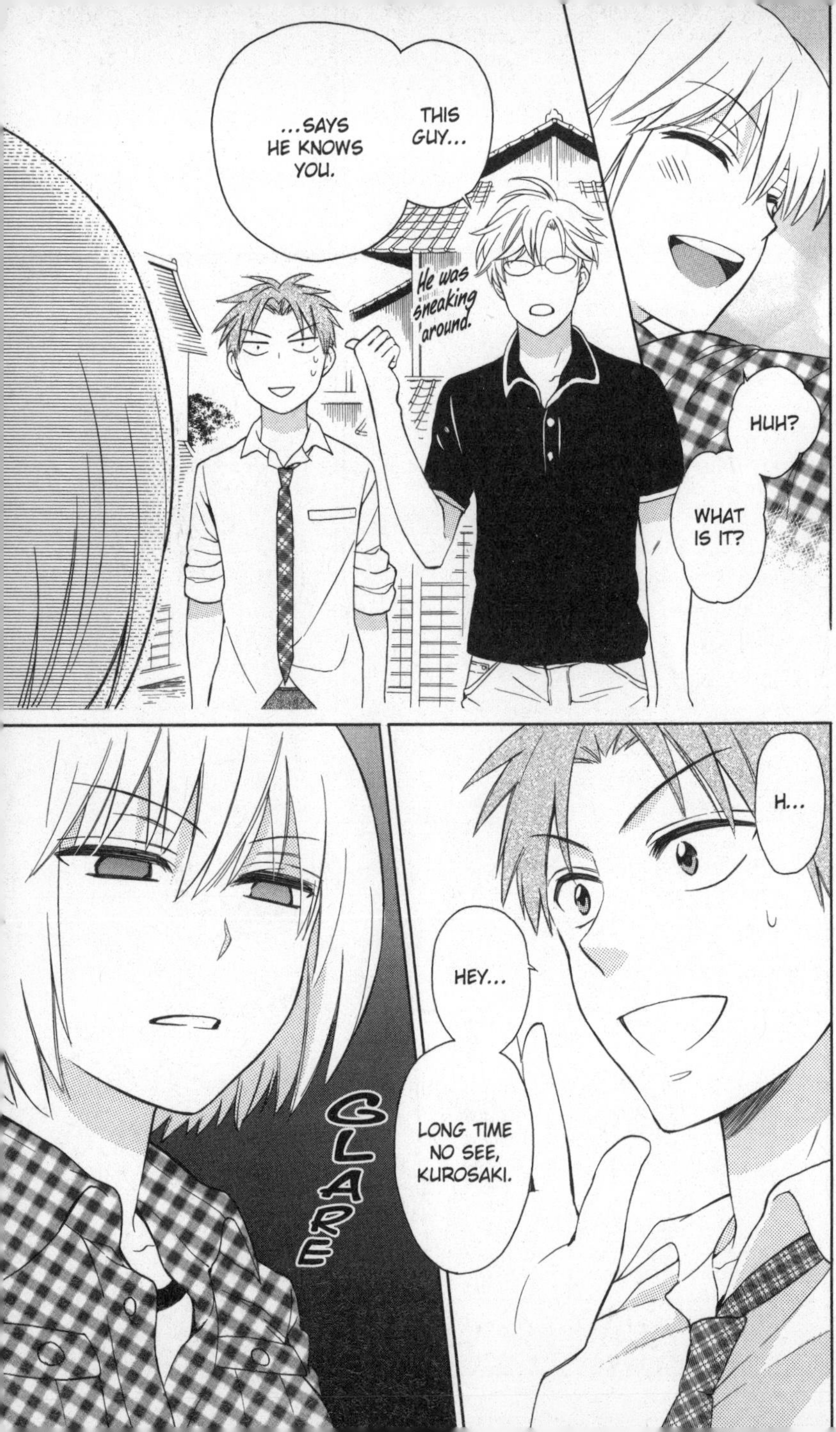
HUH?
WHAT IS IT?
THIS GUY...
...SAYS HE KNOWS YOU.
He was sneaking around.
H...
HEY...
LONG TIME NO SEE, KUROSAKI.
GLARE

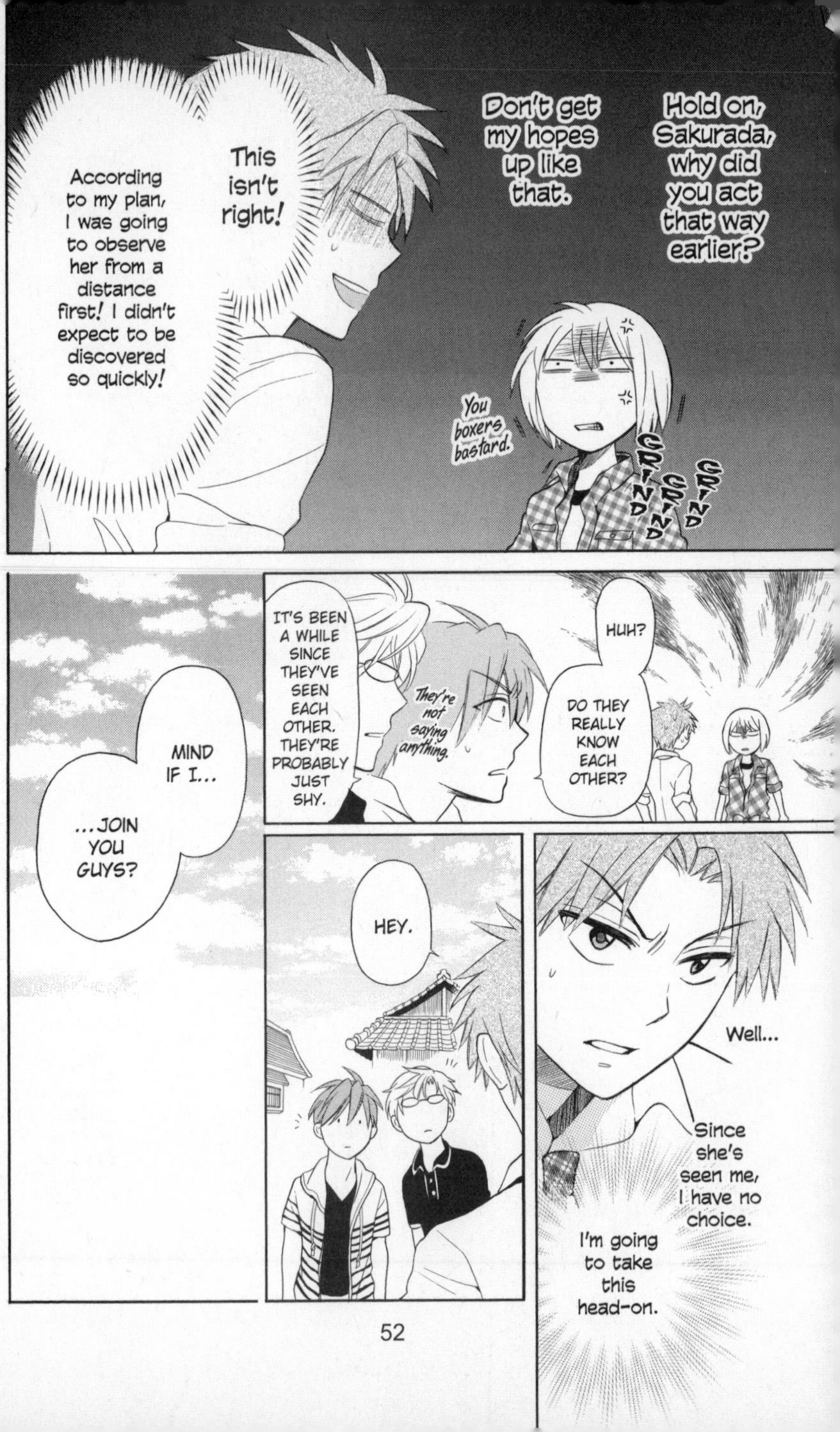
Hold on, Sakurada, why did you act that way earlier?
Don't get my hopes up like that.
This isn't right!
According to my plan, I was going to observe her from a distance first! I didn't expect to be discovered so quickly!
GRIND GRIND GRIND
You boxers bastard.
HUH?
DO THEY REALLY KNOW EACH OTHER?
They're not saying anything.
IT'S BEEN A WHILE SINCE THEY'VE SEEN EACH OTHER. THEY'RE PROBABLY JUST SHY.
Well...
Since she's seen me, I have no choice.
I'm going to take this head-on.
HEY.
MIND IF I...
...JOIN YOU GUYS?

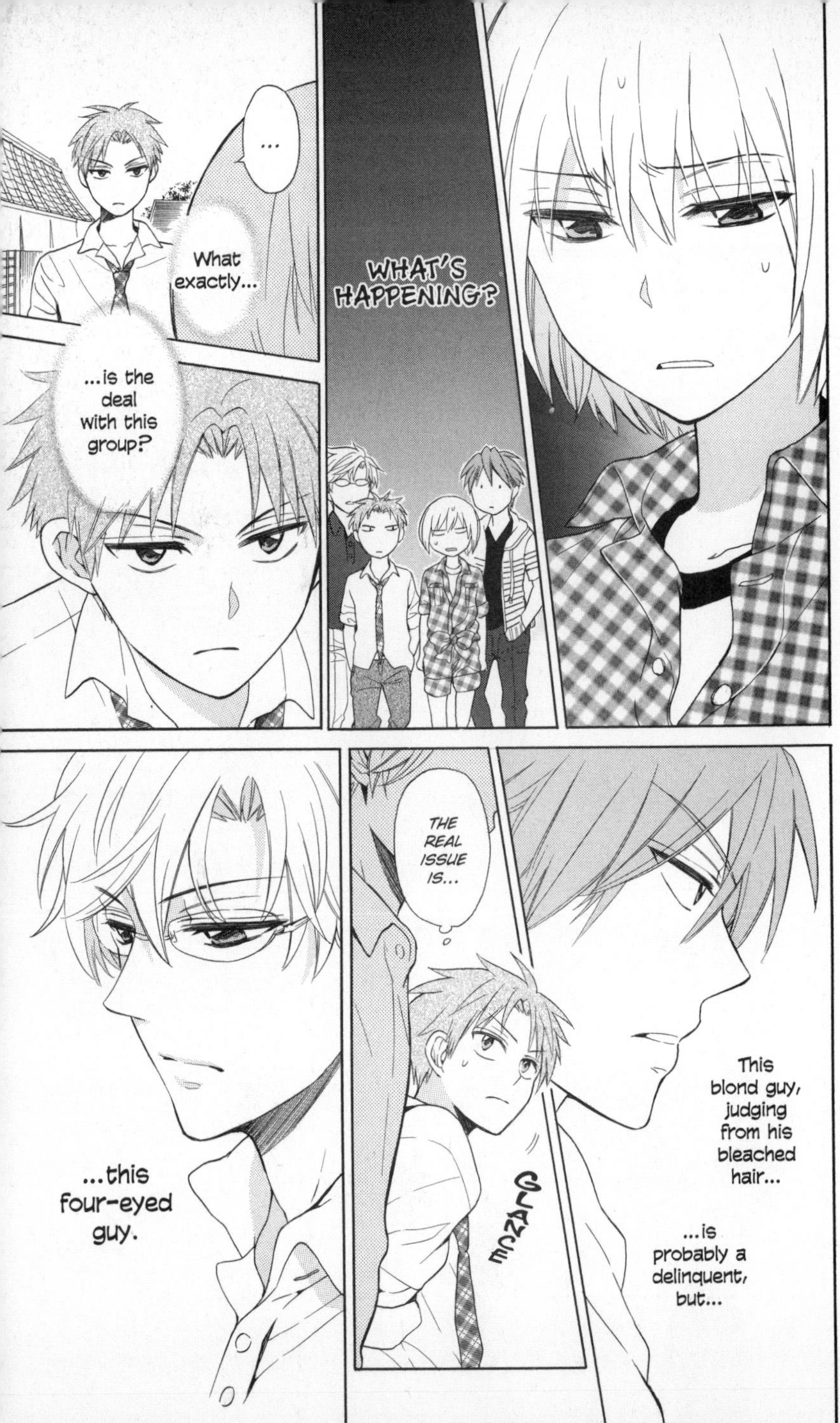
WHAT'S HAPPENING?
...
What exactly...
...is the deal with this group?
This blond guy, judging from his bleached hair...
...is probably a delinquent, but...
GLANCE
THE REAL ISSUE IS...
...this four-eyed guy.

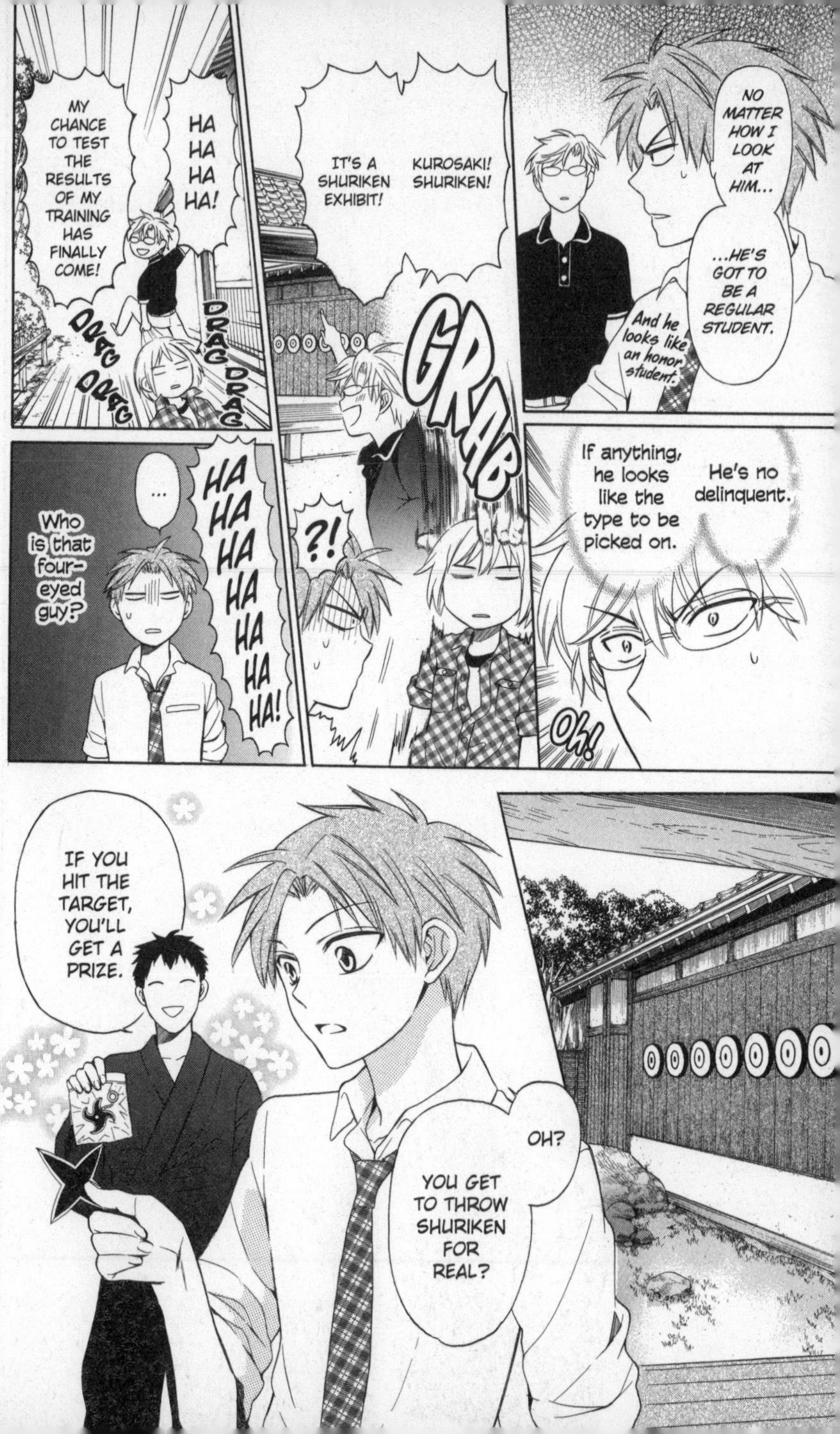
NO MATTER HOW I LOOK AT HIM...
...HE'S GOT TO BE A REGULAR STUDENT.
And he looks like an honor student.
KUROSAKI! SHURIKEN!
IT'S A SHURIKEN EXHIBIT!
GRAB
HA HA HA HA!
MY CHANCE TO TEST THE RESULTS OF MY TRAINING HAS FINALLY COME!
DRAG DRAG DRAG DRAG
He's no delinquent.
If anything, he looks like the type to be picked on.
Oh!
?!
HA HA HA HA HA HA HA!
...
Who is that four-eyed guy?
OH?
YOU GET TO THROW SHURIKEN FOR REAL?
IF YOU HIT THE TARGET, YOU'LL GET A PRIZE.

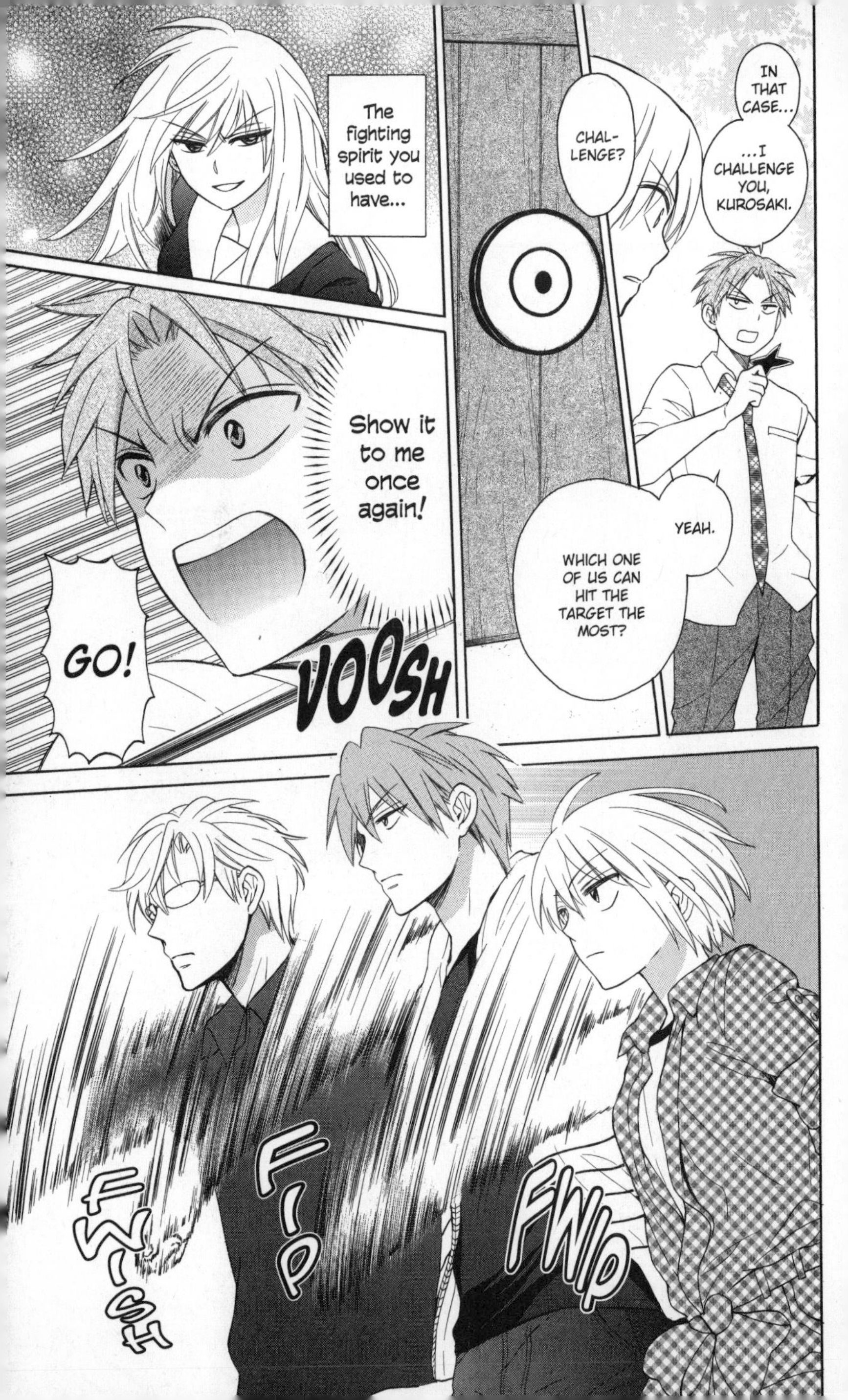
IN THAT CASE...
...I CHALLENGE YOU, KUROSAKI.
CHAL-LENGE?
YEAH.
WHICH ONE OF US CAN HIT THE TARGET THE MOST?
The fighting spirit you used to have...
Show it to me once again!
GO!
VOOSH
FWIP
FLIP
FWISH

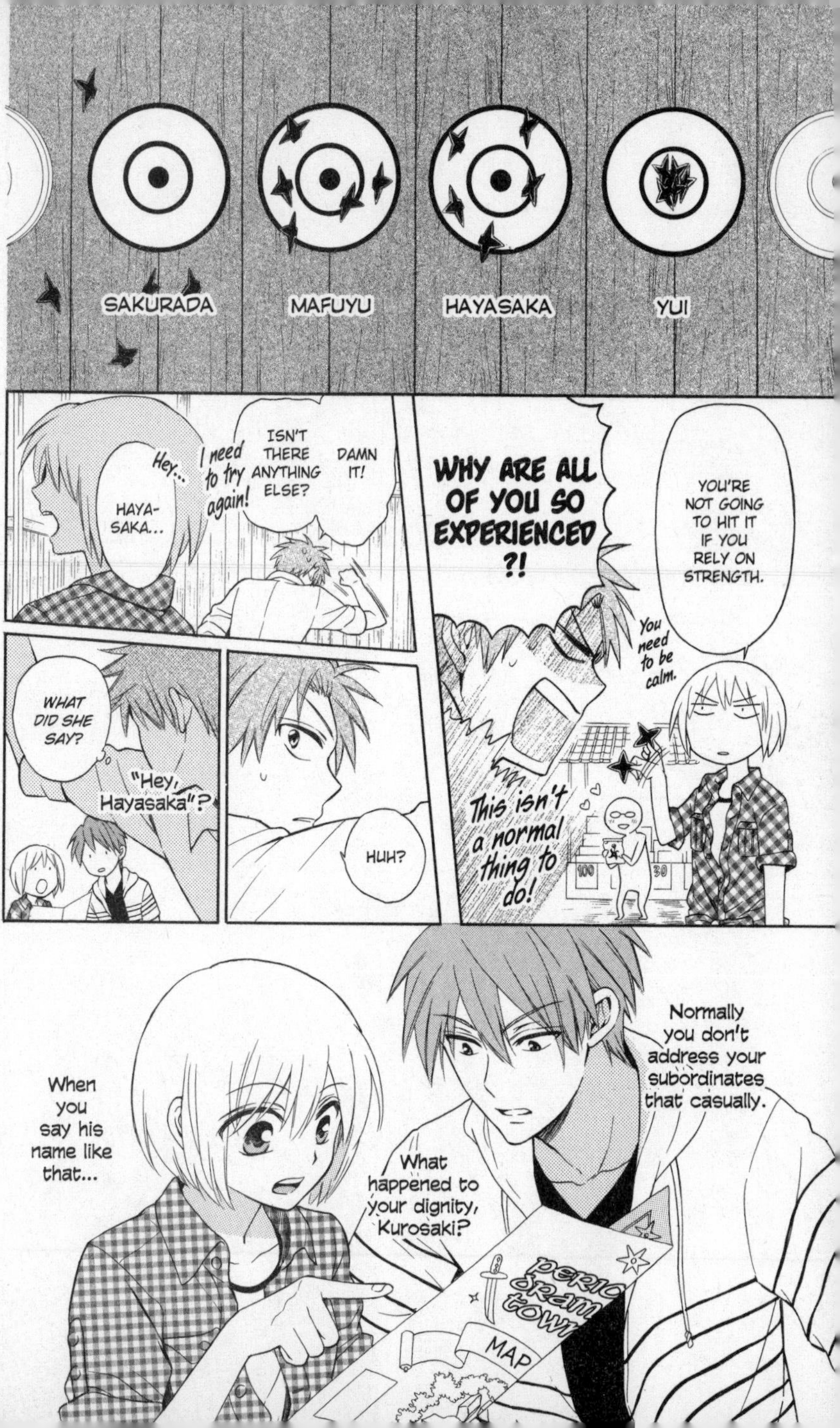
YUI
HAYASAKA
MAFUYU
SAKURADA
YOU'RE NOT GOING TO HIT IT IF YOU RELY ON STRENGTH.
You need to be calm.
WHY ARE ALL OF YOU SO EXPERIENCED ?!
This isn't a normal thing to do!
DAMN IT!
ISN'T THERE ANYTHING ELSE?
I need to try again!
Hey...
HAYA-SAKA...
HUH?
WHAT DID SHE SAY?
"Hey, Hayasaka"?
Normally you don't address your subordinates that casually.
What happened to your dignity, Kurosaki?
When you say his name like that...
MAP

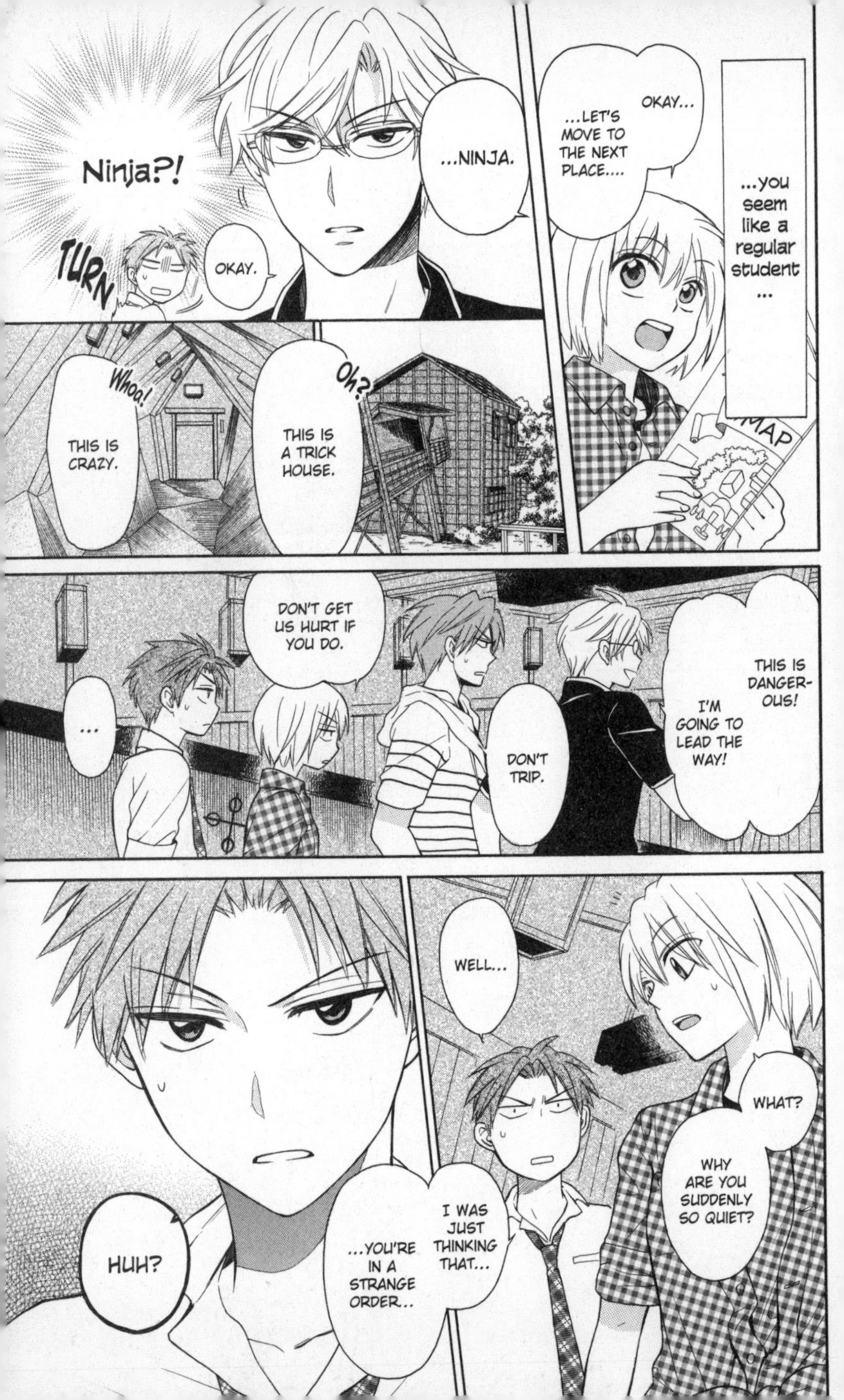
...you seem like a regular student ...
OKAY...
...LET'S MOVE TO THE NEXT PLACE....
...NINJA.
Ninja?!
OKAY.
TURN
Oh?
THIS IS A TRICK HOUSE.
Whoa!
THIS IS CRAZY.
THIS IS DANGER-OUS!
I'M GOING TO LEAD THE WAY!
DON'T TRIP.
DON'T GET US HURT IF YOU DO.
...
WHAT?
WHY ARE YOU SUDDENLY SO QUIET?
WELL...
I WAS JUST THINKING THAT...
...YOU'RE IN A STRANGE ORDER...
HUH?

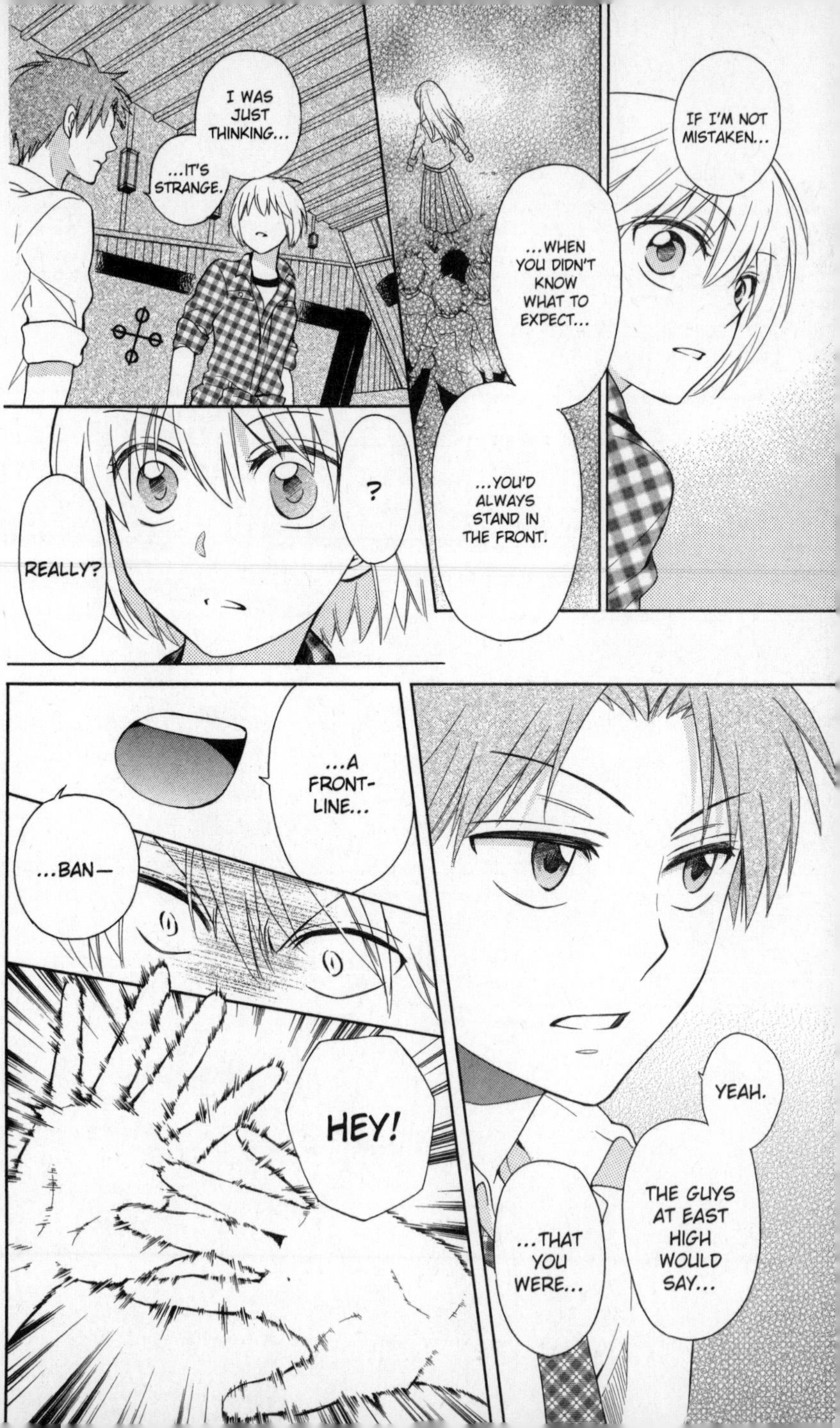
IF I'M NOT MISTAKEN...
...WHEN YOU DIDN'T KNOW WHAT TO EXPECT...
...YOU'D ALWAYS STAND IN THE FRONT.
I WAS JUST THINKING...
...IT'S STRANGE.
?
REALLY?
YEAH.
THE GUYS AT EAST HIGH WOULD SAY...
...THAT YOU WERE...
...A FRONT-LINE...
...BAN—
HEY!

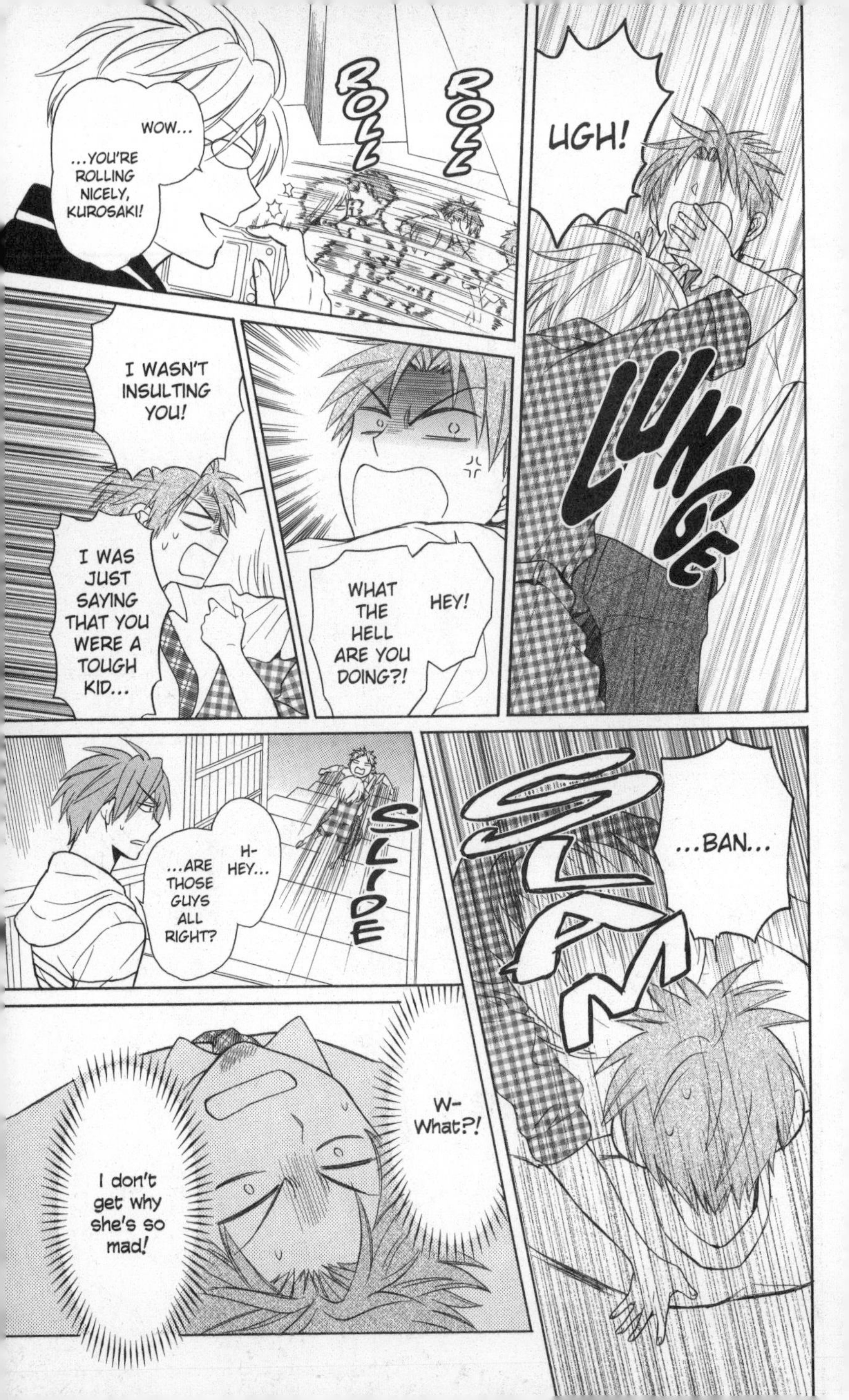
UGH!
LUNGE
ROLL
ROLL
WOW...
...YOU'RE ROLLING NICELY, KUROSAKI!
HEY!
WHAT THE HELL ARE YOU DOING?!
I WASN'T INSULTING YOU!
I WAS JUST SAYING THAT YOU WERE A TOUGH KID...
SLAM
...BAN...
SLIDE
H-HEY...
...ARE THOSE GUYS ALL RIGHT?
W-What?!
I don't get why she's so mad!

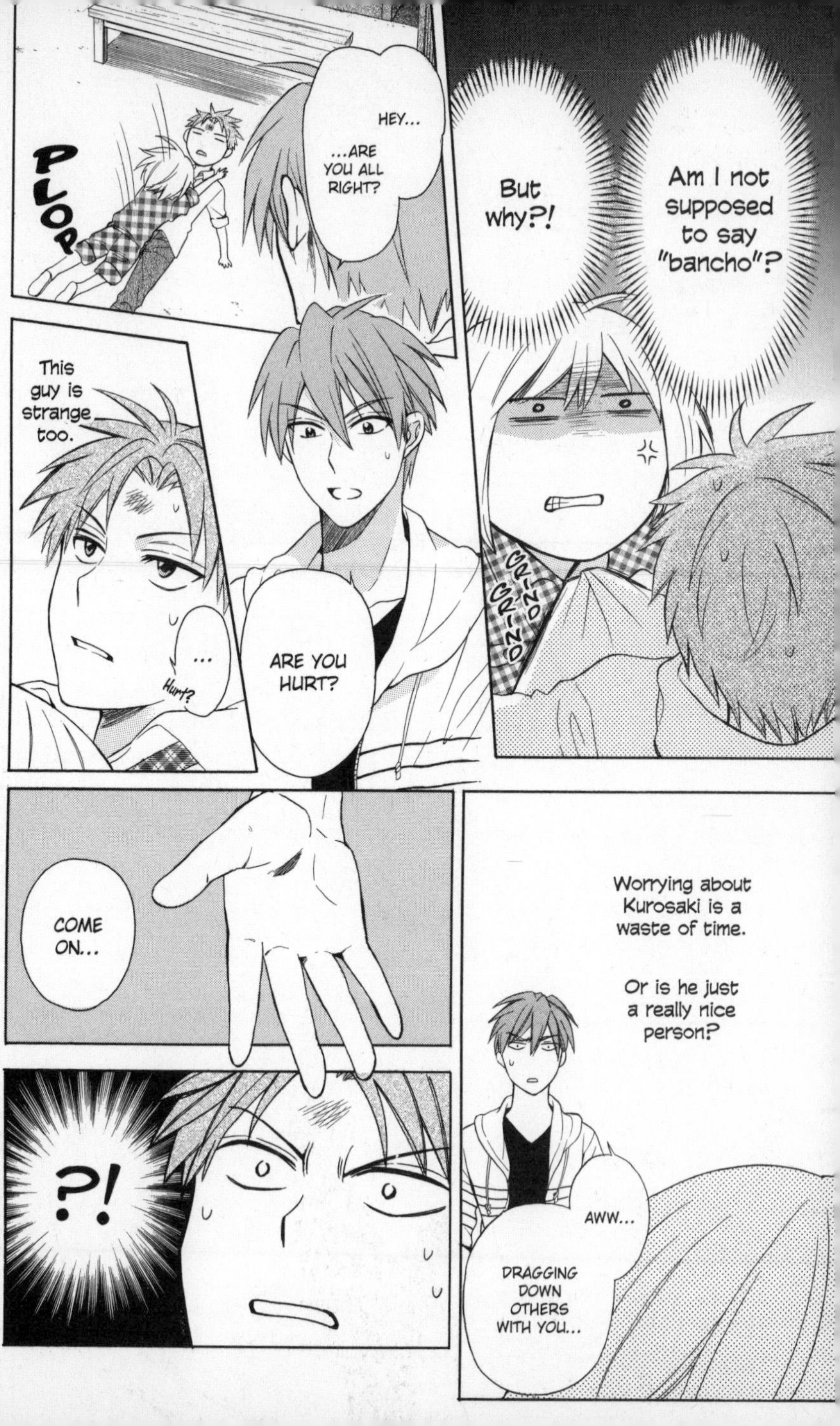

Am I not supposed to say "bancho"?
But why?!
GRIND GRIND
PLOP
HEY...
...ARE YOU ALL RIGHT?
ARE YOU HURT?
...
Hurt?
This guy is strange too.
Worrying about Kurosaki is a waste of time.
Or is he just a really nice person?
AWW...
DRAGGING DOWN OTHERS WITH YOU...
COME ON...
?!

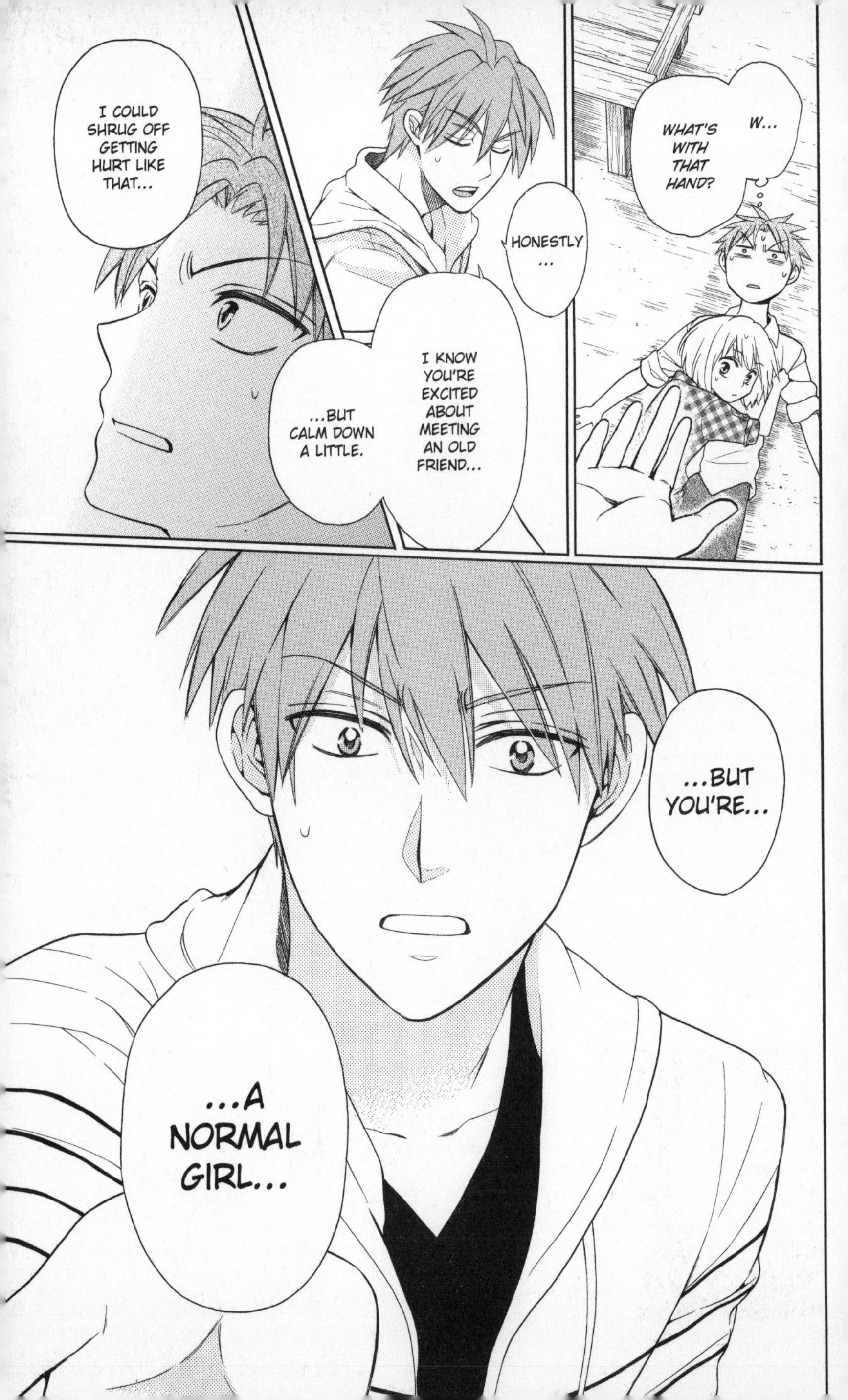
W...
WHAT'S WITH THAT HAND?
HONESTLY...
I KNOW YOU'RE EXCITED ABOUT MEETING AN OLD FRIEND...
...BUT CALM DOWN A LITTLE.
I COULD SHRUG OFF GETTING HURT LIKE THAT...
...BUT YOU'RE...
...A NORMAL GIRL...

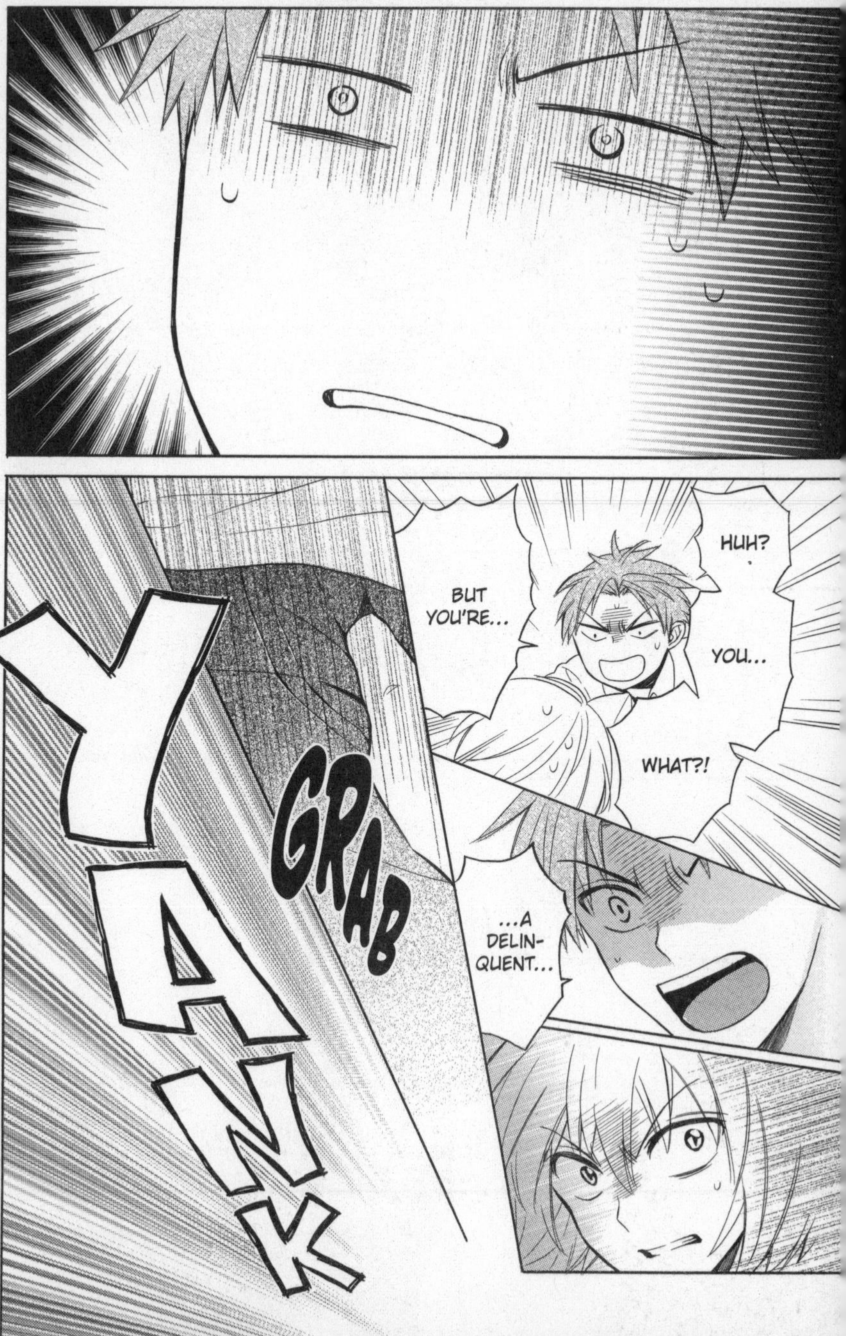
HUH?
YOU...
WHAT?!
BUT YOU'RE...
...A DELIN-QUENT...
GRAB
YANK

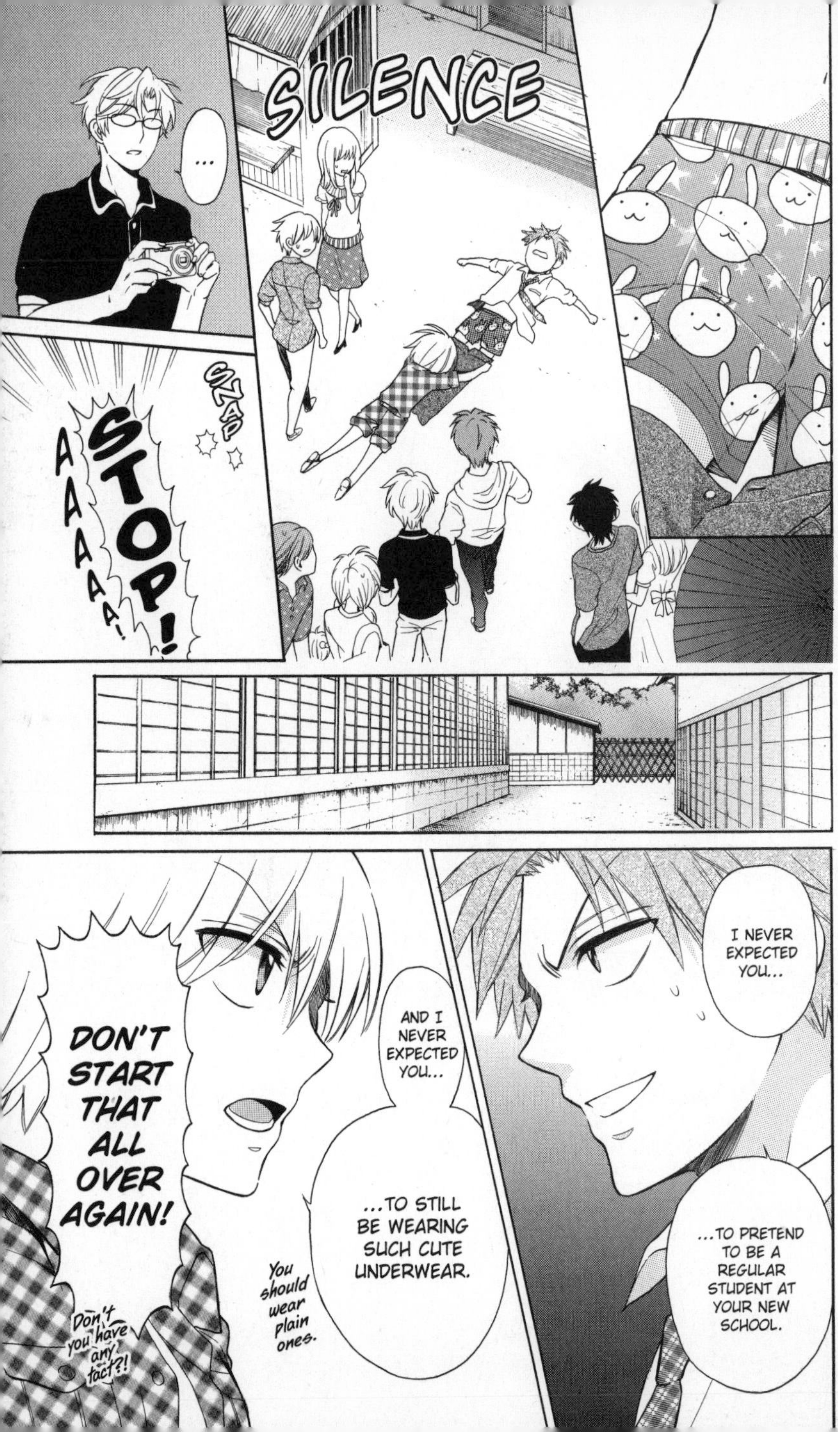
SILENCE
...
SNAP
STOP! AAAAAA!
I NEVER EXPECTED YOU...
...TO PRETEND TO BE A REGULAR STUDENT AT YOUR NEW SCHOOL.
AND I NEVER EXPECTED YOU...
...TO STILL BE WEARING SUCH CUTE UNDERWEAR.
You should wear plain ones.
DON'T START THAT ALL OVER AGAIN!
Don't you have any tact?!

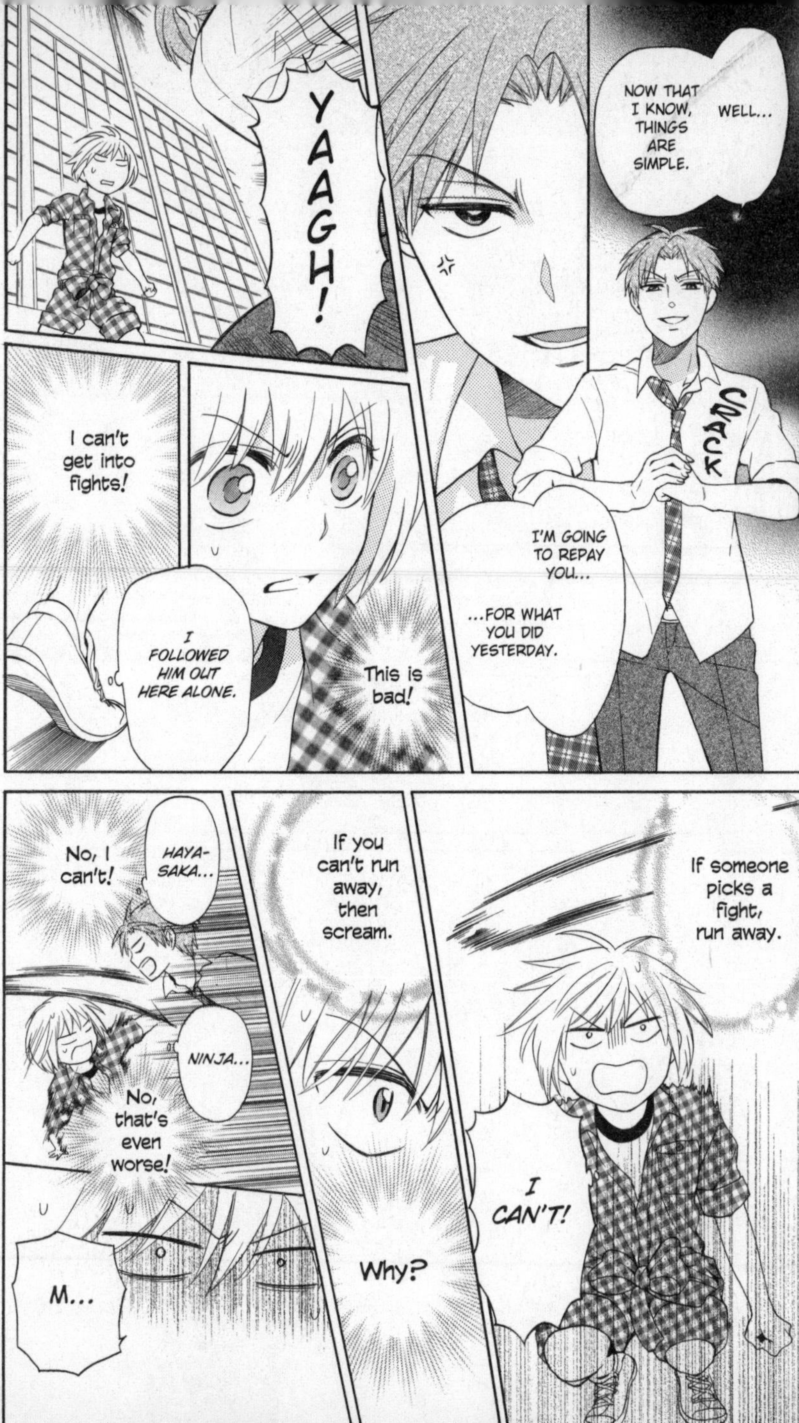
WELL...
NOW THAT I KNOW, THINGS ARE SIMPLE.
CRACK
I'M GOING TO REPAY YOU...
...FOR WHAT YOU DID YESTERDAY.
YAAGH!
This is bad!
I FOLLOWED HIM OUT HERE ALONE.
I can't get into fights!
If someone picks a fight, run away.
I CAN'T!
If you can't run away, then scream.
Why?
HAYA-SAKA...
No, I can't!
NINJA...
No, that's even worse!
M...

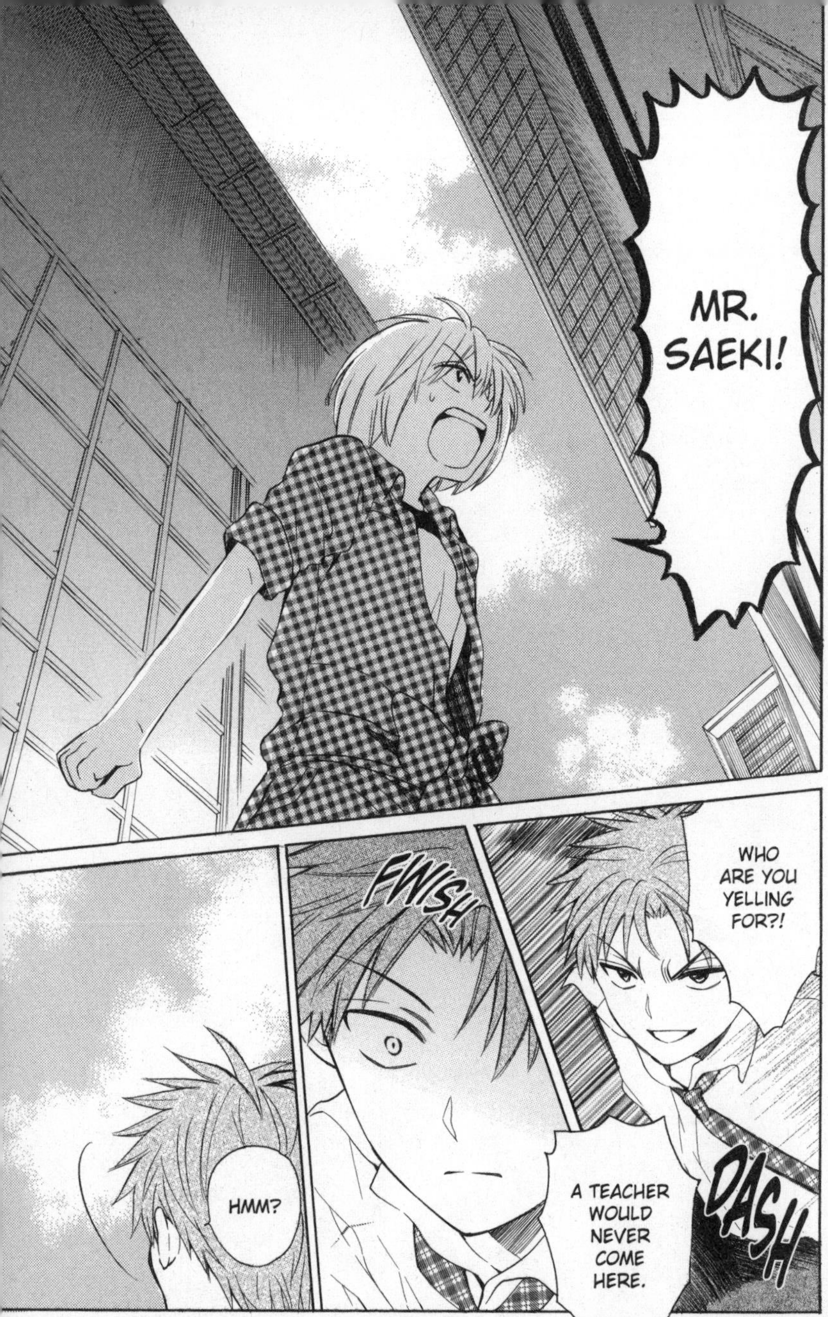
MR. SAEKI!
WHO ARE YOU YELLING FOR?!
DASH
FWISH
A TEACHER WOULD NEVER COME HERE.
HMM?

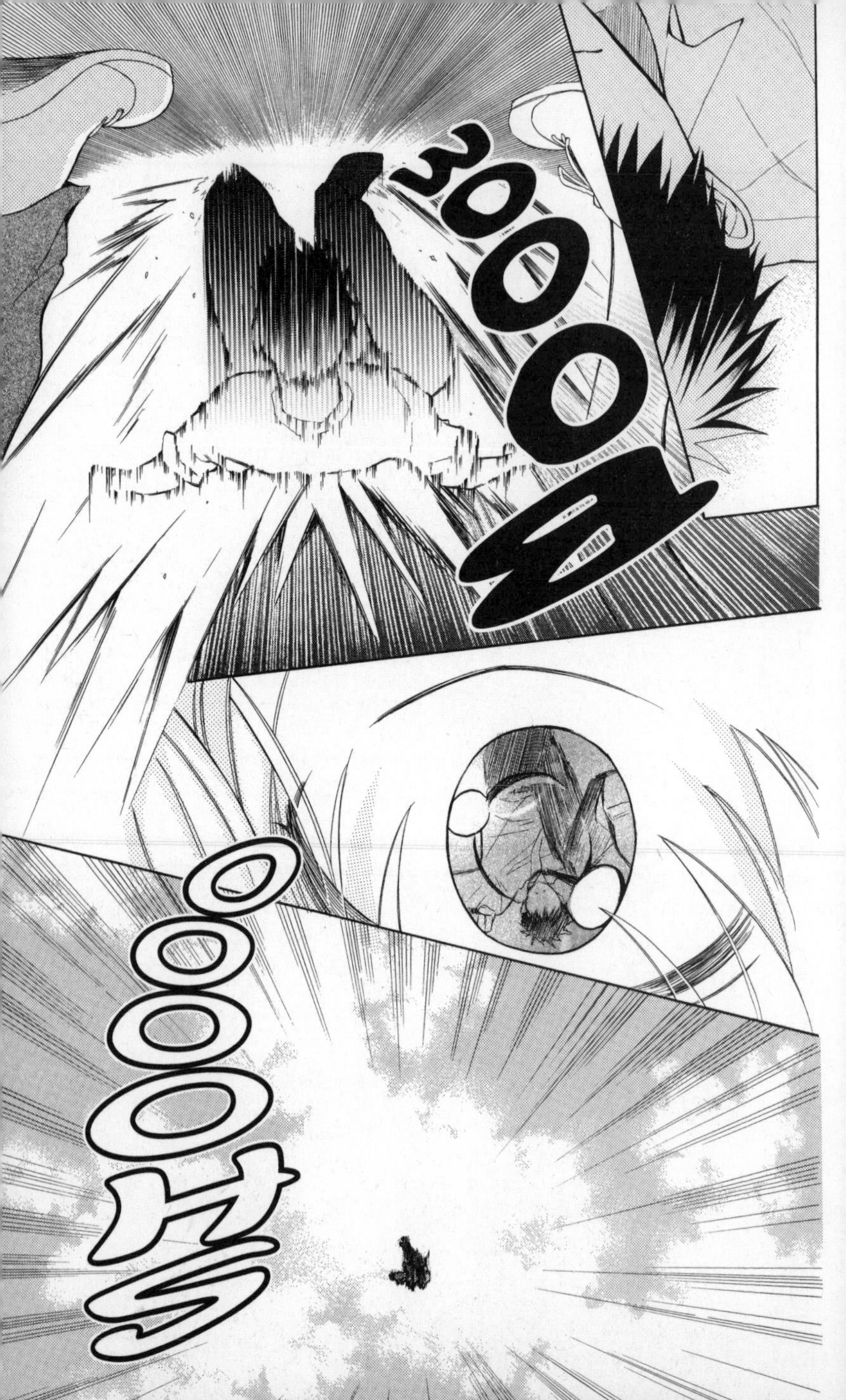
BOOOM
SHOOOO

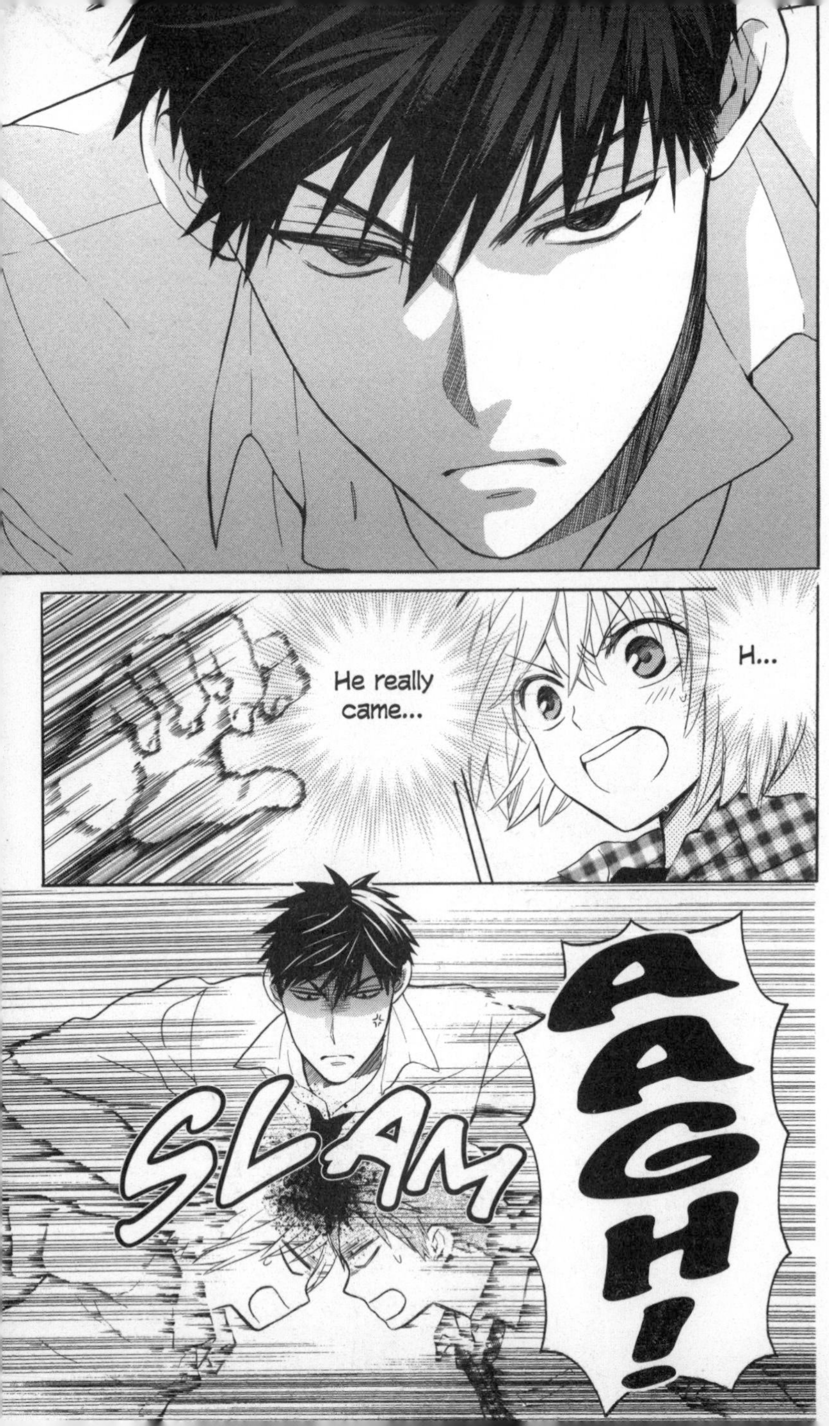
H...
He really came...
AAGH!
SLAM

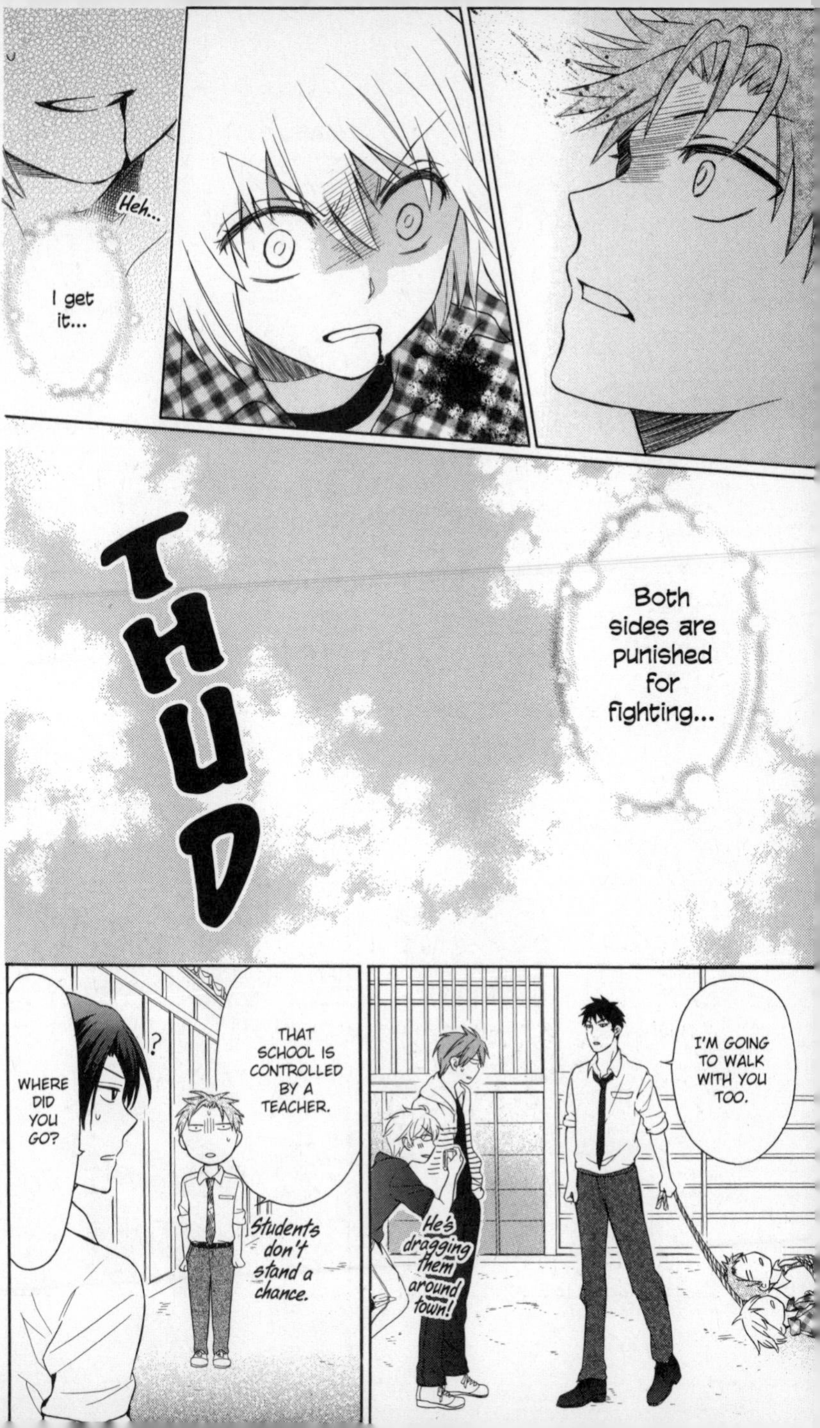
Heh...
I get it...
Both sides are punished for fighting...
THUD
I'M GOING TO WALK WITH YOU TOO.
He's dragging them around town!
THAT SCHOOL IS CONTROLLED BY A TEACHER.
Students don't stand a chance.
?
WHERE DID YOU GO?

MAFUYU, THE NORMAL PERSON

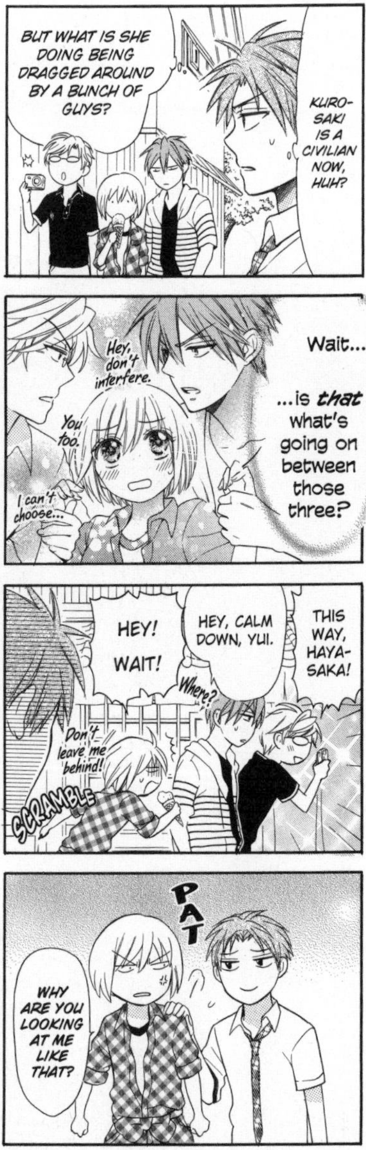
KURO-SAKI IS A CIVILIAN NOW, HUH?
BUT WHAT IS SHE DOING BEING DRAGGED AROUND BY A BUNCH OF GUYS?
Wait...
...is *that* what's going on between those three?
Hey, don't interfere.
You too.
I can't choose...
THIS WAY, HAYA-SAKA!
HEY, CALM DOWN, YUI.
HEY! WAIT!
Where?
Don't leave me behind!
SCRAMBLE
PAT
WHY ARE YOU LOOKING AT ME LIKE THAT?

THE TASTE OF DEFEAT

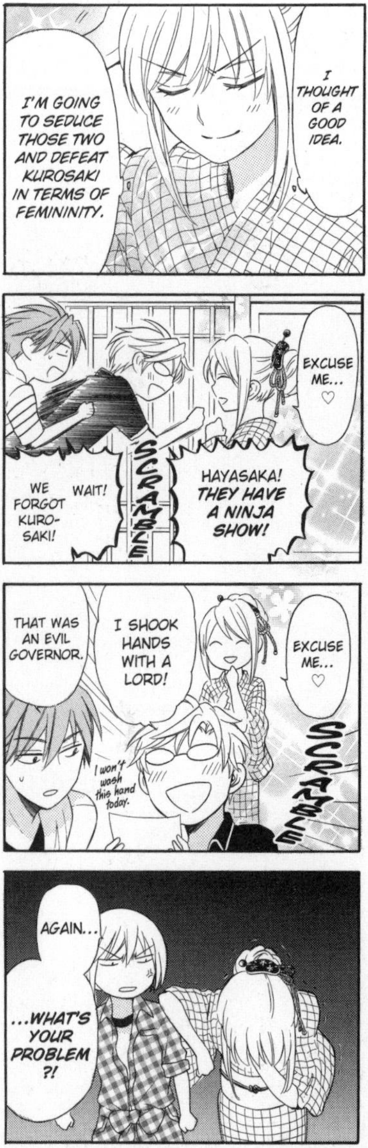
I THOUGHT OF A GOOD IDEA.
I'M GOING TO SEDUCE THOSE TWO AND DEFEAT KUROSAKI IN TERMS OF FEMININITY.
EXCUSE ME... ♡
HAYASAKA! THEY HAVE A NINJA SHOW!
SCRAMBLE
WAIT!
WE FORGOT KURO-SAKI!
EXCUSE ME... ♡
SCRAMBLE
I SHOOK HANDS WITH A LORD!
THAT WAS AN EVIL GOVERNOR.
I won't wash this hand today.
AGAIN...
...WHAT'S YOUR PROBLEM ?!

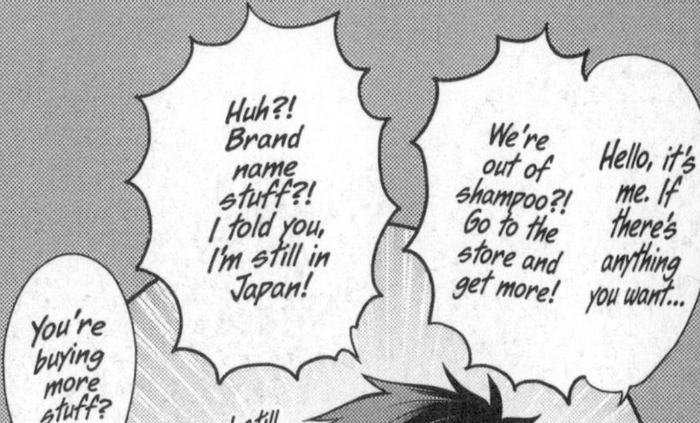
Hello, it's me. If there's anything you want...
We're out of shampoo?! Go to the store and get more!
Huh?! Brand name stuff?! I told you, I'm still in Japan!
I still have to pay sales tax!
You're buying more stuff?

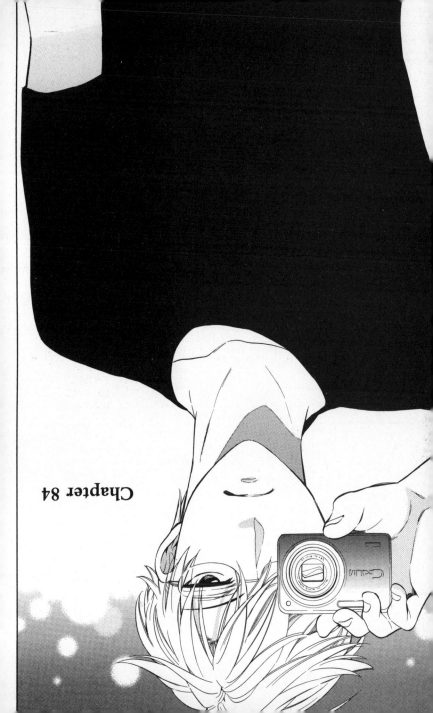

Chapter 84

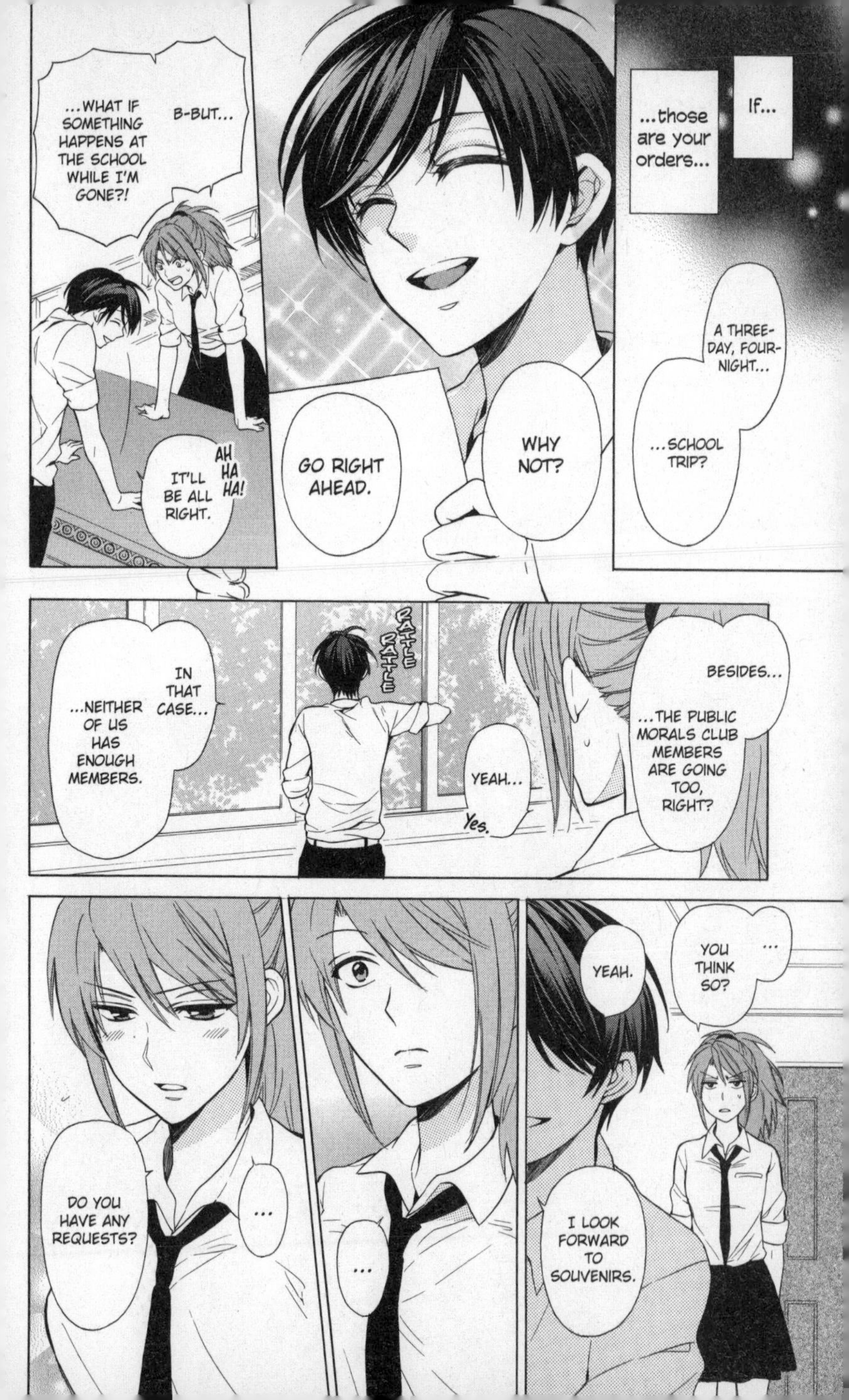
IF...
...those are your orders...
A THREE-DAY, FOUR-NIGHT...
...SCHOOL TRIP?
WHY NOT?
GO RIGHT AHEAD.
B-BUT...
...WHAT IF SOMETHING HAPPENS AT THE SCHOOL WHILE I'M GONE?!
AH HA HA!
IT'LL BE ALL RIGHT.
BESIDES...
...THE PUBLIC MORALS CLUB MEMBERS ARE GOING TOO, RIGHT?
YEAH...
Yes.
RATTLE RATTLE
IN THAT CASE...
...NEITHER OF US HAS ENOUGH MEMBERS.
...
YOU THINK SO?
YEAH.
I LOOK FORWARD TO SOUVENIRS.
...
...
DO YOU HAVE ANY REQUESTS?

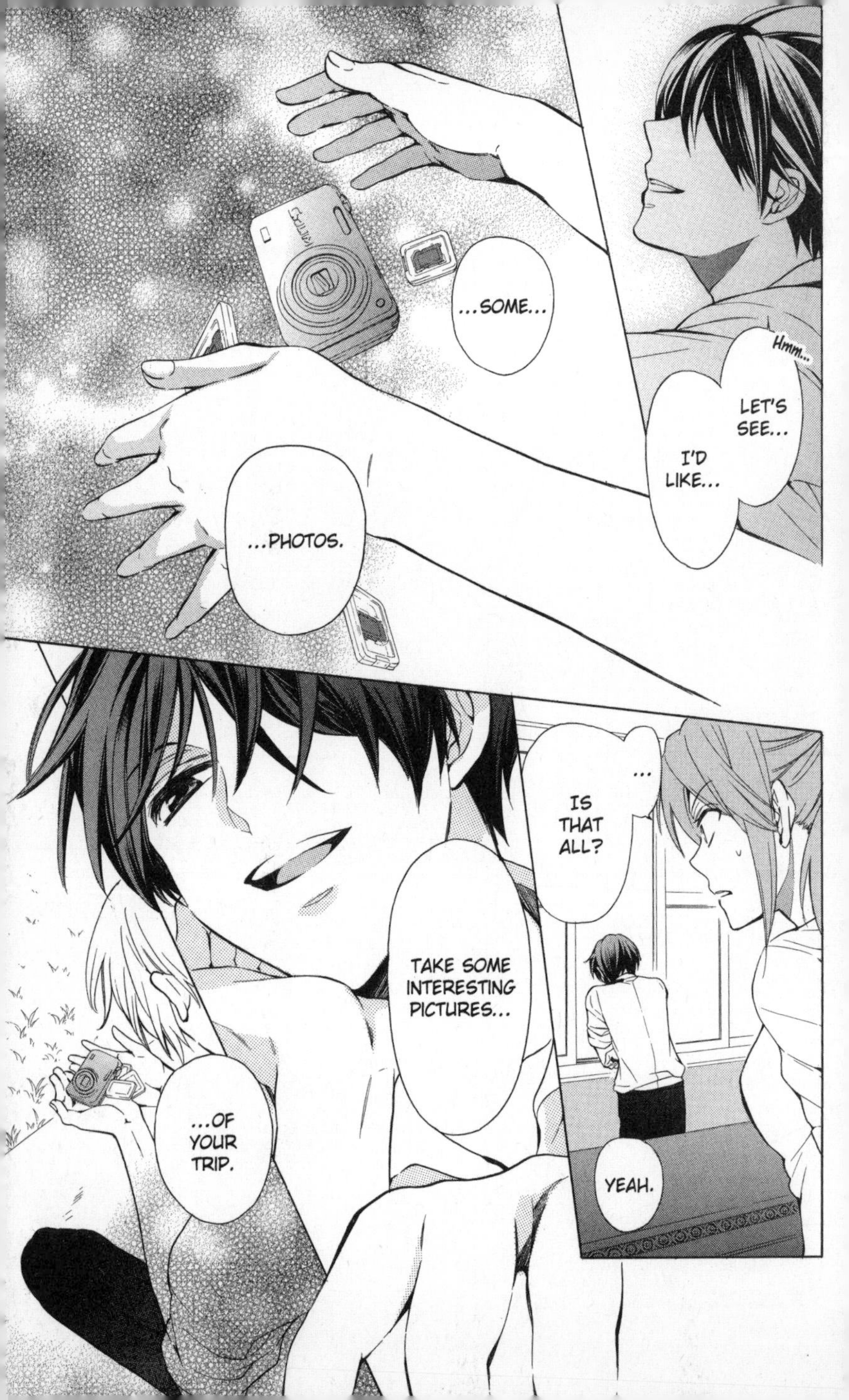
Hmm...
LET'S SEE...
I'D LIKE...
...SOME...
...PHOTOS.
...
IS THAT ALL?
TAKE SOME INTERESTING PICTURES...
...OF YOUR TRIP.
YEAH.

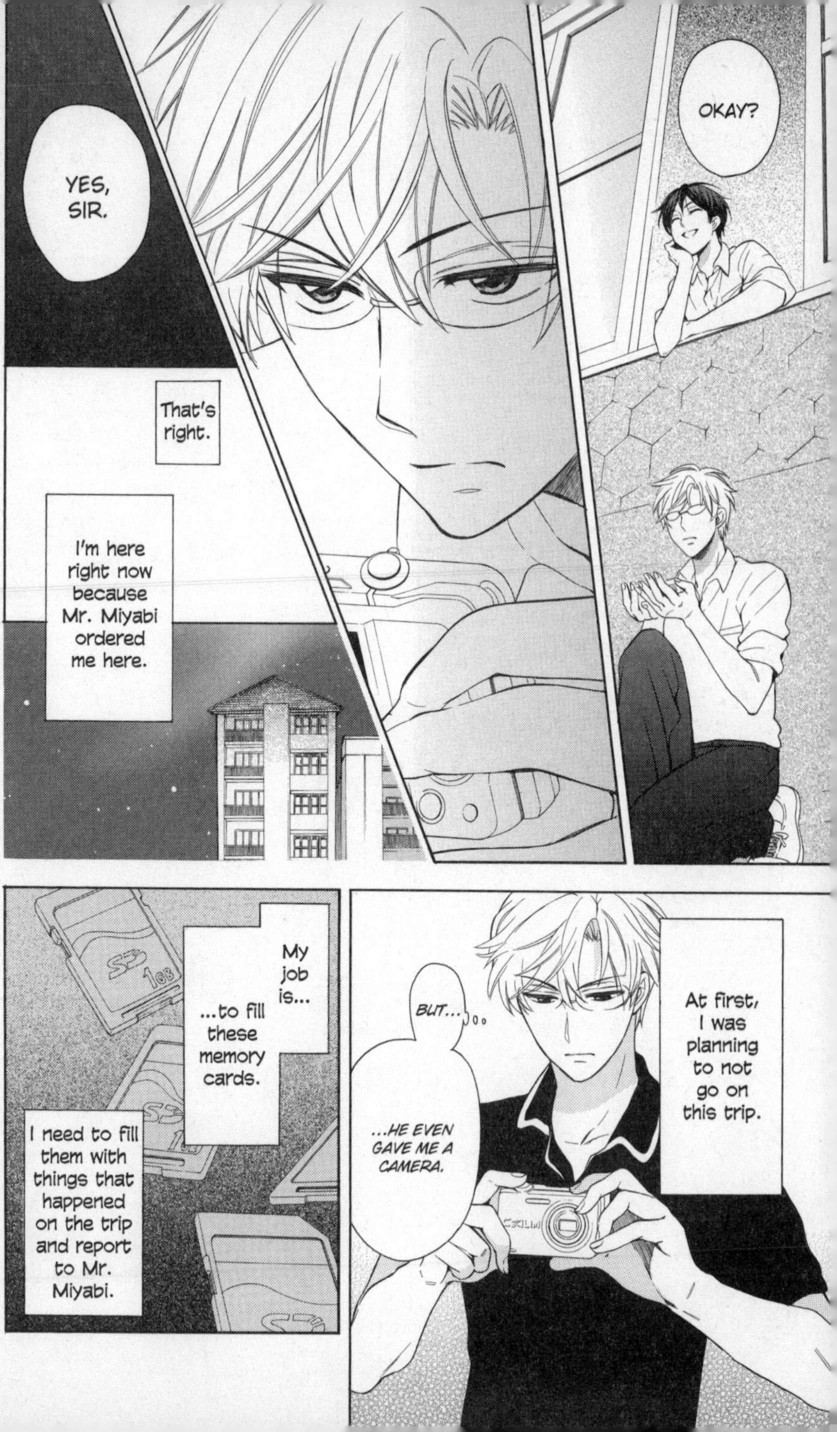
OKAY?
YES, SIR.
That's right.
I'm here right now because Mr. Miyabi ordered me here.
At first, I was planning to not go on this trip.
BUT...
...HE EVEN GAVE ME A CAMERA.
My job is...
...to fill these memory cards.
I need to fill them with things that happened on the trip and report to Mr. Miyabi.

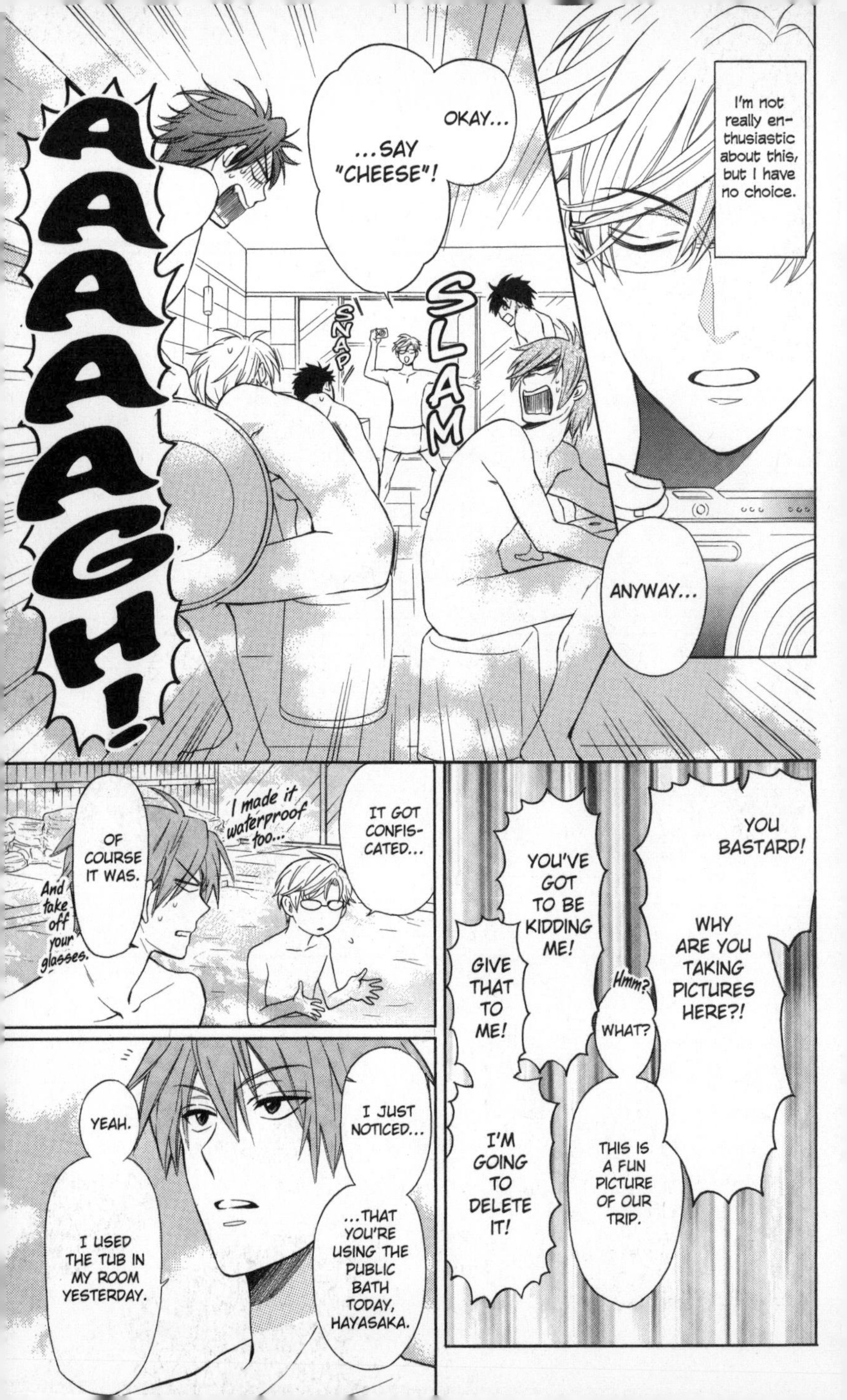
I'm not really en-thusiastic about this, but I have no choice.
ANYWAY...
OKAY...
...SAY "CHEESE"!
SNAP
SLAM
AAAAGH!
YOU BASTARD!
WHY ARE YOU TAKING PICTURES HERE?!
Hmm?
WHAT?
THIS IS A FUN PICTURE OF OUR TRIP.
YOU'VE GOT TO BE KIDDING ME!
GIVE THAT TO ME!
I'M GOING TO DELETE IT!
IT GOT CONFIS-CATED...
I made it waterproof too...
OF COURSE IT WAS.
And take off your glasses.
I JUST NOTICED...
...THAT YOU'RE USING THE PUBLIC BATH TODAY, HAYASAKA.
YEAH.
I USED THE TUB IN MY ROOM YESTERDAY.

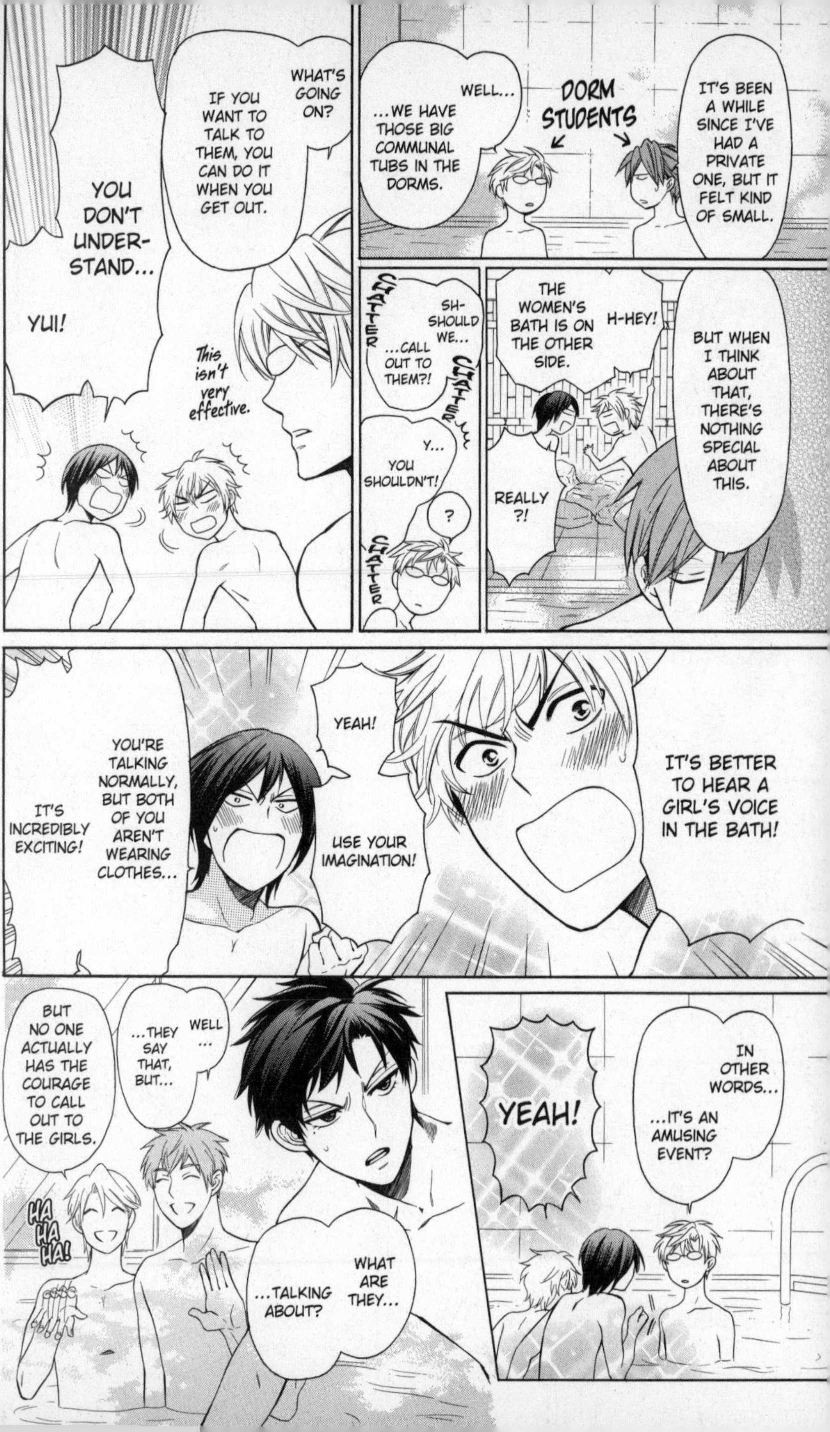
It's been a while since I've had a private one, but it felt kind of small.
DORM STUDENTS
Well...
...we have those big communal tubs in the dorms.
What's going on?
If you want to talk to them, you can do it when you get out.
You don't under-stand...
Yui!
This isn't very effective.
But when I think about that, there's nothing special about this.
H-hey!
The women's bath is on the other side.
Really?!
Sh-should we...
...call out to them?!
CHATTER
CHATTER
Y... You shouldn't!
?
CHATTER
It's better to hear a girl's voice in the bath!
Yeah!
Use your imagination!
You're talking normally, but both of you aren't wearing clothes...
It's incredibly exciting!
In other words...
...it's an amusing event?
YEAH!
But no one actually has the courage to call out to the girls.
Well...
...they say that, but...
HA HA HA!
What are they...
...talking about?

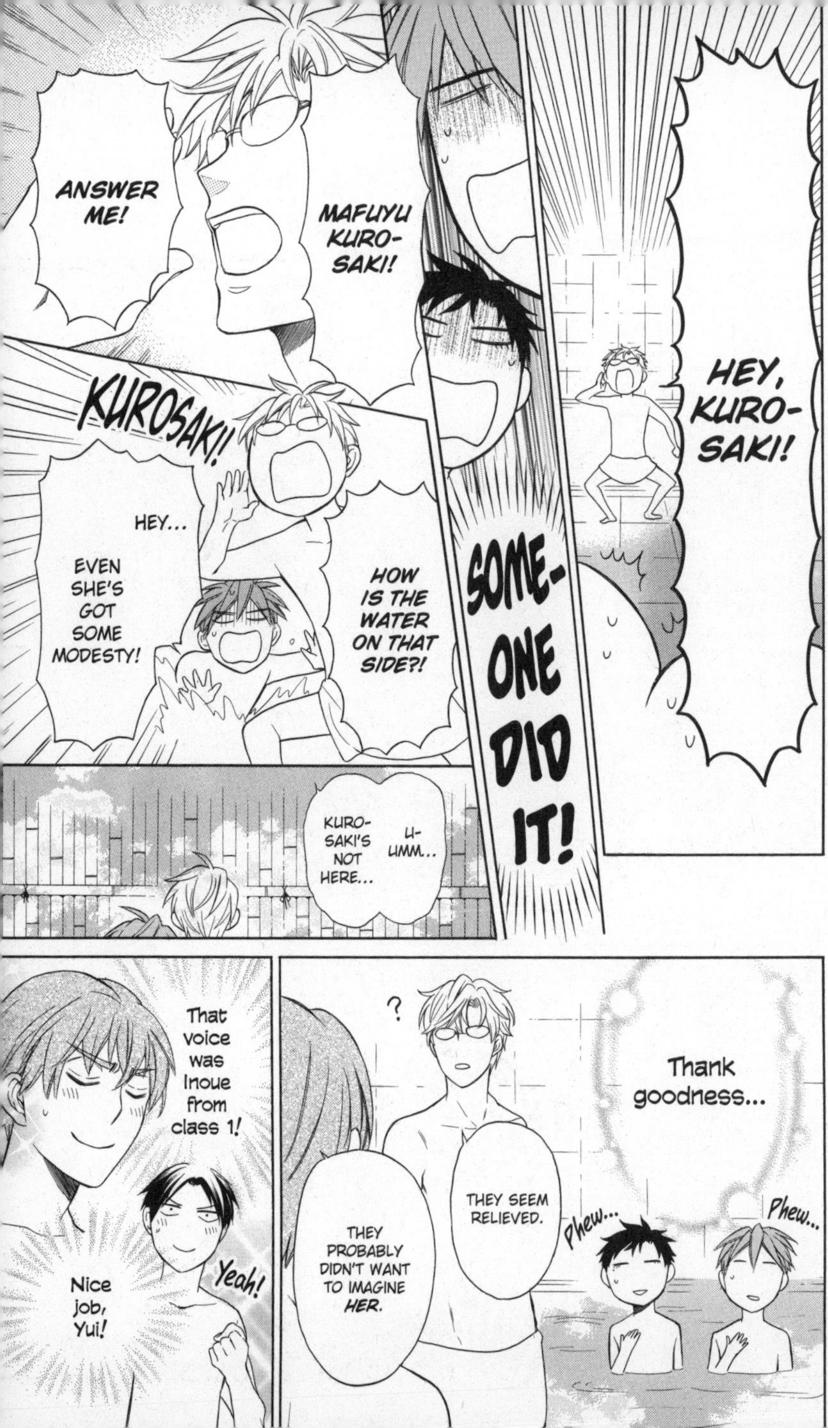
HEY, KURO-SAKI!
SOME-ONE DID IT!
MAFUYU KURO-SAKI!
ANSWER ME!
KUROSAKI!!
HOW IS THE WATER ON THAT SIDE?!
HEY...
EVEN SHE'S GOT SOME MODESTY!
U-UMM...
KURO-SAKI'S NOT HERE...
Thank goodness...
Phew...
Phew...
?
THEY SEEM RELIEVED.
THEY PROBABLY DIDN'T WANT TO IMAGINE HER.
That voice was Inoue from class 1!
Yeah!
Nice job, Yui!

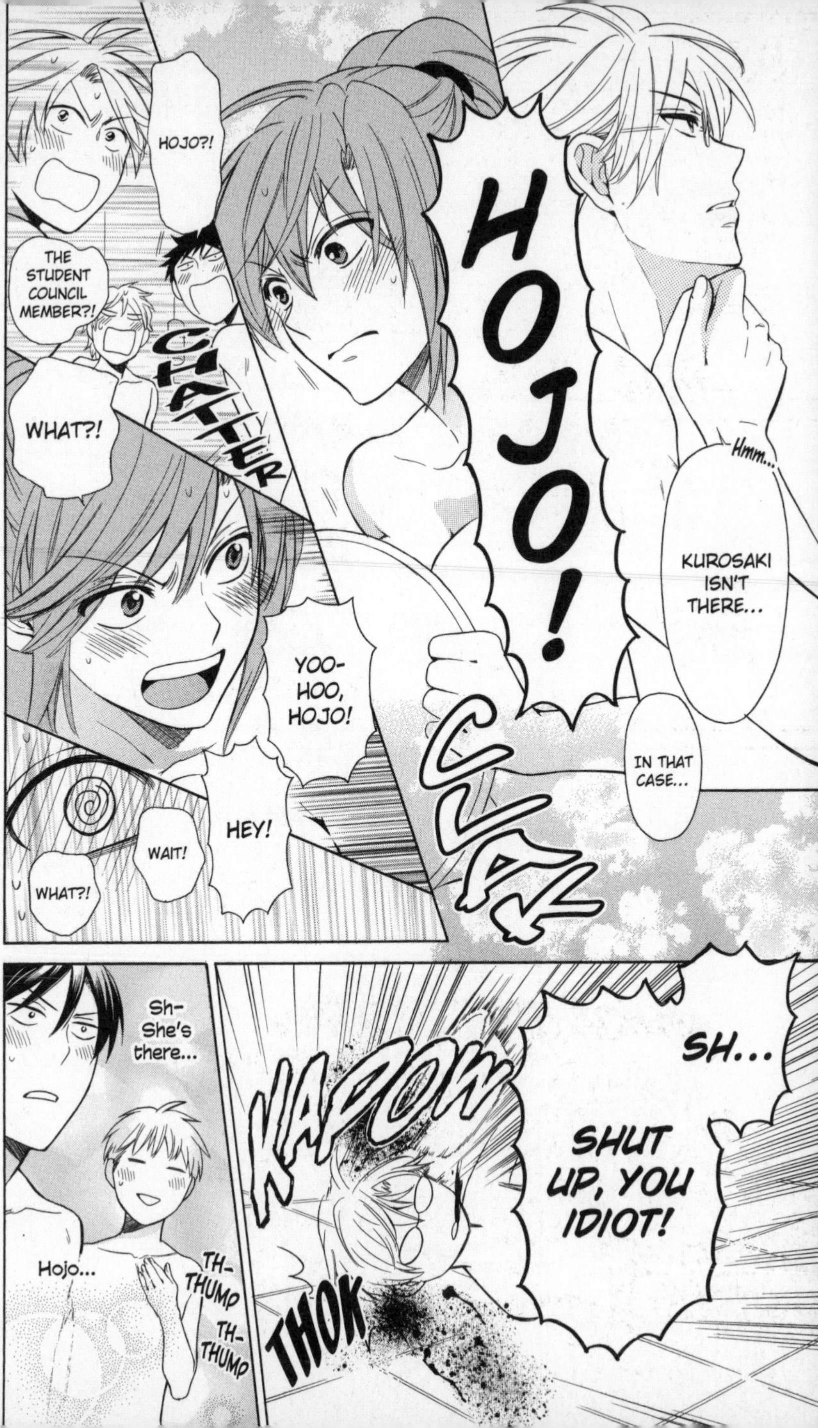
Hmm...
KUROSAKI ISN'T THERE...
IN THAT CASE...
HOJO!
CLACK
HOJO?!
THE STUDENT COUNCIL MEMBER?!
CHATTER
WHAT?!
YOO-HOO, HOJO!
HEY!
WAIT!
WHAT?!
SH...
SHUT UP, YOU IDIOT!
KAPOW
THOK
Sh- She's there...
Hojo...
TH-THUMP
TH-THUMP

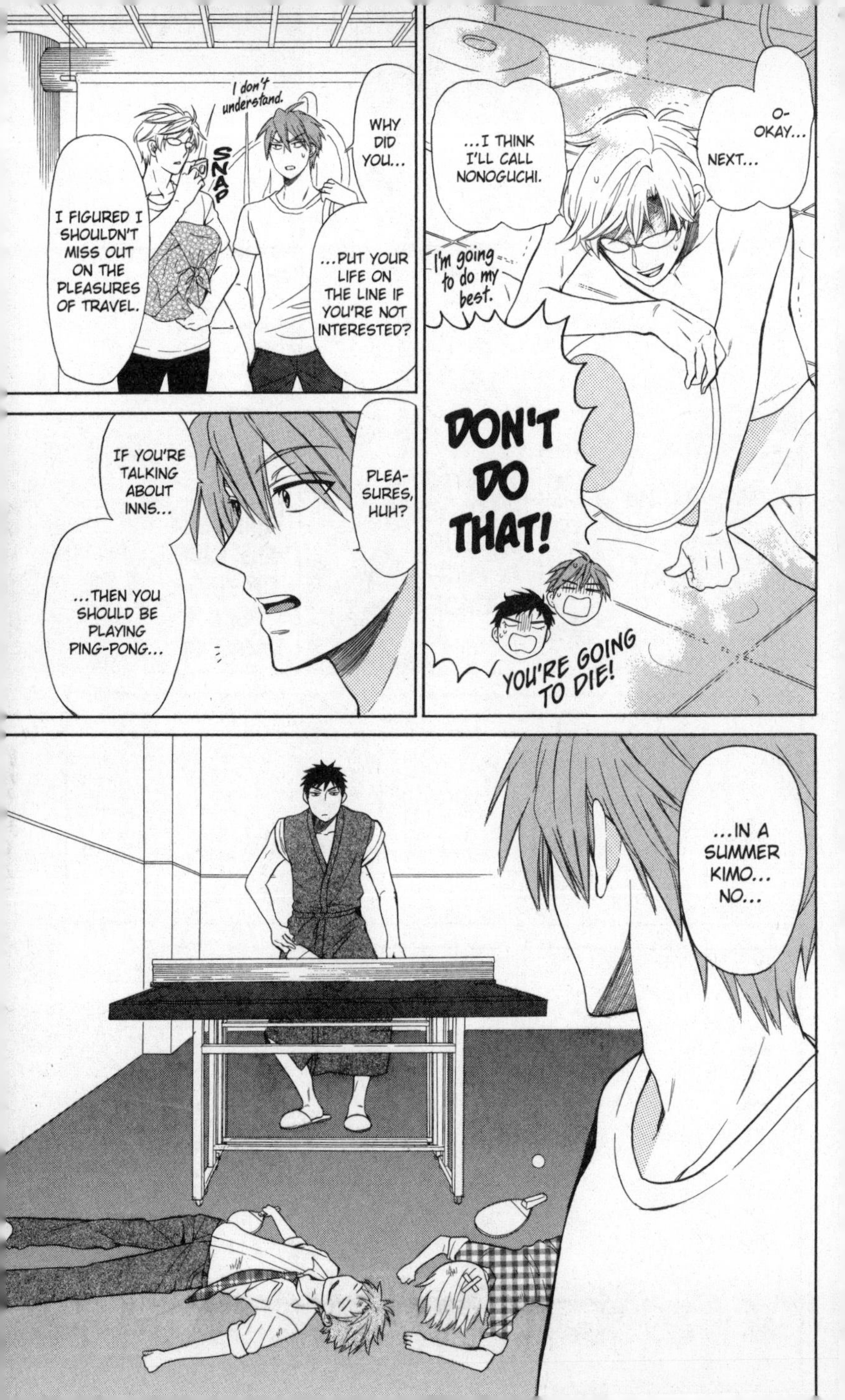
O-OKAY...
NEXT...
...I THINK I'LL CALL NONOGUCHI.
I'm going to do my best.
DON'T DO THAT!
YOU'RE GOING TO DIE!
WHY DID YOU...
...PUT YOUR LIFE ON THE LINE IF YOU'RE NOT INTERESTED?
I don't understand.
SNAP
I FIGURED I SHOULDN'T MISS OUT ON THE PLEASURES OF TRAVEL.
PLEA-SURES, HUH?
IF YOU'RE TALKING ABOUT INNS...
...THEN YOU SHOULD BE PLAYING PING-PONG...
...IN A SUMMER KIMO... NO...

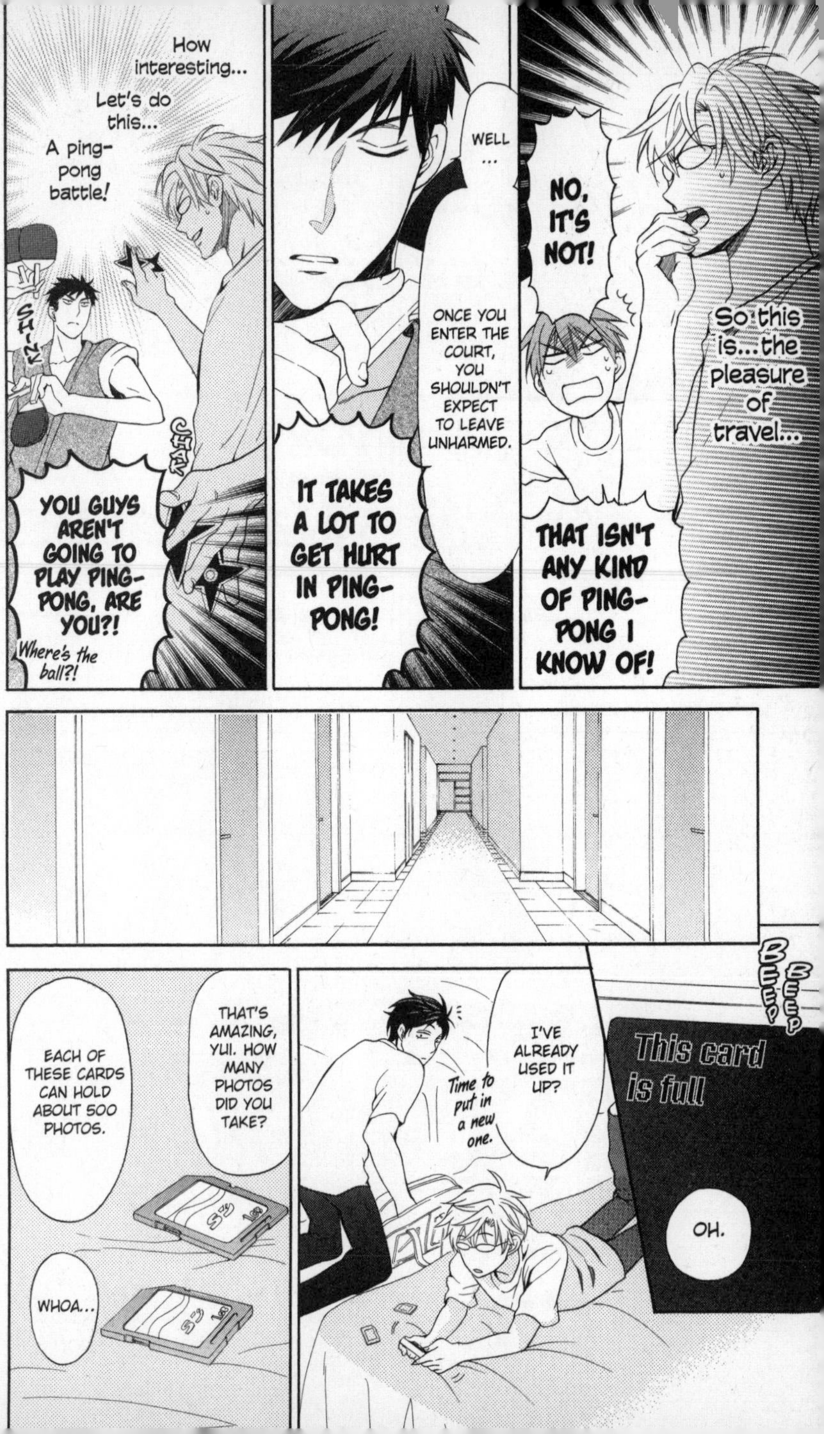
So this is...the pleasure of travel...
NO, IT'S NOT!
THAT ISN'T ANY KIND OF PING-PONG I KNOW OF!
WELL ...
ONCE YOU ENTER THE COURT, YOU SHOULDN'T EXPECT TO LEAVE UNHARMED.
IT TAKES A LOT TO GET HURT IN PING-PONG!
How interesting...
Let's do this...
A ping-pong battle!
SHINK
CHAK
YOU GUYS AREN'T GOING TO PLAY PING-PONG, ARE YOU?!
Where's the ball?!
BEEP BEEP
This card is full
OH.
I'VE ALREADY USED IT UP?
Time to put in a new one.
THAT'S AMAZING, YUI. HOW MANY PHOTOS DID YOU TAKE?
EACH OF THESE CARDS CAN HOLD ABOUT 500 PHOTOS.
WHOA...

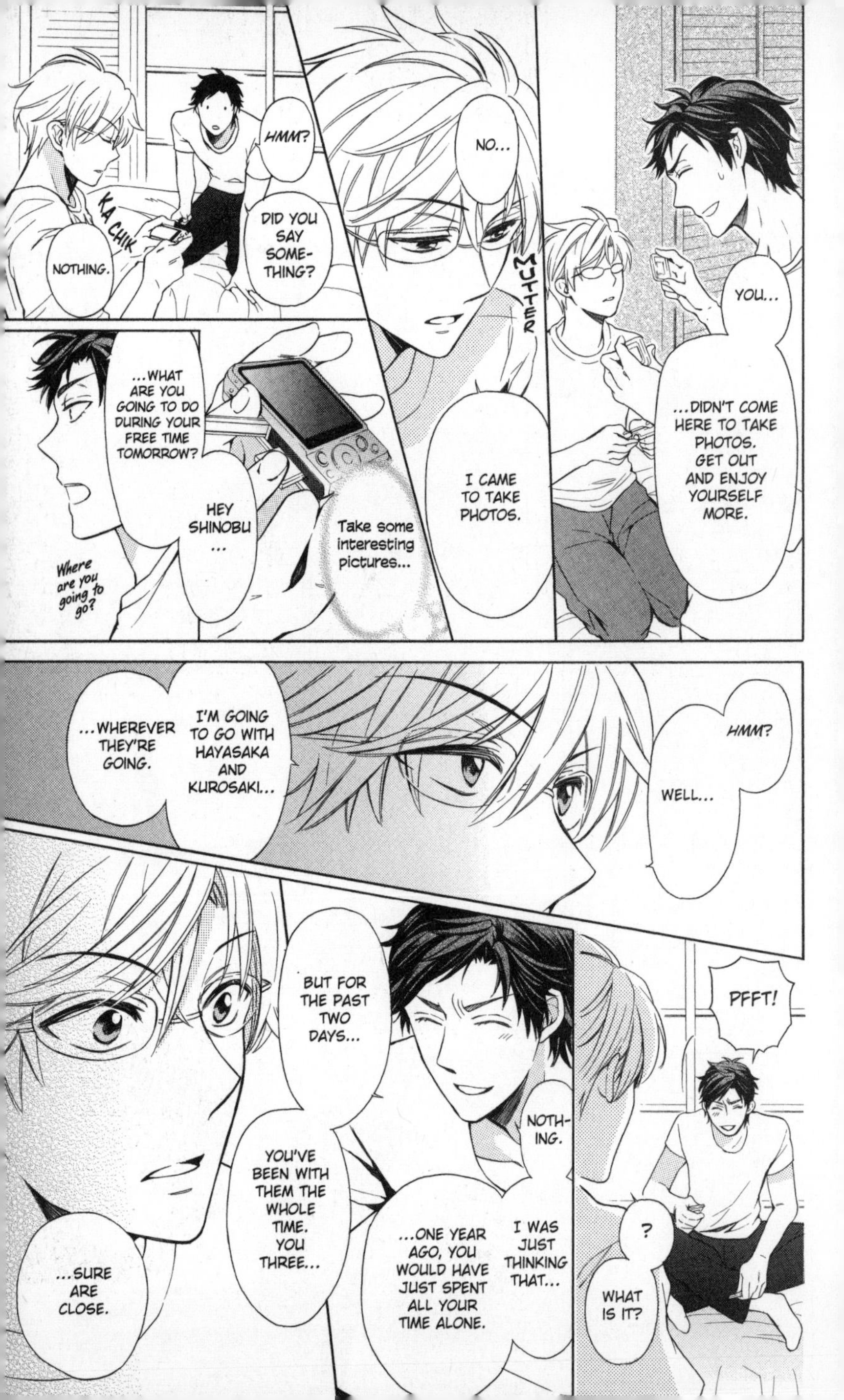
YOU...
...DIDN'T COME HERE TO TAKE PHOTOS. GET OUT AND ENJOY YOURSELF MORE.
NO...
MUTTER
I CAME TO TAKE PHOTOS.
HMM?
DID YOU SAY SOME-THING?
KA CHIK
NOTHING.
...WHAT ARE YOU GOING TO DO DURING YOUR FREE TIME TOMORROW?
HEY SHINOBU ...
Take some interesting pictures...
Where are you going to go?
HMM?
WELL...
I'M GOING TO GO WITH HAYASAKA AND KUROSAKI...
...WHEREVER THEY'RE GOING.
PFFT!
?
WHAT IS IT?
NOTH-ING.
I WAS JUST THINKING THAT...
...ONE YEAR AGO, YOU WOULD HAVE JUST SPENT ALL YOUR TIME ALONE.
BUT FOR THE PAST TWO DAYS...
YOU'VE BEEN WITH THEM THE WHOLE TIME. YOU THREE...
...SURE ARE CLOSE.

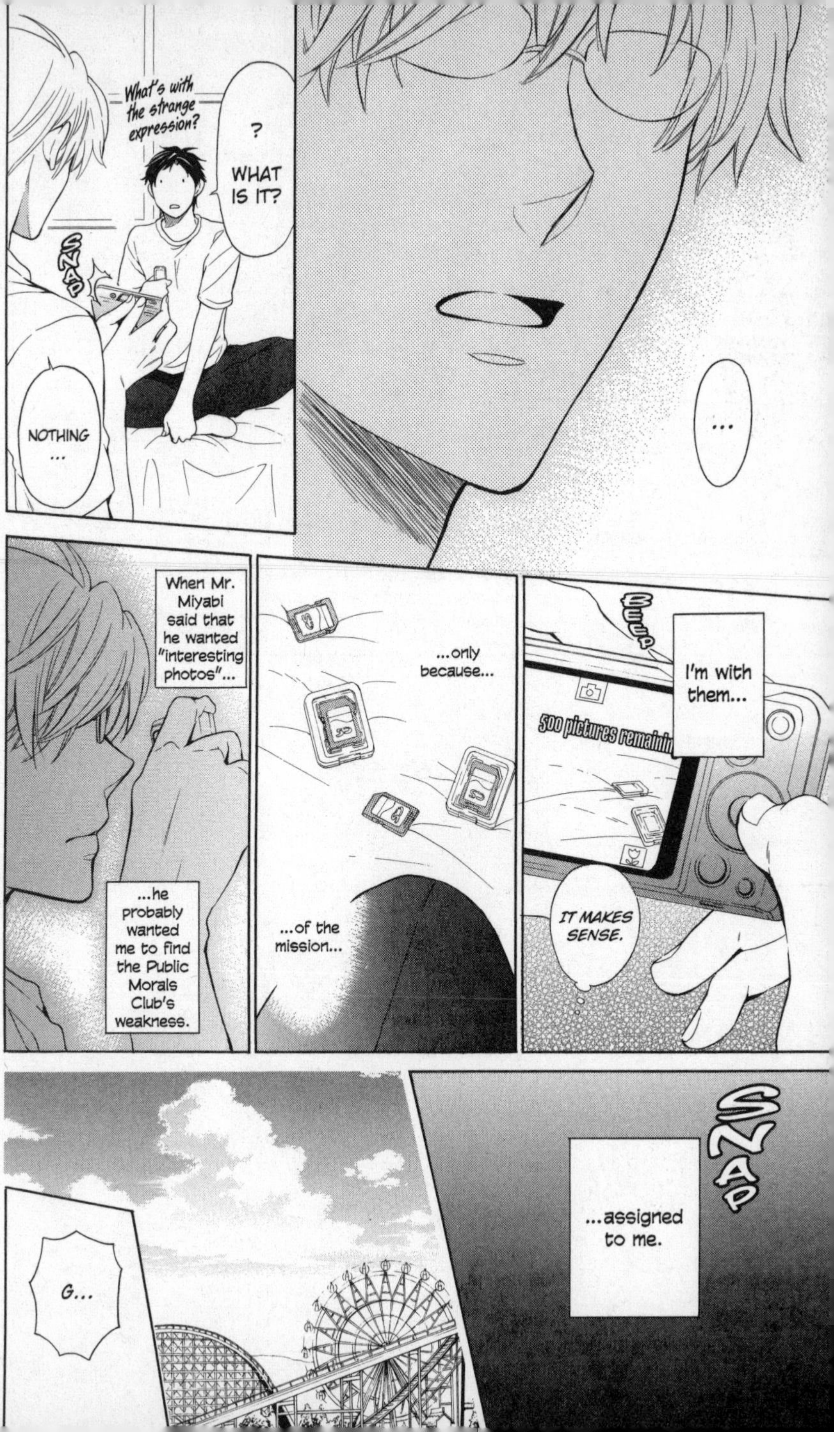
...
?
WHAT IS IT?
What's with the strange expression?
SNAP
NOTHING ...
I'm with them...
BEEP
500 pictures remainin
IT MAKES SENSE.
...only because...
...of the mission...
When Mr. Miyabi said that he wanted "interesting photos"...
...he probably wanted me to find the Public Morals Club's weakness.
SNAP
...assigned to me.
G...

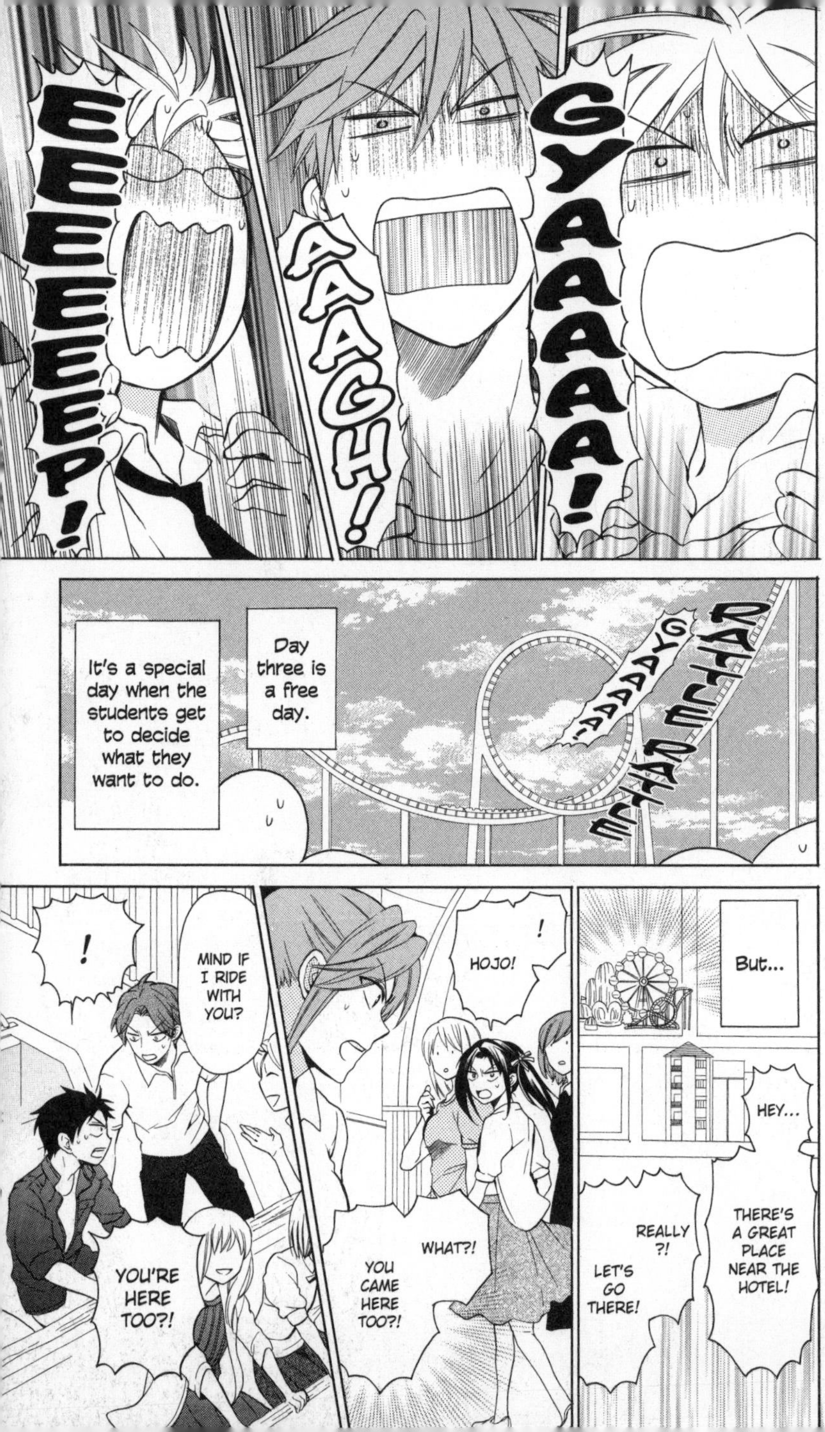
GYAAAAA!
AAAGH!
EEEEEEP!
RATTLE RATTLE
GYAAAAA!
Day three is a free day.
It's a special day when the students get to decide what they want to do.
But...
HEY...
THERE'S A GREAT PLACE NEAR THE HOTEL!
REALLY?!
LET'S GO THERE!
!
HOJO!
WHAT?!
YOU CAME HERE TOO?!
!
MIND IF I RIDE WITH YOU?
YOU'RE HERE TOO?!

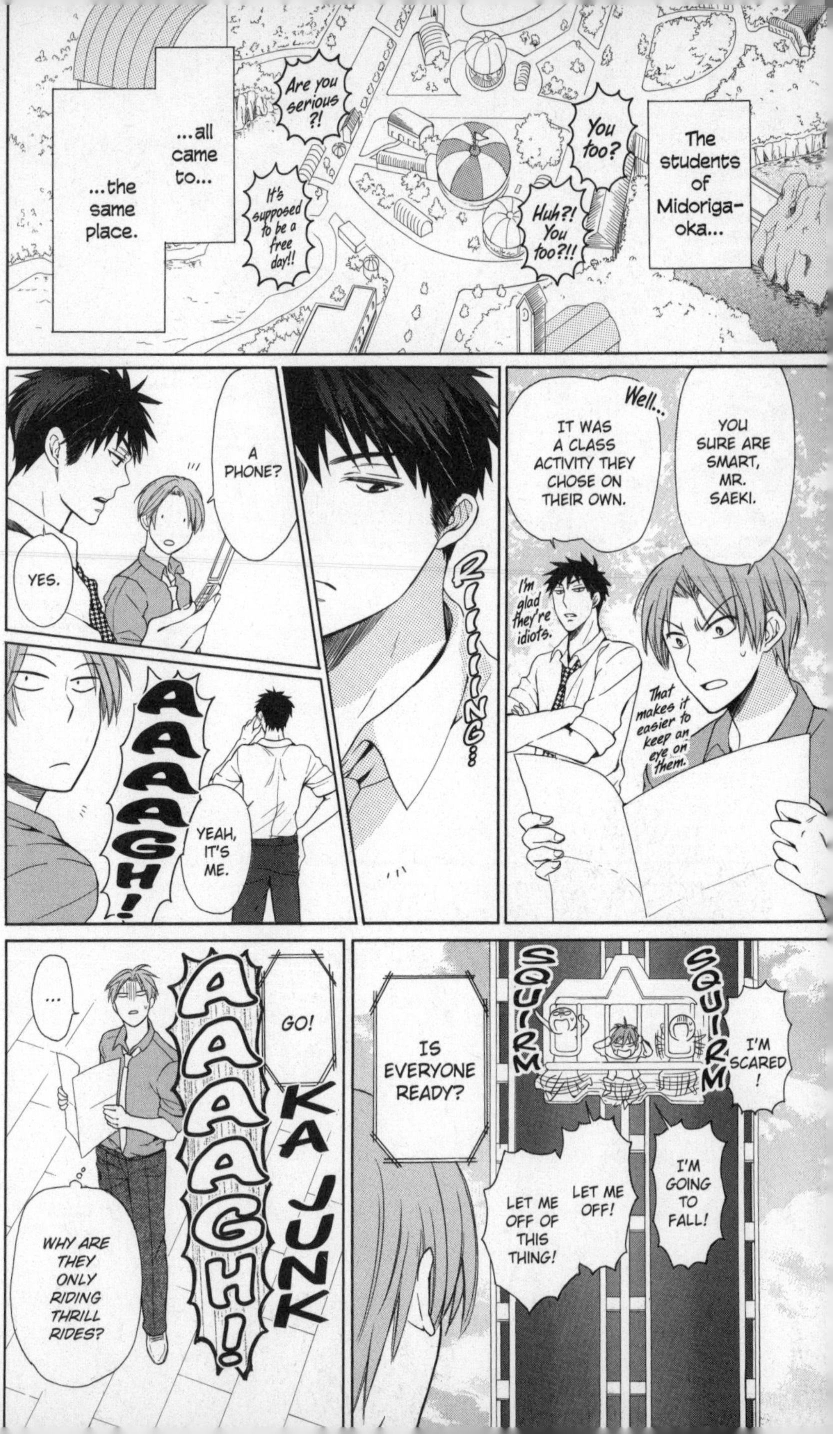
The students of Midoriga-oka...
You too?
Huh?! You too?!!
Are you serious?!
It's supposed to be a free day!!
...all came to...
...the same place.
YOU SURE ARE SMART, MR. SAEKI.
Well...
IT WAS A CLASS ACTIVITY THEY CHOSE ON THEIR OWN.
I'm glad they're idiots.
That makes it easier to keep an eye on them.
RIIIIING...
A PHONE?
YES.
YEAH, IT'S ME.
AAAAAGH!
SQUIRM SQUIRM
I'M SCARED!
I'M GOING TO FALL!
LET ME OFF!
LET ME OFF OF THIS THING!
IS EVERYONE READY?
GO!
KA JUNK
AAAAAGH!
...
WHY ARE THEY ONLY RIDING THRILL RIDES?

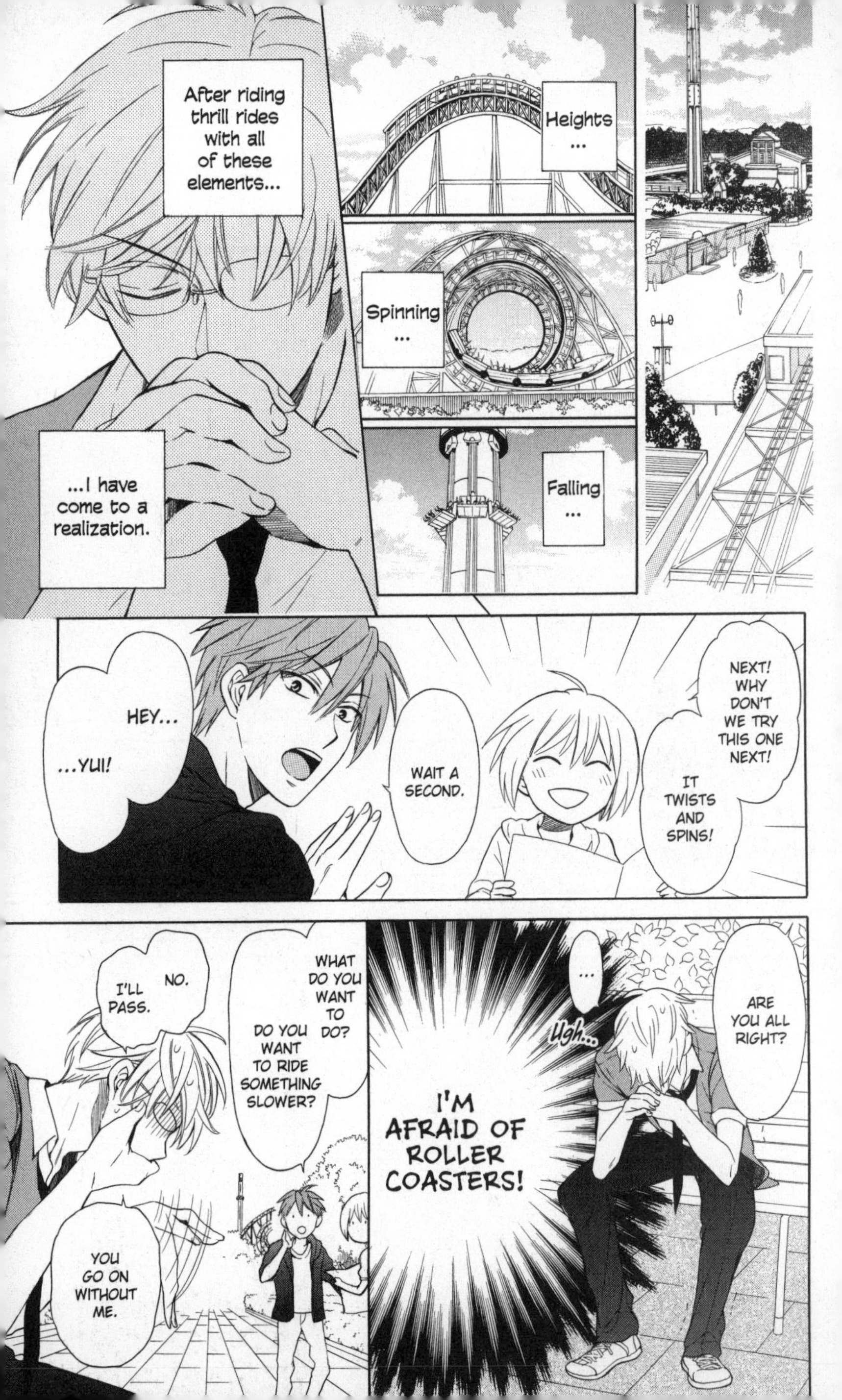
After riding thrill rides with all of these elements...
Heights...
Spinning...
Falling...
...I have come to a realization.
NEXT! WHY DON'T WE TRY THIS ONE NEXT!
IT TWISTS AND SPINS!
WAIT A SECOND.
HEY...
...YUI!
ARE YOU ALL RIGHT?
...
Ugh...
I'M AFRAID OF ROLLER COASTERS!
WHAT DO YOU WANT TO DO?
DO YOU WANT TO RIDE SOMETHING SLOWER?
NO.
I'LL PASS.
YOU GO ON WITHOUT ME.

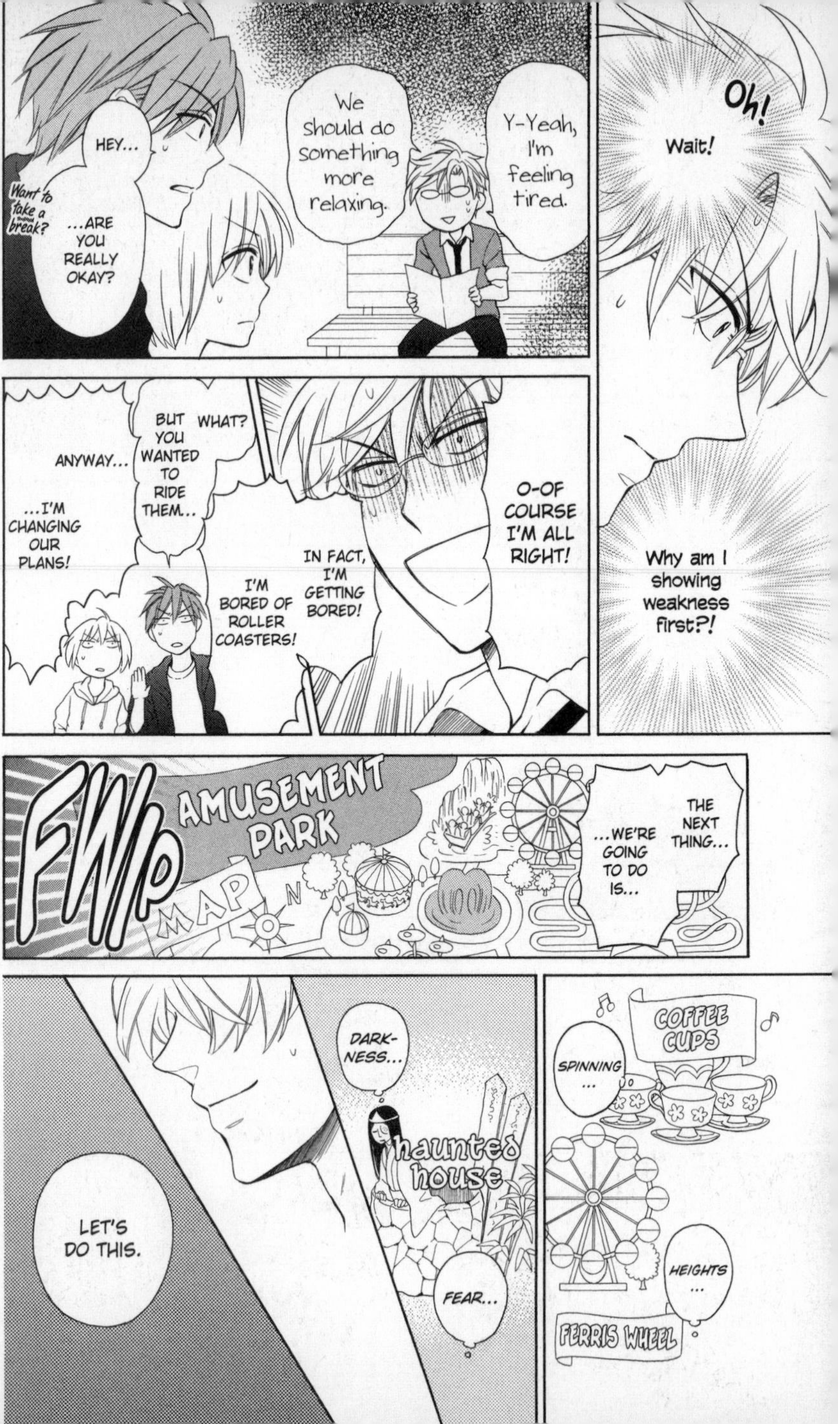
Oh!
Wait!
Why am I showing weakness first?!
Y-Yeah, I'm feeling tired.
We should do something more relaxing.
HEY...
...ARE YOU REALLY OKAY?
Want to take a break?
O-OF COURSE I'M ALL RIGHT!
IN FACT, I'M GETTING BORED!
I'M BORED OF ROLLER COASTERS!
WHAT?
BUT YOU WANTED TO RIDE THEM...
ANYWAY...
...I'M CHANGING OUR PLANS!
THE NEXT THING...
...WE'RE GOING TO DO IS...
AMUSEMENT PARK
MAP
N
FWIP
COFFEE CUPS
SPINNING...
HEIGHTS...
FERRIS WHEEL
DARKNESS...
haunted house
FEAR...
LET'S DO THIS.

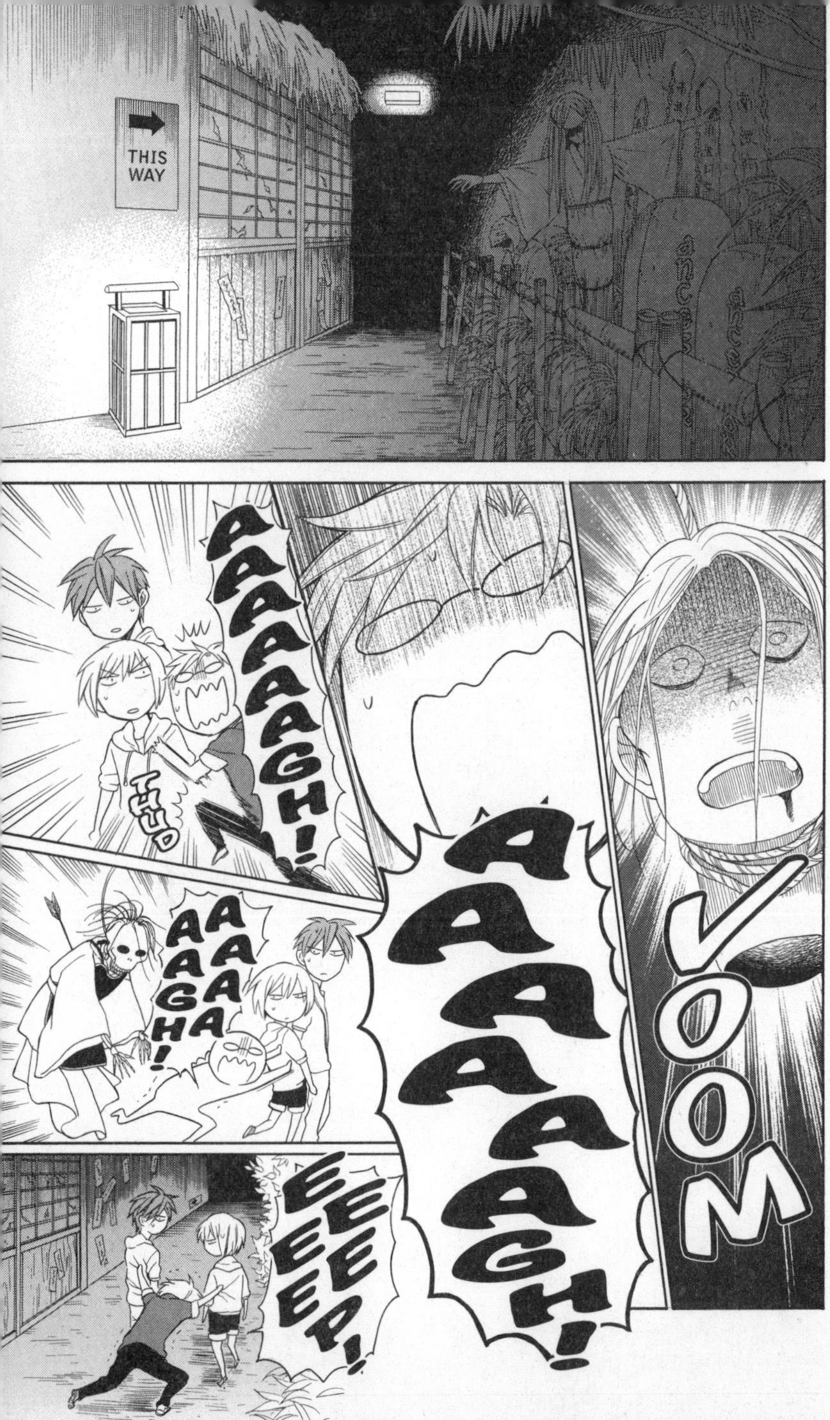
THIS WAY
VOOM
AAAAAAGH!
AAAAAAAGH!
THUD
AAAAAAAGH!
EEEEEP!

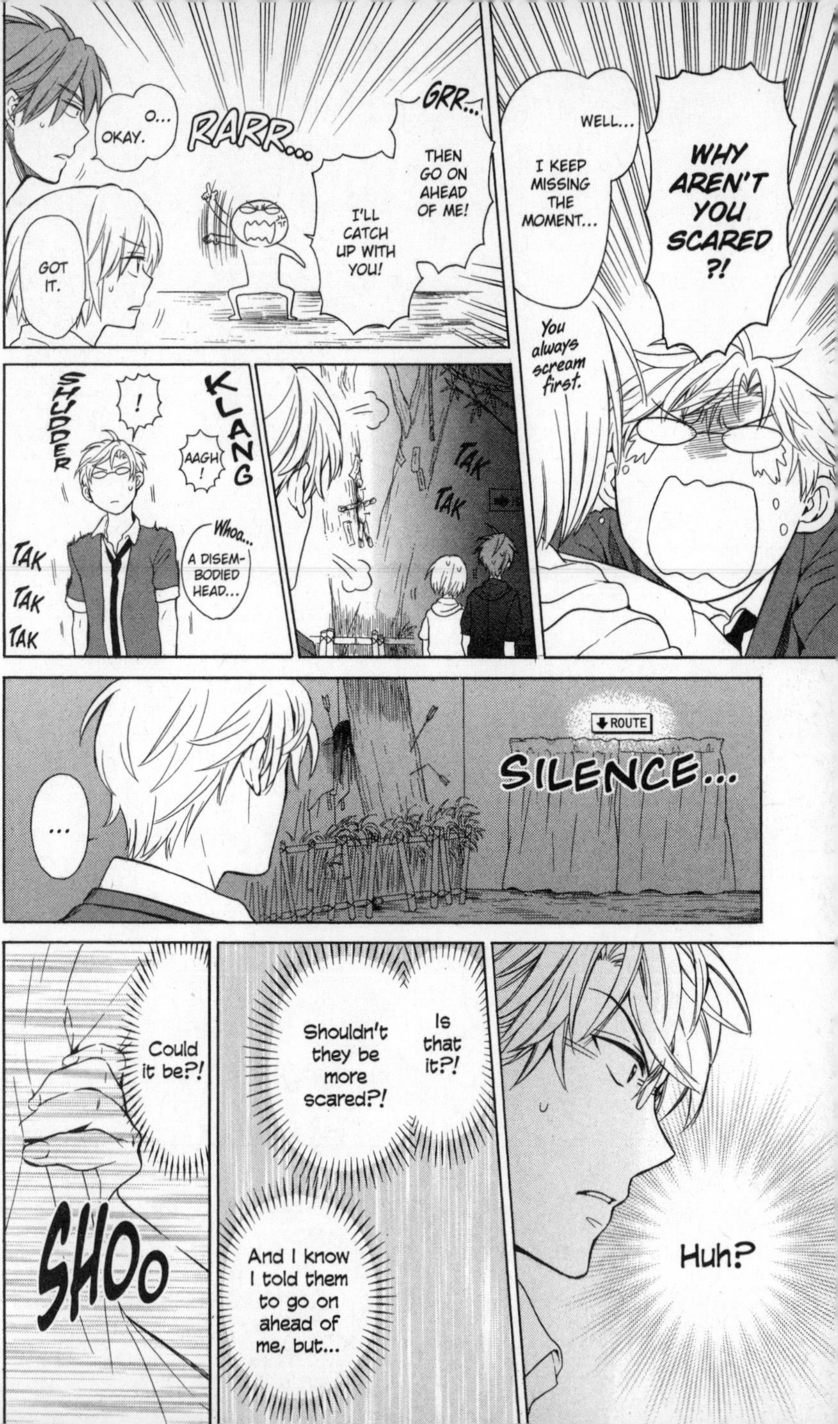
WHY AREN'T YOU SCARED ?!
WELL...
I KEEP MISSING THE MOMENT...
You always scream first.
GRR...
THEN GO ON AHEAD OF ME!
I'LL CATCH UP WITH YOU!
RARR...
O... OKAY.
GOT IT.
TAK
TAK
KLANG
AAGH!
!
SHUDDER
Whoa...
A DISEMBODIED HEAD...
TAK
TAK
TAK
ROUTE
SILENCE...
...
Huh?
Is that it?!
Shouldn't they be more scared?!
And I know I told them to go on ahead of me, but...
Could it be?!
SHOO

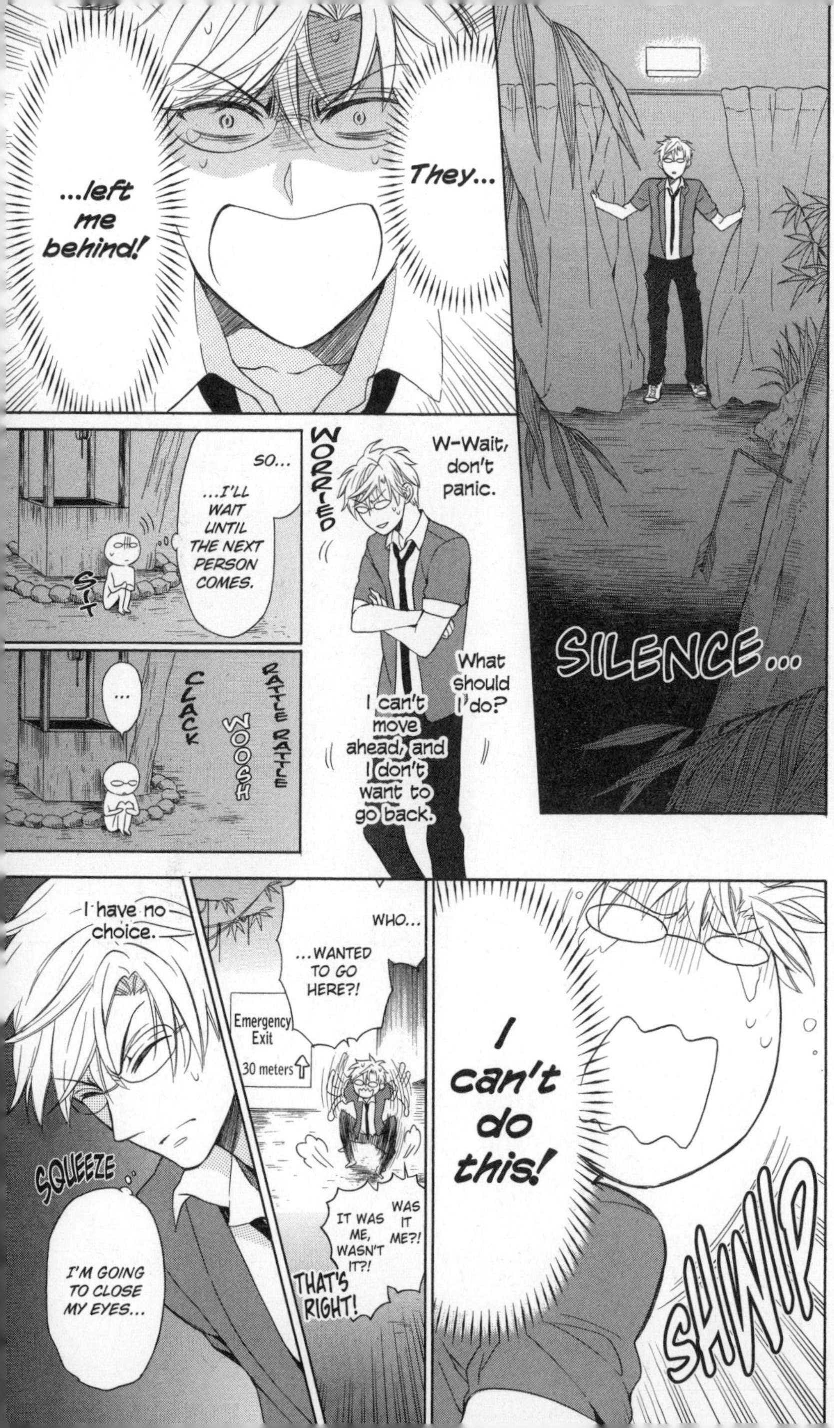
SILENCE...
They...
...left me behind!
W-Wait, don't panic.
WORRIED
What should I do?
I can't move ahead, and I don't want to go back.
SO...
...I'LL WAIT UNTIL THE NEXT PERSON COMES.
SIT
RATTLE RATTLE
WOOSH
CLACK
...
I can't do this!
SHWIP
WHO...
...WANTED TO GO HERE?!
Emergency Exit
30 meters
WAS IT ME?!
IT WAS ME, WASN'T IT?!
THAT'S RIGHT!
I have no choice.
SQUEEZE
I'M GOING TO CLOSE MY EYES...

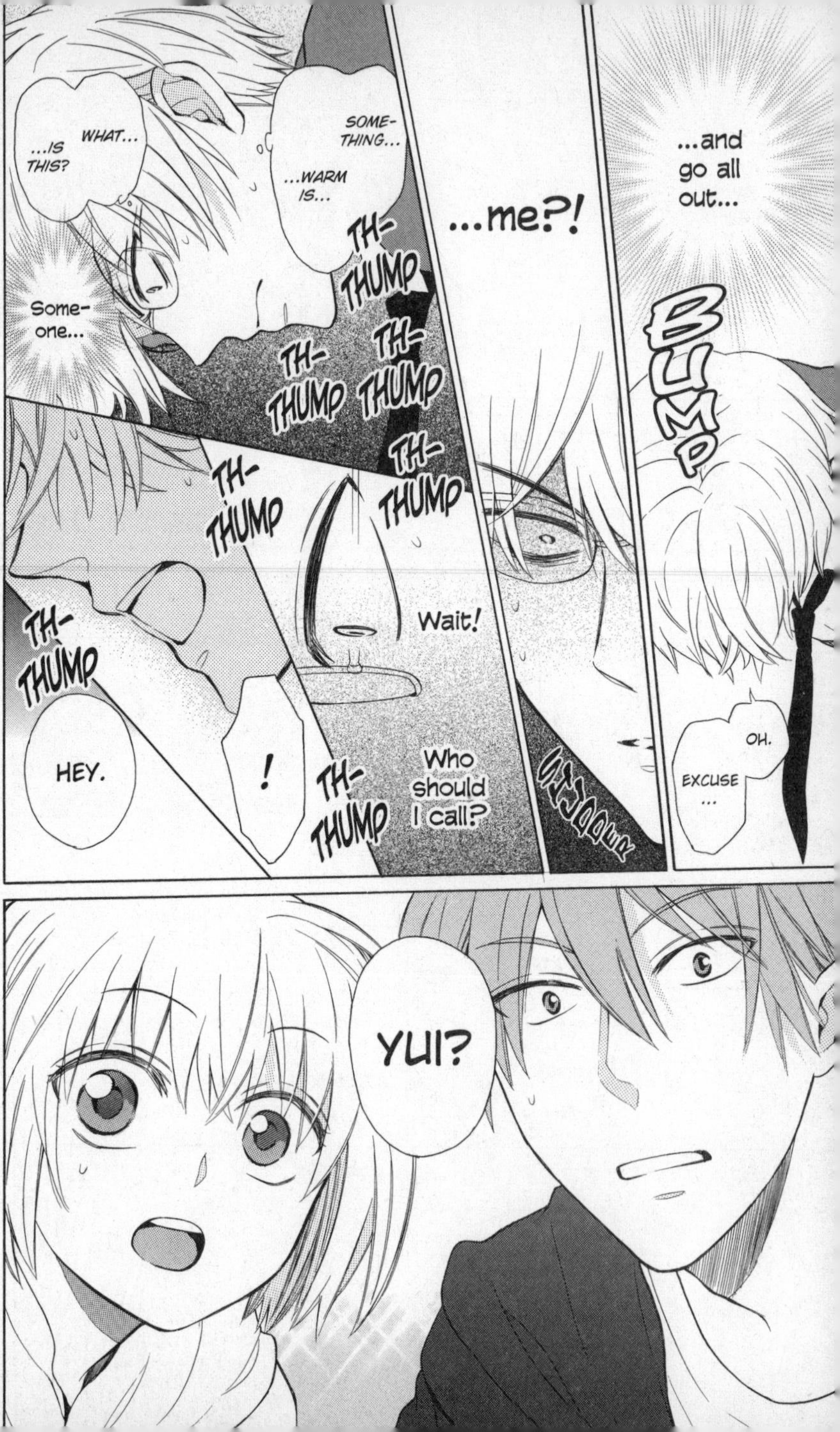
...and go all out...
BUMP
OH.
EXCUSE ...
...me?!
Who should I call?
TH-THUMP
Wait!
TH-THUMP
TH-THUMP
HEY.
!
TH-THUMP
SOME-THING...
...WARM IS...
TH-THUMP
TH-THUMP TH-THUMP
WHAT...
...IS THIS?
Some-one...
YUI?

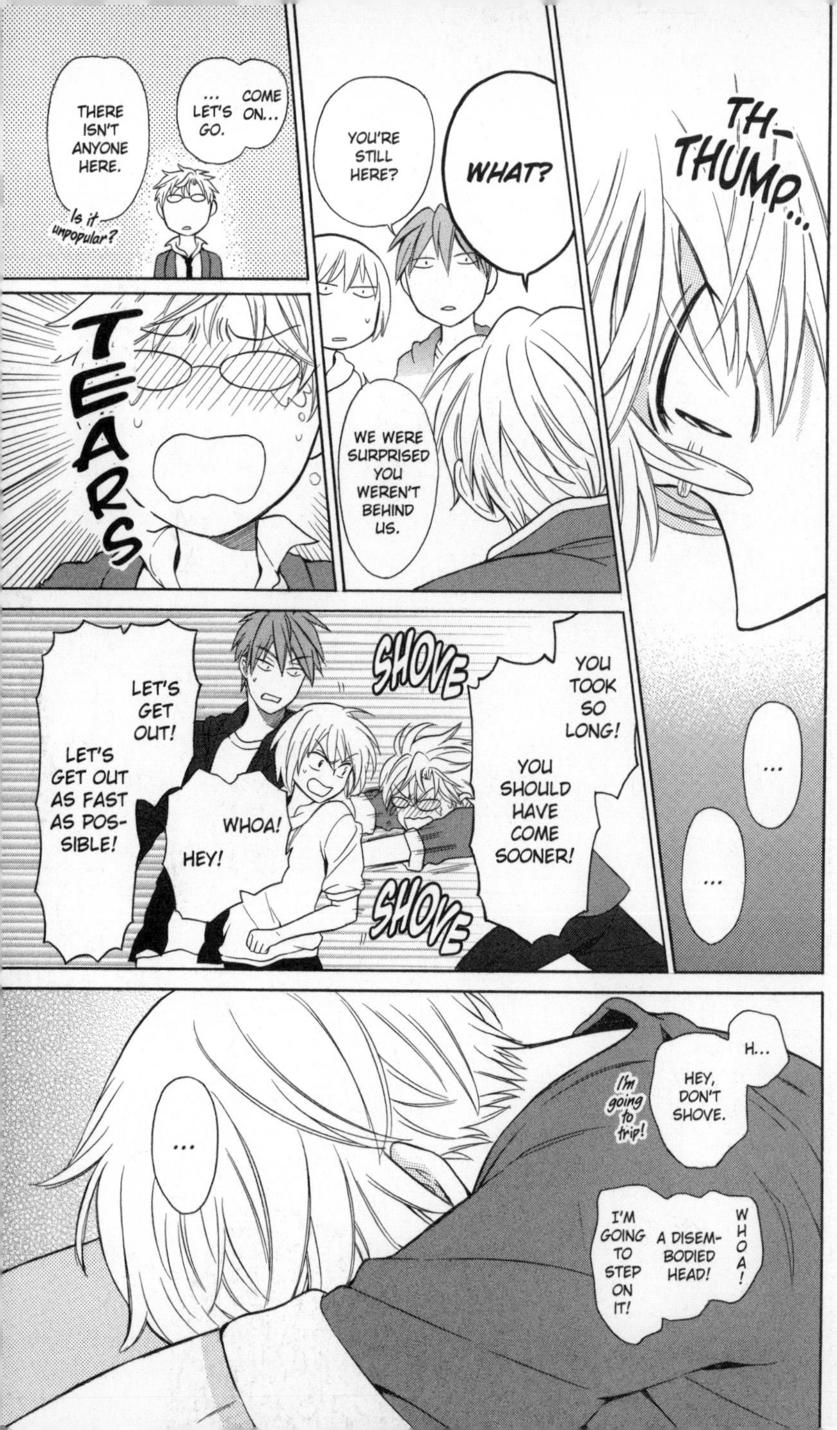
TH-THUMP...
...
...
WHAT?
YOU'RE STILL HERE?
WE WERE SURPRISED YOU WEREN'T BEHIND US.
COME ON... ...LET'S GO.
THERE ISN'T ANYONE HERE.
Is it unpopular?
TEARS
YOU TOOK SO LONG!
SHOVE
YOU SHOULD HAVE COME SOONER!
SHOVE
LET'S GET OUT!
LET'S GET OUT AS FAST AS POSSIBLE!
WHOA!
HEY!
H...
HEY, DON'T SHOVE.
I'm going to trip!
WHOA!
A DISEMBODIED HEAD!
I'M GOING TO STEP ON IT!
...

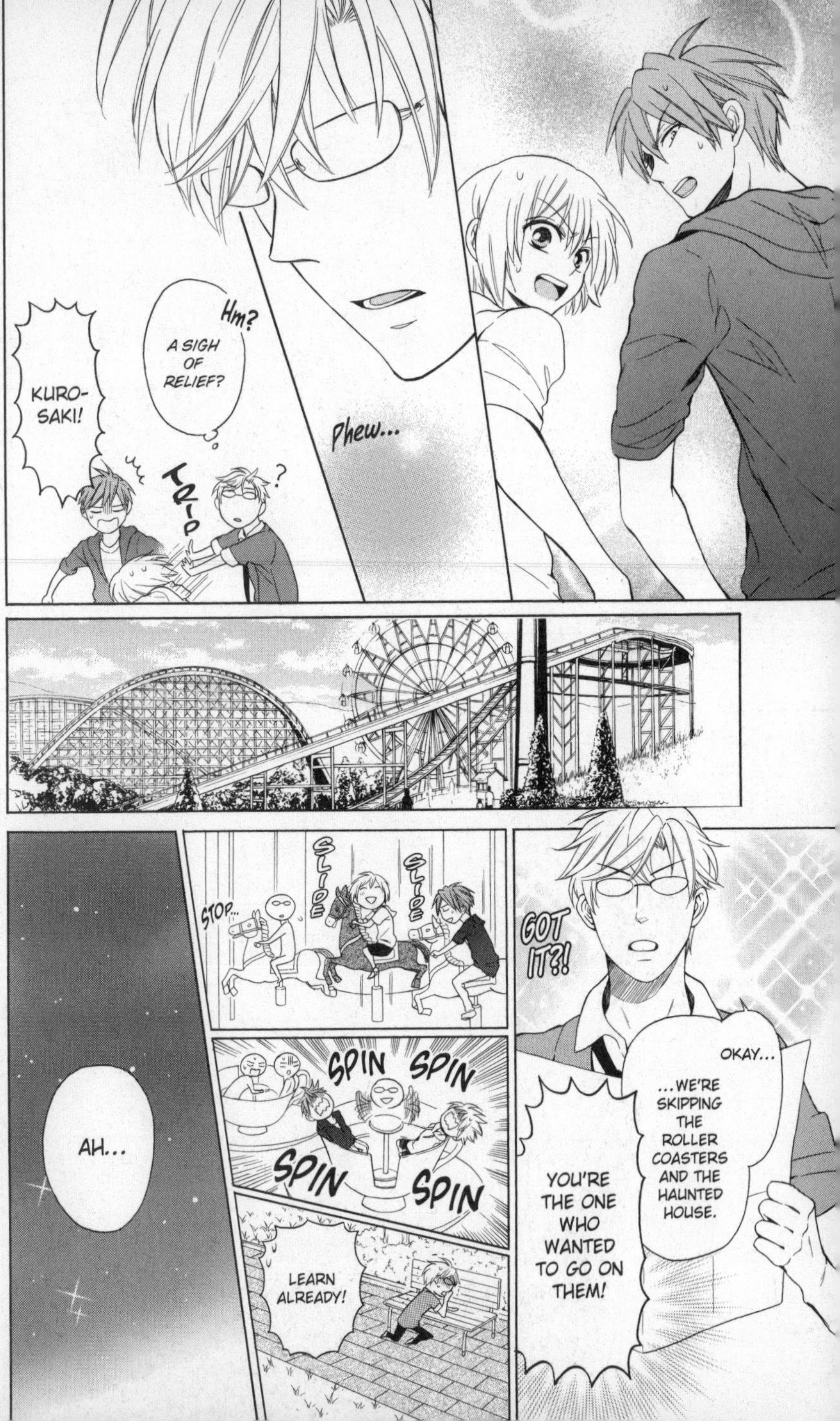
Phew...
Hm?
A SIGH OF RELIEF?
TRIP
?
KURO-SAKI!
GOT IT?!
OKAY...
...WE'RE SKIPPING THE ROLLER COASTERS AND THE HAUNTED HOUSE.
YOU'RE THE ONE WHO WANTED TO GO ON THEM!
SLIDE
SLIDE
STOP...
SPIN SPIN
SPIN SPIN
LEARN ALREADY!
AH...

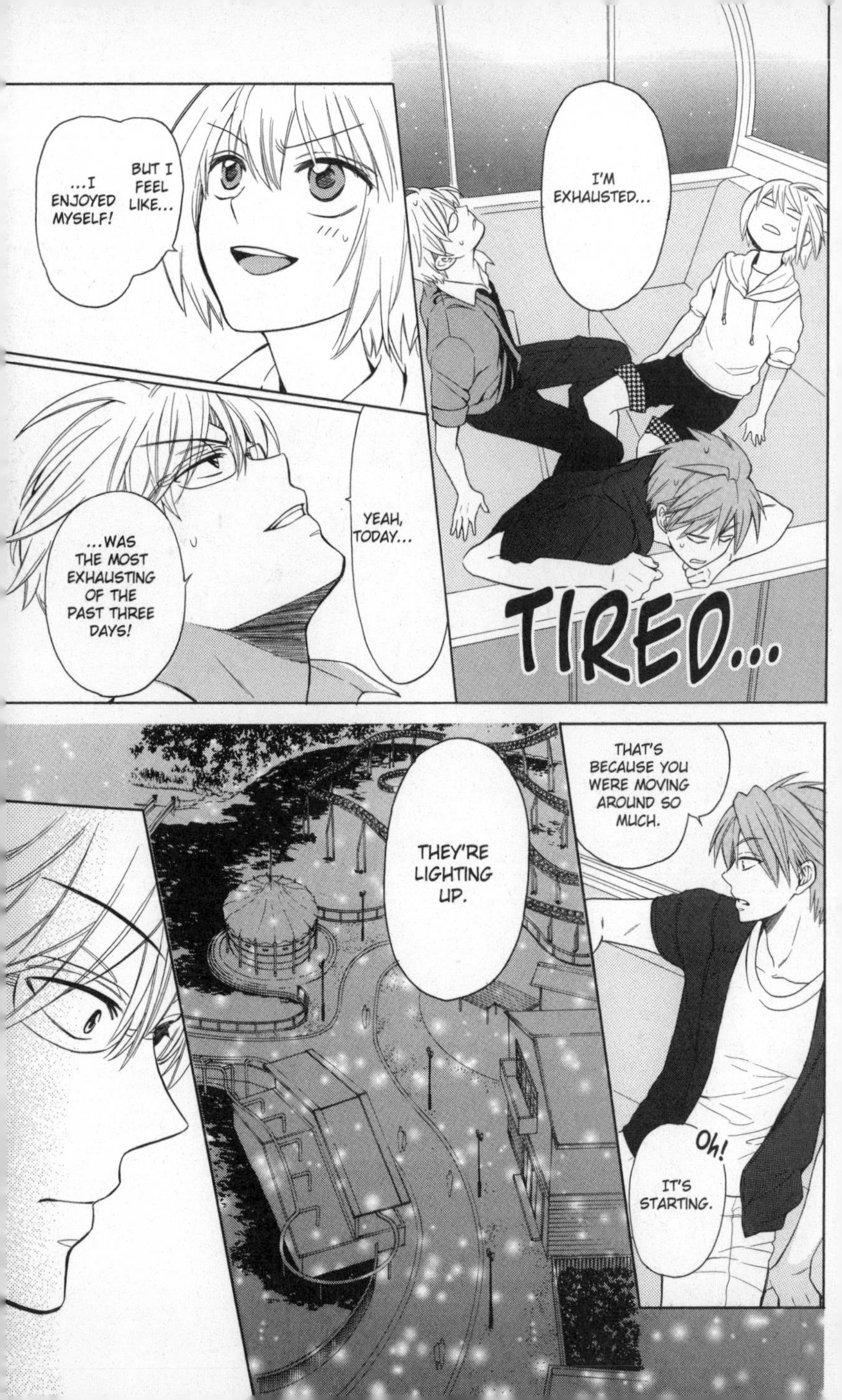
I'M EXHAUSTED...
TIRED...
BUT I FEEL LIKE...
...I ENJOYED MYSELF!
YEAH, TODAY...
...WAS THE MOST EXHAUSTING OF THE PAST THREE DAYS!
THAT'S BECAUSE YOU WERE MOVING AROUND SO MUCH.
Oh!
IT'S STARTING.
THEY'RE LIGHTING UP.

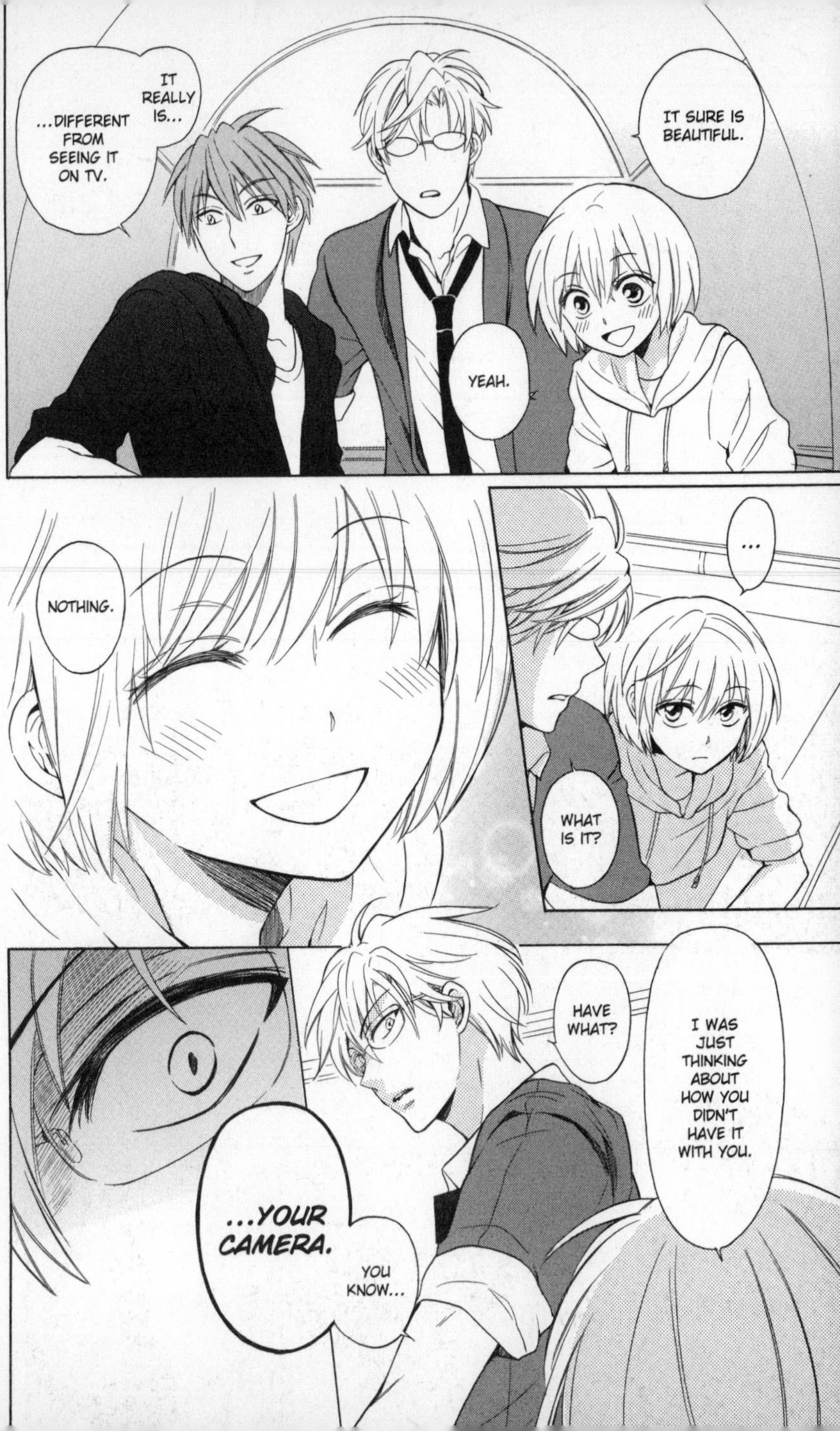
IT SURE IS BEAUTIFUL.
YEAH.
IT REALLY IS...
...DIFFERENT FROM SEEING IT ON TV.
...
WHAT IS IT?
NOTHING.
I WAS JUST THINKING ABOUT HOW YOU DIDN'T HAVE IT WITH YOU.
HAVE WHAT?
...YOUR CAMERA.
YOU KNOW...

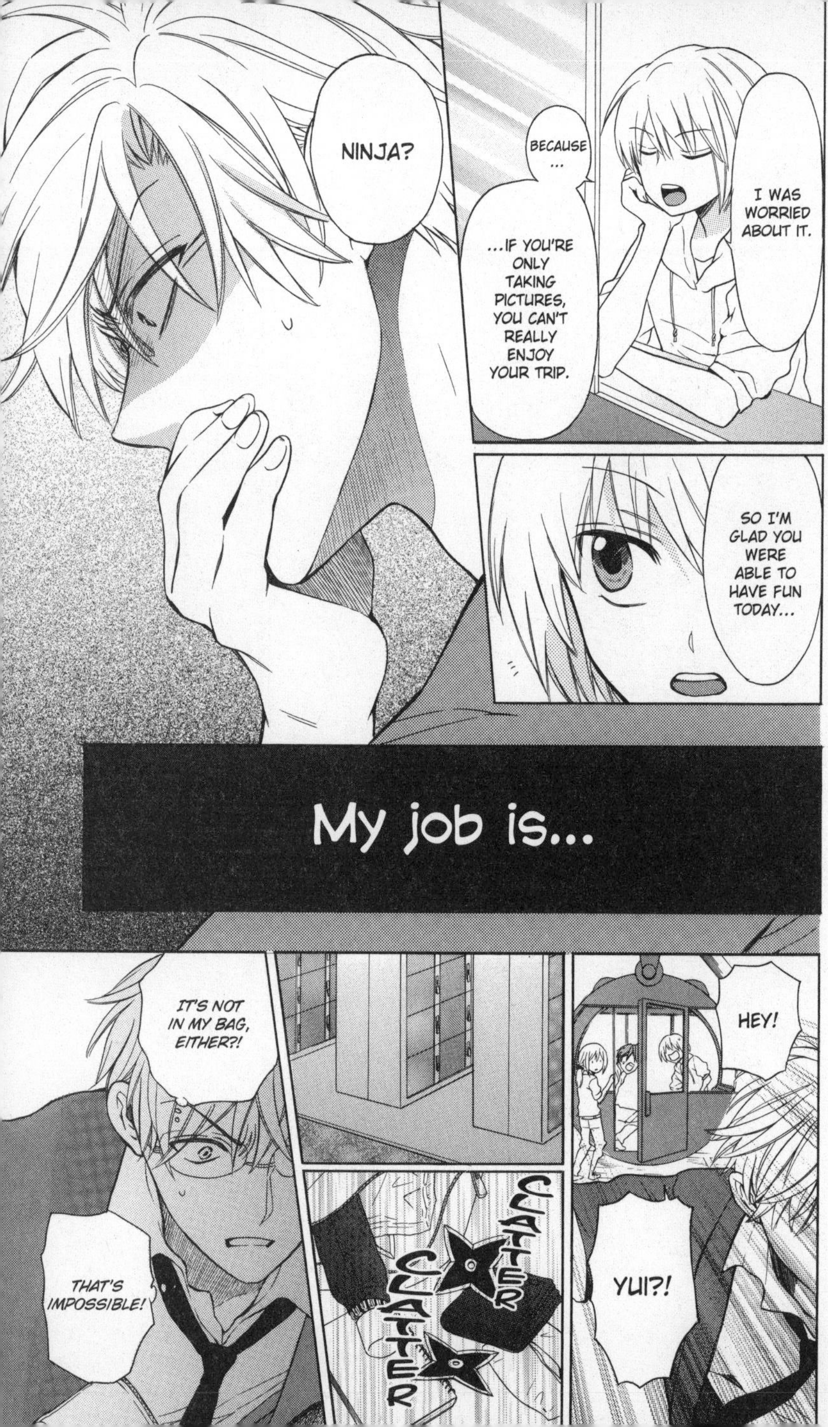
I WAS WORRIED ABOUT IT.
BECAUSE ...
...IF YOU'RE ONLY TAKING PICTURES, YOU CAN'T REALLY ENJOY YOUR TRIP.
NINJA?
SO I'M GLAD YOU WERE ABLE TO HAVE FUN TODAY...
My job is...
HEY!
YUI?!
IT'S NOT IN MY BAG, EITHER?!
CLATTER CLATTER
THAT'S IMPOSSIBLE!

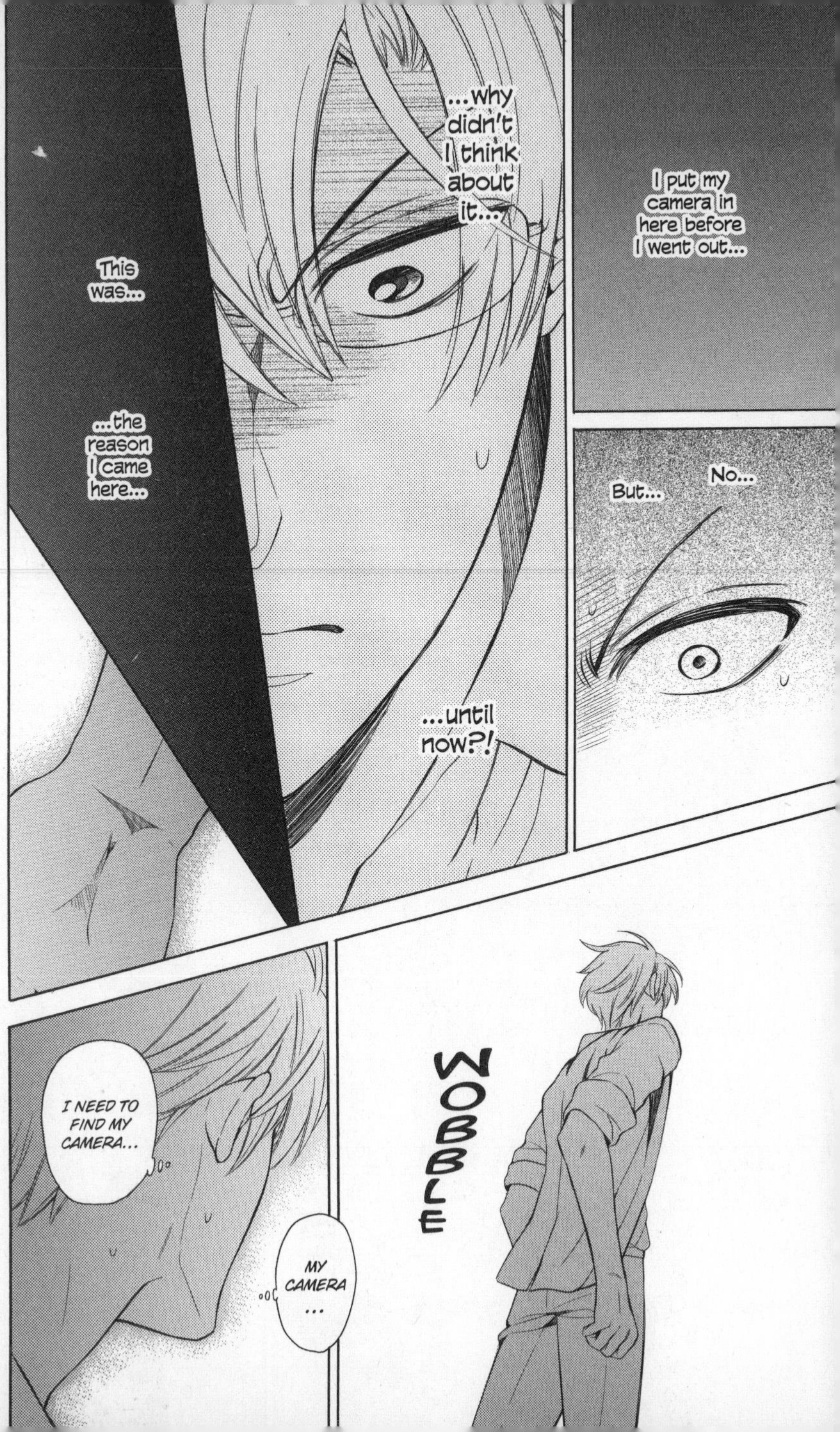
I put my camera in here before I went out...
No...
But...
...why didn't I think about it...
This was...
...the reason I came here...
...until now?!
WOBBLE
MY CAMERA ...
I NEED TO FIND MY CAMERA...

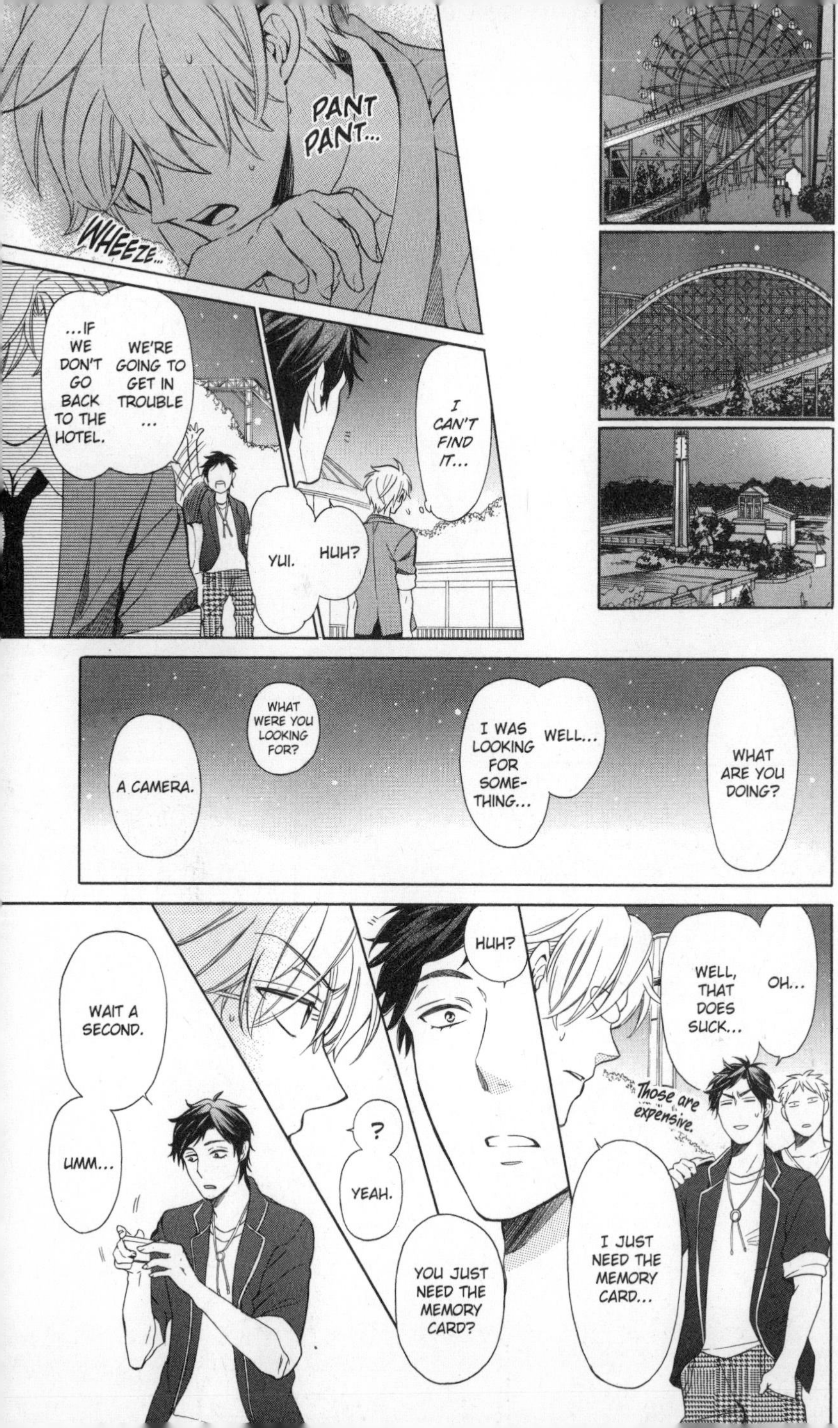
PANT PANT...
WHEEZE...
I CAN'T FIND IT...
HUH?
YUI.
WE'RE GOING TO GET IN TROUBLE...
...IF WE DON'T GO BACK TO THE HOTEL.
WHAT ARE YOU DOING?
WELL...
I WAS LOOKING FOR SOME-THING...
WHAT WERE YOU LOOKING FOR?
A CAMERA.
OH...
WELL, THAT DOES SUCK...
Those are expensive.
I JUST NEED THE MEMORY CARD...
HUH?
YOU JUST NEED THE MEMORY CARD?
?
YEAH.
WAIT A SECOND.
UMM...

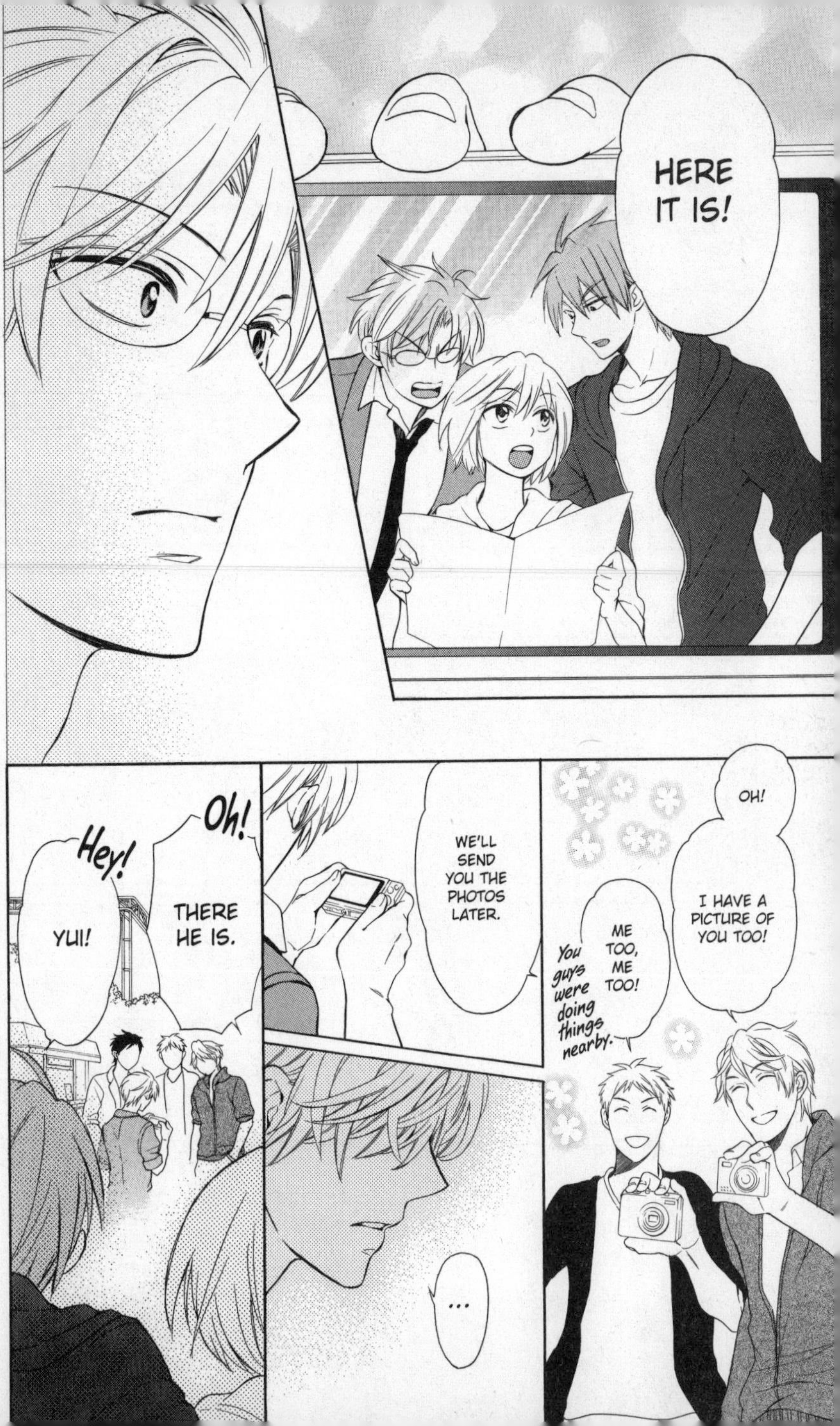
HERE IT IS!
OH!
I HAVE A PICTURE OF YOU TOO!
ME TOO, ME TOO!
You guys were doing things nearby.
WE'LL SEND YOU THE PHOTOS LATER.
...
Oh!
THERE HE IS.
Hey!
YUI!

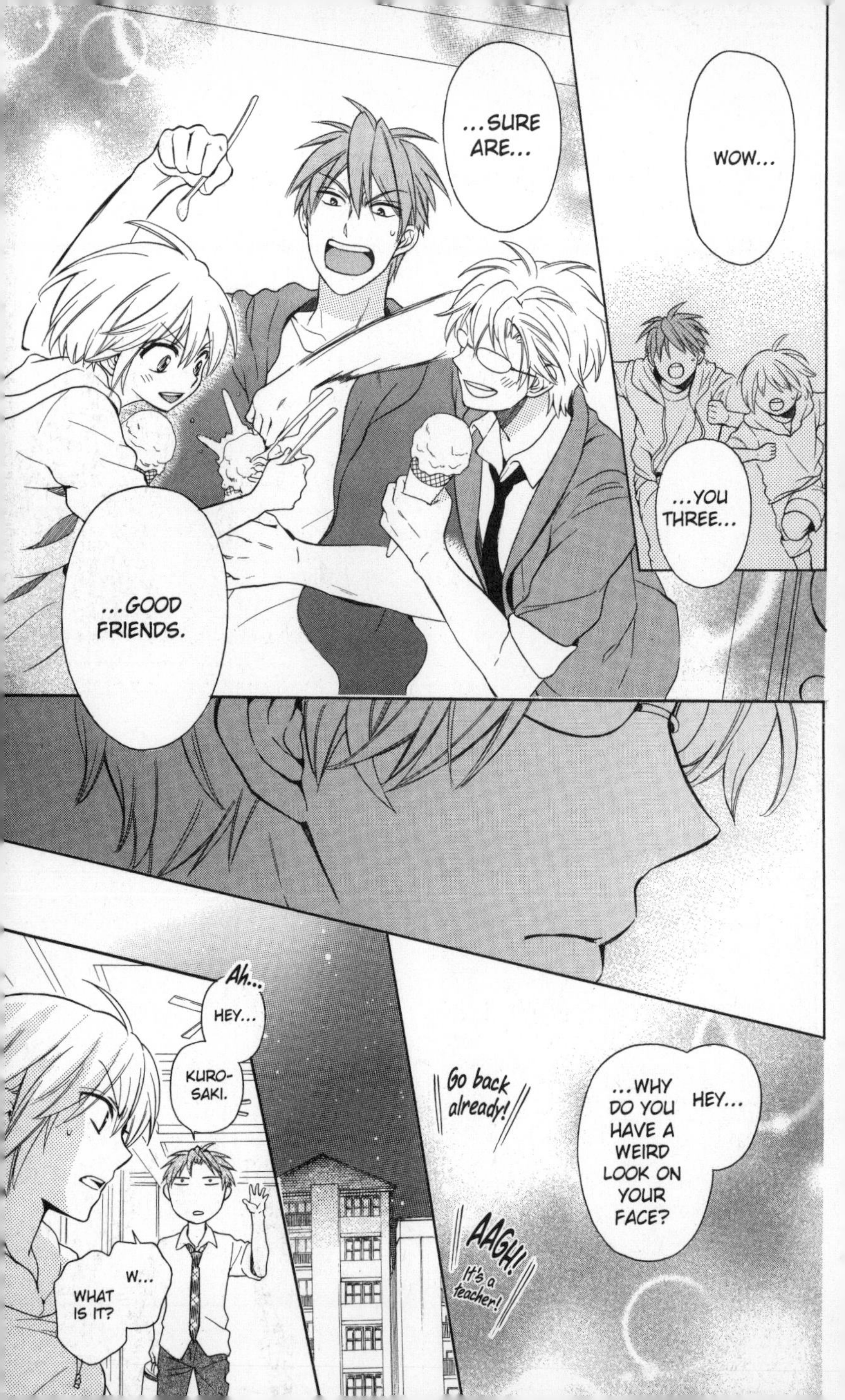
WOW...
...YOU THREE...
...SURE ARE...
...GOOD FRIENDS.
HEY...
...WHY DO YOU HAVE A WEIRD LOOK ON YOUR FACE?
Go back already!
AAGH! It's a teacher!
Ah... HEY...
KURO-SAKI.
W... WHAT IS IT?

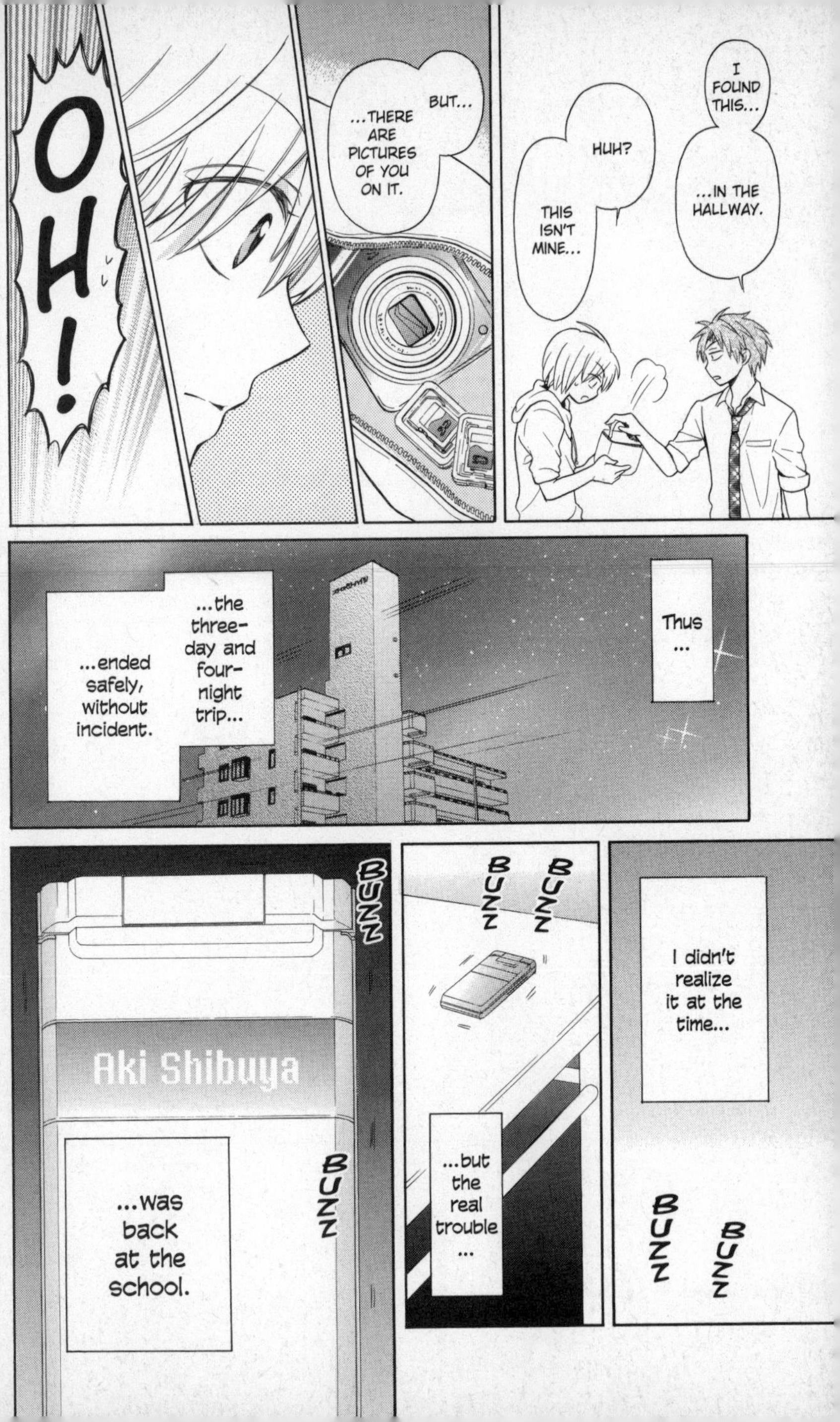
I FOUND THIS...
...IN THE HALLWAY.
HUH?
THIS ISN'T MINE...
BUT...
...THERE ARE PICTURES OF YOU ON IT.
OH!
Thus ...
...the three-day and four-night trip...
...ended safely, without incident.
I didn't realize it at the time...
BUZZ
BUZZ
BUZZ
BUZZ
...but the real trouble ...
BUZZ
Aki Shibuya
BUZZ
...was back at the school.

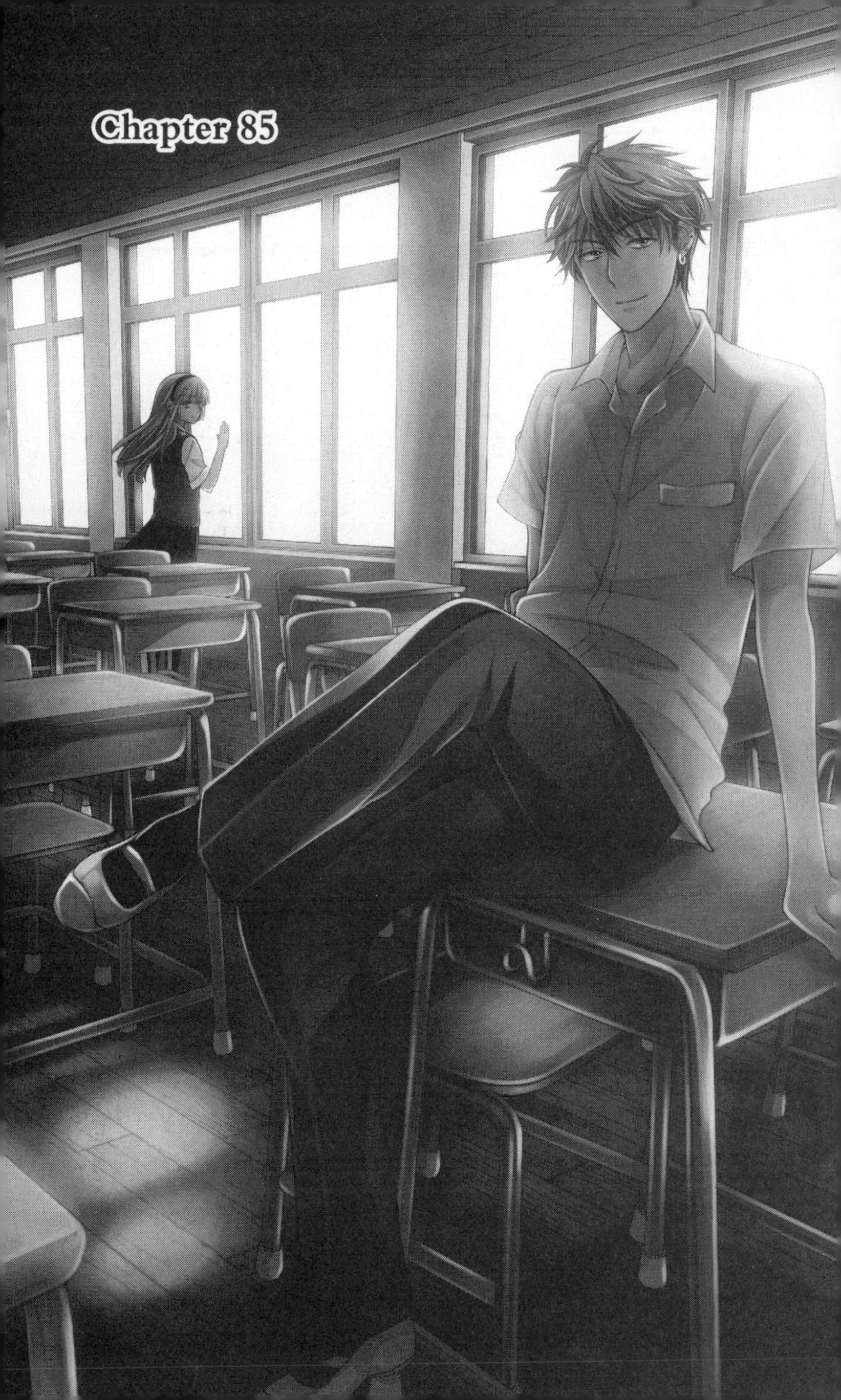
Chapter 85

INSIDE THE COURT

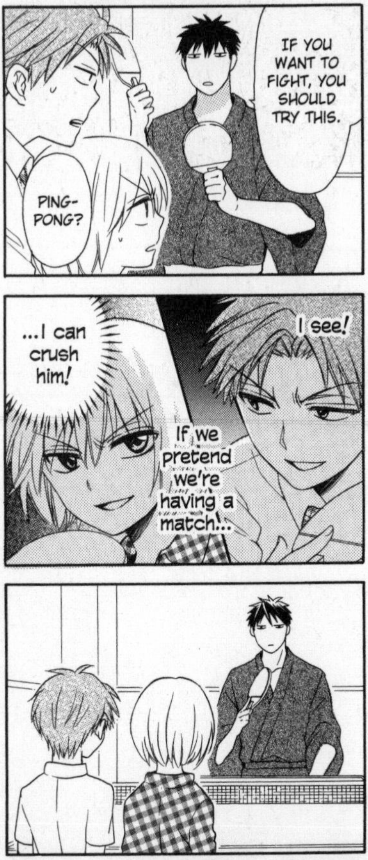
IF YOU WANT TO FIGHT, YOU SHOULD TRY THIS.
PING-PONG?
I see!
If we pretend we're having a match...
...I can crush him!
There's...
...another enemy here!

NEW AND OLD

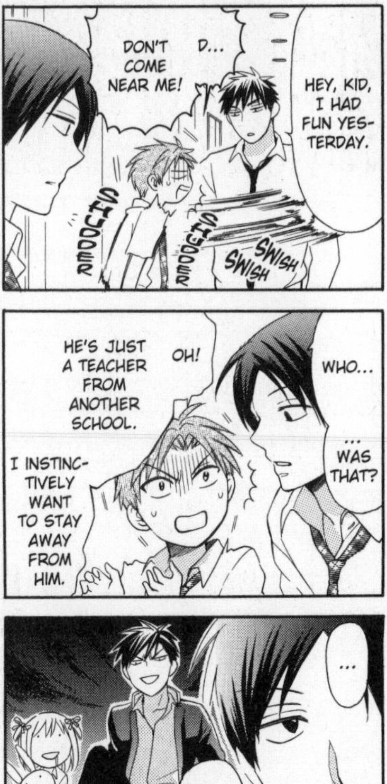
HEY, KID, I HAD FUN YESTERDAY.
D...
DON'T COME NEAR ME!
SHUDDER
SHUDDER
SWISH
SWISH
WHO...
...WAS THAT?
OH!
HE'S JUST A TEACHER FROM ANOTHER SCHOOL.
I INSTINCTIVELY WANT TO STAY AWAY FROM HIM.
...
THAT FACE...
West
I WONDER IF THAT MEANS THAT THE BLOOD OF THE WEST HIGH BANCHO RUNS THICK IN YOUR VEINS.
YUP.
WHAT?!
DON'T PRAISE ME OUT OF THE BLUE!
It's embarrassing!

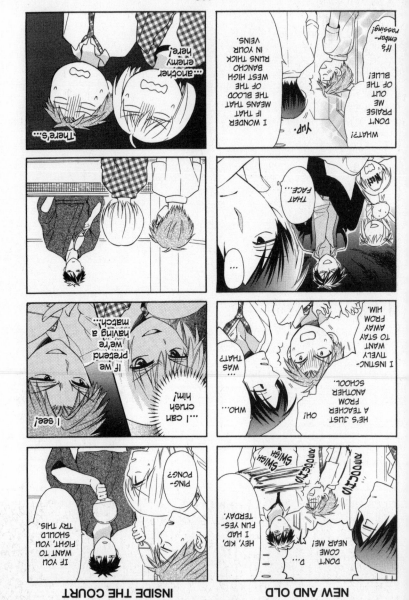

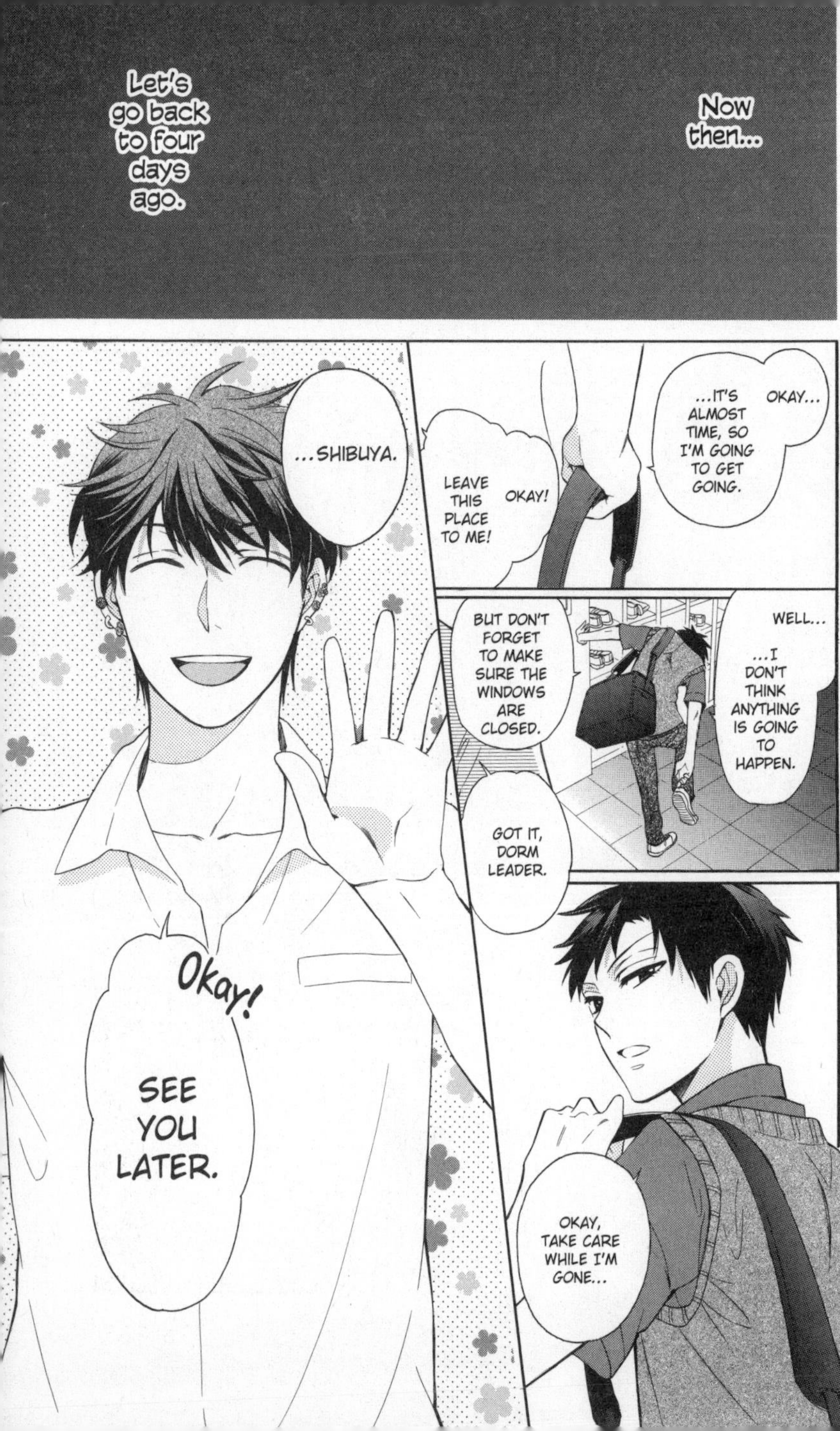
Now then...
Let's go back to four days ago.
...IT'S ALMOST TIME, SO I'M GOING TO GET GOING.
OKAY...
LEAVE THIS PLACE TO ME!
OKAY!
WELL...
...I DON'T THINK ANYTHING IS GOING TO HAPPEN.
BUT DON'T FORGET TO MAKE SURE THE WINDOWS ARE CLOSED.
GOT IT, DORM LEADER.
OKAY, TAKE CARE WHILE I'M GONE...
...SHIBUYA.
Okay!
SEE YOU LATER.

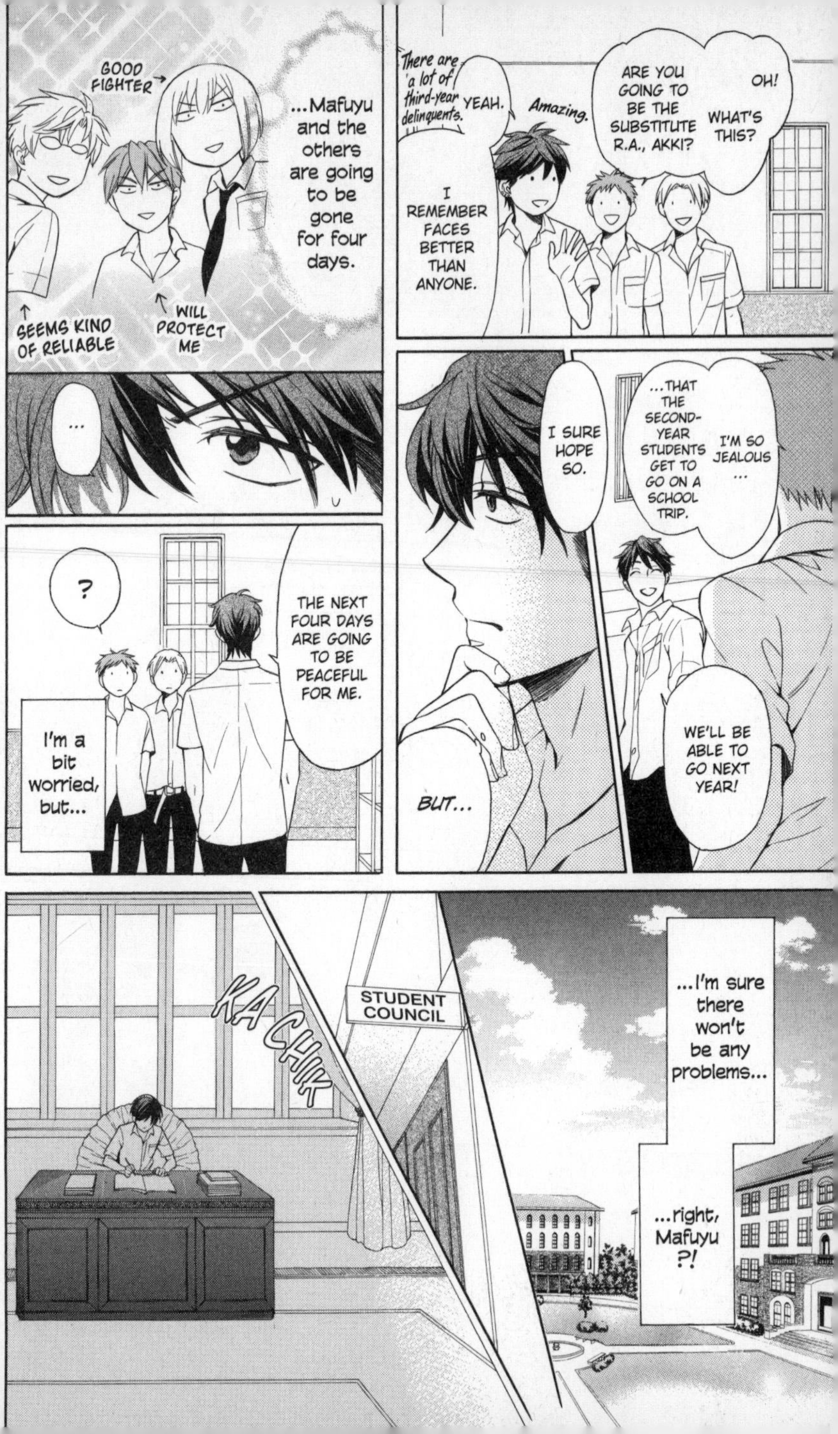
OH!
WHAT'S THIS?
ARE YOU GOING TO BE THE SUBSTITUTE R.A., AKKI?
Amazing.
YEAH.
There are a lot of third-year delinquents.
I REMEMBER FACES BETTER THAN ANYONE.
...Mafuyu and the others are going to be gone for four days.
GOOD FIGHTER
WILL PROTECT ME
SEEMS KIND OF RELIABLE
...THAT THE SECOND-YEAR STUDENTS GET TO GO ON A SCHOOL TRIP.
I'M SO JEALOUS ...
WE'LL BE ABLE TO GO NEXT YEAR!
I SURE HOPE SO.
BUT...
...
THE NEXT FOUR DAYS ARE GOING TO BE PEACEFUL FOR ME.
?
I'm a bit worried, but...
...I'm sure there won't be any problems...
...right, Mafuyu?!
STUDENT COUNCIL
KA CHIK

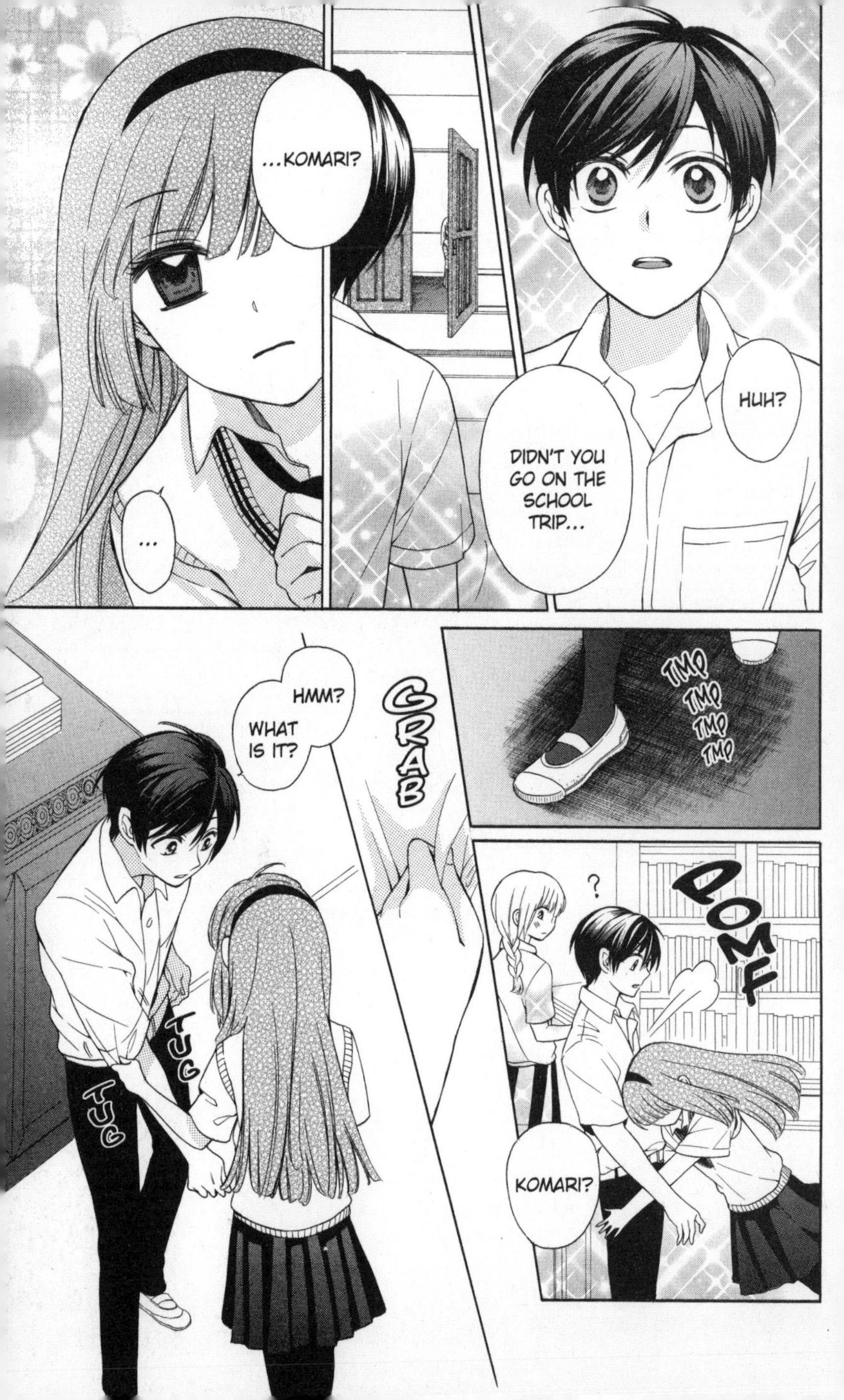
HUH?
DIDN'T YOU GO ON THE SCHOOL TRIP...
...KOMARI?
...
TMP TMP TMP TMP
?
POMF
KOMARI?
GRAB
HMM? WHAT IS IT?
TUG
TUG

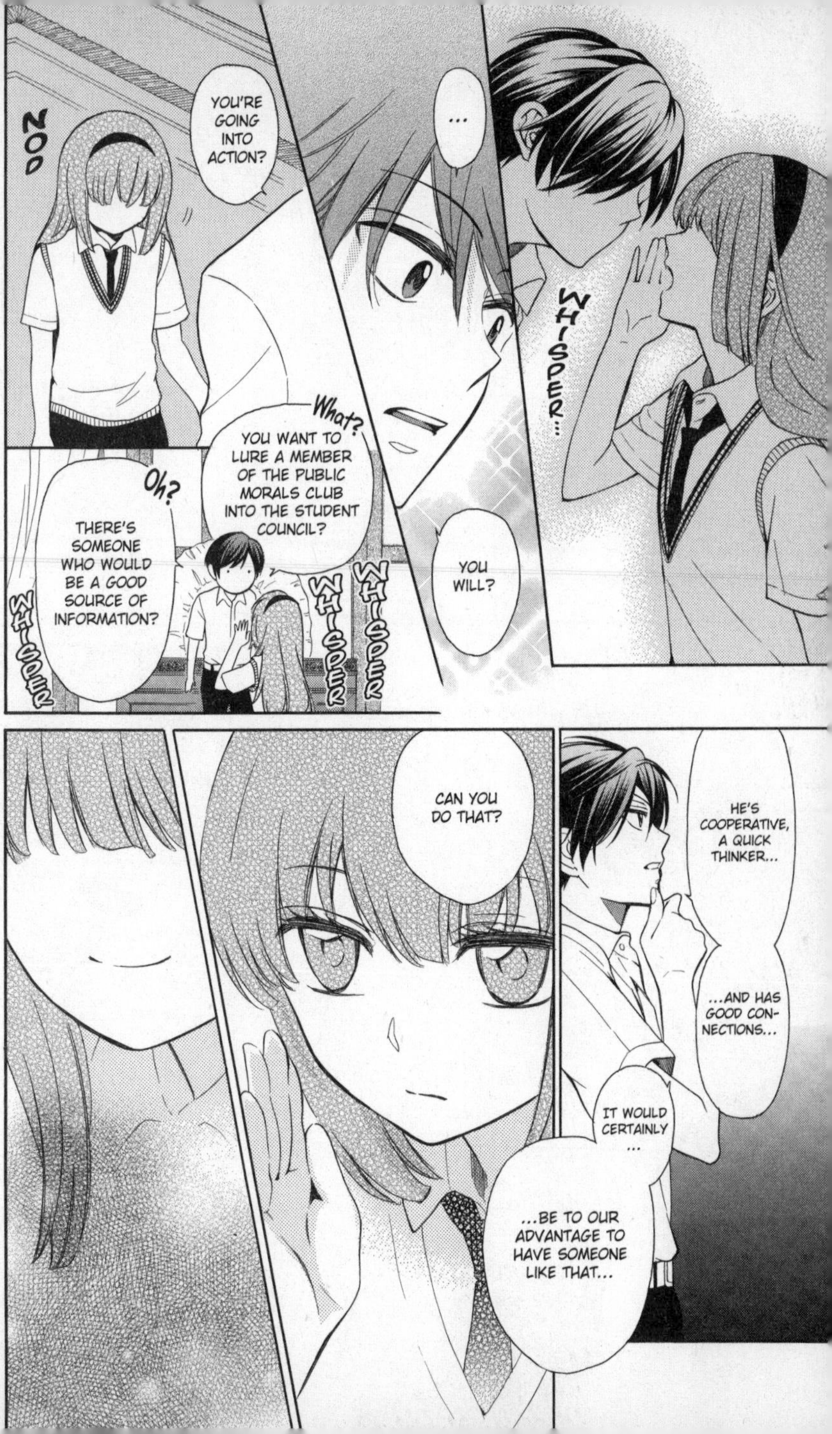
WHISPER...
...
YOU WILL?
YOU'RE GOING INTO ACTION?
NOD
What?
YOU WANT TO LURE A MEMBER OF THE PUBLIC MORALS CLUB INTO THE STUDENT COUNCIL?
WHISPER
WHISPER
Oh?
THERE'S SOMEONE WHO WOULD BE A GOOD SOURCE OF INFORMATION?
WHISPER
HE'S COOPERATIVE, A QUICK THINKER...
...AND HAS GOOD CON-NECTIONS...
IT WOULD CERTAINLY ...
...BE TO OUR ADVANTAGE TO HAVE SOMEONE LIKE THAT...
CAN YOU DO THAT?

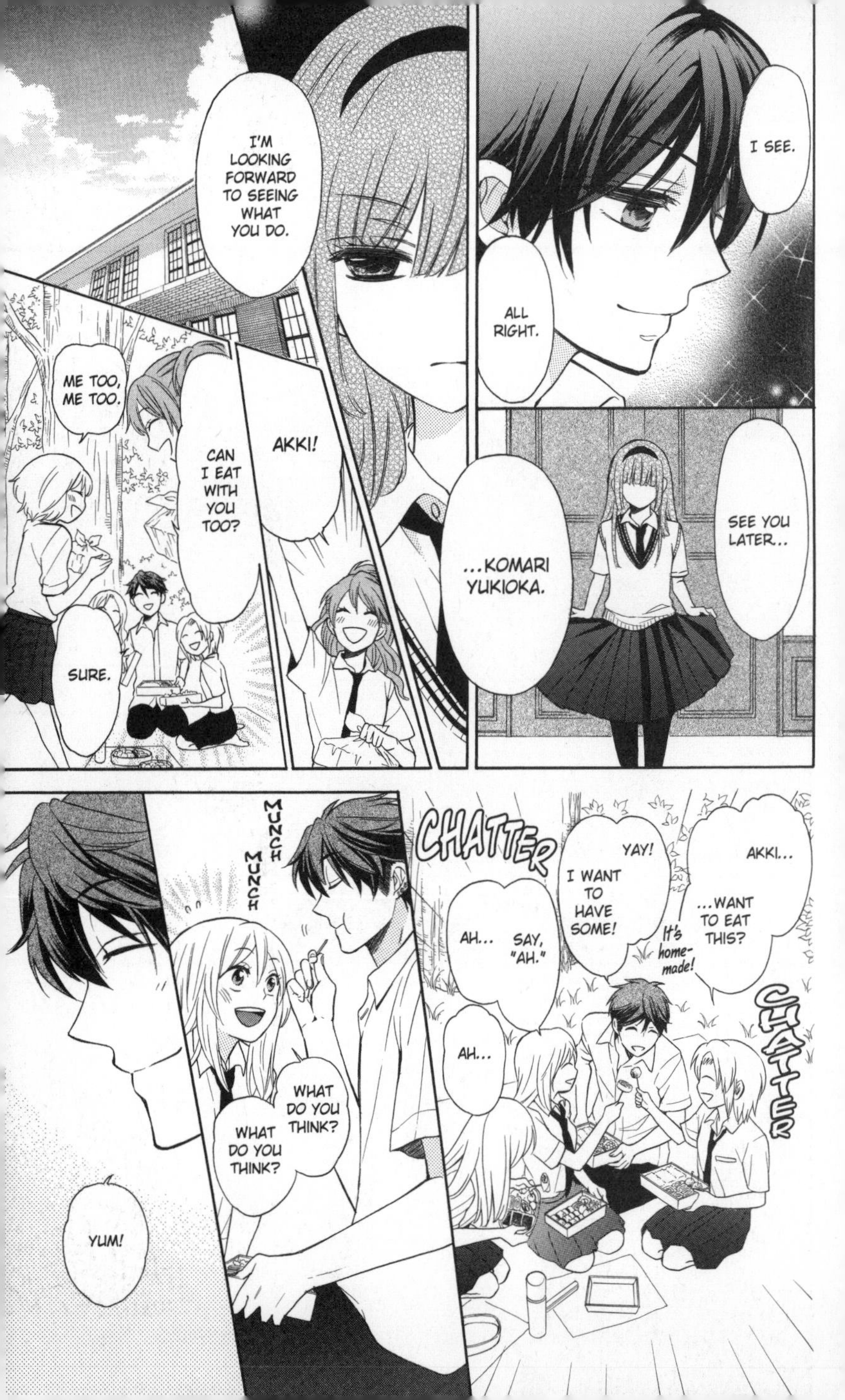
I SEE.
ALL RIGHT.
SEE YOU LATER...
...KOMARI YUKIOKA.
I'M LOOKING FORWARD TO SEEING WHAT YOU DO.
AKKI!
CAN I EAT WITH YOU TOO?
ME TOO, ME TOO.
SURE.
CHATTER
AKKI...
...WANT TO EAT THIS?
It's home-made!
YAY!
I WANT TO HAVE SOME!
SAY, "AH."
AH...
AH...
CHATTER
MUNCH
MUNCH
WHAT DO YOU THINK?
WHAT DO YOU THINK?
YUM!

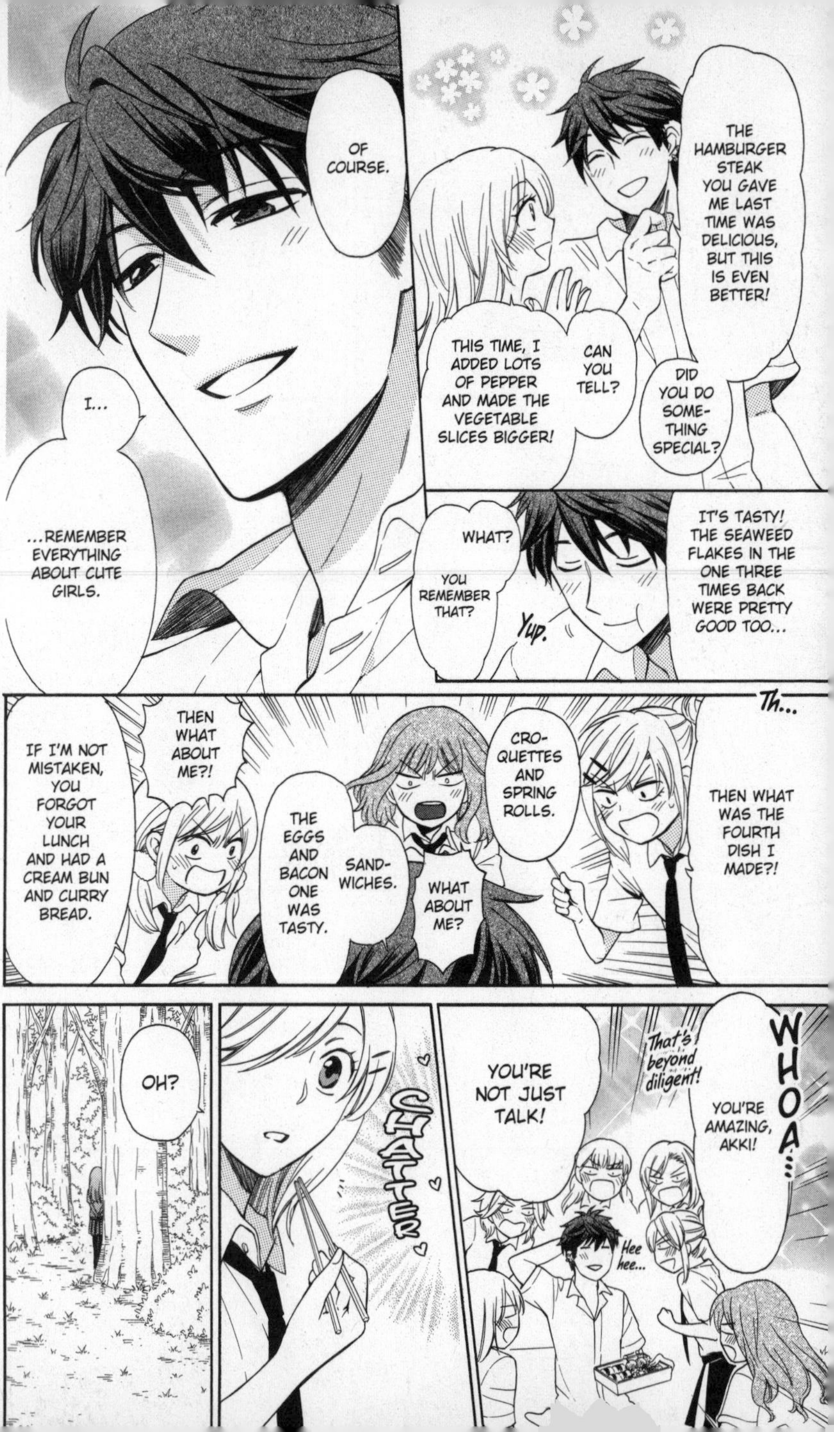
THE HAMBURGER STEAK YOU GAVE ME LAST TIME WAS DELICIOUS, BUT THIS IS EVEN BETTER!
DID YOU DO SOME-THING SPECIAL?
CAN YOU TELL?
THIS TIME, I ADDED LOTS OF PEPPER AND MADE THE VEGETABLE SLICES BIGGER!
IT'S TASTY! THE SEAWEED FLAKES IN THE ONE THREE TIMES BACK WERE PRETTY GOOD TOO...
WHAT?
YOU REMEMBER THAT?
Yup.
OF COURSE.
I...
...REMEMBER EVERYTHING ABOUT CUTE GIRLS.
Th...
THEN WHAT WAS THE FOURTH DISH I MADE?!
CRO-QUETTES AND SPRING ROLLS.
WHAT ABOUT ME?
THE EGGS AND BACON ONE WAS TASTY.
SAND-WICHES.
THEN WHAT ABOUT ME?!
IF I'M NOT MISTAKEN, YOU FORGOT YOUR LUNCH AND HAD A CREAM BUN AND CURRY BREAD.
WHOA...
YOU'RE AMAZING, AKKI!
That's beyond diligent!
YOU'RE NOT JUST TALK!
Hee hee...
CHATTER
OH?

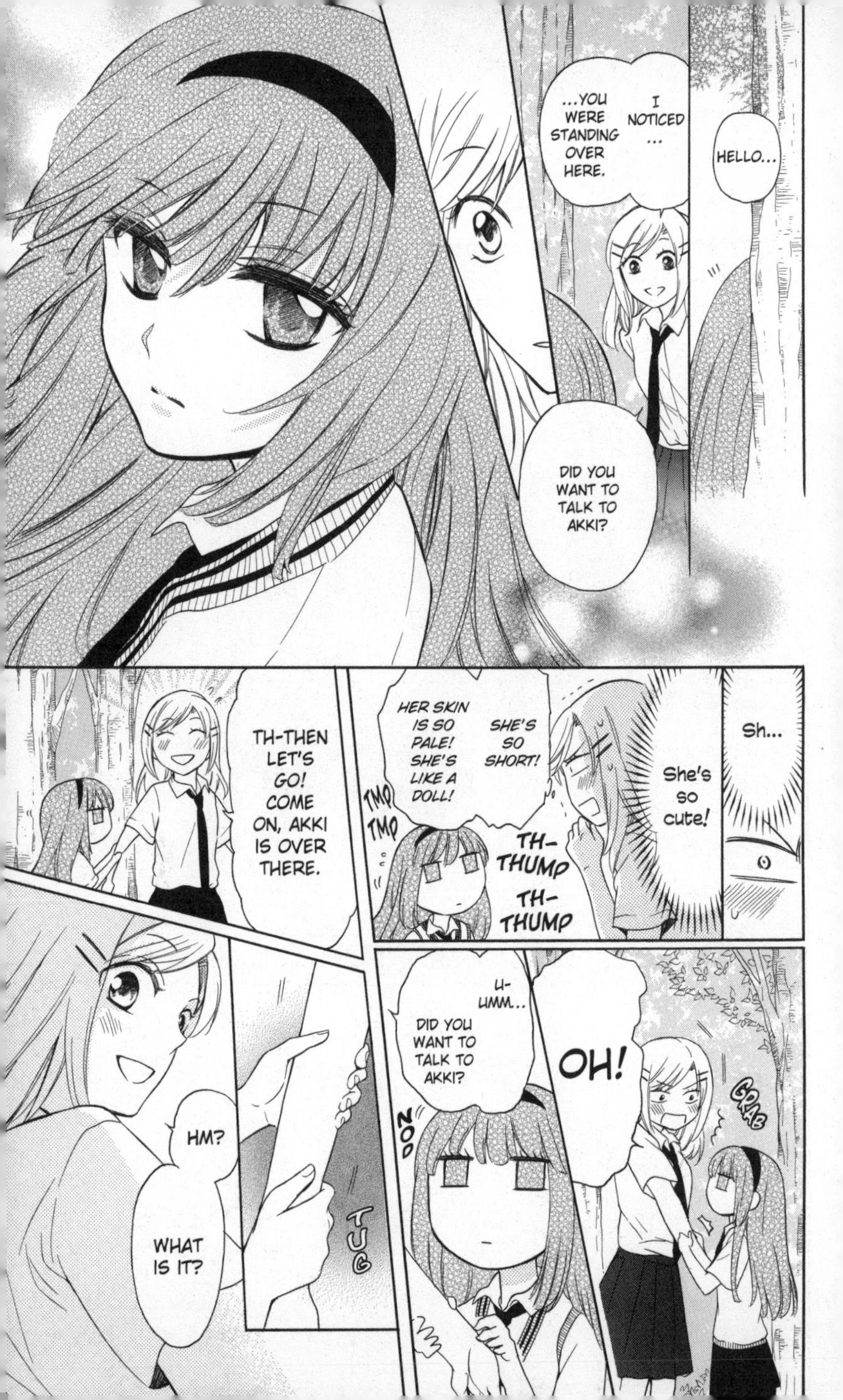
HELLO...
I NOTICED ...
...YOU WERE STANDING OVER HERE.
DID YOU WANT TO TALK TO AKKI?
Sh...
She's so cute!
HER SKIN IS SO PALE! SHE'S LIKE A DOLL!
SHE'S SO SHORT!
TMP TMP
TH-THUMP TH-THUMP
TH-THEN LET'S GO! COME ON, AKKI IS OVER THERE.
GRAB
OH!
U-UMM...
DID YOU WANT TO TALK TO AKKI?
NOD
TUG
HM?
WHAT IS IT?

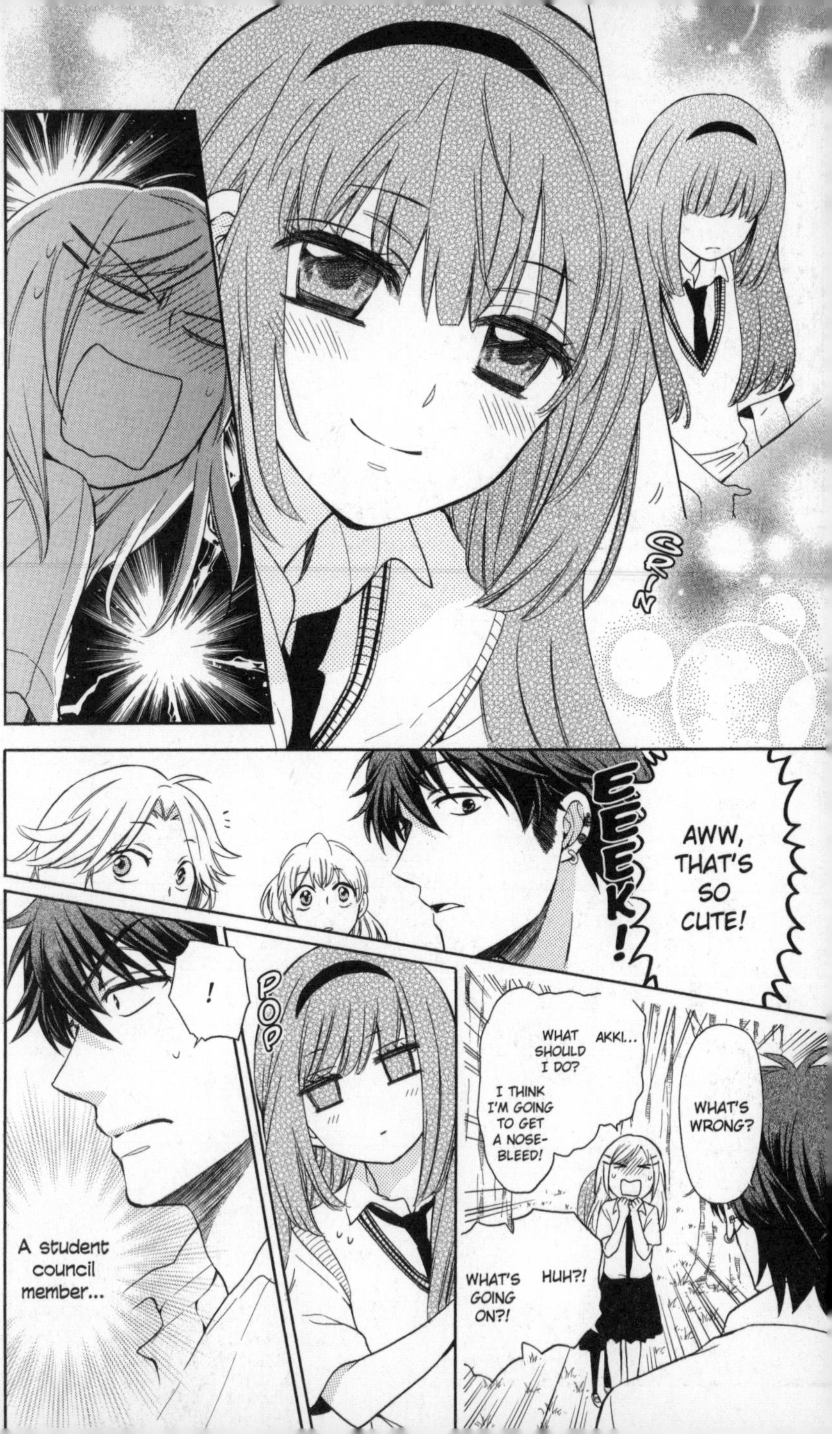
GRIN
AWW, THAT'S SO CUTE!
EEEEK!
WHAT'S WRONG?
AKKI...
WHAT SHOULD I DO?
I THINK I'M GOING TO GET A NOSE-BLEED!
HUH?!
WHAT'S GOING ON?!
POP
!
A student council member...

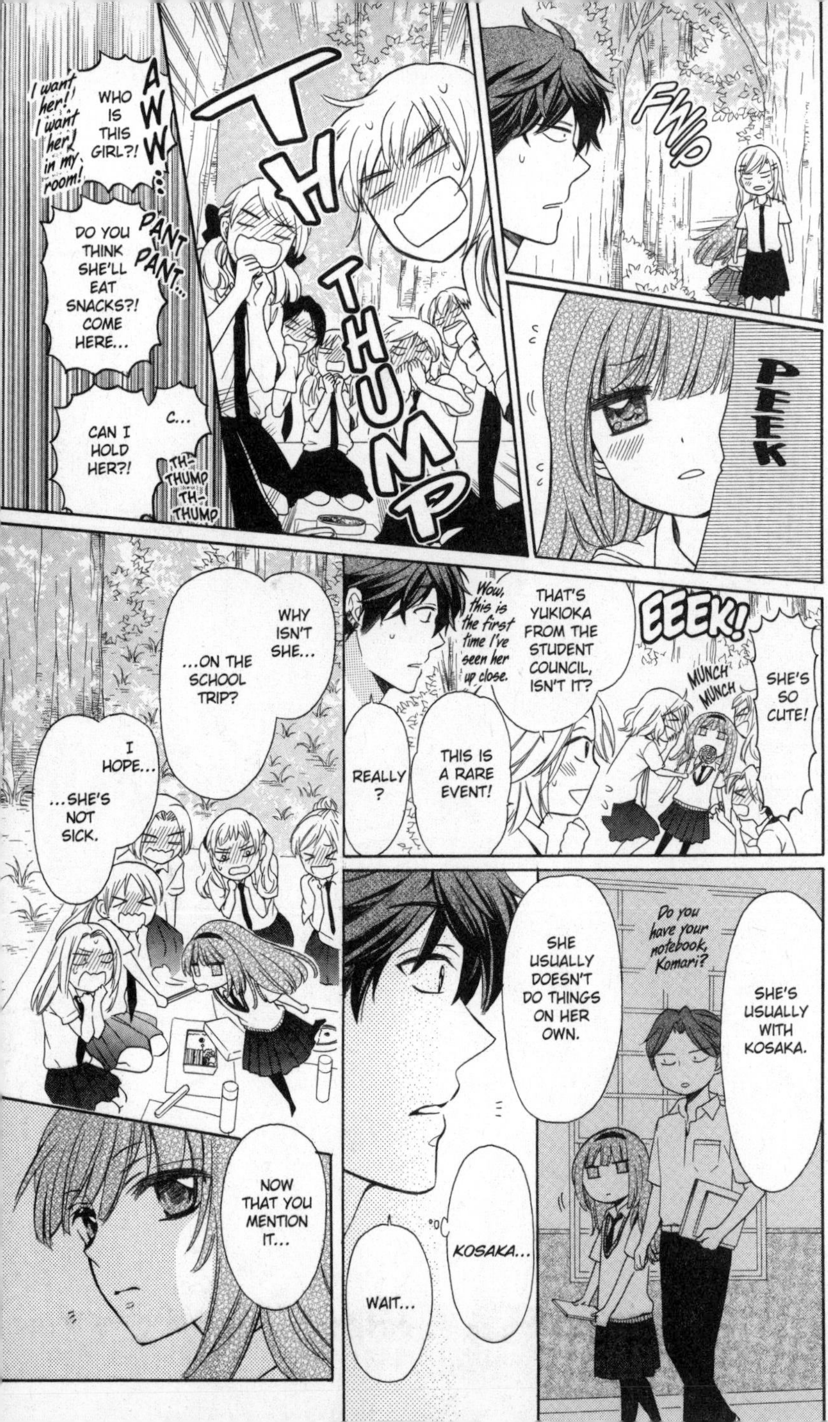
FWIP
PEEK
THUMP
AWW...
WHO IS THIS GIRL?!
I want her! I want her in my room!
PANT PANT...
DO YOU THINK SHE'LL EAT SNACKS?! COME HERE...
C...
CAN I HOLD HER?!
TH-THUMP TH-THUMP
EEEK!
SHE'S SO CUTE!
MUNCH MUNCH
THAT'S YUKIOKA FROM THE STUDENT COUNCIL, ISN'T IT?
Wow, this is the first time I've seen her up close.
THIS IS A RARE EVENT!
REALLY?
WHY ISN'T SHE...
...ON THE SCHOOL TRIP?
I HOPE...
...SHE'S NOT SICK.
SHE'S USUALLY WITH KOSAKA.
Do you have your notebook, Komari?
SHE USUALLY DOESN'T DO THINGS ON HER OWN.
KOSAKA...
WAIT...
NOW THAT YOU MENTION IT...

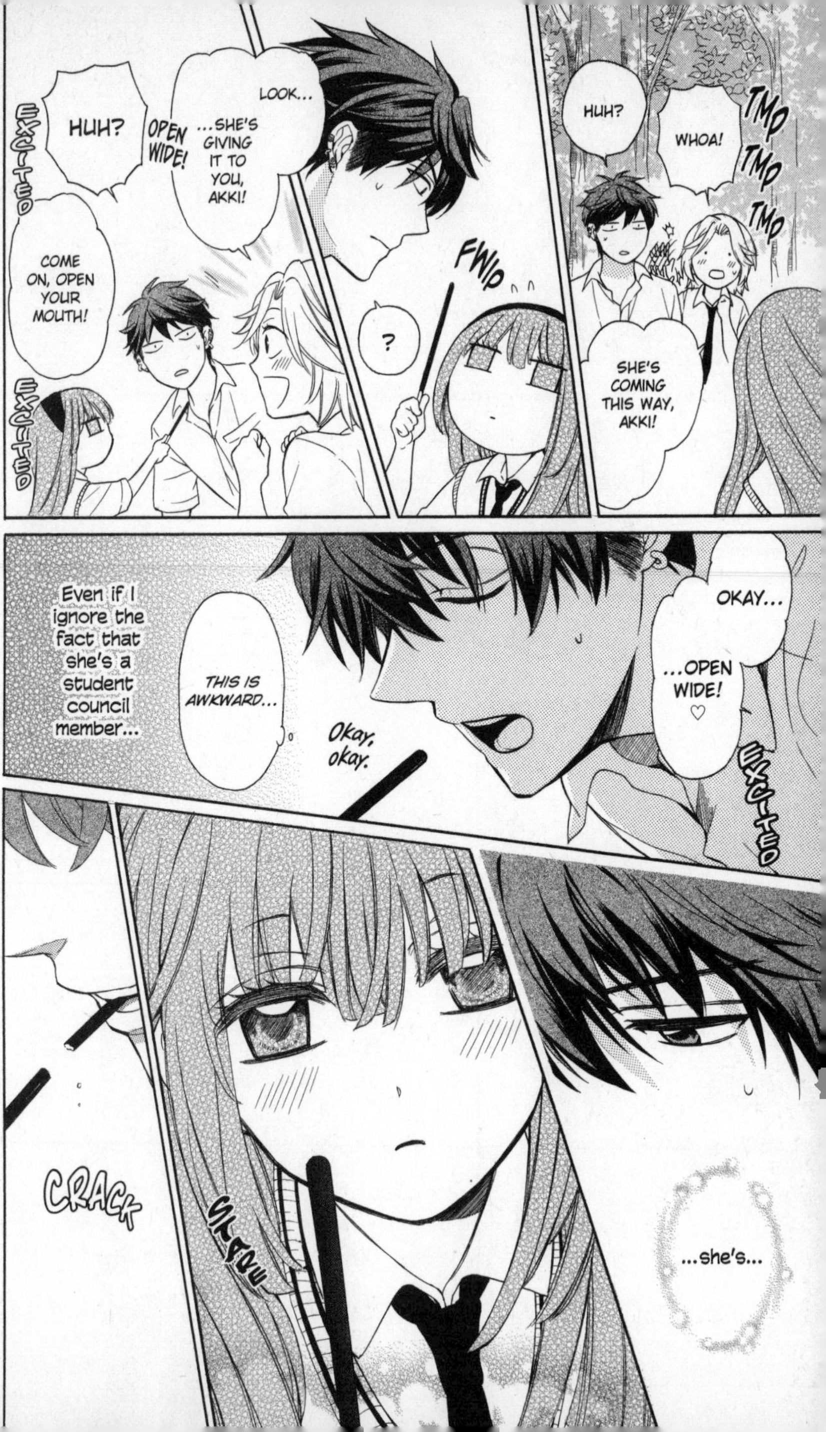

TMP TMP TMP
WHOA!
HUH?
SHE'S COMING THIS WAY, AKKI!
FWIP
?
LOOK...
...SHE'S GIVING IT TO YOU, AKKI!
OPEN WIDE!
HUH?
EXCITED
COME ON, OPEN YOUR MOUTH!
EXCITED
OKAY...
...OPEN WIDE! ♡
EXCITED
Okay, okay.
THIS IS AWKWARD...
Even if I ignore the fact that she's a student council member...
...she's...
STARE
CRACK

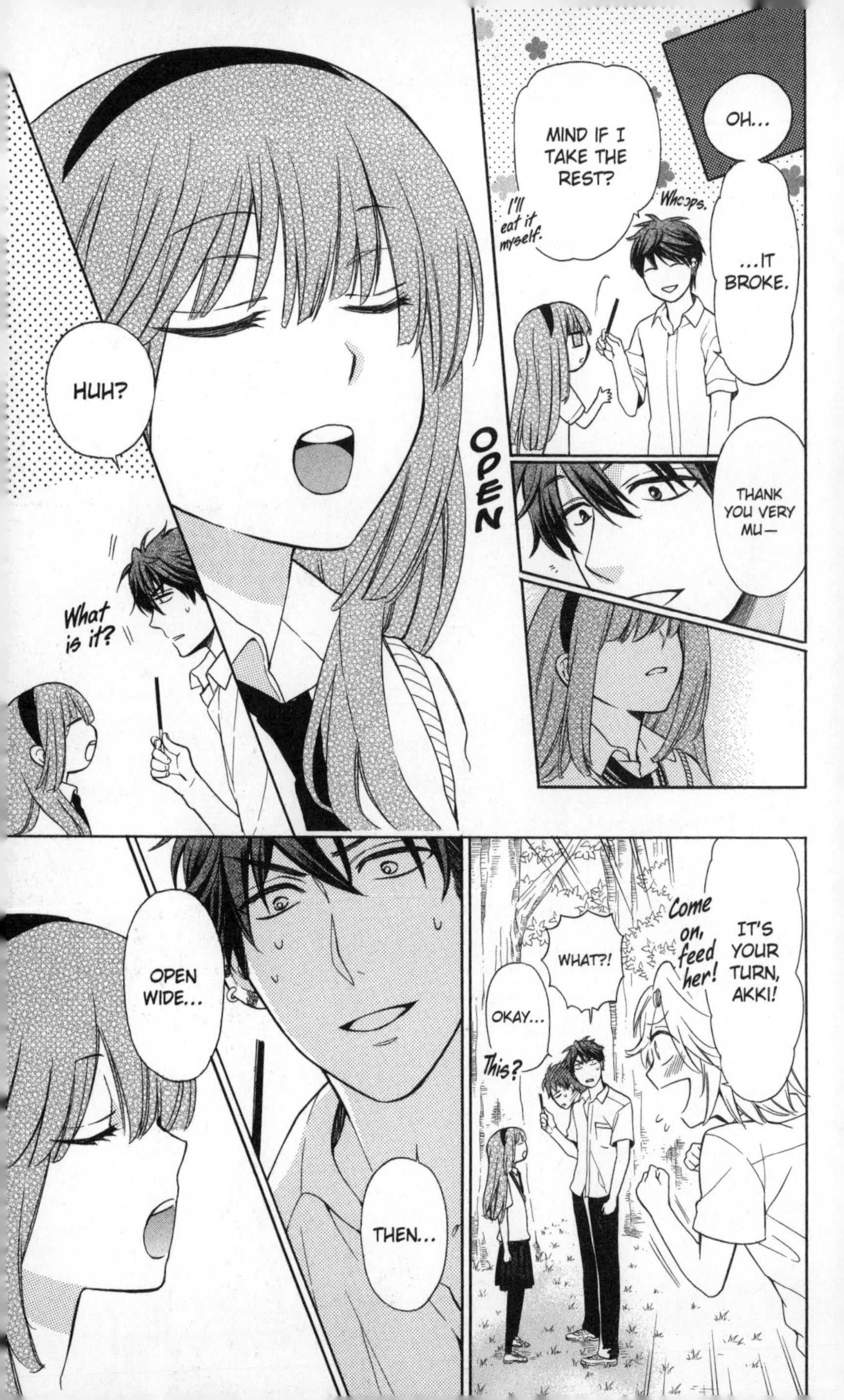
OH...
...IT BROKE.
Whoops.
MIND IF I TAKE THE REST?
I'll eat it myself.
THANK YOU VERY MU—
OPEN
HUH?
What is it?
IT'S YOUR TURN, AKKI!
Come on, feed her!
WHAT?!
OKAY...
This?
OPEN WIDE...
THEN...

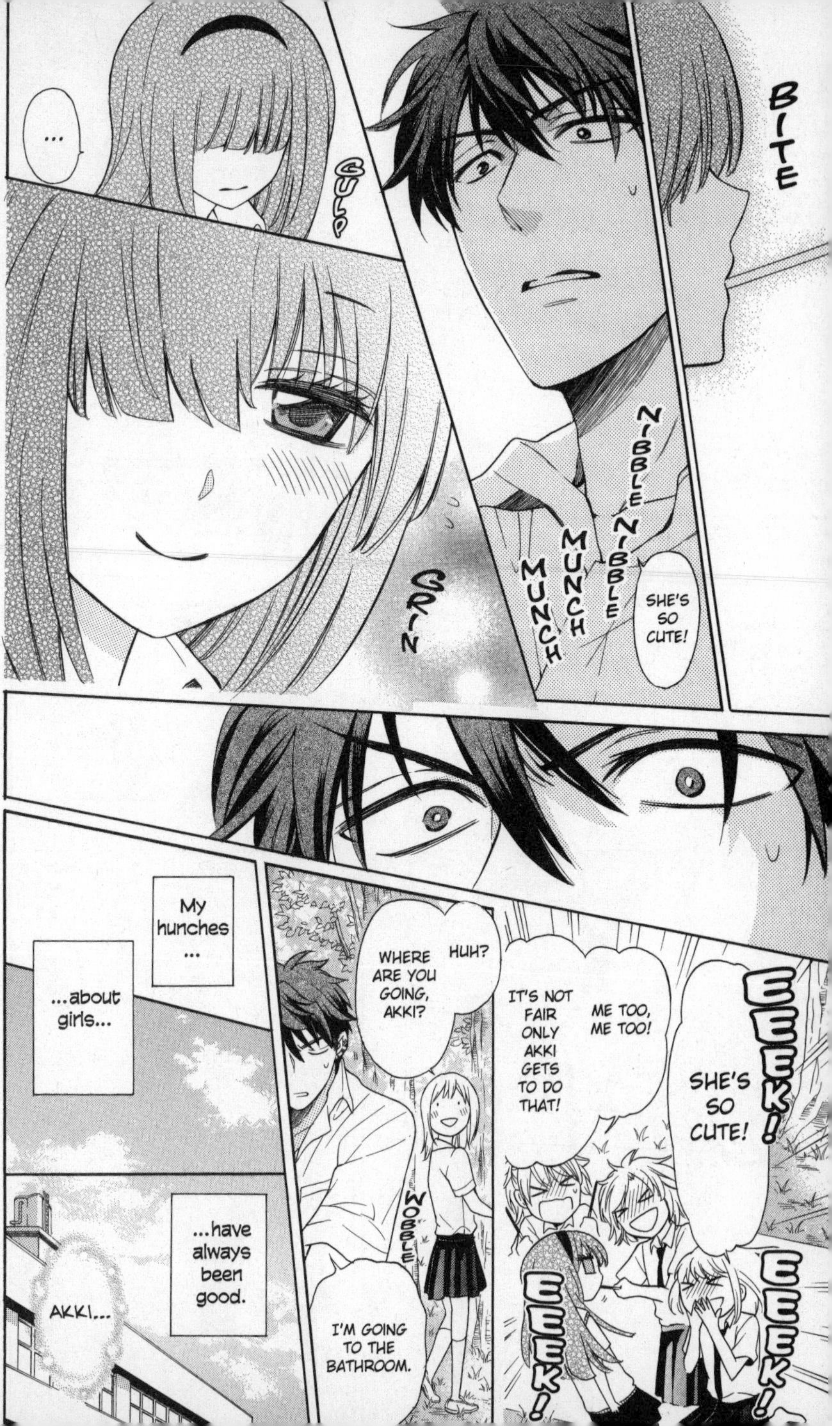
BITE
NIBBLE NIBBLE
MUNCH MUNCH
SHE'S SO CUTE!
GULP
...
GRIN
EEEEK!
SHE'S SO CUTE!
ME TOO, ME TOO!
IT'S NOT FAIR ONLY AKKI GETS TO DO THAT!
EEEEK!
EEEEK!
HUH?
WHERE ARE YOU GOING, AKKI?
WOBBLE
I'M GOING TO THE BATHROOM.
My hunches ...
...about girls...
...have always been good.
AKKI...

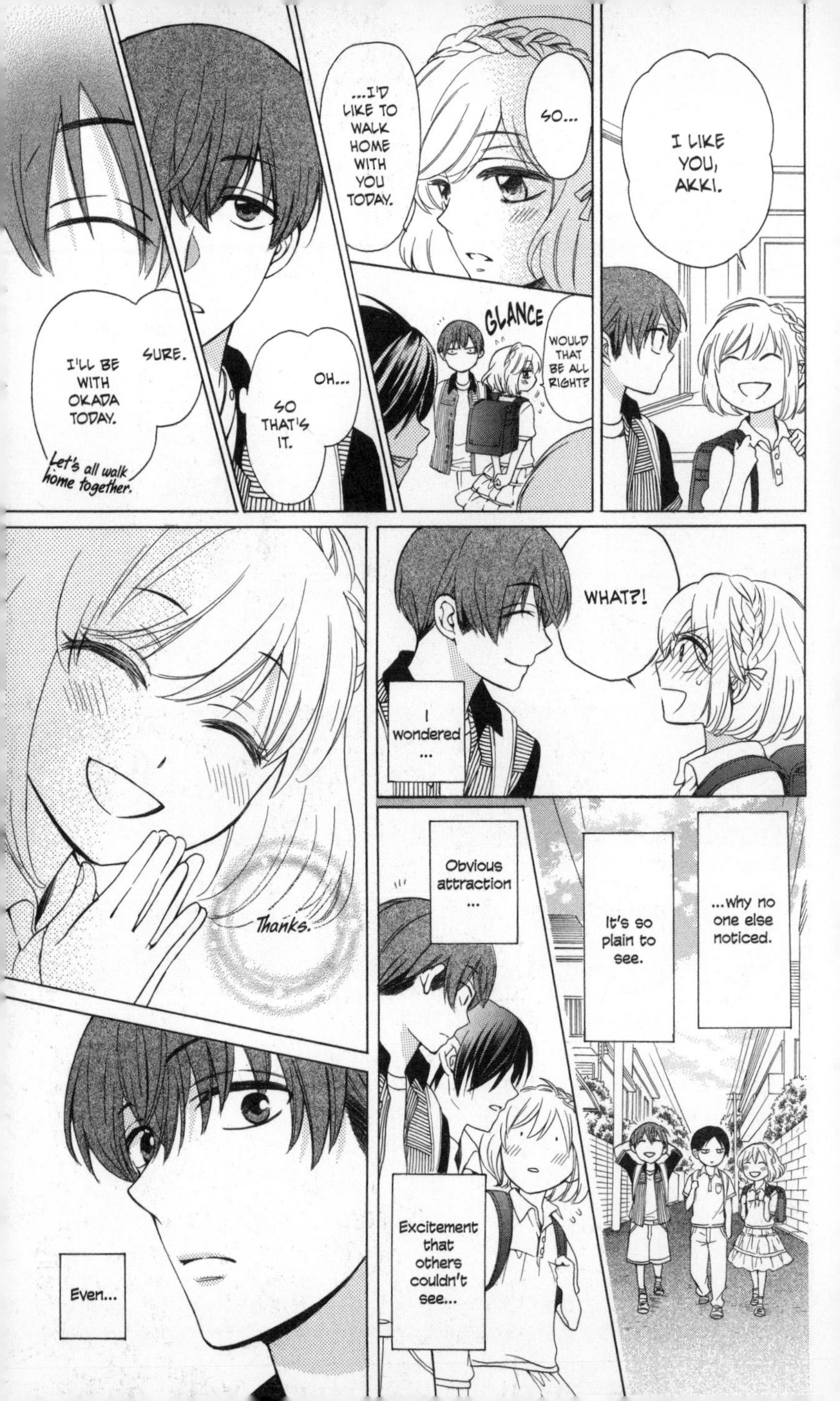
I LIKE YOU, AKKI.
SO...
...I'D LIKE TO WALK HOME WITH YOU TODAY.
WOULD THAT BE ALL RIGHT?
GLANCE
OH...
SO THAT'S IT.
SURE.
I'LL BE WITH OKADA TODAY.
Let's all walk home together.
WHAT?!
I wondered...
Thanks.
...why no one else noticed.
It's so plain to see.
Obvious attraction...
Excitement that others couldn't see...
Even...

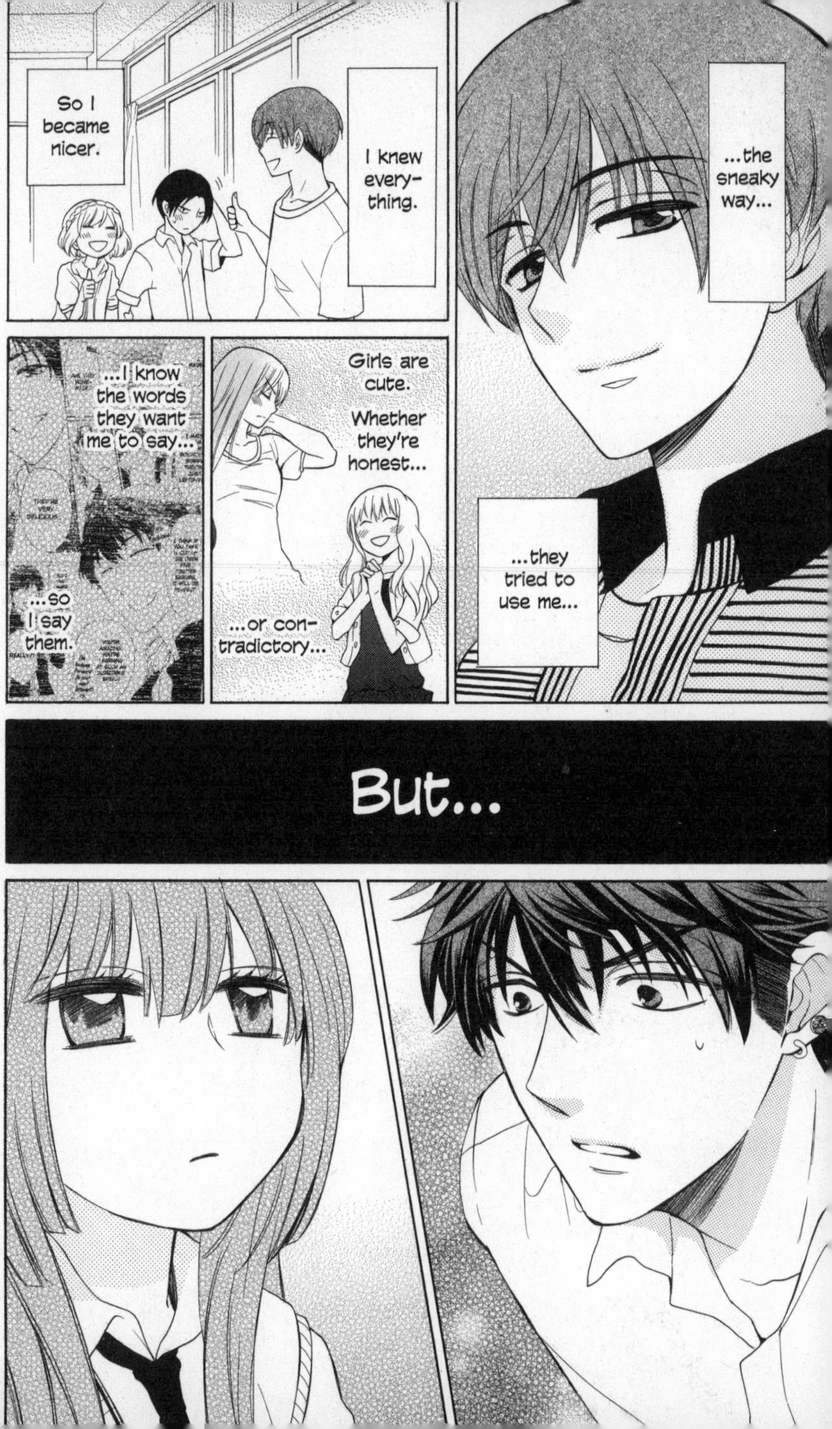
...the sneaky way...
...they tried to use me...
I knew every-thing.
So I became nicer.
Girls are cute.
Whether they're honest...
...or con-tradictory...
...I know the words they want me to say...
...so I say them.
But...

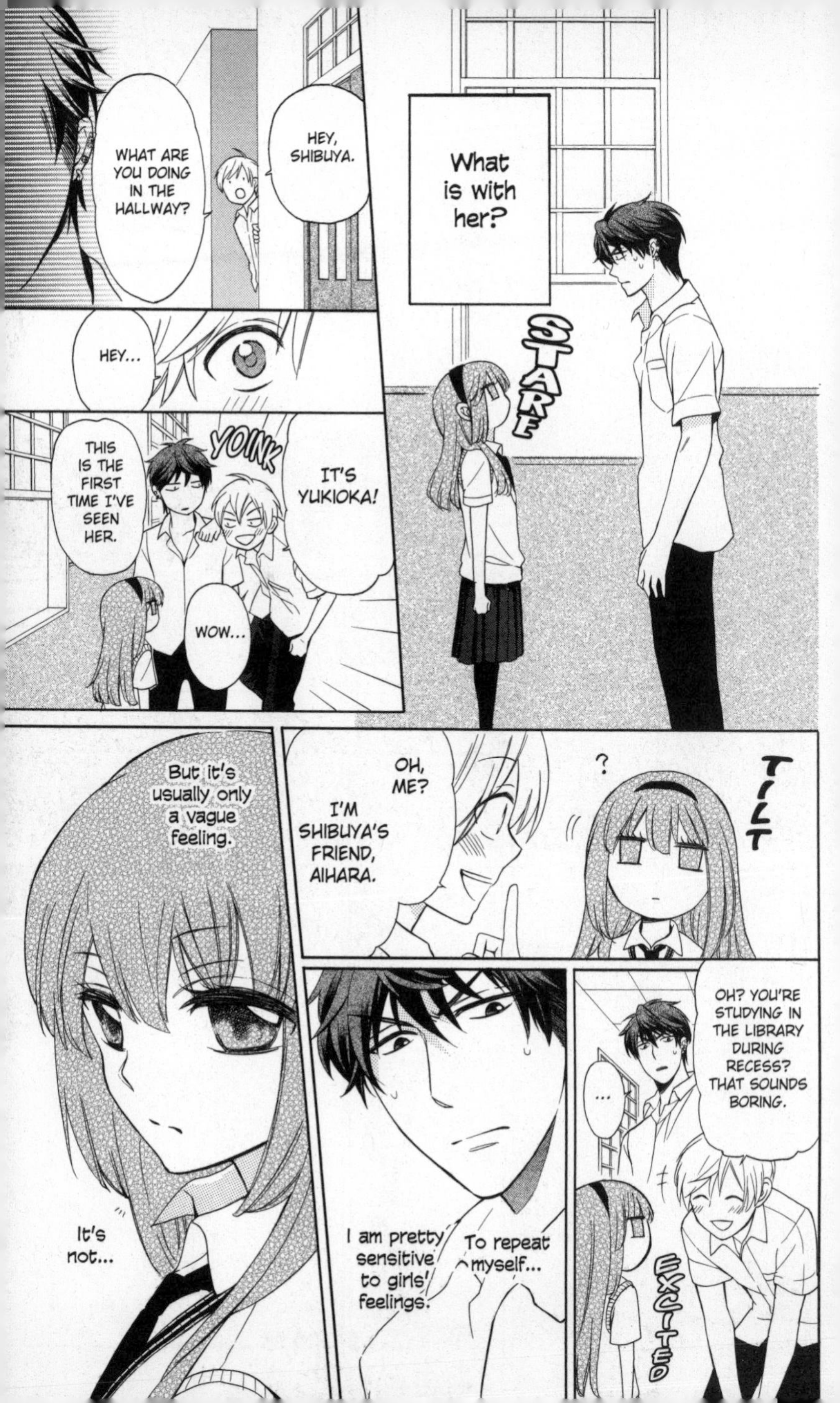
What is with her?
STARE
HEY, SHIBUYA.
WHAT ARE YOU DOING IN THE HALLWAY?
HEY...
IT'S YUKIOKA!
YOINK
THIS IS THE FIRST TIME I'VE SEEN HER.
WOW...
TILT
?
OH, ME?
I'M SHIBUYA'S FRIEND, AIHARA.
OH? YOU'RE STUDYING IN THE LIBRARY DURING RECESS? THAT SOUNDS BORING.
...
EXCITED
To repeat myself...
I am pretty sensitive to girls' feelings.
But it's usually only a vague feeling.
It's not...

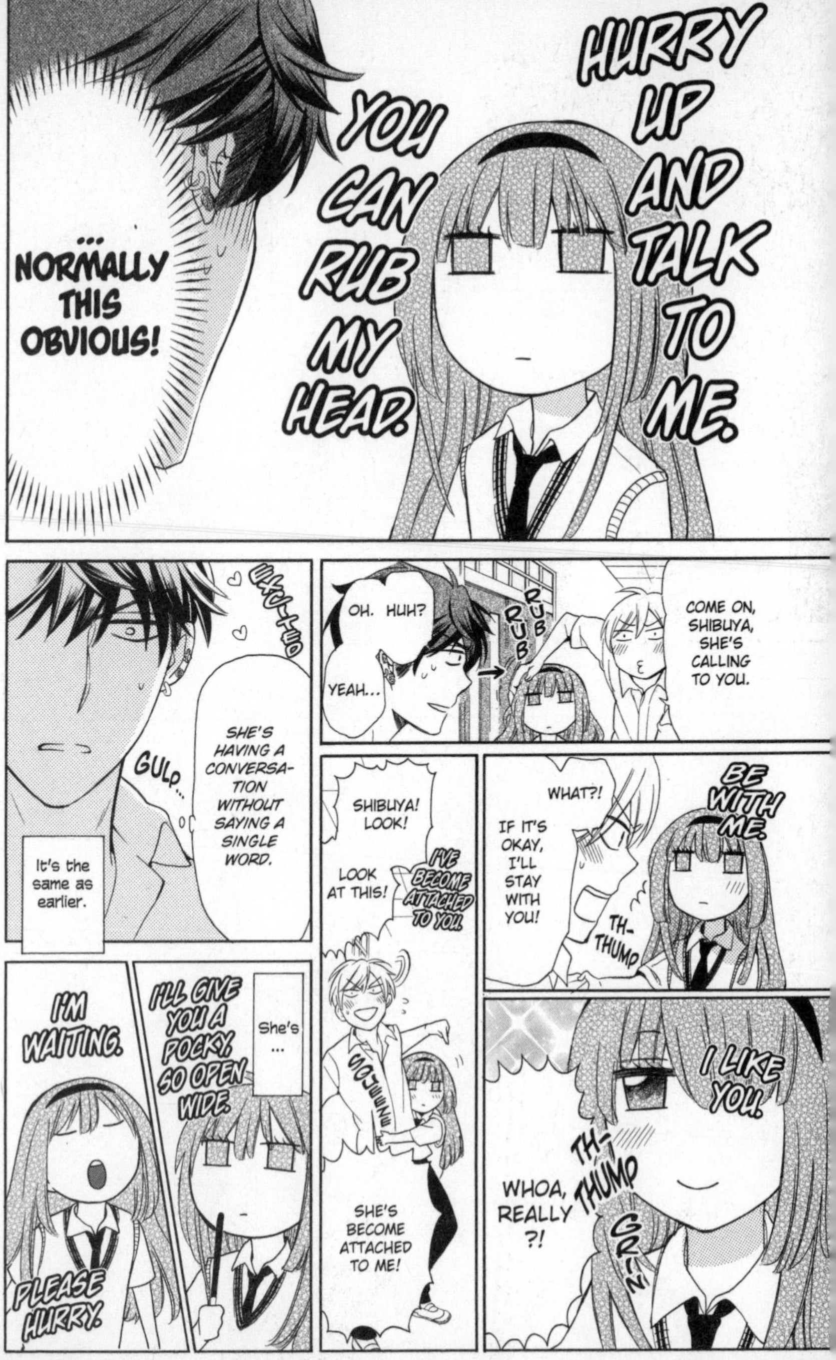
HURRY UP AND TALK TO ME.
YOU CAN RUB MY HEAD.
... NORMALLY THIS OBVIOUS!
COME ON, SHIBUYA, SHE'S CALLING TO YOU.
RUB RUB
OH. HUH?
YEAH...
EXCITED
SHE'S HAVING A CONVERSATION WITHOUT SAYING A SINGLE WORD.
GULP...
It's the same as earlier.
BE WITH ME.
WHAT?!
IF IT'S OKAY, I'LL STAY WITH YOU!
TH-THUMP
I LIKE YOU.
TH-THUMP
WHOA, REALLY?!
GRIN
SHIBUYA! LOOK!
LOOK AT THIS!
I'VE BECOME ATTACHED TO YOU.
SHE'S BECOME ATTACHED TO ME!
She's ...
I'LL GIVE YOU A POCKY, SO OPEN WIDE.
I'M WAITING.
PLEASE HURRY.

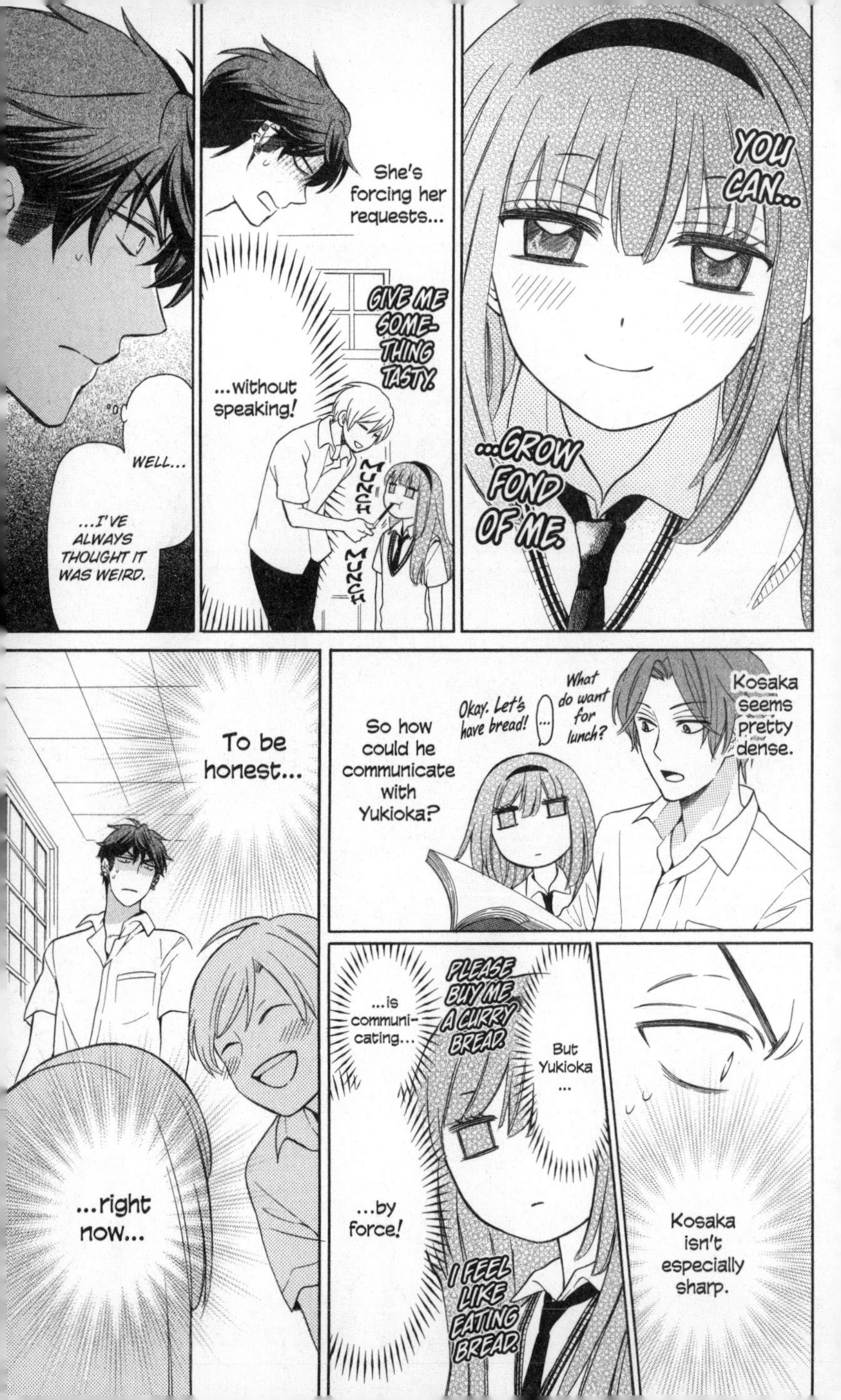
YOU CAN...
...GROW FOND OF ME.
She's forcing her requests...
GIVE ME SOME-THING TASTY.
...without speaking!
MUNCH
MUNCH
WELL...
...I'VE ALWAYS THOUGHT IT WAS WEIRD.
Kosaka seems pretty dense.
What do want for lunch?
...
Okay. Let's have bread!
So how could he communicate with Yukioka?
Kosaka isn't especially sharp.
But Yukioka ...
PLEASE BUY ME A CURRY BREAD.
...is communi-cating...
...by force!
I FEEL LIKE EATING BREAD.
To be honest...
...right now...

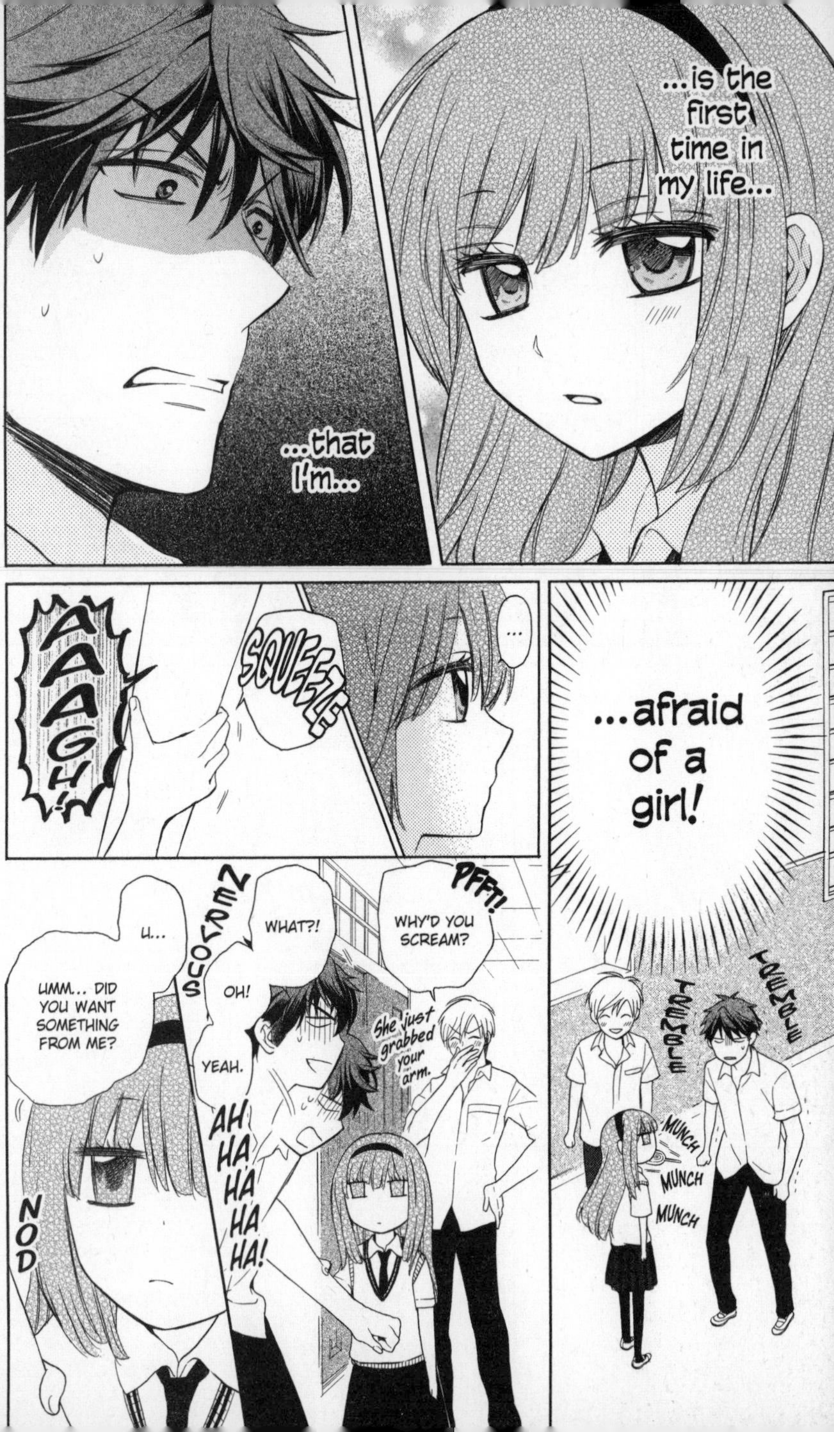
...is the first time in my life...
...that I'm...
...afraid of a girl!
TREMBLE
TREMBLE
MUNCH
MUNCH
MUNCH
...
SQUEEZE
AAAGH!!
PFFT!
WHY'D YOU SCREAM?
She just grabbed your arm.
WHAT?!
NERVOUS
OH!
YEAH.
AH HA HA HA HA!
U...
UMM... DID YOU WANT SOMETHING FROM ME?
NOD

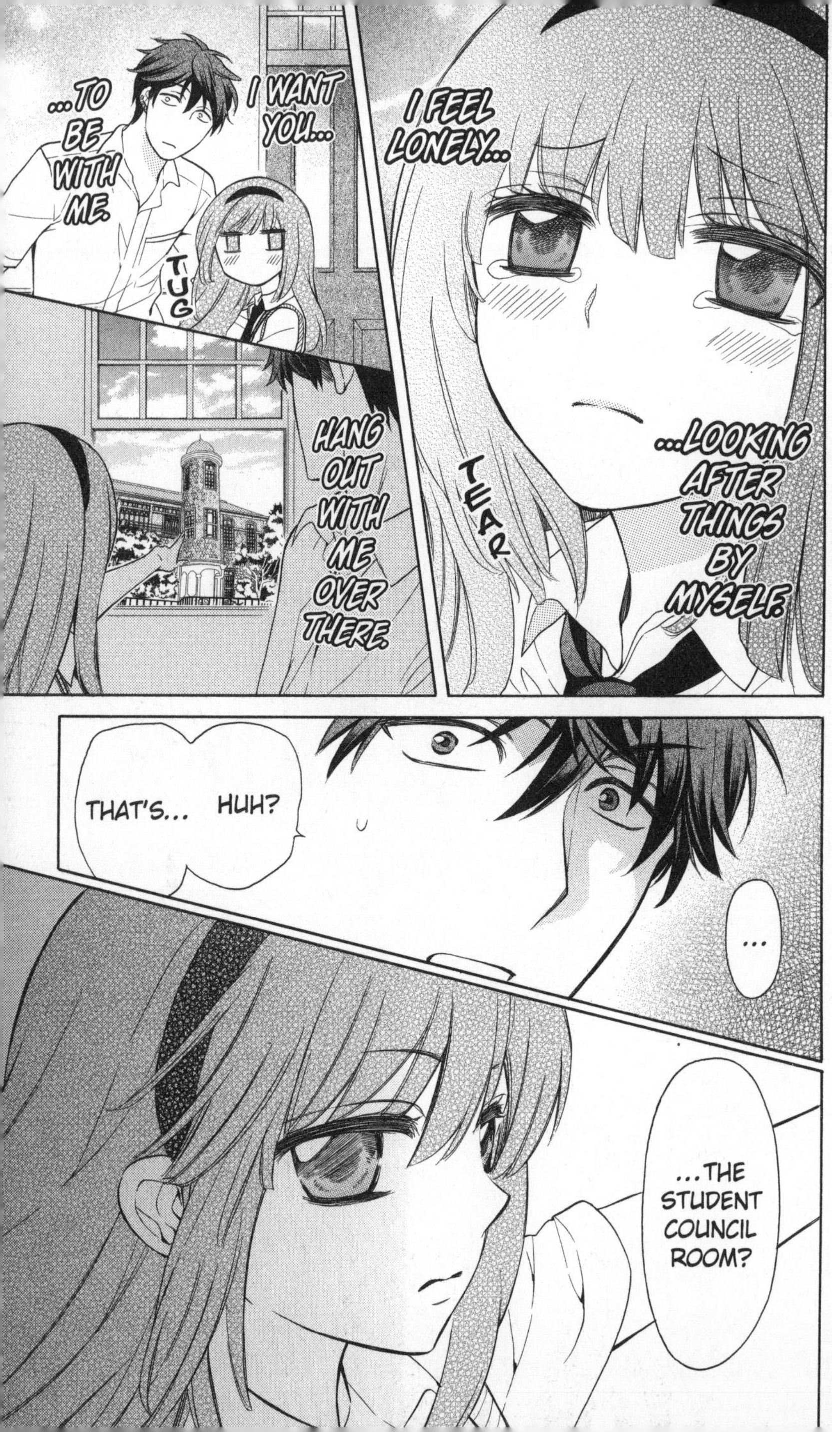
I FEEL LONELY...
...LOOKING AFTER THINGS BY MYSELF.
TEAR
I WANT YOU...
...TO BE WITH ME.
TUG
HANG OUT WITH ME OVER THERE.
THAT'S... HUH?
...
...THE STUDENT COUNCIL ROOM?

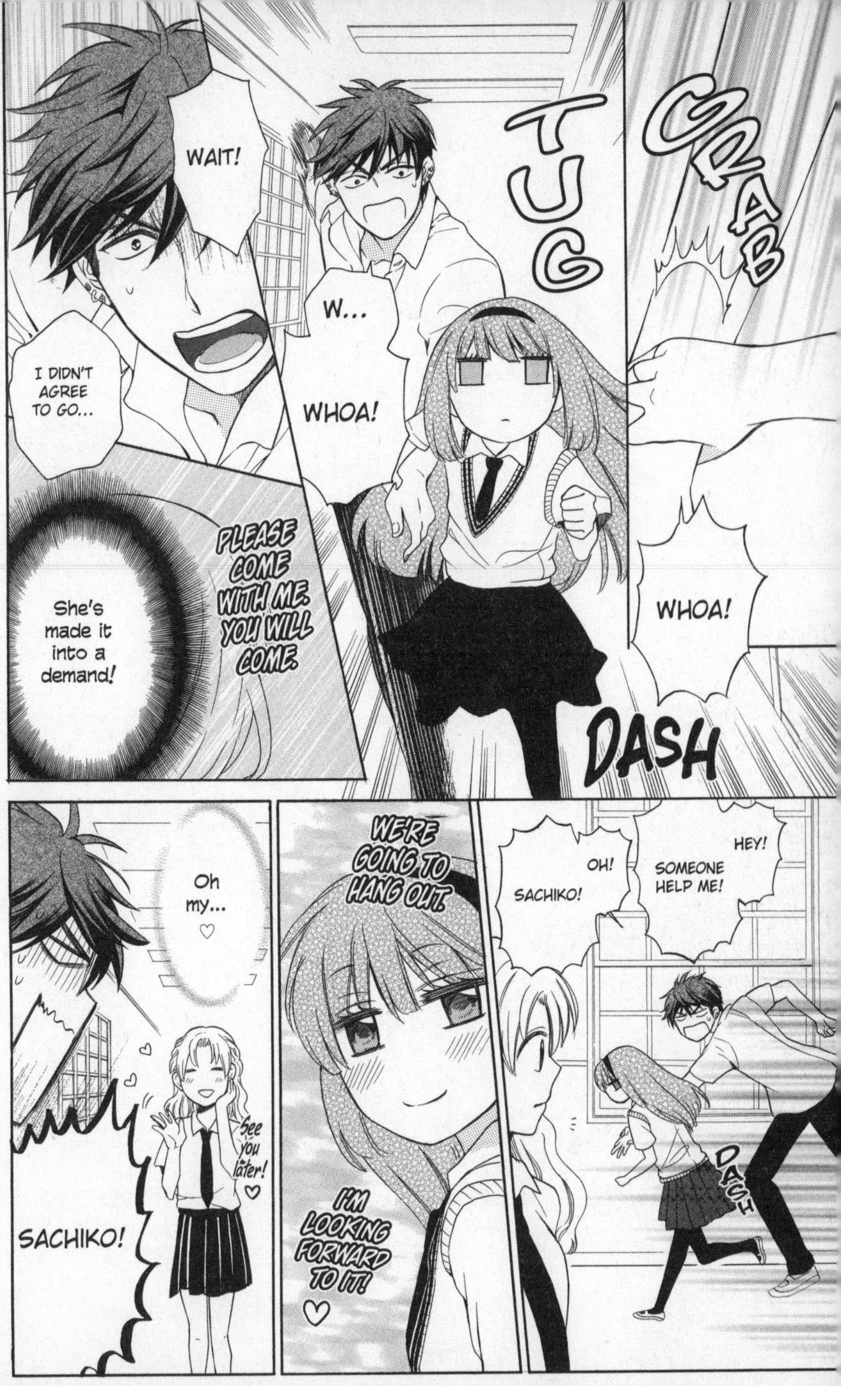
GRAB
WHOA!
DASH
TUG
W...
WHOA!
PLEASE COME WITH ME. YOU WILL COME.
WAIT!
I DIDN'T AGREE TO GO...
She's made it into a demand!
HEY! SOMEONE HELP ME!
OH! SACHIKO!
DASH
WE'RE GOING TO HANG OUT.
I'M LOOKING FORWARD TO IT! ♡
Oh my... ♡
See you later! ♡
SACHIKO!

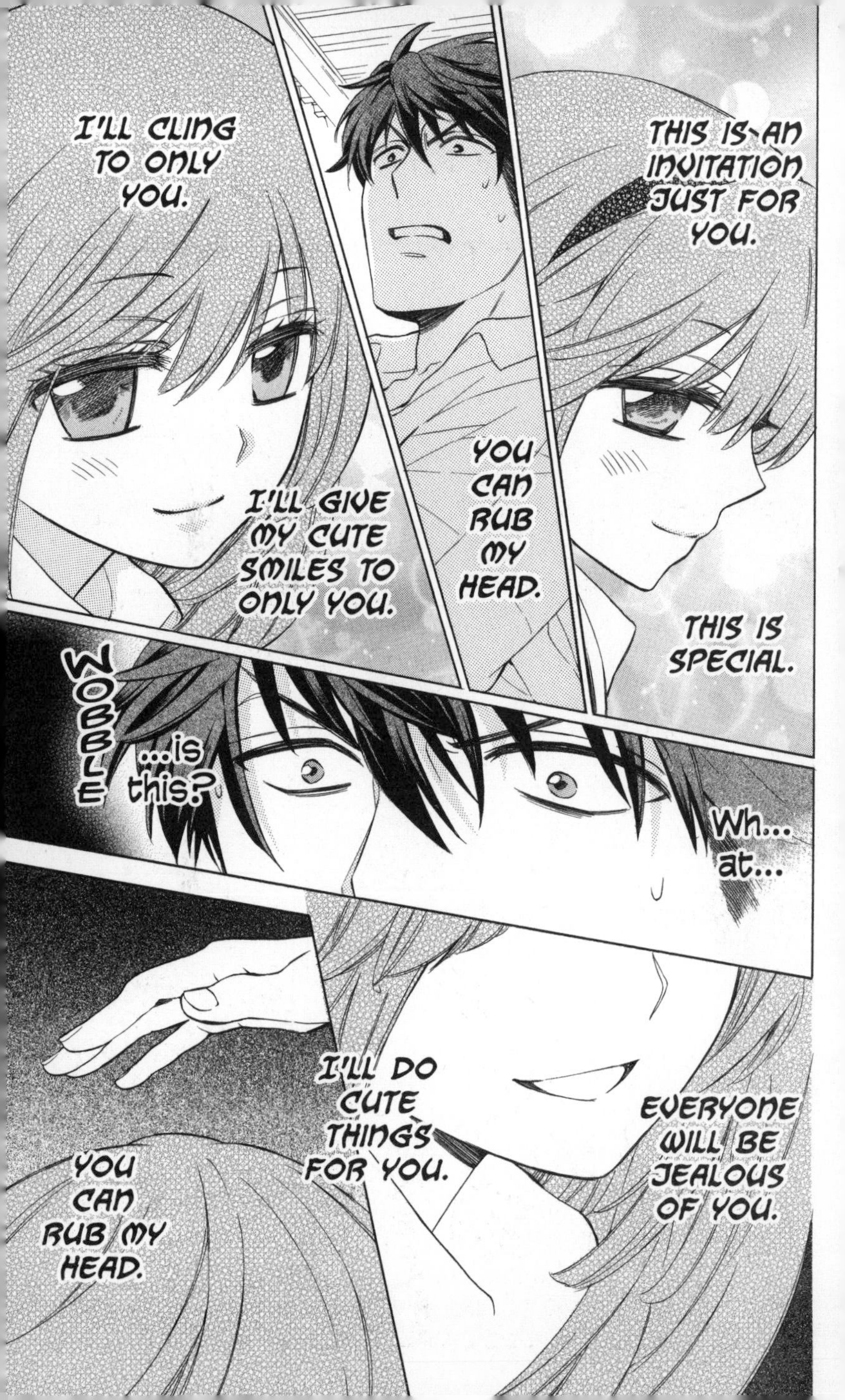
THIS IS AN INVITATION JUST FOR YOU.
THIS IS SPECIAL.
YOU CAN RUB MY HEAD.
I'LL CLING TO ONLY YOU.
I'LL GIVE MY CUTE SMILES TO ONLY YOU.
Wh... at...
...is this?
WOBBLE
EVERYONE WILL BE JEALOUS OF YOU.
I'LL DO CUTE THINGS FOR YOU.
YOU CAN RUB MY HEAD.

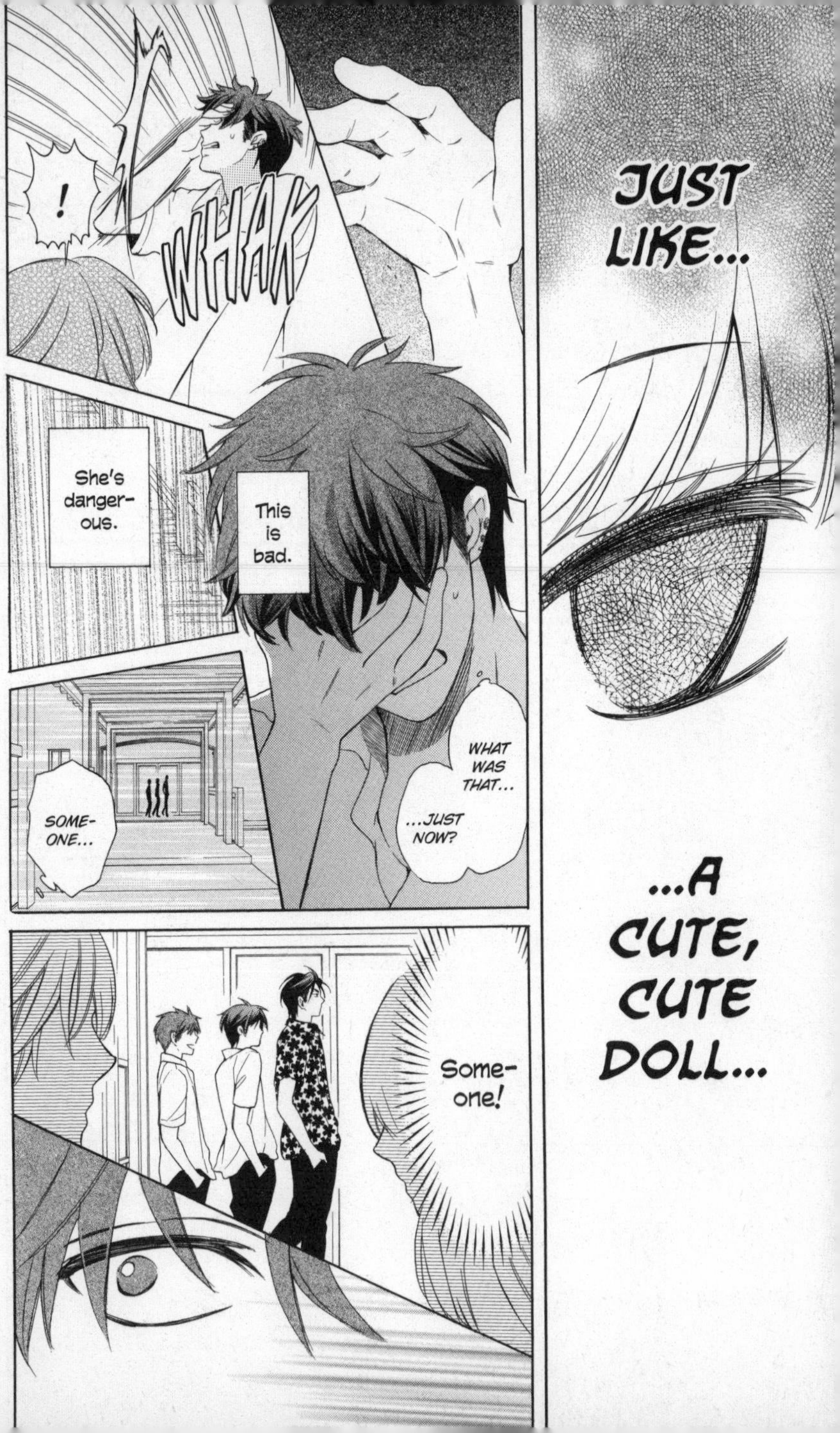
JUST LIKE...
...A CUTE, CUTE DOLL...
!
WHAK
She's danger-ous.
This is bad.
WHAT WAS THAT...
...JUST NOW?
SOME-ONE...
Some-one!

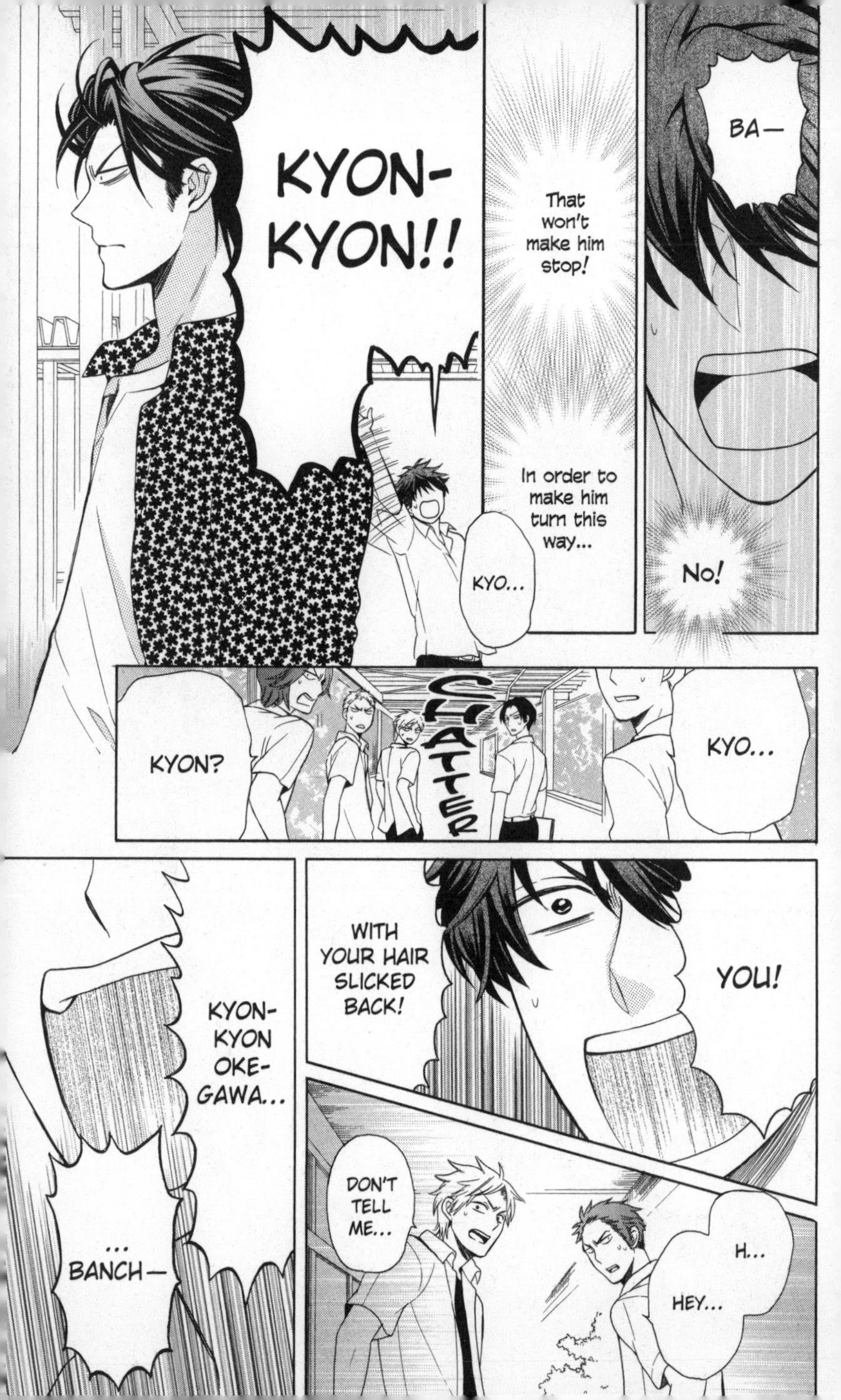

BA—
No!
That won't make him stop!
In order to make him turn this way...
KYO...
KYON-KYON!!
KYO...
CHATTER
KYON?
YOU!
WITH YOUR HAIR SLICKED BACK!
H...
HEY...
DON'T TELL ME...
KYON-KYON OKE-GAWA...
... BANCH—

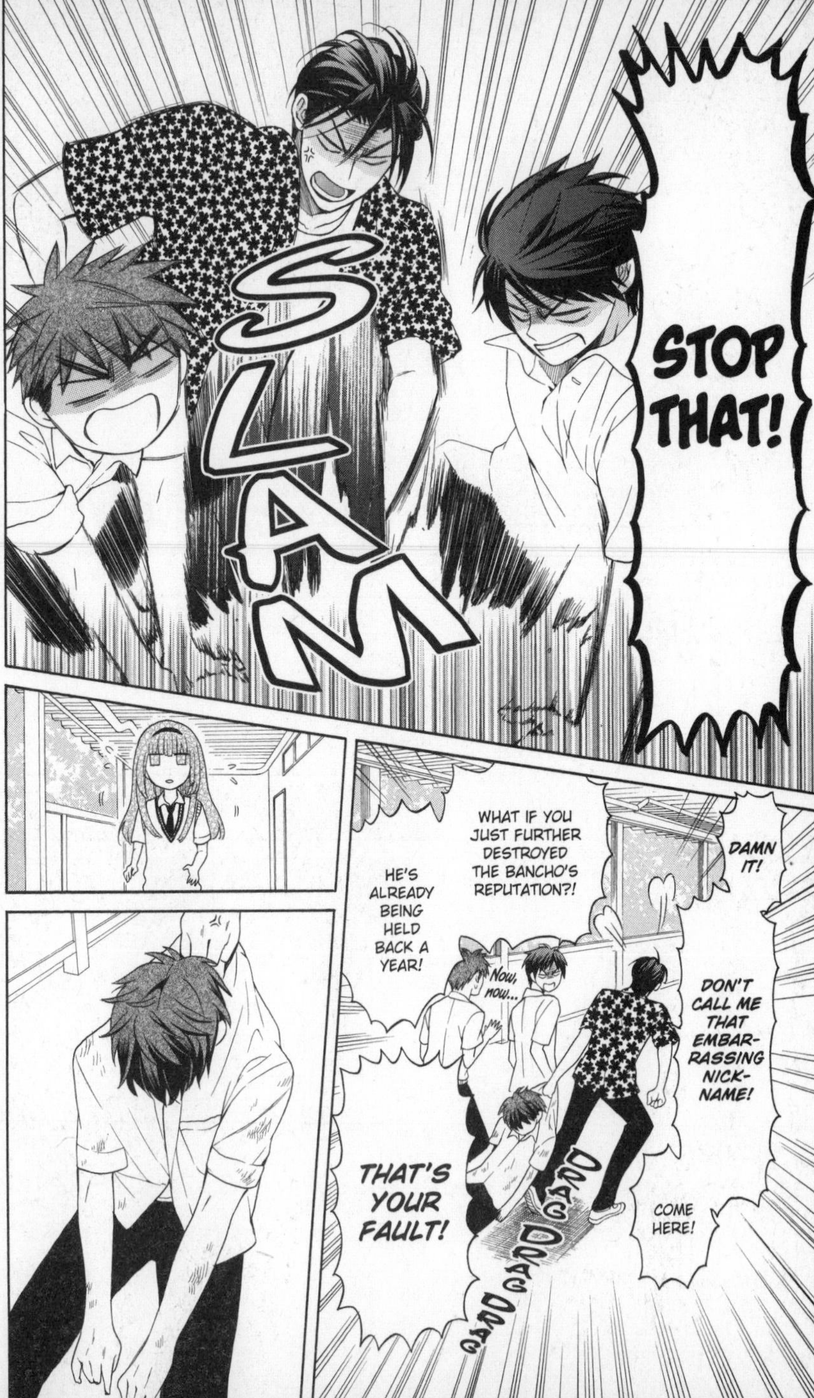
STOP THAT!
SLAM
DAMN IT!
WHAT IF YOU JUST FURTHER DESTROYED THE BANCHO'S REPUTATION?!
HE'S ALREADY BEING HELD BACK A YEAR!
Now, now...
DON'T CALL ME THAT EMBAR-RASSING NICK-NAME!
COME HERE!
THAT'S YOUR FAULT!
DRAG DRAG DRAG DRAG

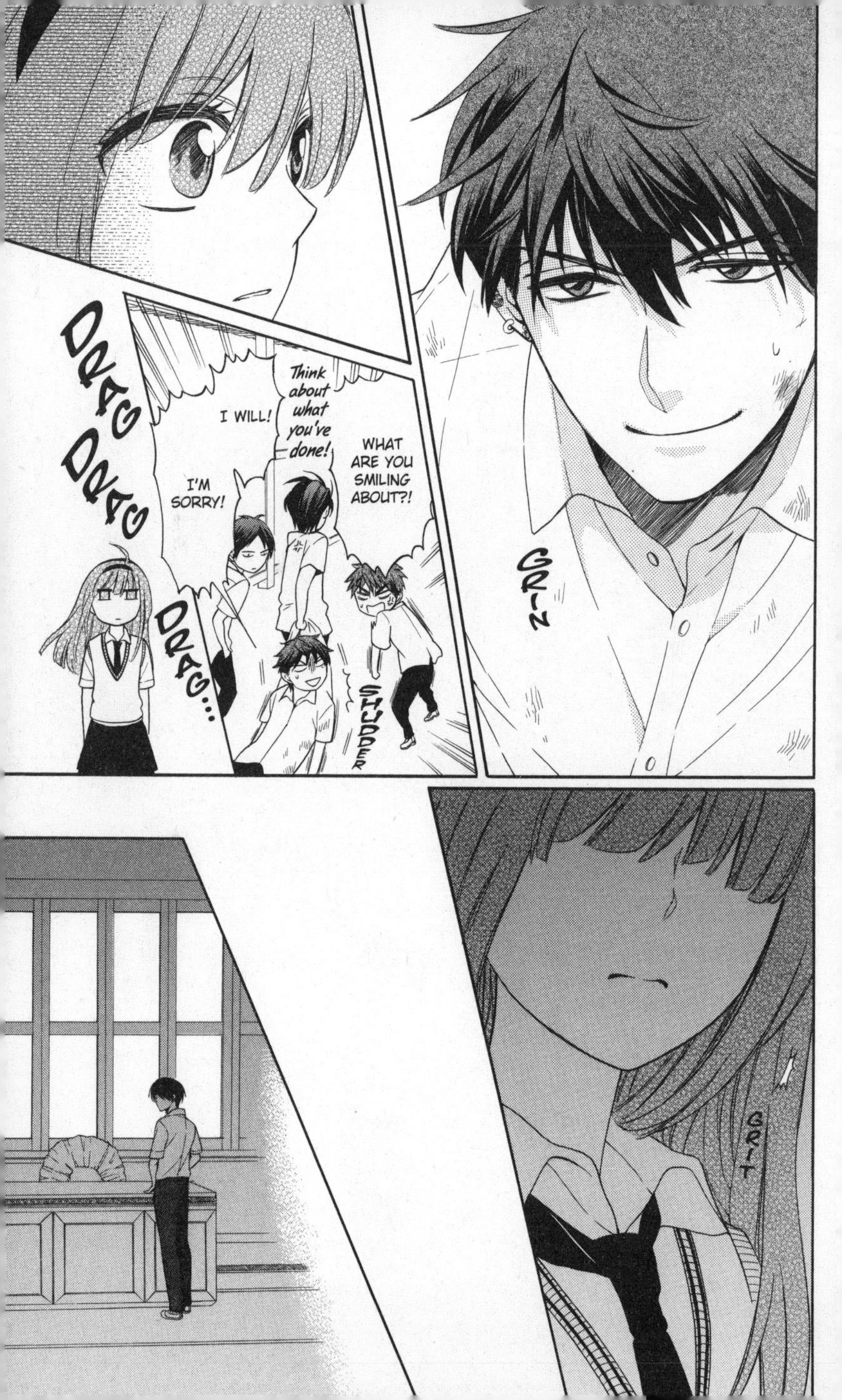
GRIN
WHAT ARE YOU SMILING ABOUT?!
SHUDDER
Think about what you've done!
I WILL!
I'M SORRY!
DRAG DRAG
DRAG...
GRIT

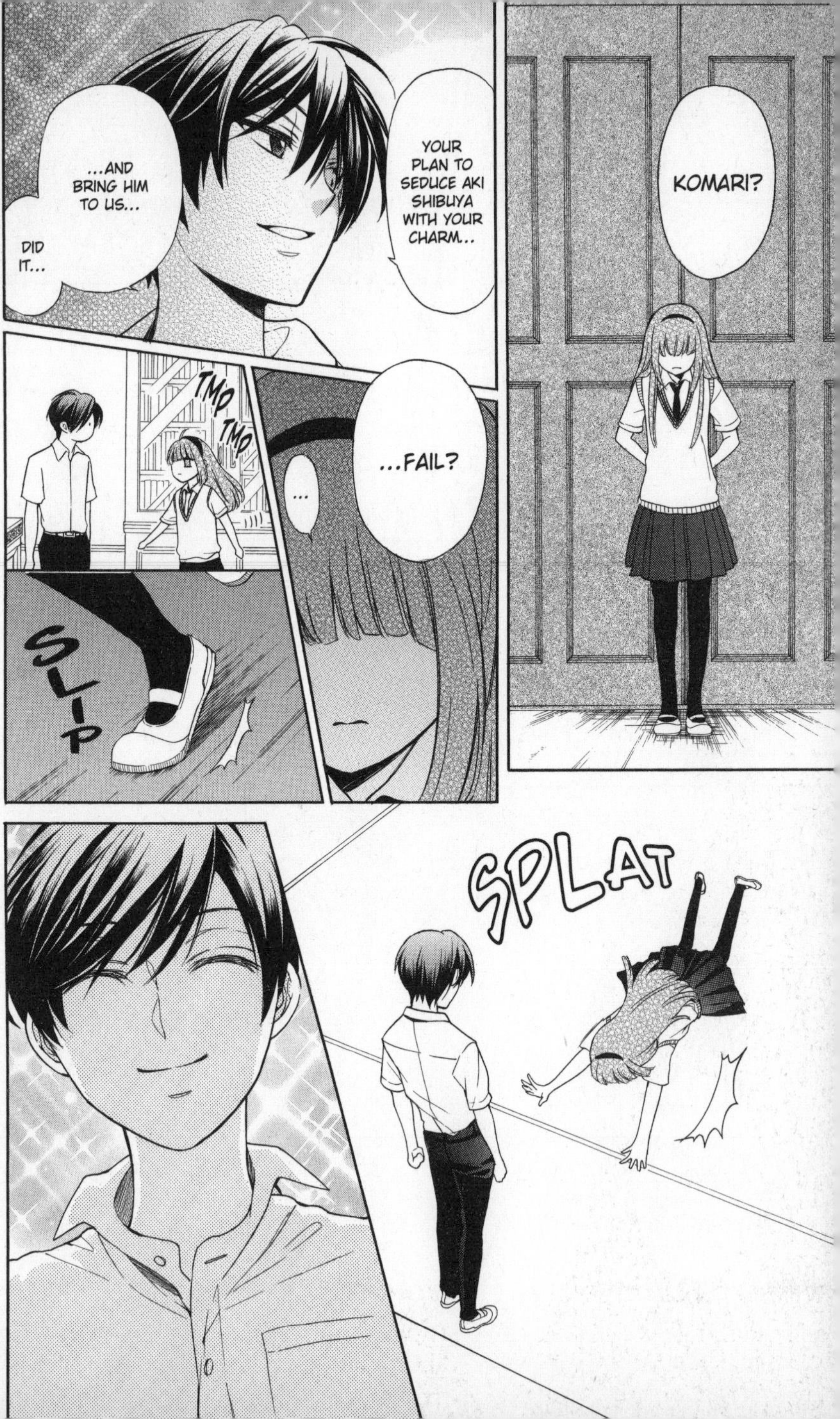
KOMARI?
YOUR PLAN TO SEDUCE AKI SHIBUYA WITH YOUR CHARM...
...AND BRING HIM TO US...
DID IT...
...FAIL?
...
TMP TMP
SLIP
SPLAT

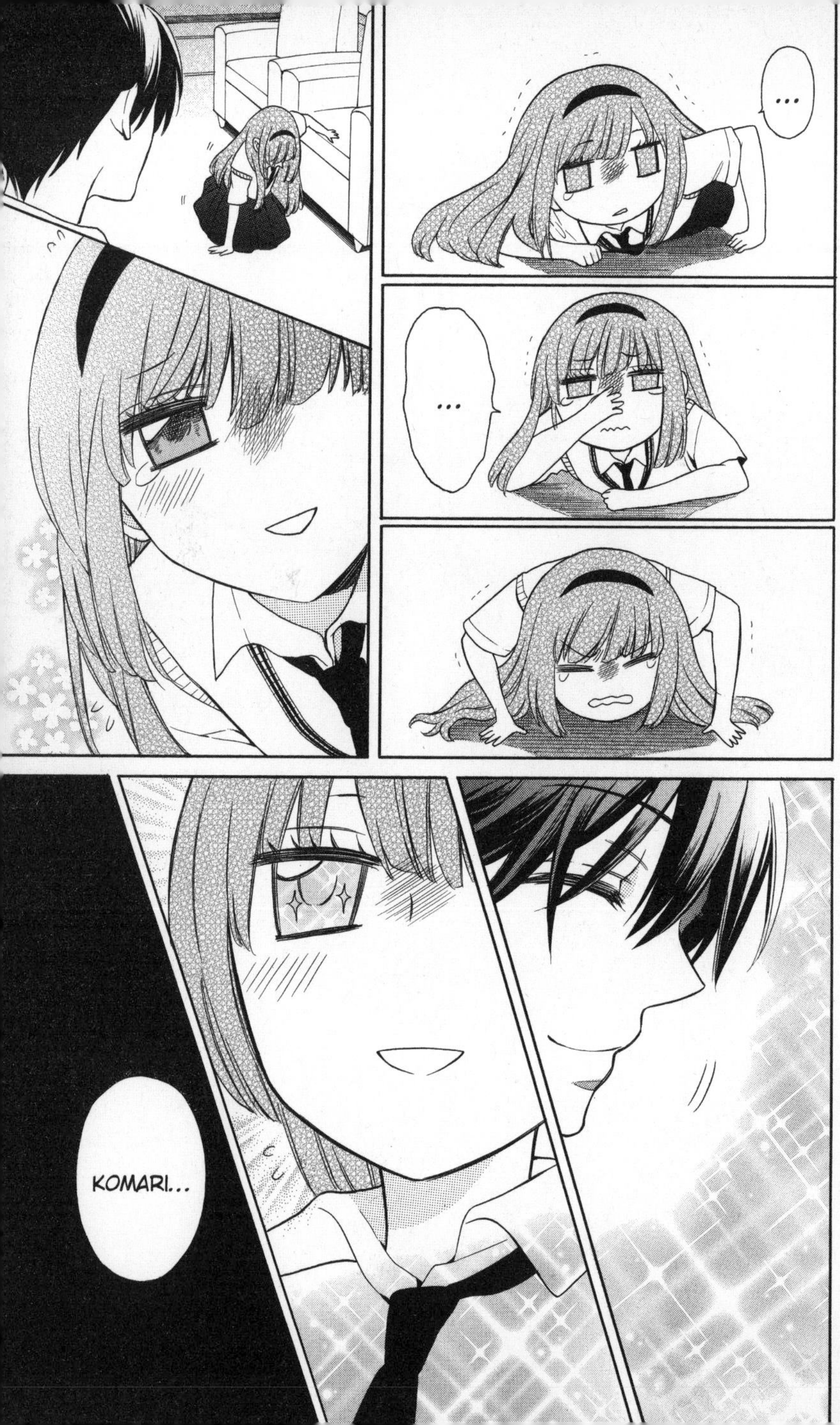
...
...
KOMARI...

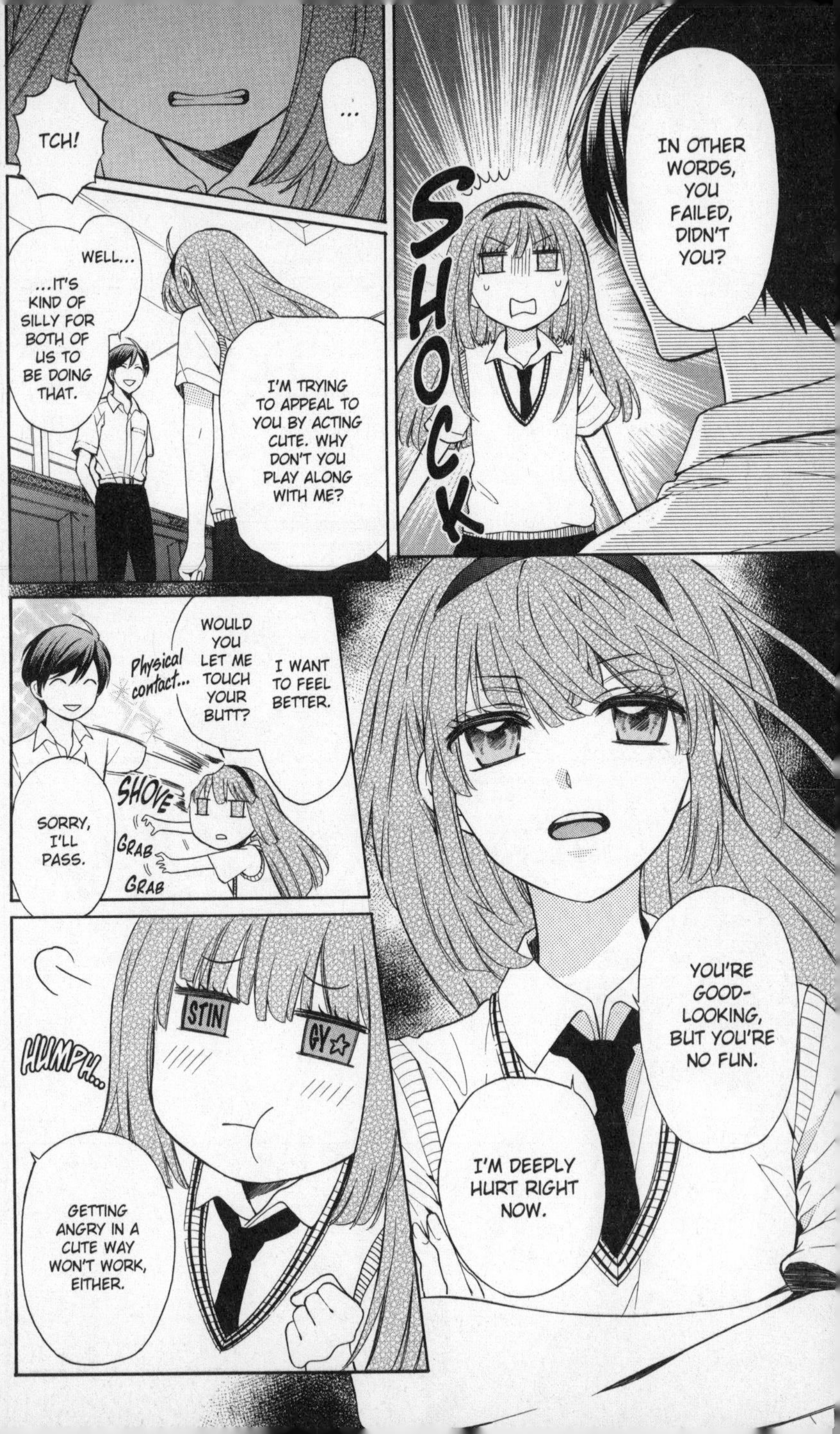
IN OTHER WORDS, YOU FAILED, DIDN'T YOU?
SHOCK
...
TCH!
I'M TRYING TO APPEAL TO YOU BY ACTING CUTE. WHY DON'T YOU PLAY ALONG WITH ME?
WELL...
...IT'S KIND OF SILLY FOR BOTH OF US TO BE DOING THAT.
YOU'RE GOOD-LOOKING, BUT YOU'RE NO FUN.
I'M DEEPLY HURT RIGHT NOW.
I WANT TO FEEL BETTER.
WOULD YOU LET ME TOUCH YOUR BUTT?
Physical contact...
SHOVE
SORRY, I'LL PASS.
GRAB
GRAB
STIN
GY☆
HUMPH...
GETTING ANGRY IN A CUTE WAY WON'T WORK, EITHER.

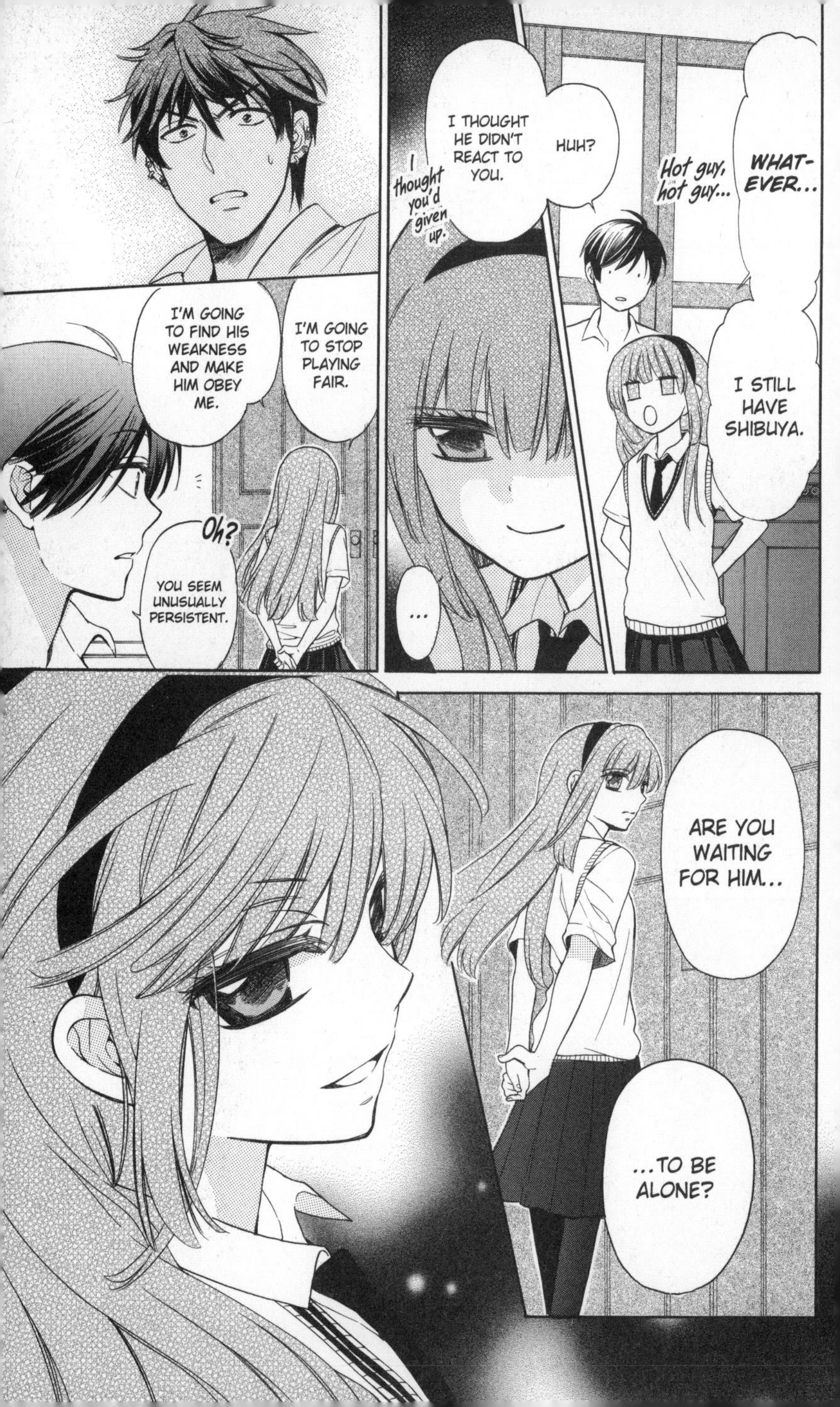
WHAT-EVER...
Hot guy, hot guy...
I STILL HAVE SHIBUYA.
HUH?
I THOUGHT HE DIDN'T REACT TO YOU.
I thought you'd given up.
...
I'M GOING TO STOP PLAYING FAIR.
I'M GOING TO FIND HIS WEAKNESS AND MAKE HIM OBEY ME.
Oh?
YOU SEEM UNUSUALLY PERSISTENT.
ARE YOU WAITING FOR HIM...
...TO BE ALONE?

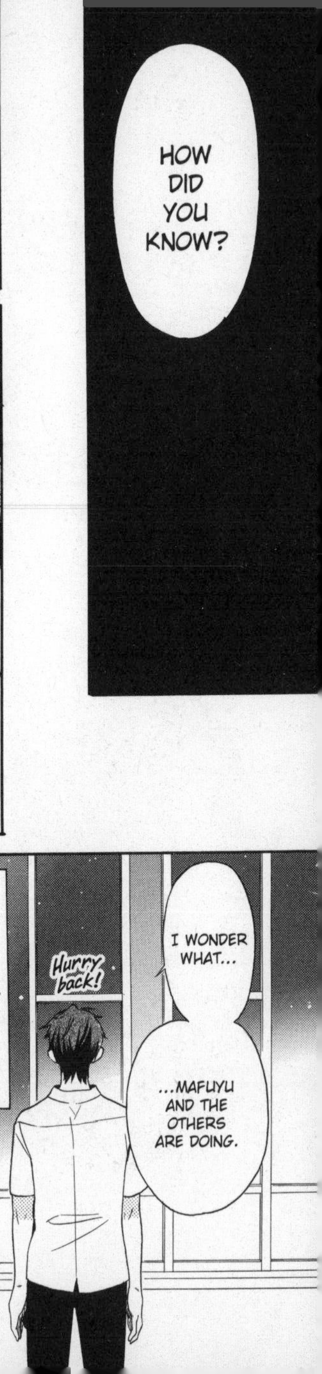
HOW DID YOU KNOW?

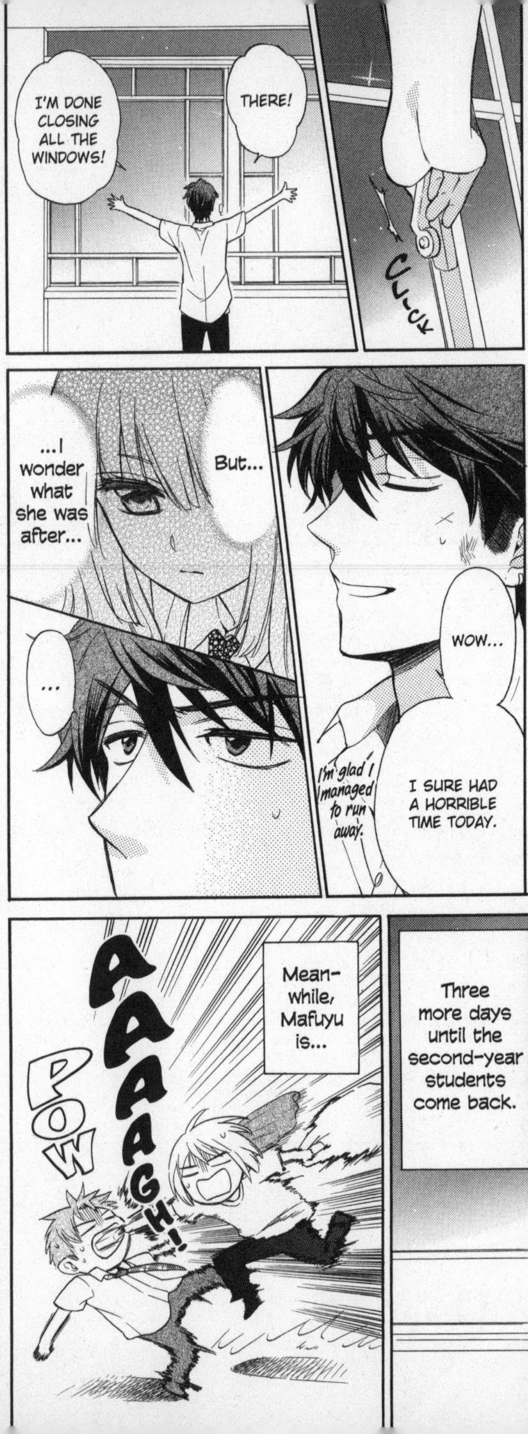
Click
THERE!
I'M DONE CLOSING ALL THE WINDOWS!
WOW...
I SURE HAD A HORRIBLE TIME TODAY.
I'm glad I managed to run away.
But...
...I wonder what she was after...
...
I WONDER WHAT...
...MAFUYU AND THE OTHERS ARE DOING.
Hurry back!
Three more days until the second-year students come back.
Mean-while, Mafuyu is...
AAAAAGH!
POW

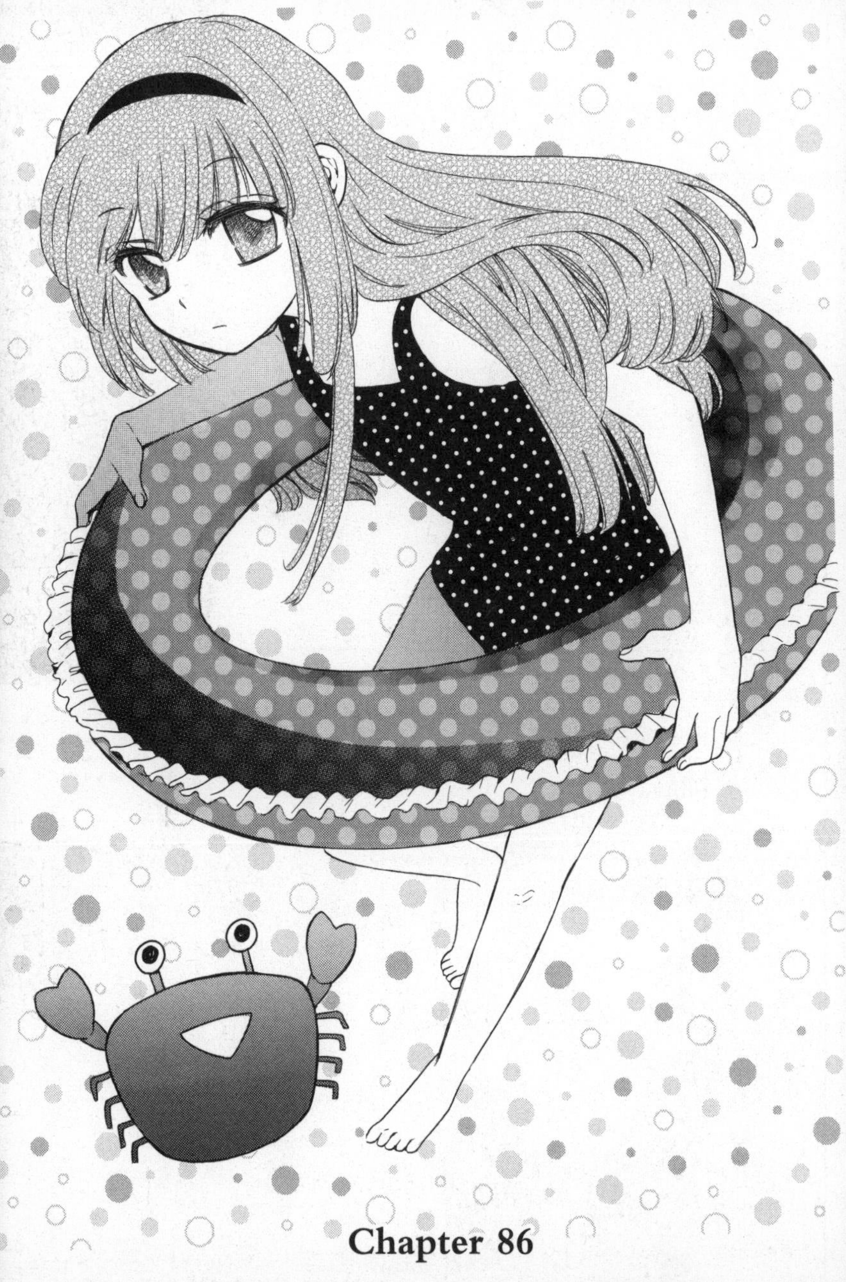

Chapter 86

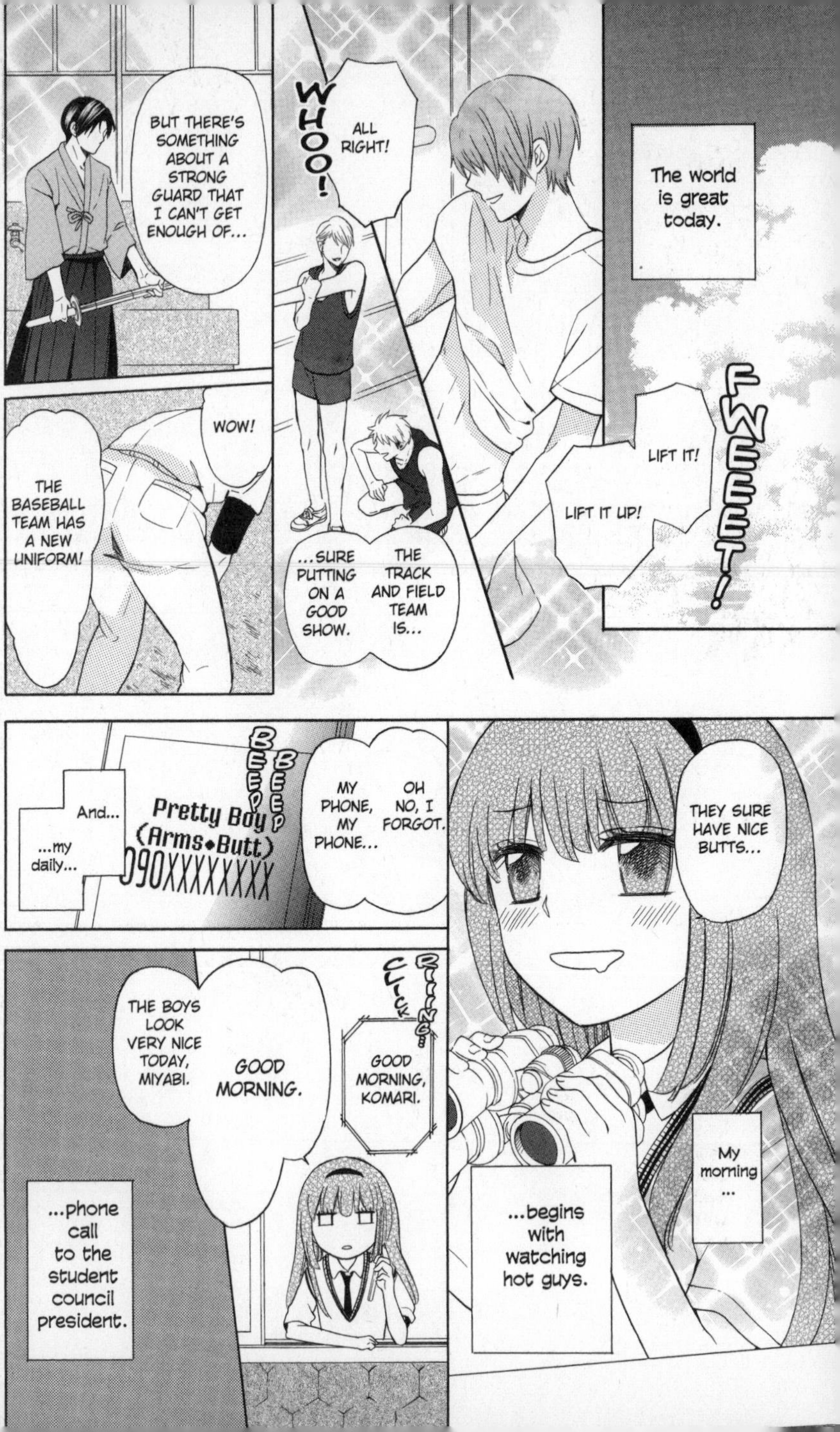
The world is great today.
LIFT IT!
LIFT IT UP!
FWEEET!
ALL RIGHT!
WHOO!
BUT THERE'S SOMETHING ABOUT A STRONG GUARD THAT I CAN'T GET ENOUGH OF...
THE TRACK AND FIELD TEAM IS...
...SURE PUTTING ON A GOOD SHOW.
WOW!
THE BASEBALL TEAM HAS A NEW UNIFORM!
THEY SURE HAVE NICE BUTTS...
OH NO, I FORGOT.
MY PHONE, MY PHONE...
BEEP BEEP
Pretty Boy (Arms◆Butt) 090XXXXXXXX
And...
...my daily...
My morning...
...begins with watching hot guys.
RIIING!! CLICK
GOOD MORNING, KOMARI.
GOOD MORNING.
THE BOYS LOOK VERY NICE TODAY, MIYABI.
...phone call to the student council president.

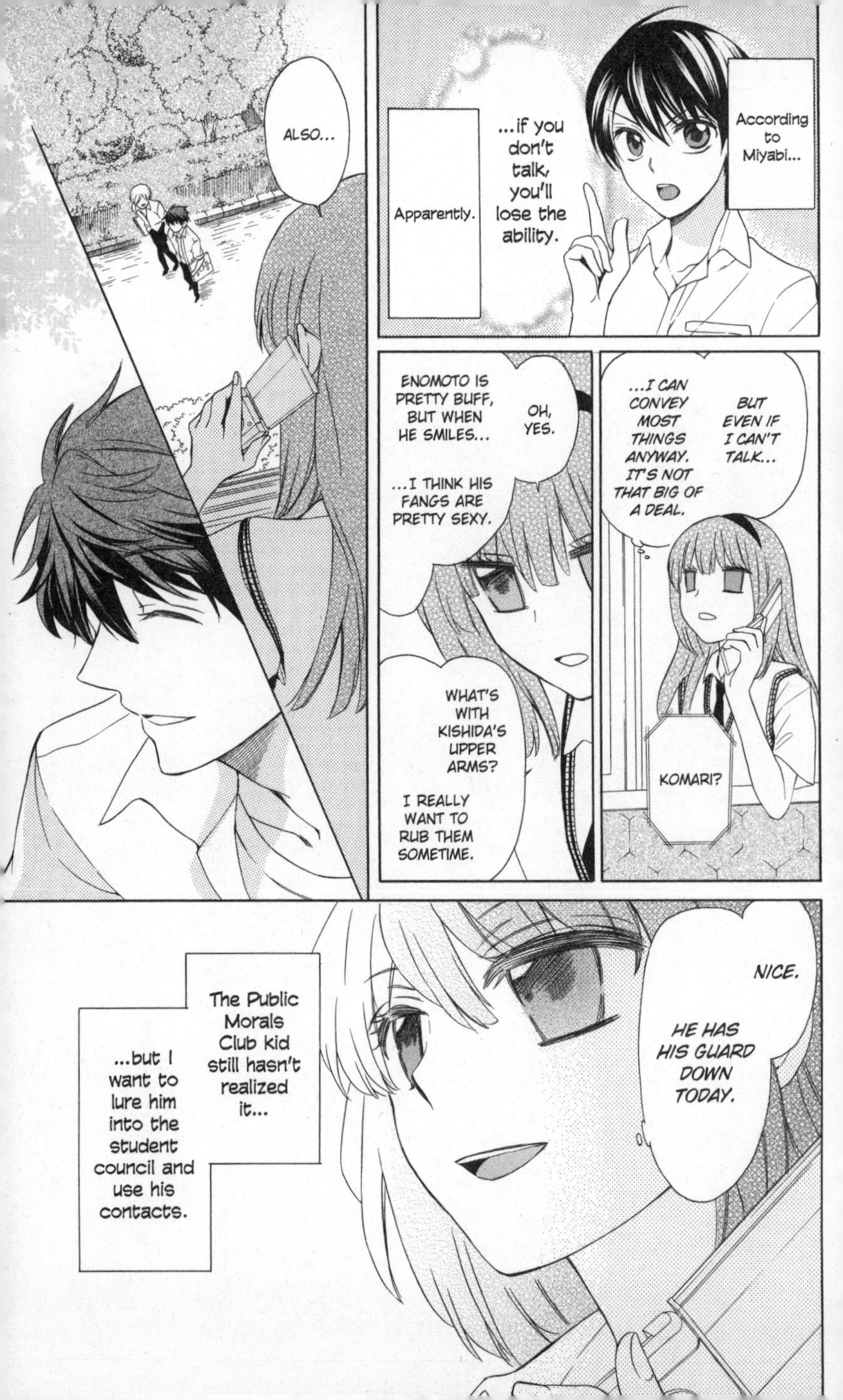
According to Miyabi...
...if you don't talk, you'll lose the ability.
Apparently.
...I CAN CONVEY MOST THINGS ANYWAY. IT'S NOT THAT BIG OF A DEAL.
BUT EVEN IF I CAN'T TALK...
KOMARI?
OH, YES.
ENOMOTO IS PRETTY BUFF, BUT WHEN HE SMILES...
...I THINK HIS FANGS ARE PRETTY SEXY.
WHAT'S WITH KISHIDA'S UPPER ARMS?
I REALLY WANT TO RUB THEM SOMETIME.
ALSO...
NICE.
HE HAS HIS GUARD DOWN TODAY.
The Public Morals Club kid still hasn't realized it...
...but I want to lure him into the student council and use his contacts.

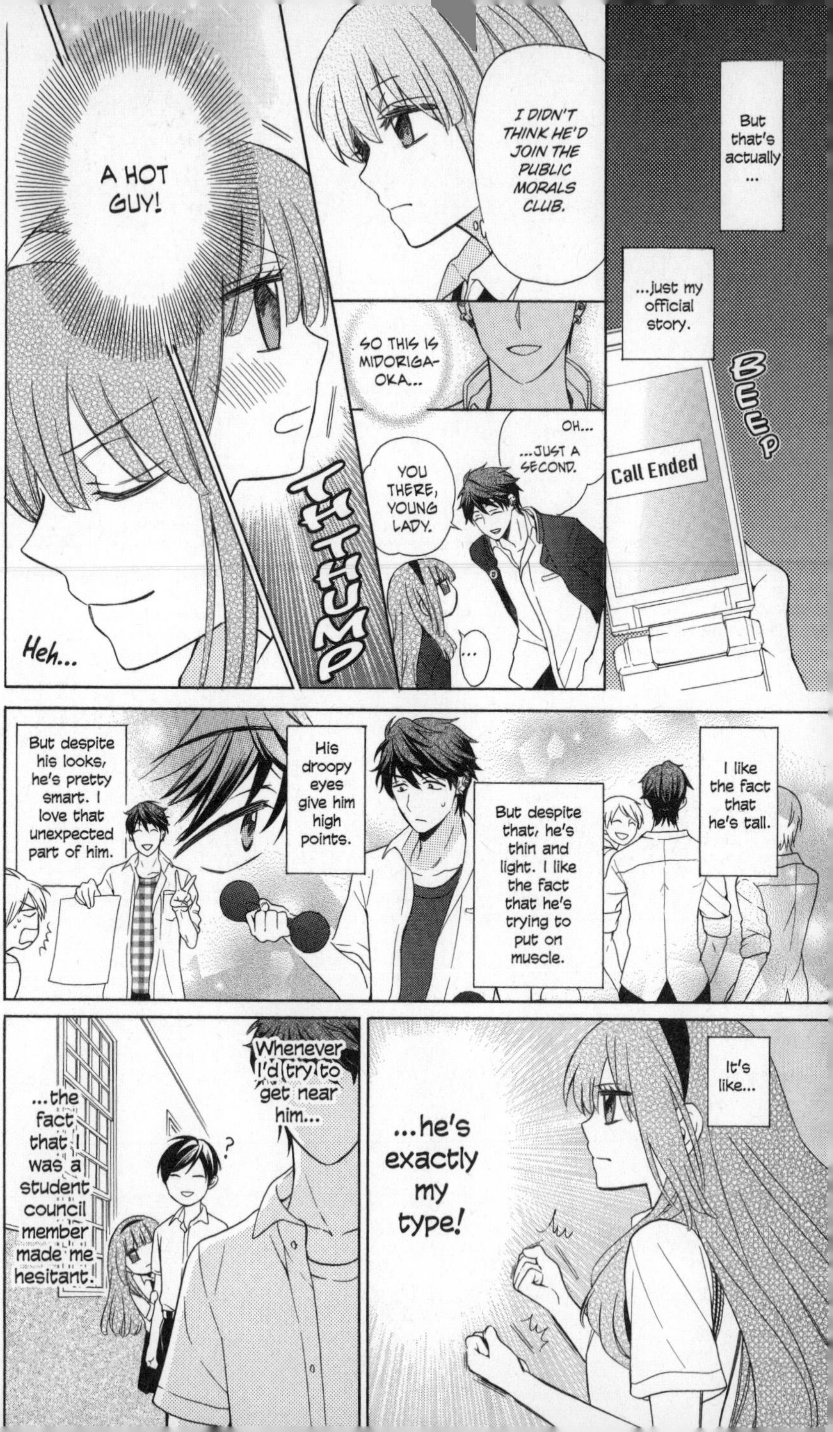
But that's actually ...
...just my official story.
BEEP
Call Ended
I DIDN'T THINK HE'D JOIN THE PUBLIC MORALS CLUB.
SO THIS IS MIDORIGA-OKA...
OH... ...JUST A SECOND.
YOU THERE, YOUNG LADY.
...
THTHUMP
A HOT GUY!
Heh...
I like the fact that he's tall.
But despite that, he's thin and light. I like the fact that he's trying to put on muscle.
His droopy eyes give him high points.
But despite his looks, he's pretty smart. I love that unexpected part of him.
It's like...
...he's exactly my type!
Whenever I'd try to get near him...
?
...the fact that I was a student council member made me hesitant.

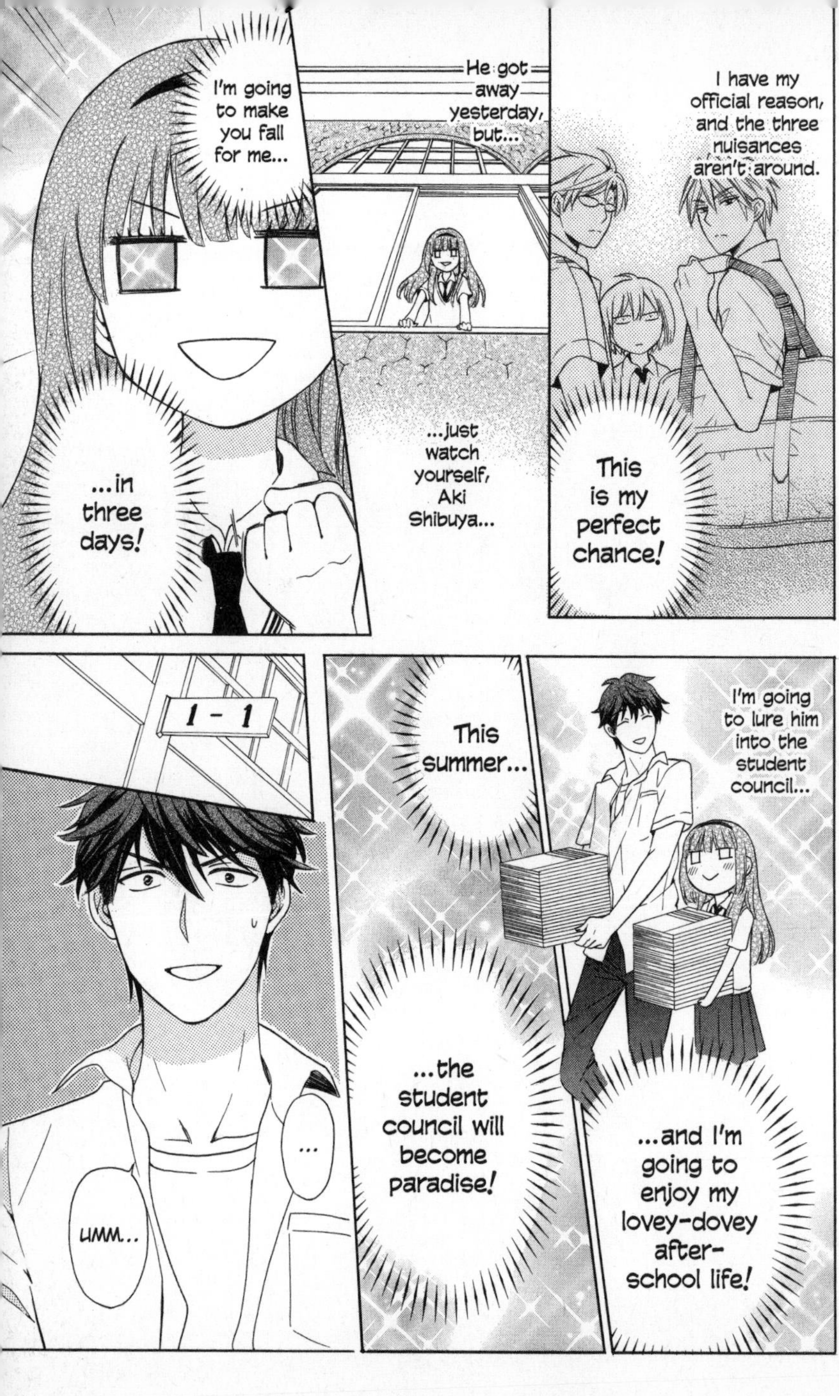
I have my official reason, and the three nuisances aren't around.
This is my perfect chance!
He got away yesterday, but...
...just watch yourself, Aki Shibuya...
I'm going to make you fall for me...
...in three days!
I'm going to lure him into the student council...
...and I'm going to enjoy my lovey-dovey after-school life!
This summer...
...the student council will become paradise!
1 - 1
...
UMM...

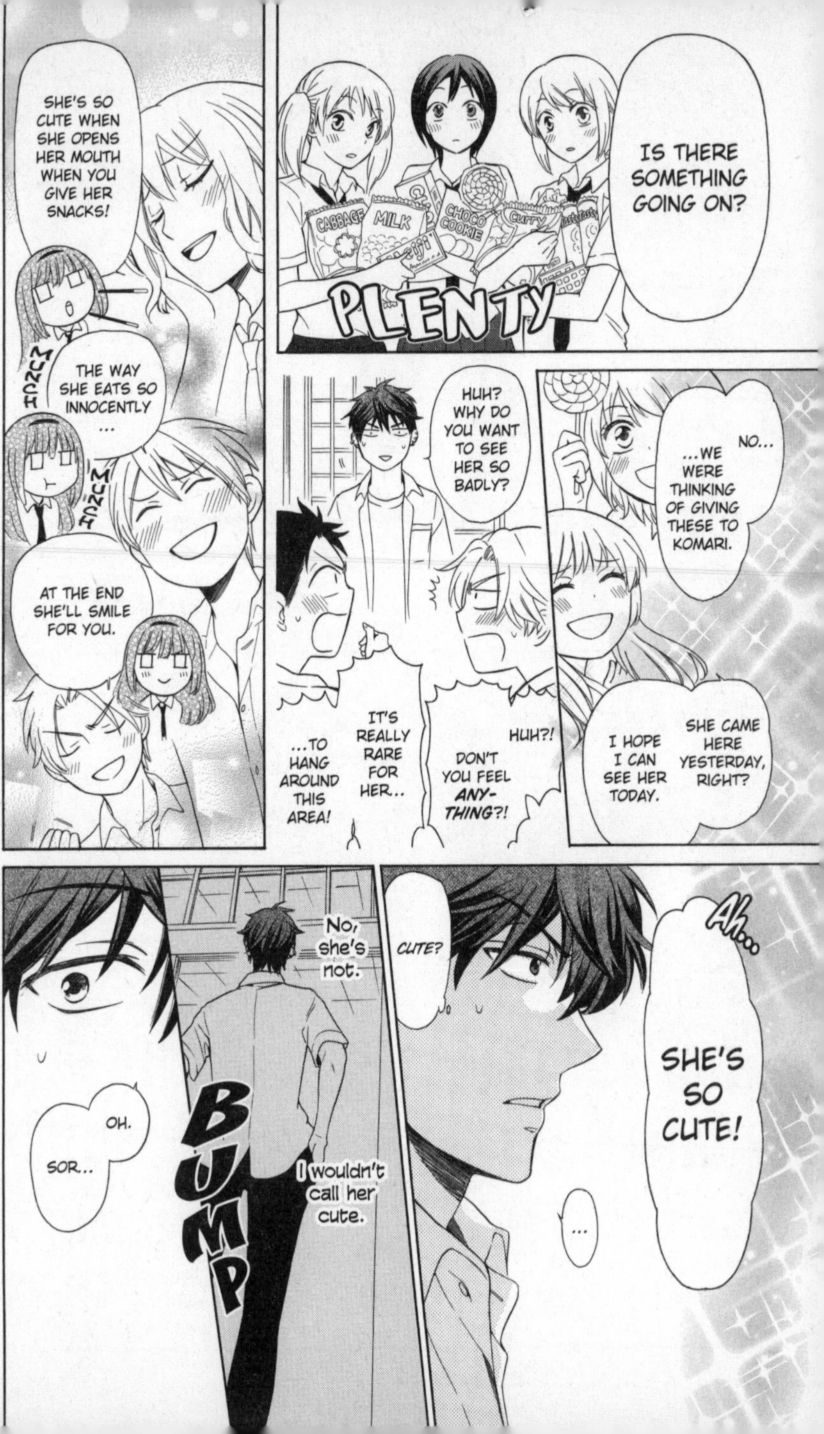
IS THERE SOMETHING GOING ON?
PLENTY
CABBAGE
MILK
CHOCO COOKIE
Curry
tasty tasty
NO... ...WE WERE THINKING OF GIVING THESE TO KOMARI.
SHE CAME HERE YESTERDAY, RIGHT?
I HOPE I CAN SEE HER TODAY.
HUH? WHY DO YOU WANT TO SEE HER SO BADLY?
HUH?!
DON'T YOU FEEL ANYTHING?!
IT'S REALLY RARE FOR HER...
...TO HANG AROUND THIS AREA!
SHE'S SO CUTE WHEN SHE OPENS HER MOUTH WHEN YOU GIVE HER SNACKS!
MUNCH
THE WAY SHE EATS SO INNOCENTLY ...
MUNCH
AT THE END SHE'LL SMILE FOR YOU.
Ah...
SHE'S SO CUTE!
CUTE?
...
No, she's not.
I wouldn't call her cute.
BUMP
OH.
SOR...

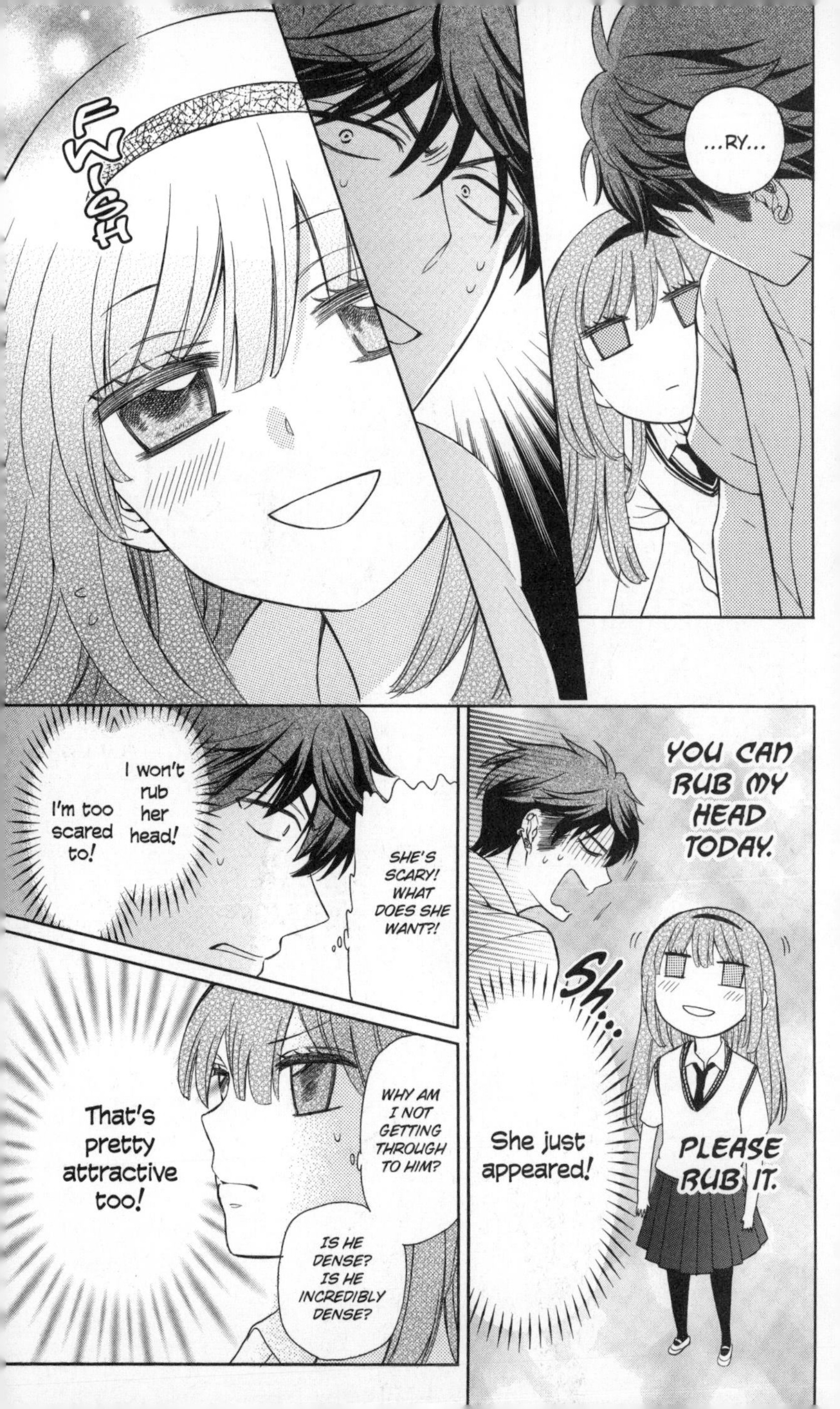
...RY...
FWISH
YOU CAN RUB MY HEAD TODAY.
PLEASE RUB IT.
SH...
She just appeared!
I won't rub her head!
I'm too scared to!
SHE'S SCARY! WHAT DOES SHE WANT?!
WHY AM I NOT GETTING THROUGH TO HIM?
IS HE DENSE? IS HE INCREDIBLY DENSE?
That's pretty attractive too!

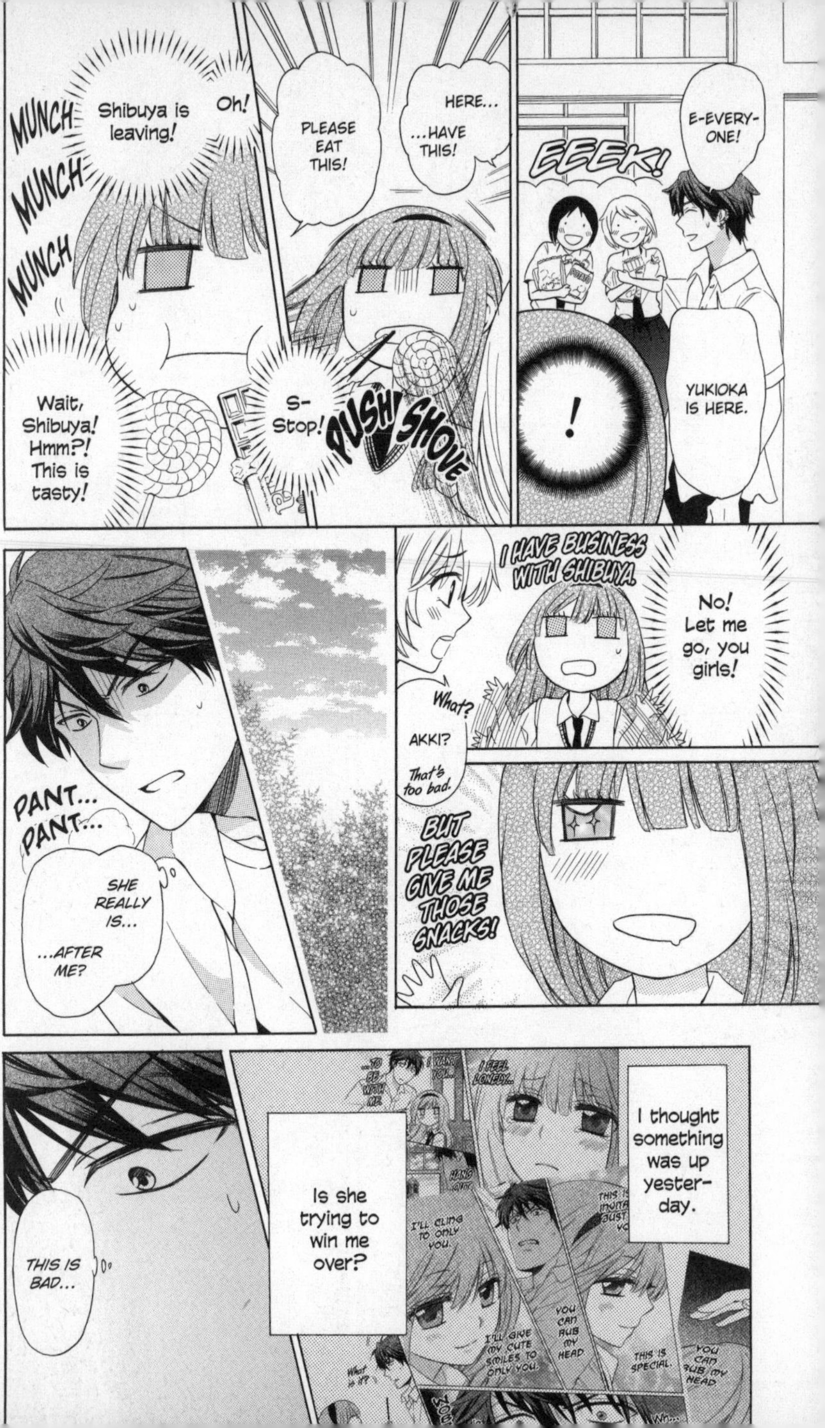
E-EVERY-ONE!
EEEK!
YUKIOKA IS HERE.
!
HERE... ...HAVE THIS!
PLEASE EAT THIS!
S-Stop!
PUSH! SHOVE
Oh!
Shibuya is leaving!
MUNCH MUNCH MUNCH
Wait, Shibuya! Hmm?! This is tasty!
I HAVE BUSINESS WITH SHIBUYA.
No! Let me go, you girls!
What?
AKKI?
That's too bad.
BUT PLEASE GIVE ME THOSE SNACKS!
PANT... PANT...
SHE REALLY IS...
...AFTER ME?
I thought something was up yester-day.
I FEEL LONELY...
I WANT YOU...
...TO BE WITH ME.
I'LL CLING TO ONLY YOU.
YOU CAN RUB MY HEAD
THIS IS SPECIAL.
YOU CAN RUB MY HEAD
I'LL GIVE MY CUTE SMILES TO ONLY YOU.
What is it?
Is she trying to win me over?
THIS IS BAD...

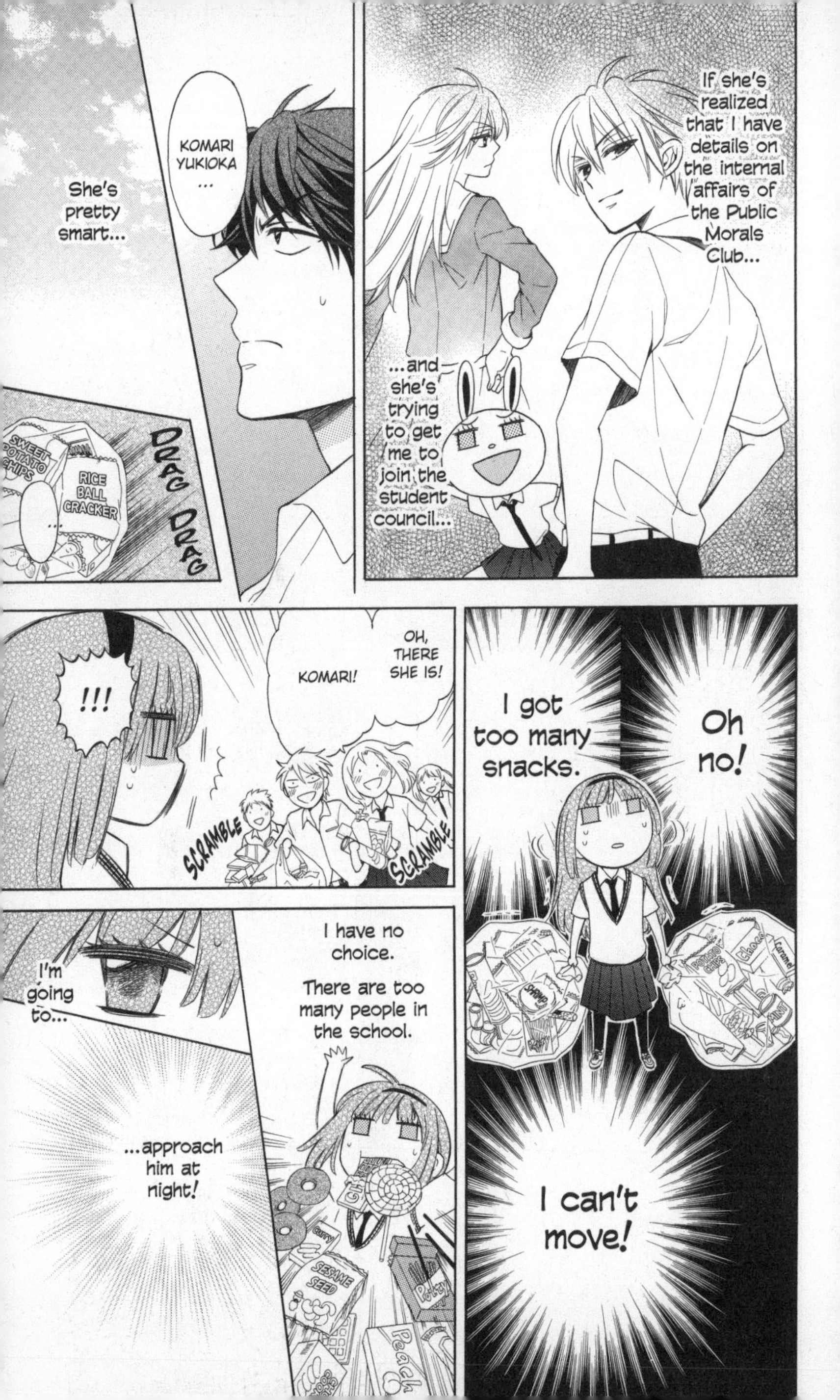
If she's realized that I have details on the internal affairs of the Public Morals Club...
...and she's trying to get me to join the student council...
KOMARI YUKIOKA ...
She's pretty smart...
SWEET POTATO CHIPS
RICE BALL CRACKER
...
DRAG DRAG
Oh no!
I got too many snacks.
POTATO CHIPS
Choco
Caramel
SHRIMP
I can't move!
KOMARI!
OH, THERE SHE IS!
!!!
SCRAMBLE
SCRAMBLE
I have no choice.
There are too many people in the school.
I'm going to...
...approach him at night!
Curry
SESAME SEED
Potty
Peach

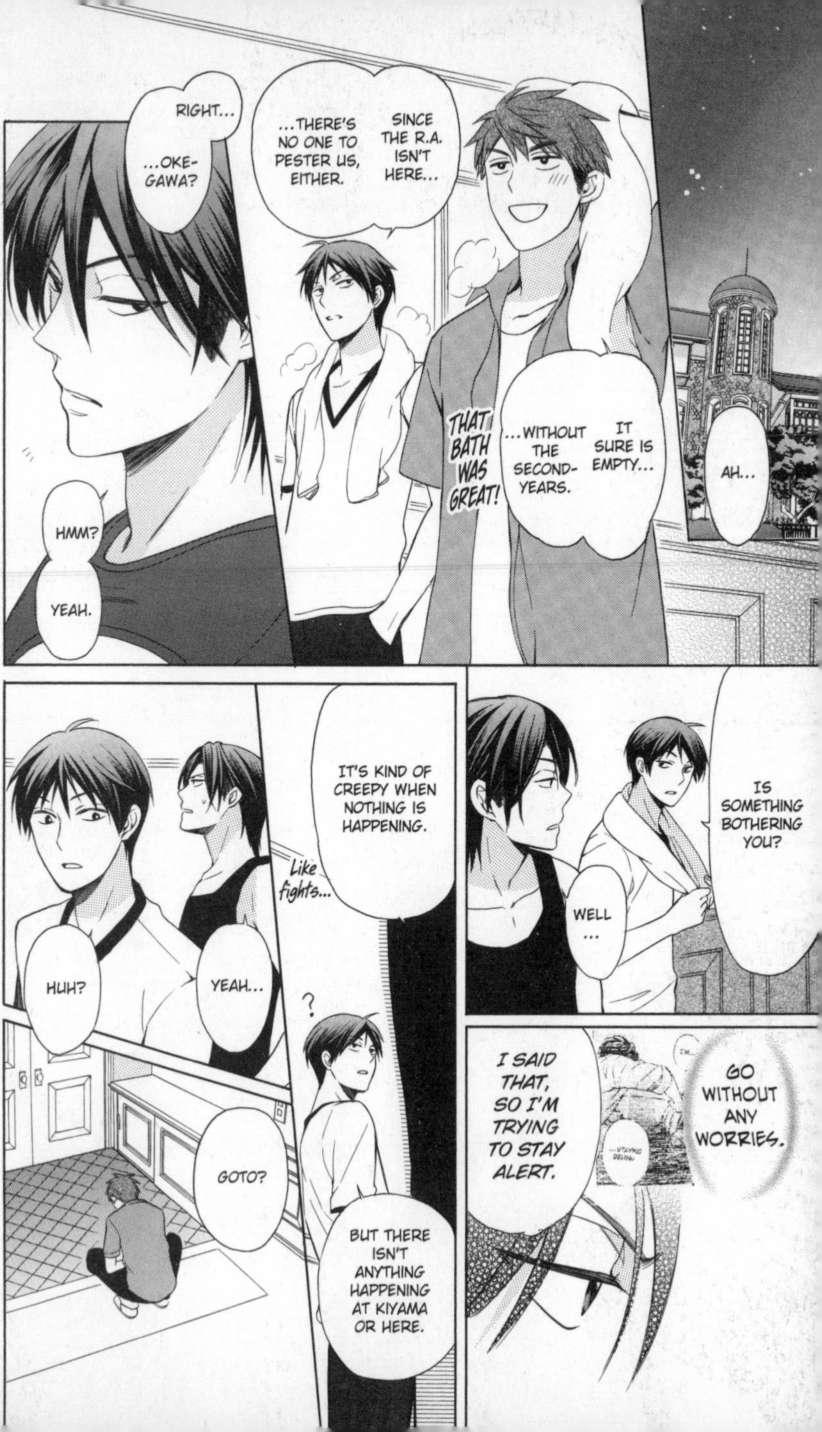
AH...
IT SURE IS EMPTY...
...WITHOUT THE SECOND-YEARS.
THAT BATH WAS GREAT!
SINCE THE R.A. ISN'T HERE...
...THERE'S NO ONE TO PESTER US, EITHER.
RIGHT...
...OKE-GAWA?
HMM?
YEAH.
IS SOMETHING BOTHERING YOU?
WELL...
GO WITHOUT ANY WORRIES.
I'M...
...STAYING BEHIND.
I SAID THAT, SO I'M TRYING TO STAY ALERT.
IT'S KIND OF CREEPY WHEN NOTHING IS HAPPENING.
Like fights...
?
BUT THERE ISN'T ANYTHING HAPPENING AT KIYAMA OR HERE.
HUH?
YEAH...
GOTO?

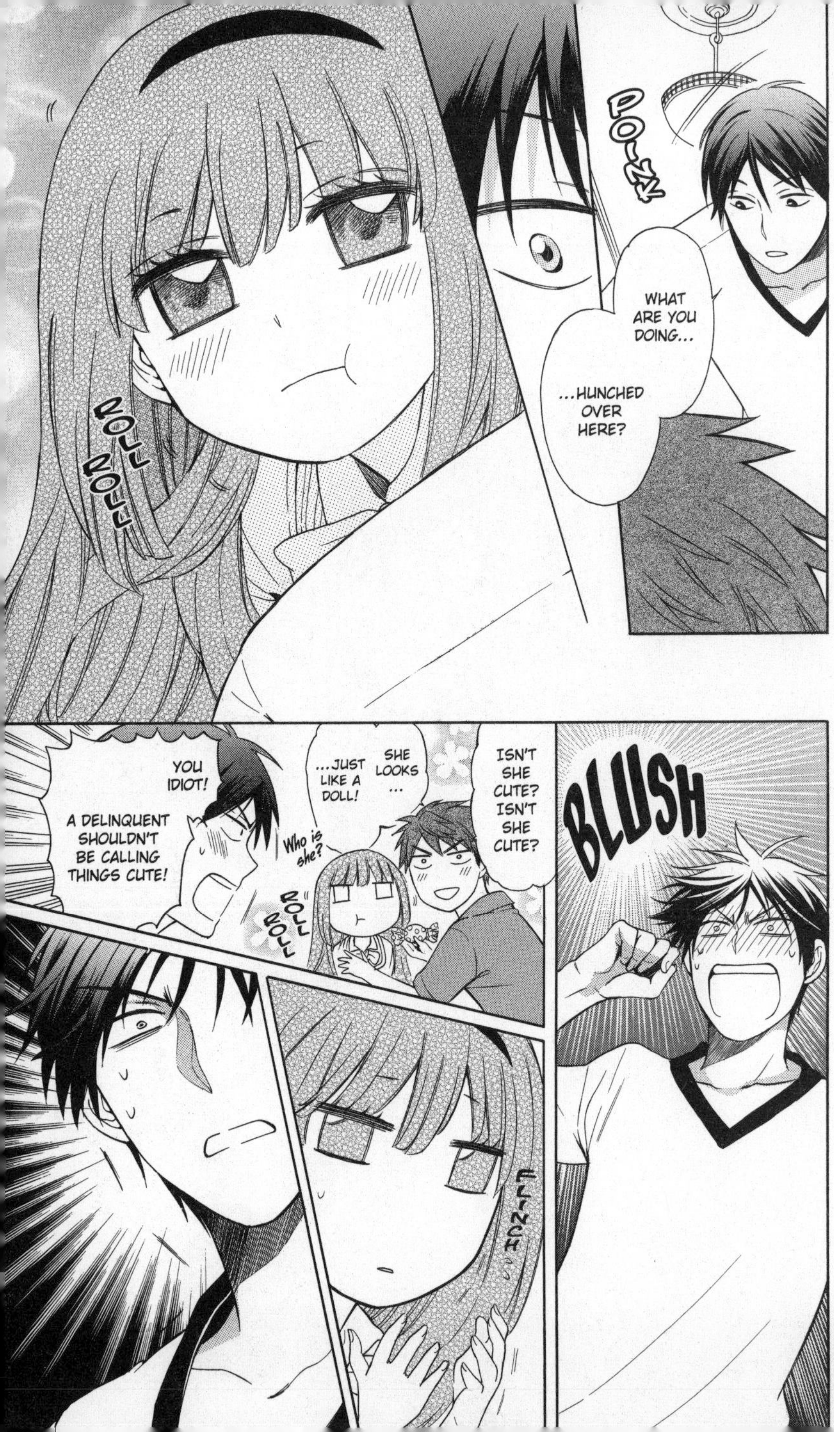
POI-N-K
WHAT ARE YOU DOING...
...HUNCHED OVER HERE?
ROLL ROLL
BLUSH
ISN'T SHE CUTE? ISN'T SHE CUTE?
SHE LOOKS ...
...JUST LIKE A DOLL!
Who is she?
ROLL ROLL
YOU IDIOT!
A DELINQUENT SHOULDN'T BE CALLING THINGS CUTE!
FLINCH

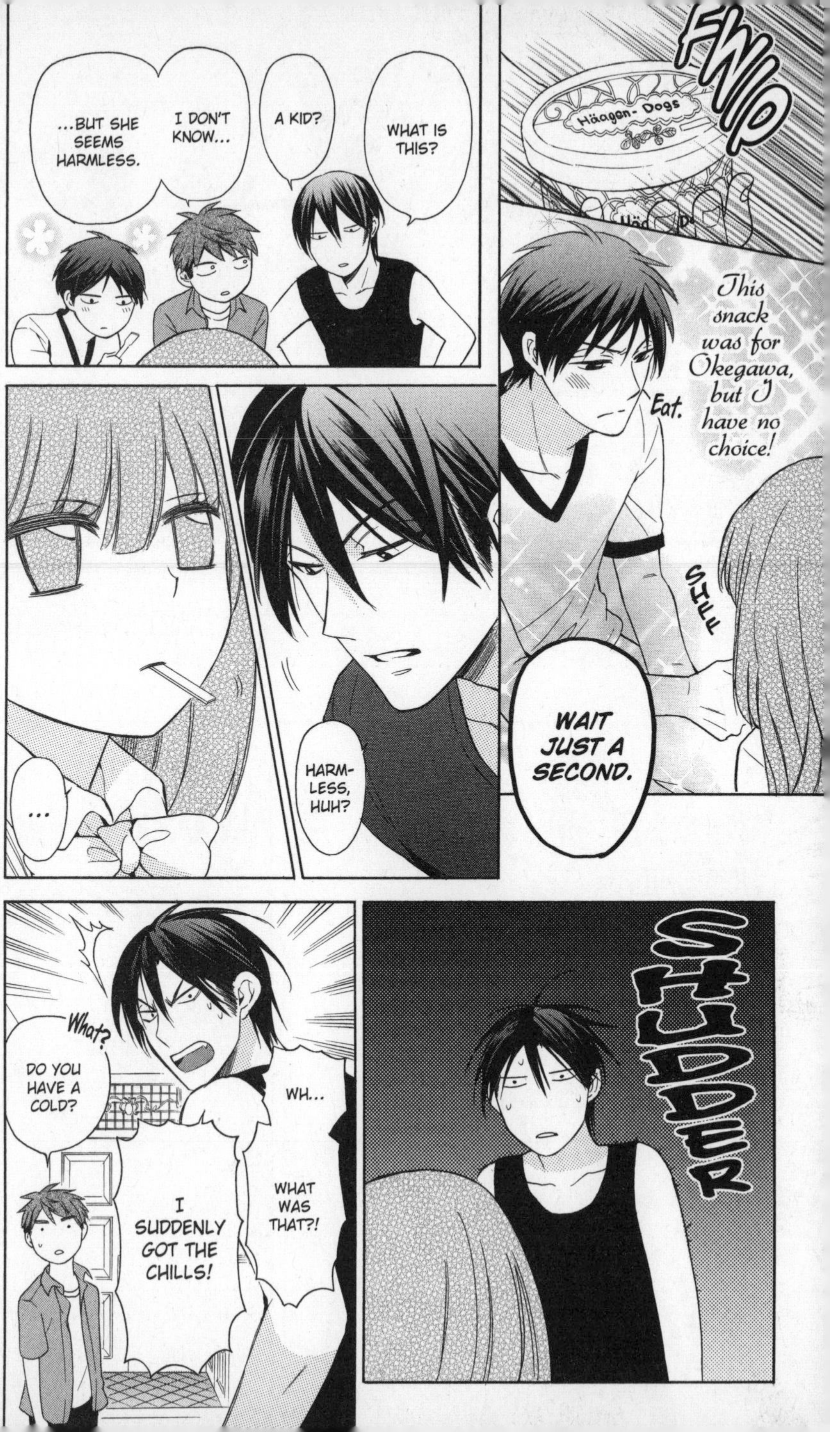
FWIP
Häagen-Dogs
This snack was for Okegawa, but I have no choice!
Eat.
SHFF
WAIT JUST A SECOND.
WHAT IS THIS?
A KID?
I DON'T KNOW...
...BUT SHE SEEMS HARMLESS.
HARM-LESS, HUH?
...
SHUDDER
What?
WH...
WHAT WAS THAT?!
I SUDDENLY GOT THE CHILLS!
DO YOU HAVE A COLD?

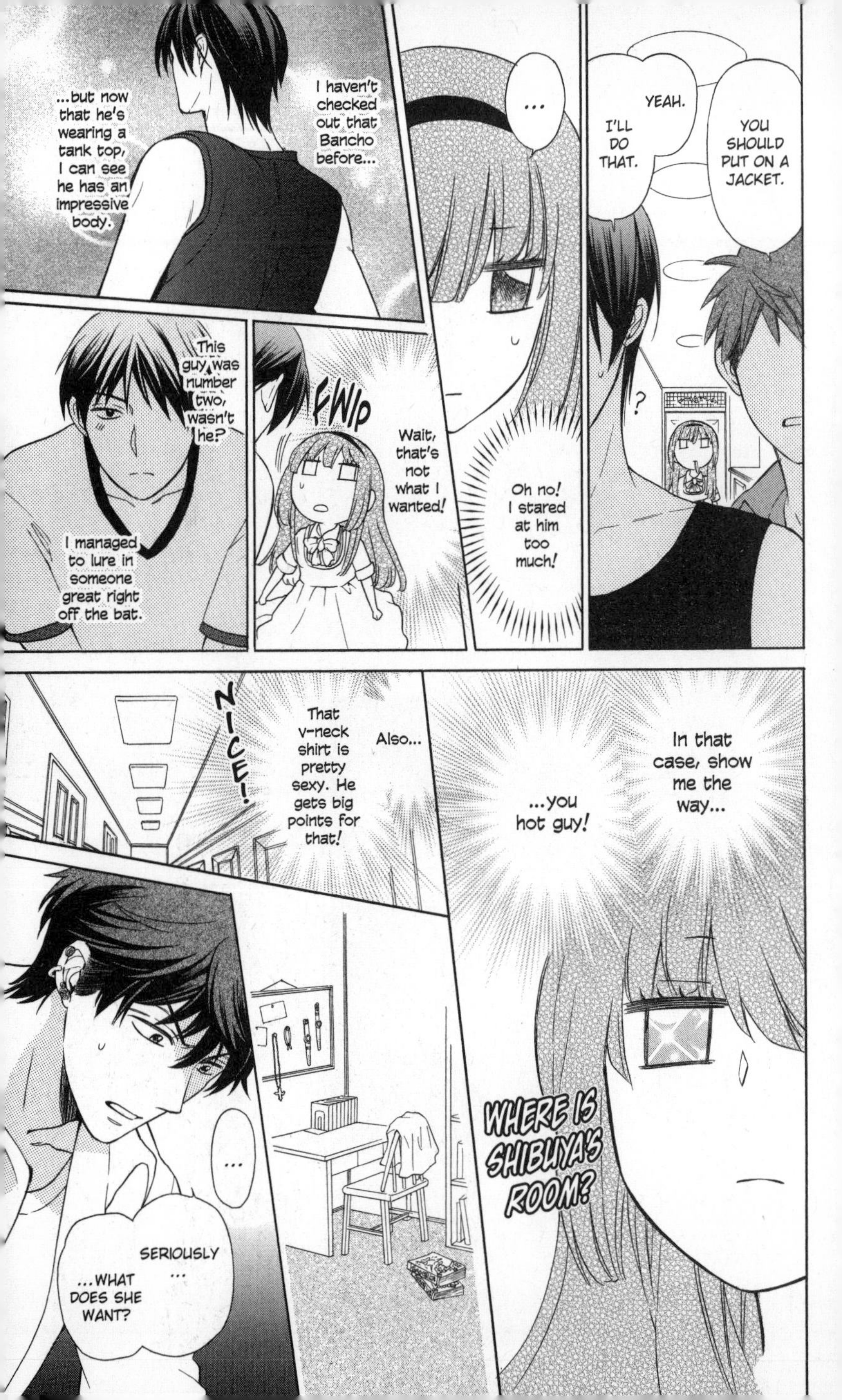
YOU SHOULD PUT ON A JACKET.
YEAH.
I'LL DO THAT.
...
Oh no! I stared at him too much!
I haven't checked out that Bancho before...
...but now that he's wearing a tank top, I can see he has an impressive body.
FWIP
Wait, that's not what I wanted!
This guy was number two, wasn't he?
I managed to lure in someone great right off the bat.
In that case, show me the way...
...you hot guy!
WHERE IS SHIBUYA'S ROOM?
Also...
That v-neck shirt is pretty sexy. He gets big points for that!
NICE!
...
SERIOUSLY ...
...WHAT DOES SHE WANT?

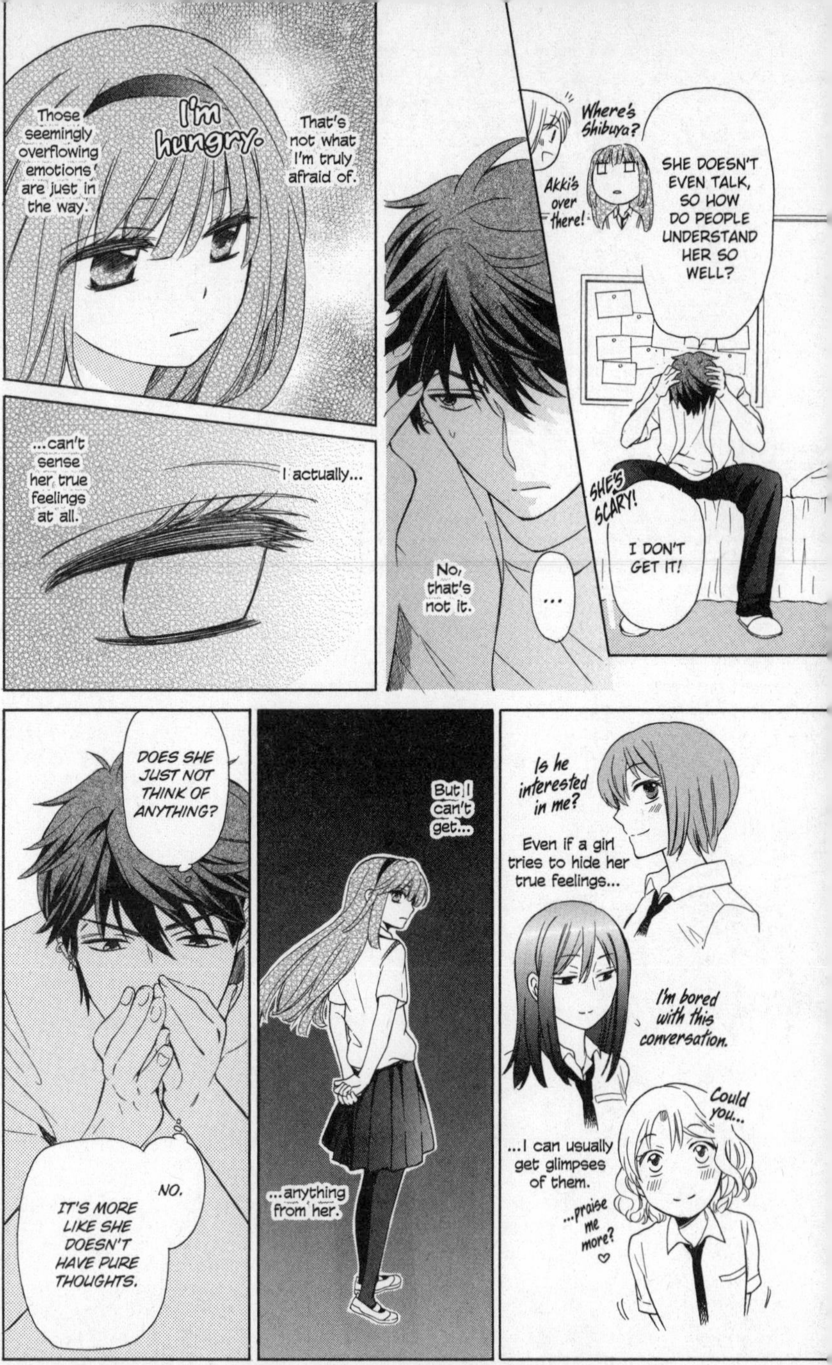
Where's Shibuya?
SHE DOESN'T EVEN TALK, SO HOW DO PEOPLE UNDERSTAND HER SO WELL?
Akki's over there!
SHE'S SCARY!
I DON'T GET IT!
...
No, that's not it.
That's not what I'm truly afraid of.
I'm hungry.
Those seemingly overflowing emotions are just in the way.
I actually...
...can't sense her true feelings at all.
Is he interested in me?
Even if a girl tries to hide her true feelings...
I'm bored with this conversation.
Could you...
...I can usually get glimpses of them.
...praise me more? ♡
But I can't get...
...anything from her.
DOES SHE JUST NOT THINK OF ANYTHING?
NO.
IT'S MORE LIKE SHE DOESN'T HAVE PURE THOUGHTS.

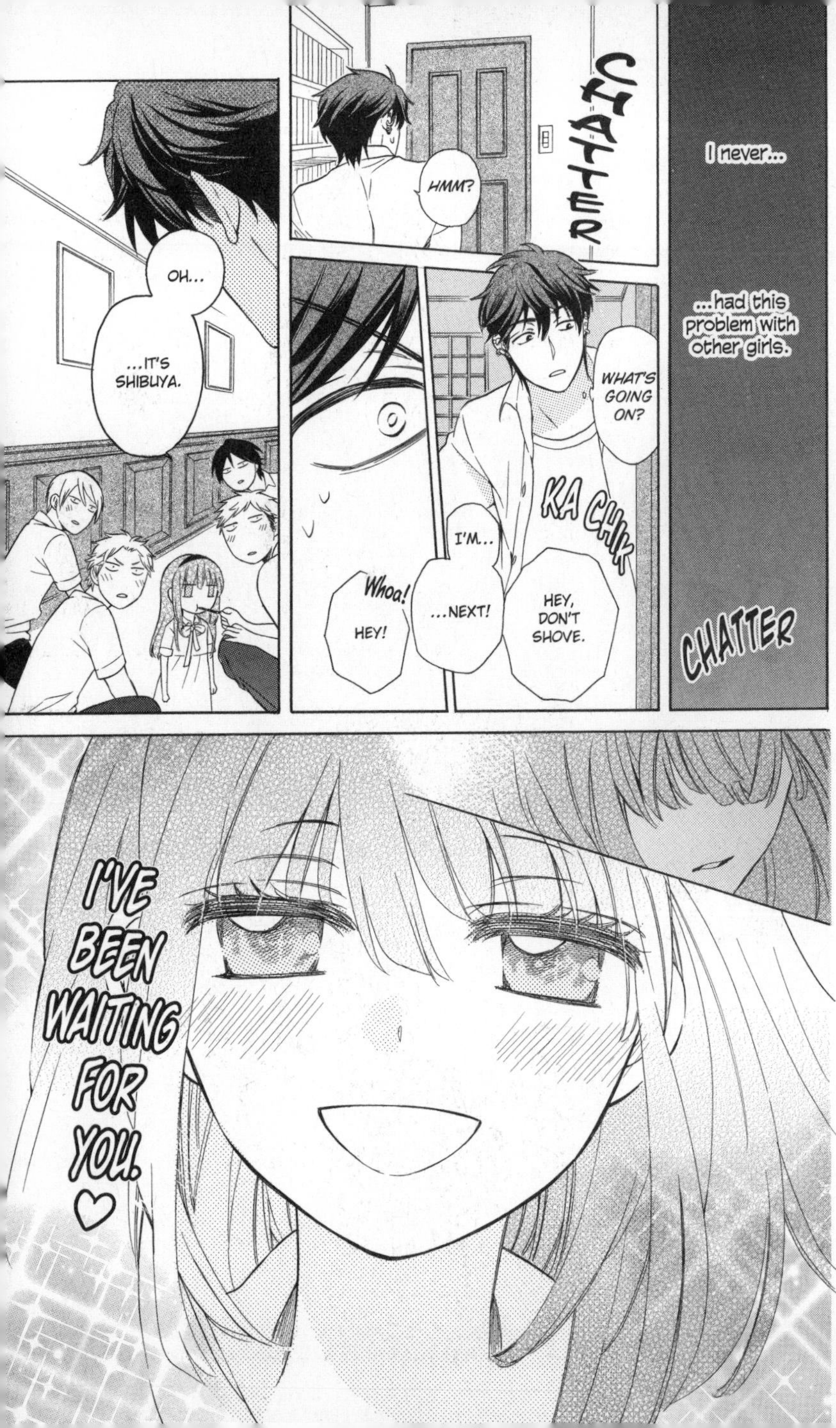
I never...
...had this problem with other girls.
CHATTER
CHATTER
HMM?
WHAT'S GOING ON?
KA CHIK
HEY, DON'T SHOVE.
I'M...
...NEXT!
Whoa!
HEY!
OH...
...IT'S SHIBUYA.
I'VE BEEN WAITING FOR YOU. ♡

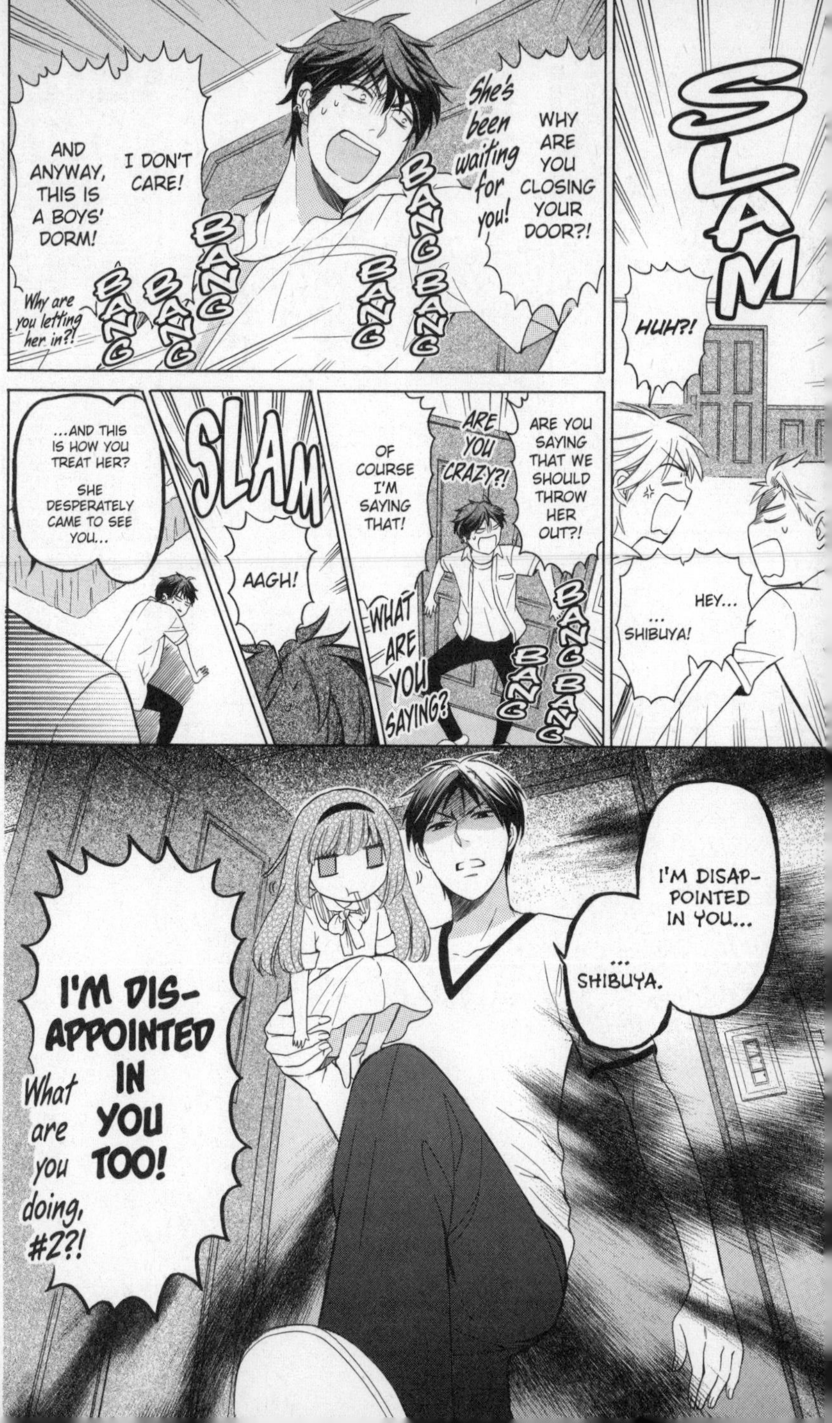
SLAM
HUH?!
HEY...
... SHIBUYA!
WHY ARE YOU CLOSING YOUR DOOR?!
She's been waiting for you!
BANG BANG
BANG
I DON'T CARE!
AND ANYWAY, THIS IS A BOYS' DORM!
BANG
BANG
BANG
Why are you letting her in?!
ARE YOU SAYING THAT WE SHOULD THROW HER OUT?!
ARE YOU CRAZY?!
BANG BANG
BANG
WHAT ARE YOU SAYING?
OF COURSE I'M SAYING THAT!
SLAM
AAGH!
...AND THIS IS HOW YOU TREAT HER?
SHE DESPERATELY CAME TO SEE YOU...
I'M DISAP-POINTED IN YOU...
... SHIBUYA.
I'M DIS-APPOINTED IN YOU TOO!
What are you doing, #2?!

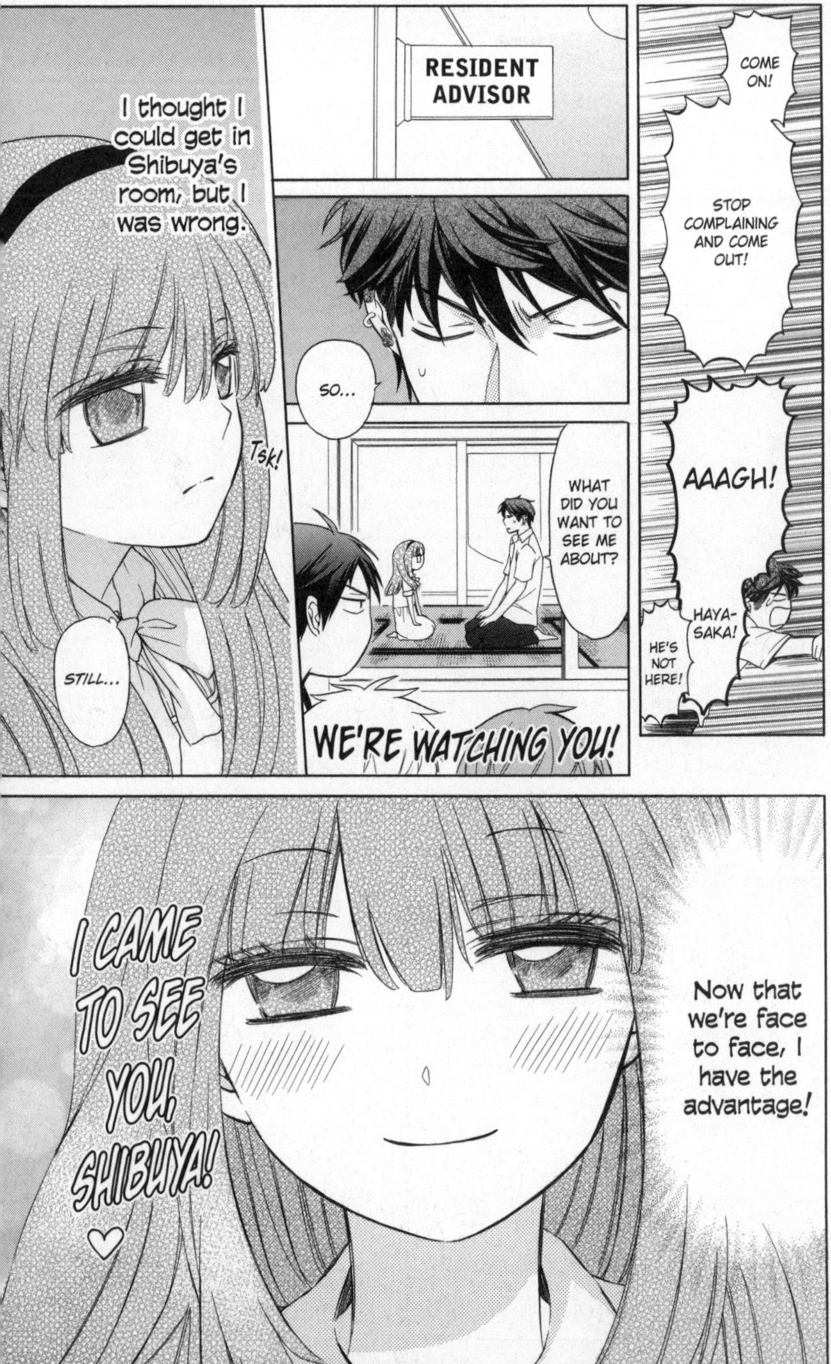
COME ON!
STOP COMPLAINING AND COME OUT!
AAAGH!
HAYA-SAKA!
HE'S NOT HERE!
RESIDENT ADVISOR
SO...
WHAT DID YOU WANT TO SEE ME ABOUT?
WE'RE WATCHING YOU!
I thought I could get in Shibuya's room, but I was wrong.
Tsk!
STILL...
Now that we're face to face, I have the advantage!
I CAME TO SEE YOU, SHIBUYA! ♥

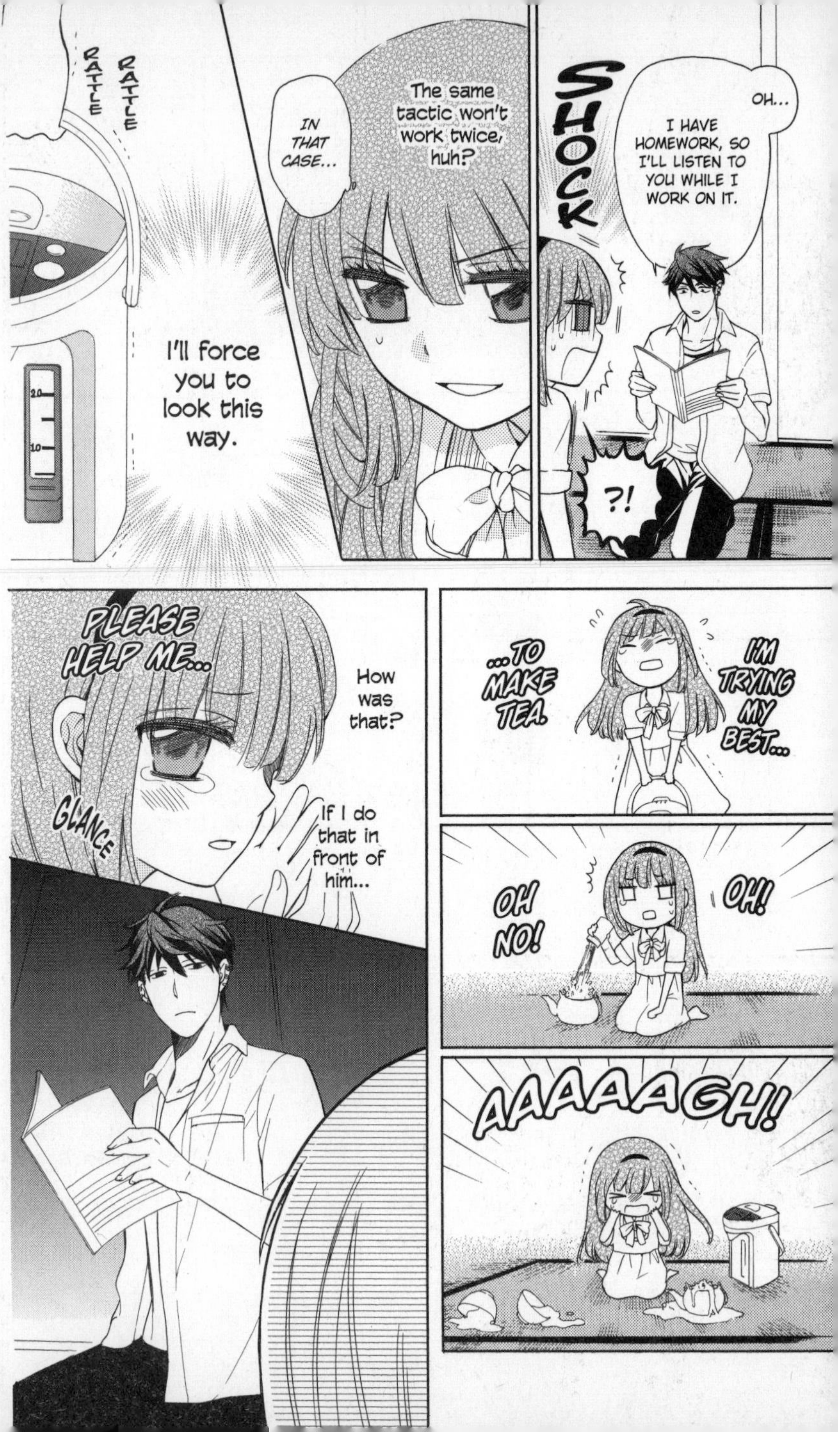
OH...
I HAVE HOMEWORK, SO I'LL LISTEN TO YOU WHILE I WORK ON IT.
SHOCK
?!
The same tactic won't work twice, huh?
IN THAT CASE...
I'll force you to look this way.
RATTLE RATTLE
I'M TRYING MY BEST...
...TO MAKE TEA.
OH!
OH NO!
AAAAAGH!
PLEASE HELP ME...
How was that?
GLANCE
If I do that in front of him...

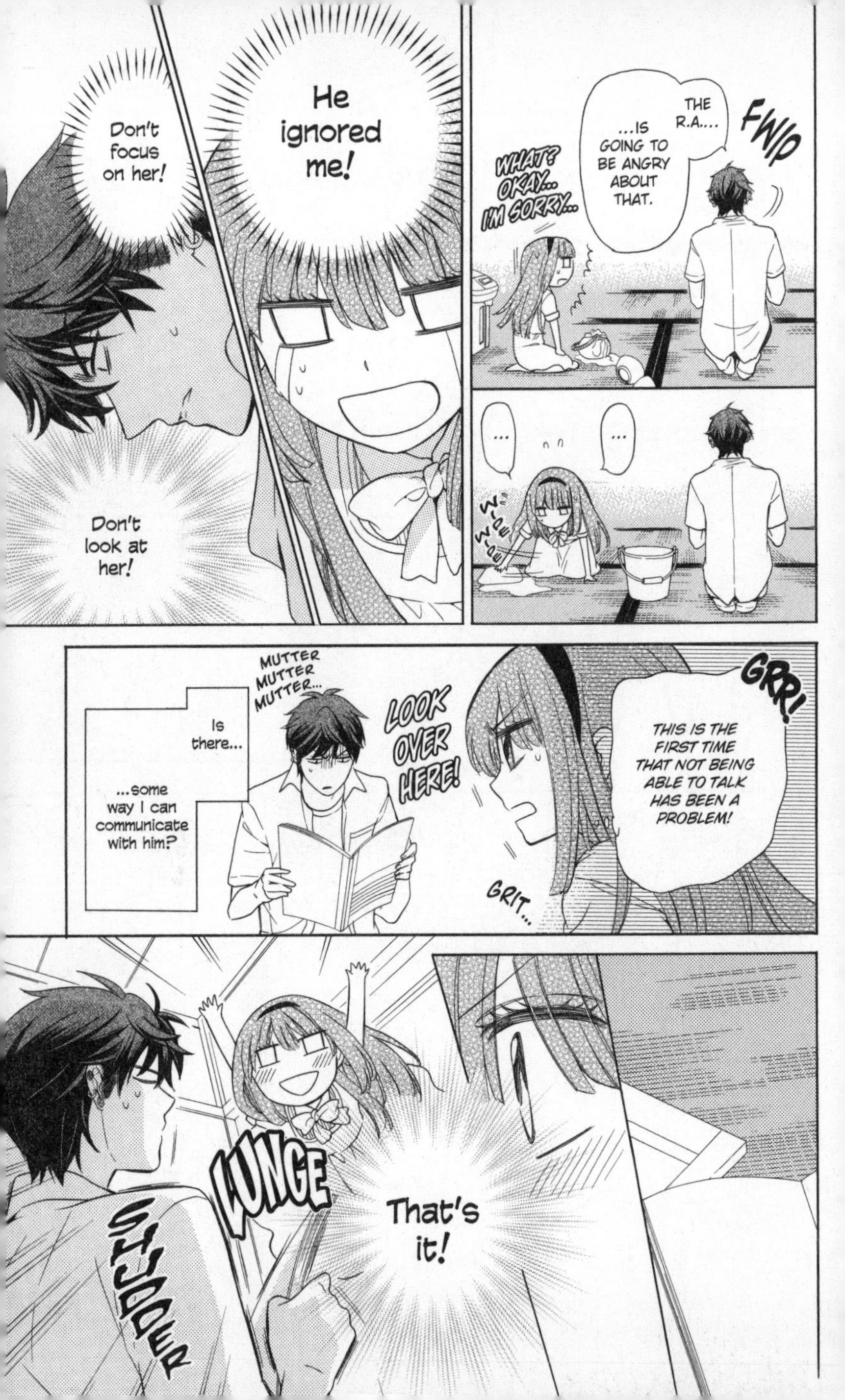
FWIP
THE R.A....
...IS GOING TO BE ANGRY ABOUT THAT.
WHAT? OKAY... I'M SORRY...
...
...
W-DE W-DE
He ignored me!
Don't focus on her!
Don't look at her!
GRRR!
THIS IS THE FIRST TIME THAT NOT BEING ABLE TO TALK HAS BEEN A PROBLEM!
GRIT...
LOOK OVER HERE!
MUTTER MUTTER MUTTER...
Is there...
...some way I can communicate with him?
That's it!
LUNGE
SHJDDER

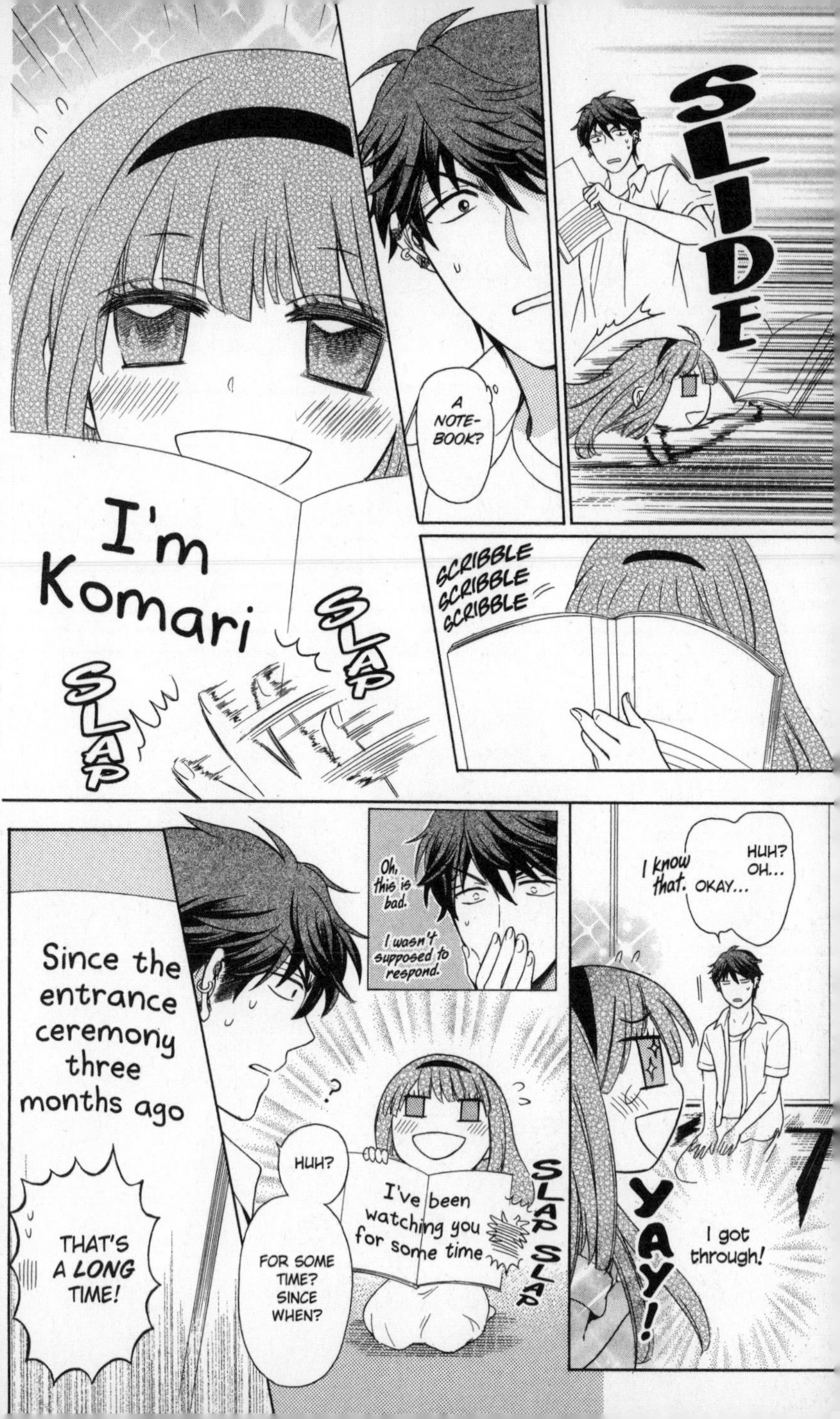
SLIDE
A NOTE-BOOK?
SCRIBBLE SCRIBBLE SCRIBBLE
I'm Komari
SLAP
SLAP
HUH? OH... OKAY...
I know that.
YAY!
I got through!
Oh, this is bad.
I wasn't supposed to respond.
SLAP SLAP
I've been watching you for some time
HUH?
FOR SOME TIME? SINCE WHEN?
Since the entrance ceremony three months ago
THAT'S A LONG TIME!

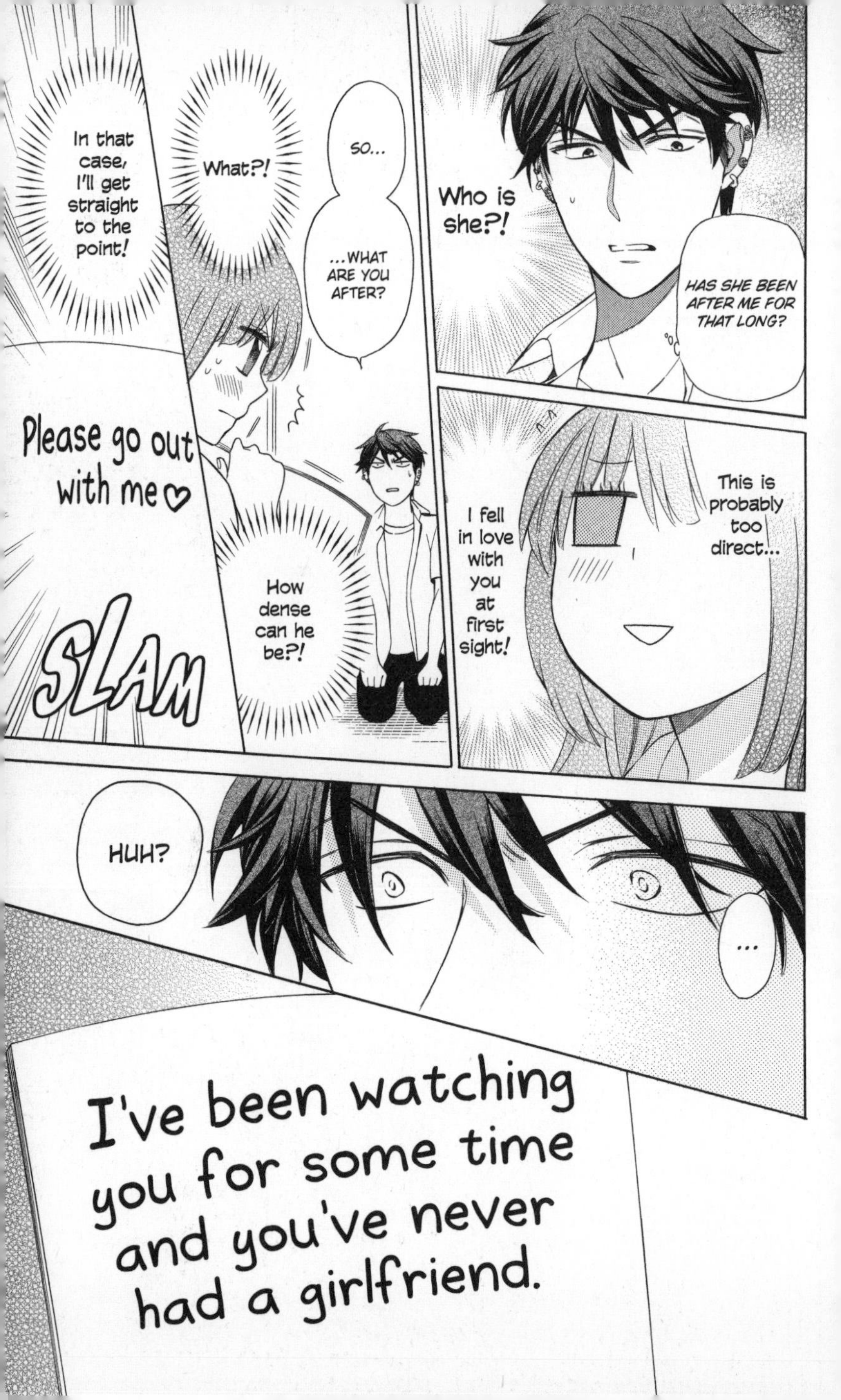
HAS SHE BEEN AFTER ME FOR THAT LONG?
Who is she?!
SO...
...WHAT ARE YOU AFTER?
What?!
In that case, I'll get straight to the point!
This is probably too direct...
I fell in love with you at first sight!
How dense can he be?!
Please go out with me ♡
SLAM
...
HUH?
I've been watching you for some time and you've never had a girlfriend.

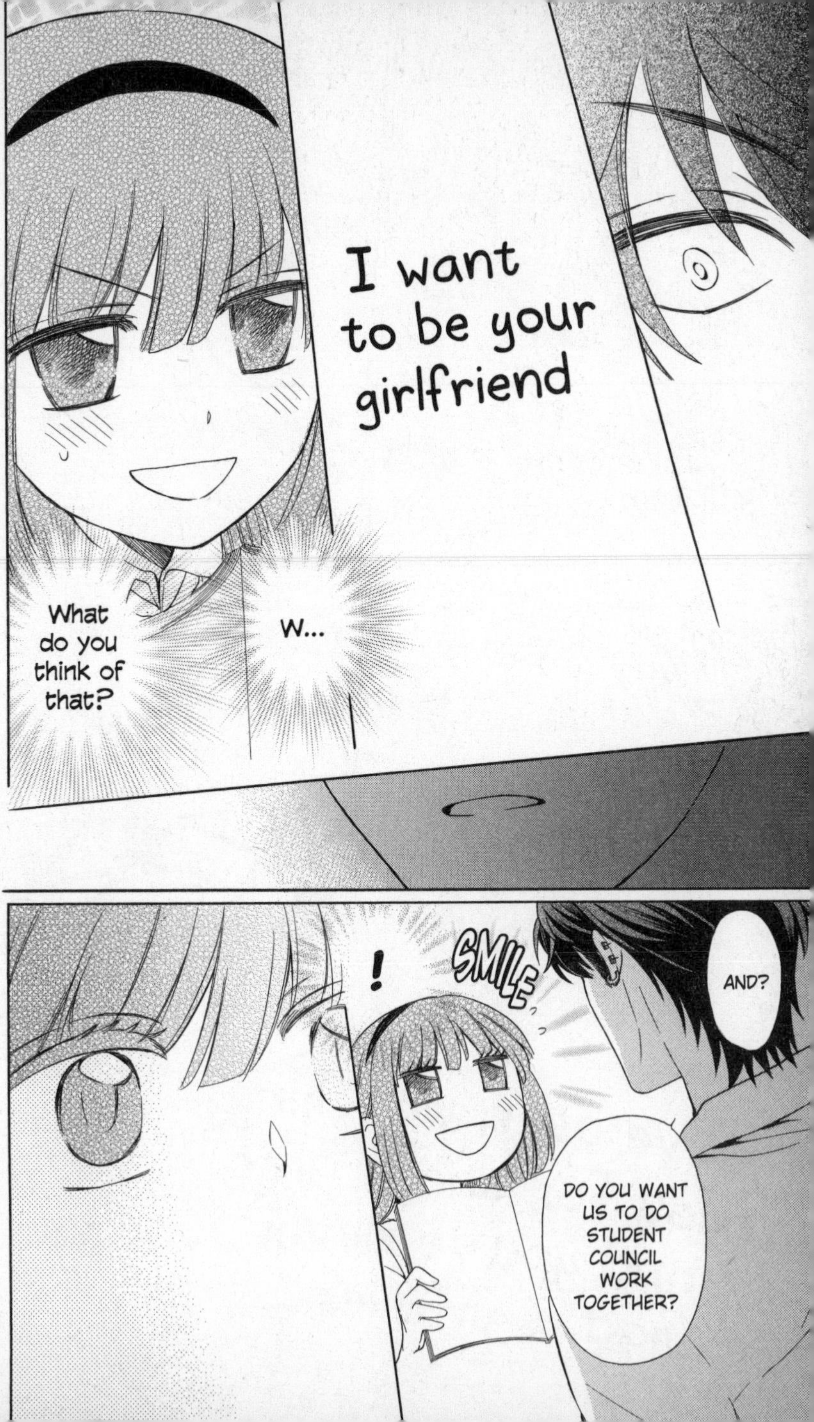
I want to be your girlfriend
What do you think of that?
W...
AND?
SMILE
!
DO YOU WANT US TO DO STUDENT COUNCIL WORK TOGETHER?

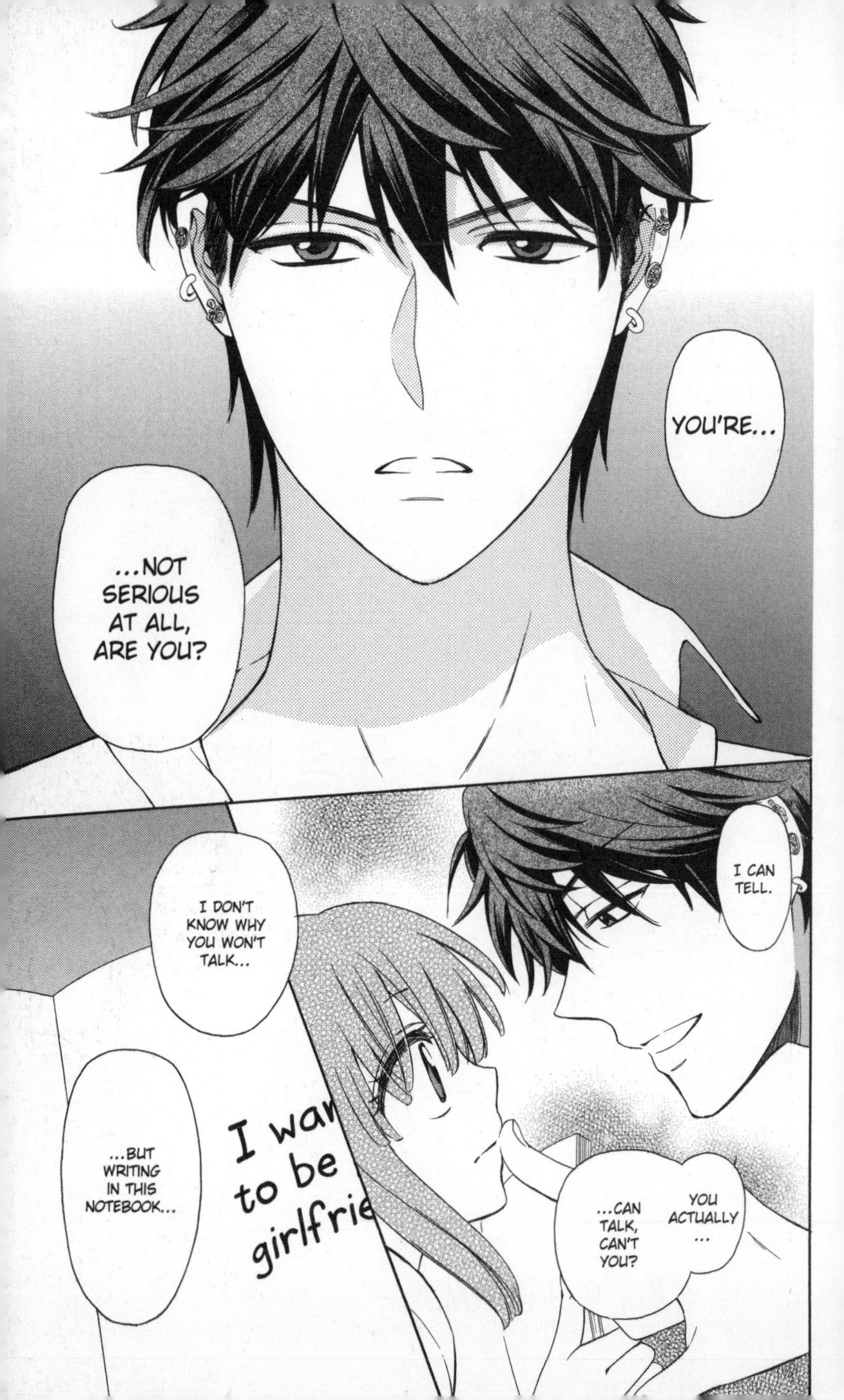
YOU'RE...
...NOT SERIOUS AT ALL, ARE YOU?
I CAN TELL.
I DON'T KNOW WHY YOU WON'T TALK...
...BUT WRITING IN THIS NOTEBOOK...
YOU ACTUALLY ...
...CAN TALK, CAN'T YOU?
I wan
to be
girlfrie

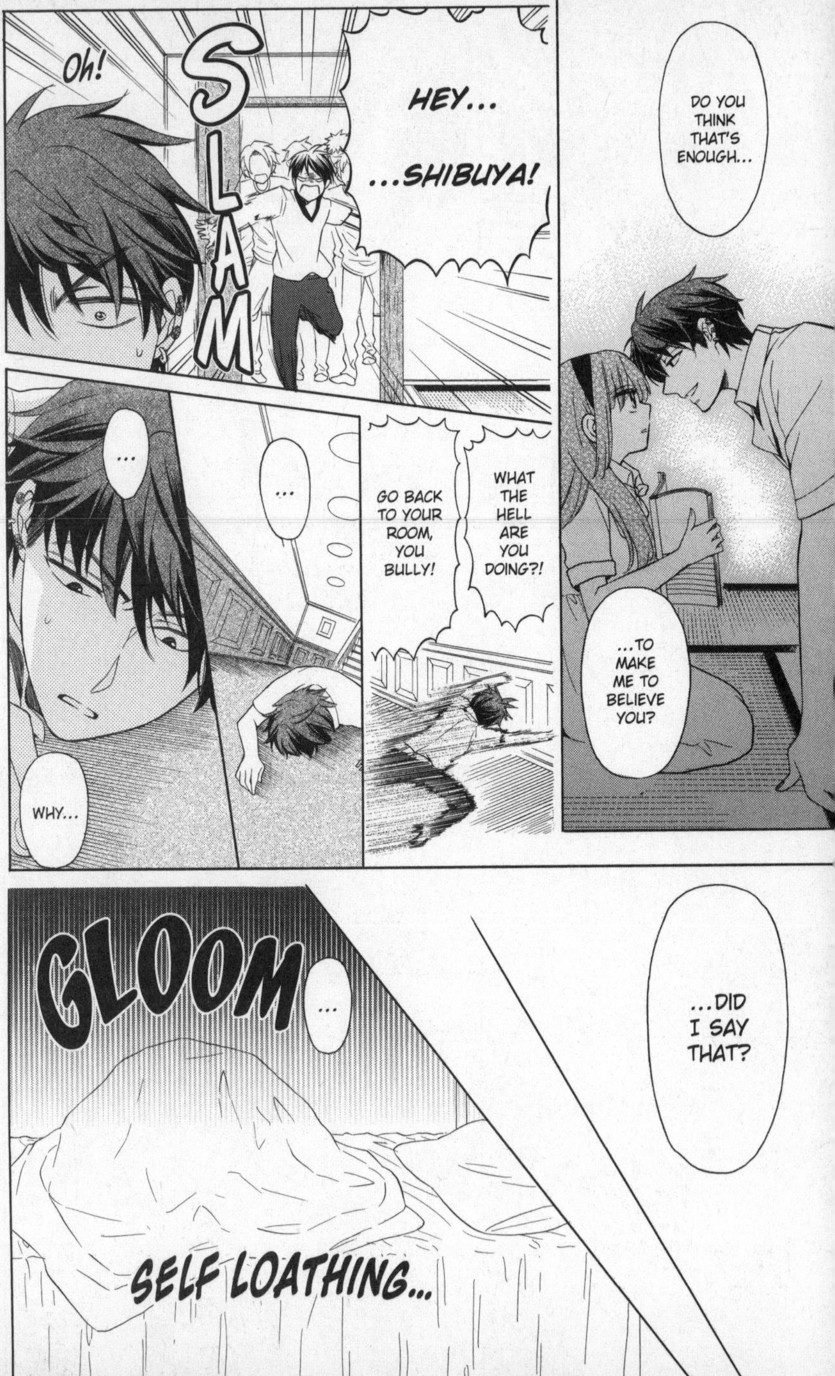
DO YOU THINK THAT'S ENOUGH...
...TO MAKE ME TO BELIEVE YOU?
HEY...
...SHIBUYA!
SLAM
Oh!
WHAT THE HELL ARE YOU DOING?!
GO BACK TO YOUR ROOM, YOU BULLY!
...
...
WHY...
...DID I SAY THAT?
...
GLOOM
SELF LOATHING...

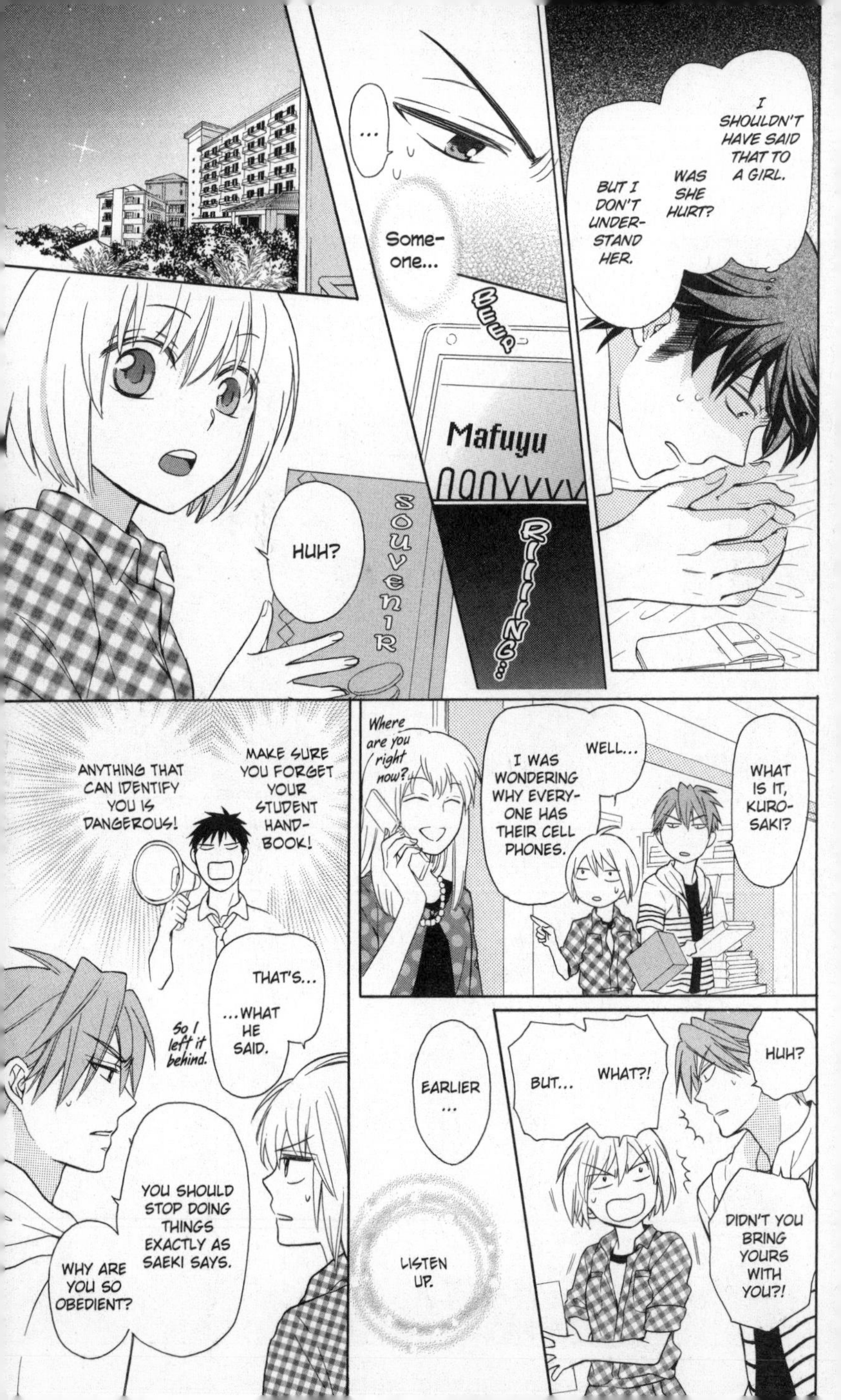

I SHOULDN'T HAVE SAID THAT TO A GIRL.
WAS SHE HURT?
BUT I DON'T UNDER-STAND HER.
...
Some-one...
Bwup
Mafuyu
RIIIING...
SOUVENIR
HUH?
WHAT IS IT, KURO-SAKI?
WELL...
I WAS WONDERING WHY EVERY-ONE HAS THEIR CELL PHONES.
Where are you right now?
HUH?
DIDN'T YOU BRING YOURS WITH YOU?!
WHAT?!
BUT...
EARLIER ...
LISTEN UP.
MAKE SURE YOU FORGET YOUR STUDENT HAND-BOOK!
ANYTHING THAT CAN IDENTIFY YOU IS DANGEROUS!
THAT'S...
...WHAT HE SAID.
So I left it behind.
YOU SHOULD STOP DOING THINGS EXACTLY AS SAEKI SAYS.
WHY ARE YOU SO OBEDIENT?

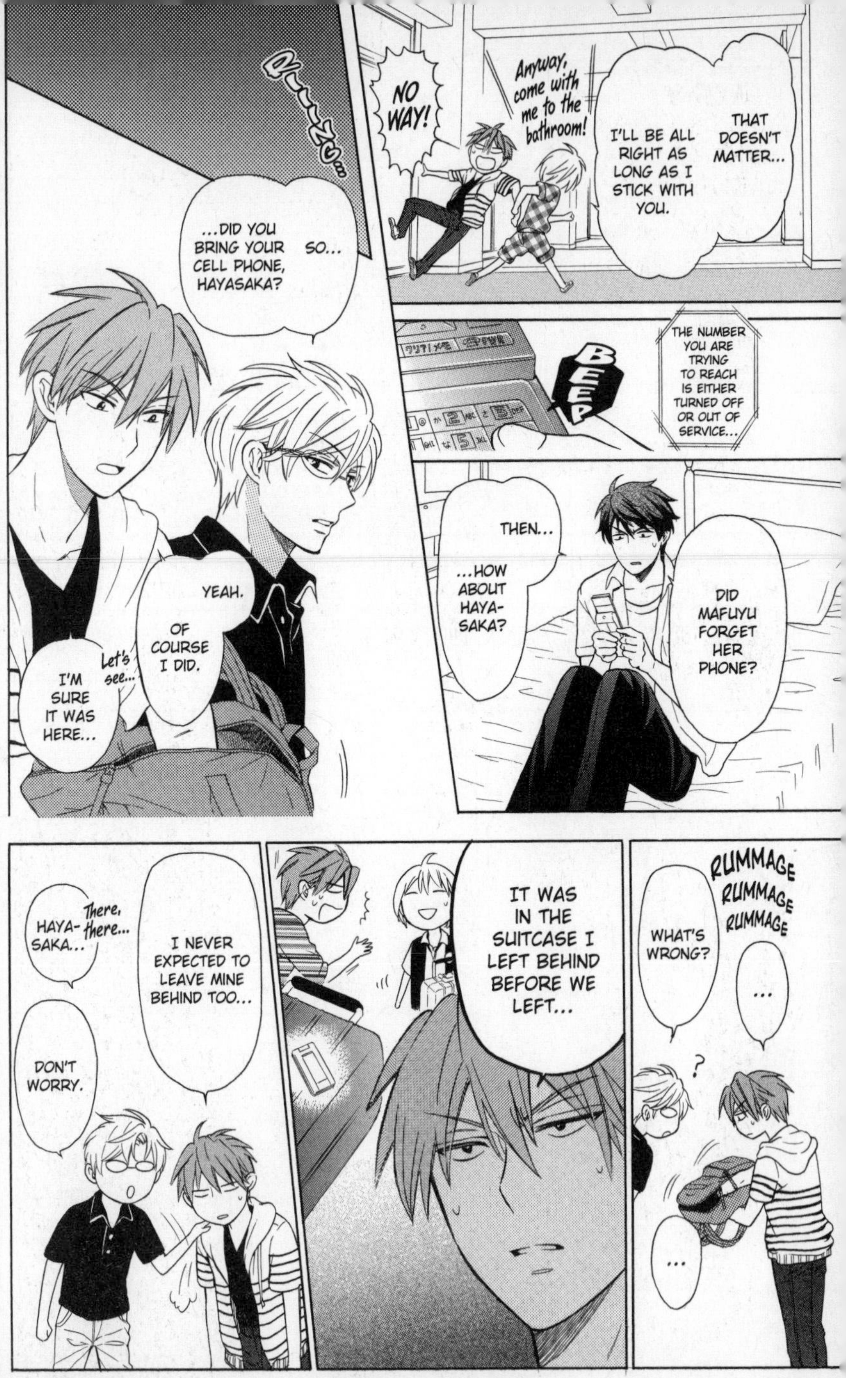
THAT DOESN'T MATTER...
I'LL BE ALL RIGHT AS LONG AS I STICK WITH YOU.
Anyway, come with me to the bathroom!
NO WAY!
THE NUMBER YOU ARE TRYING TO REACH IS EITHER TURNED OFF OR OUT OF SERVICE...
BEEP
DID MAFUYU FORGET HER PHONE?
THEN...
...HOW ABOUT HAYA-SAKA?
SO...
...DID YOU BRING YOUR CELL PHONE, HAYASAKA?
YEAH.
OF COURSE I DID.
Let's see...
I'M SURE IT WAS HERE...
RUMMAGE RUMMAGE RUMMAGE
...
WHAT'S WRONG?
?
...
IT WAS IN THE SUITCASE I LEFT BEHIND BEFORE WE LEFT...
I NEVER EXPECTED TO LEAVE MINE BEHIND TOO...
There, there...
HAYA-SAKA...
DON'T WORRY.

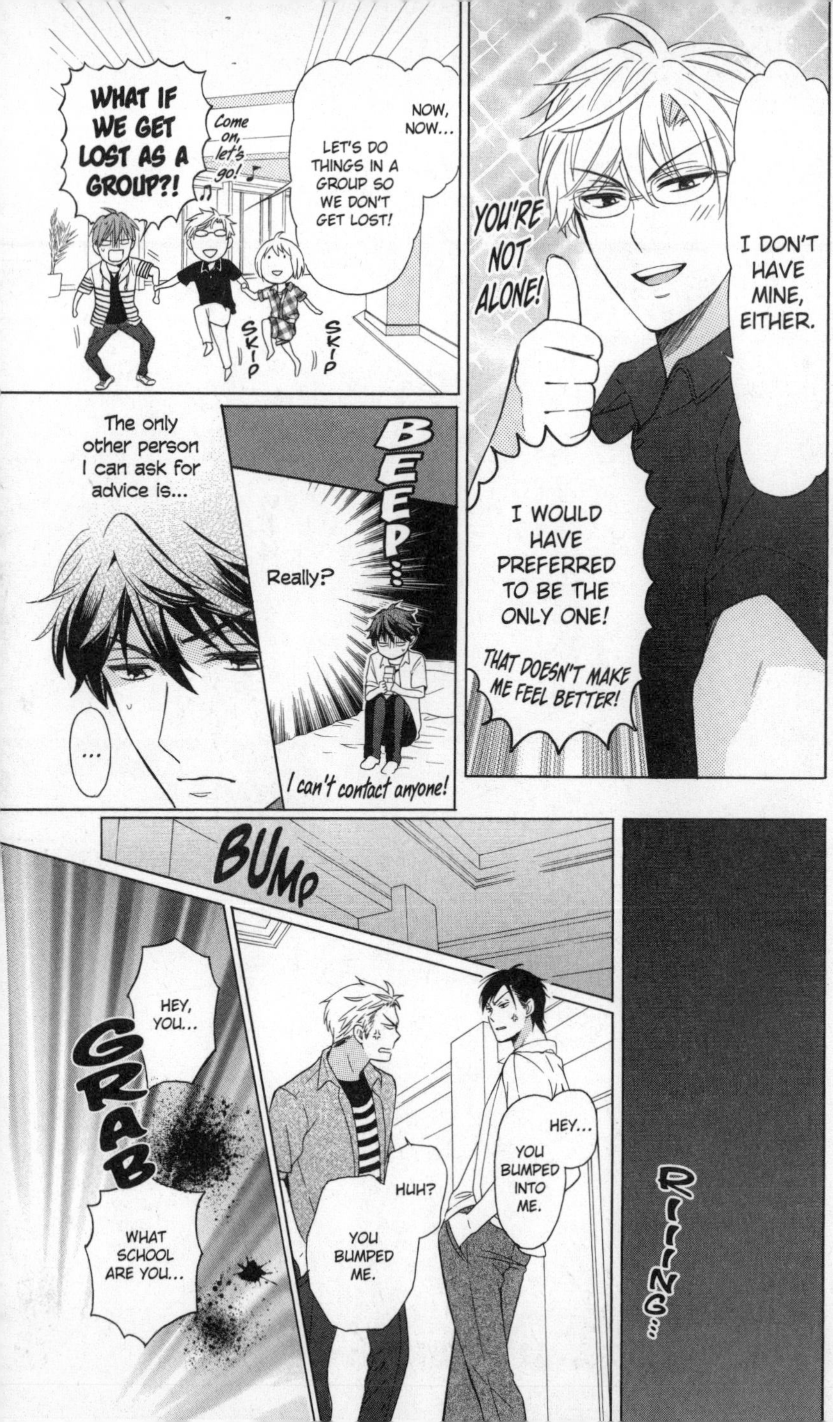
YOU'RE NOT ALONE!
I DON'T HAVE MINE, EITHER.
I WOULD HAVE PREFERRED TO BE THE ONLY ONE!
THAT DOESN'T MAKE ME FEEL BETTER!
NOW, NOW...
LET'S DO THINGS IN A GROUP SO WE DON'T GET LOST!
Come on, let's go! ♪
WHAT IF WE GET LOST AS A GROUP?!
SKIP
SKIP
BEEP...
Really?
I can't contact anyone!
The only other person I can ask for advice is...
...
RIIING...
BUMP
HEY... YOU BUMPED INTO ME.
HUH?
YOU BUMPED ME.
HEY, YOU...
GRAB
WHAT SCHOOL ARE YOU...

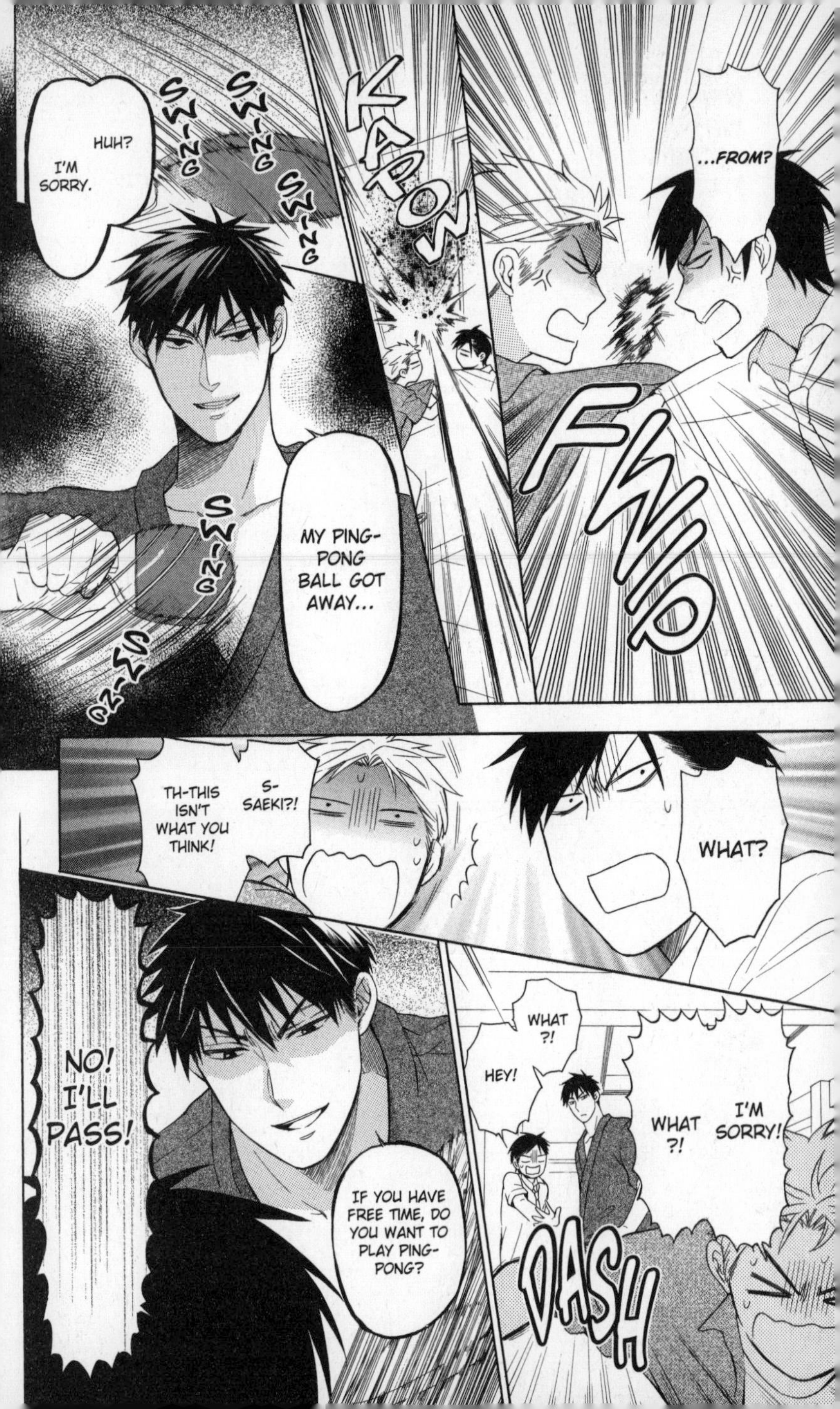
...FROM?
FWIP
KAPOW
HUH?
I'M SORRY.
SWING SWING SWING
SWING
MY PING-PONG BALL GOT AWAY...
SWING
WHAT?
S-SAEKI?!
TH-THIS ISN'T WHAT YOU THINK!
I'M SORRY!
WHAT ?!
HEY!
WHAT ?!
DASH
IF YOU HAVE FREE TIME, DO YOU WANT TO PLAY PING-PONG?
NO! I'LL PASS!

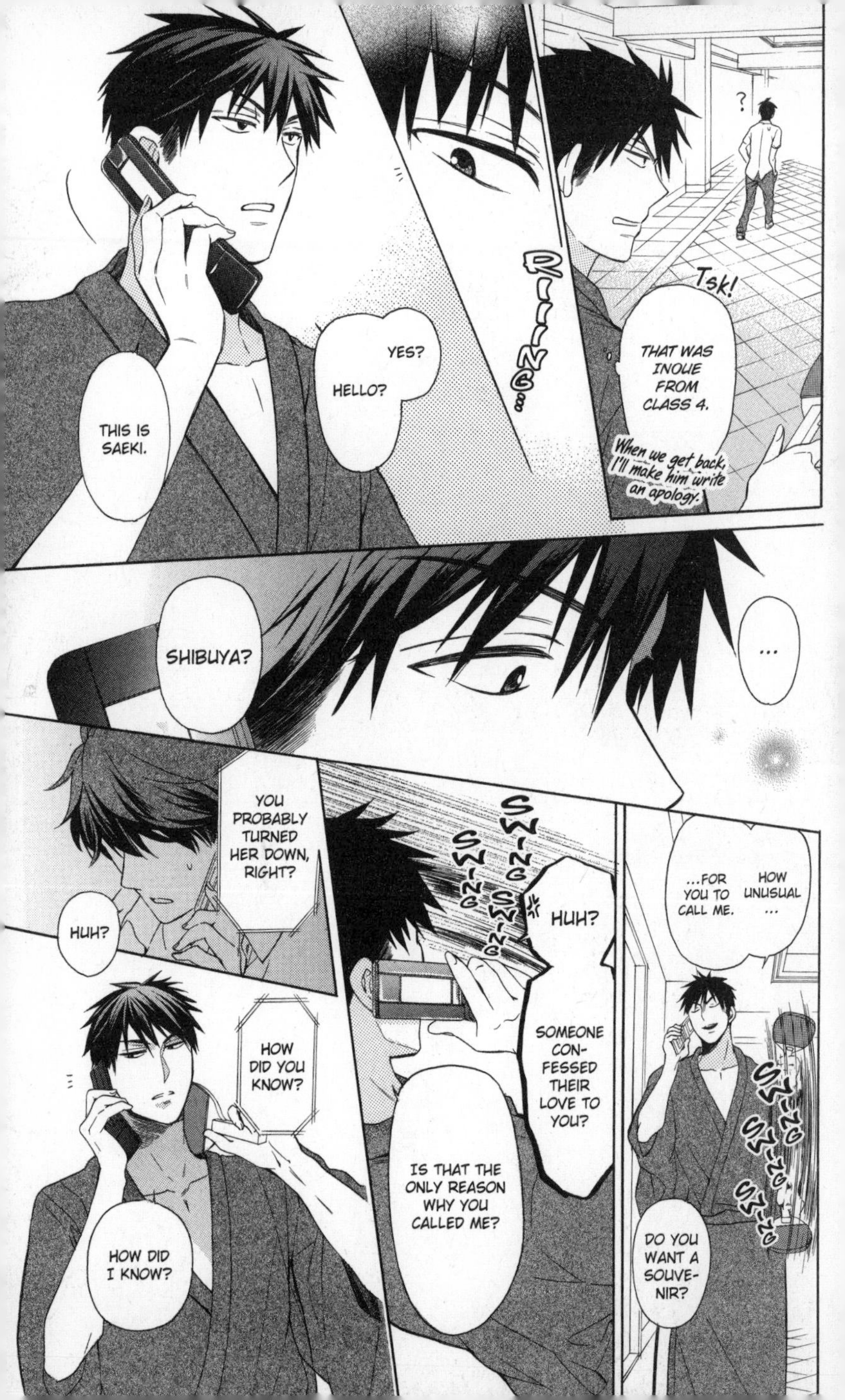
Tsk!
THAT WAS INOUE FROM CLASS 4.
When we get back, I'll make him write an apology.
RIIING...
YES?
HELLO?
THIS IS SAEKI.
...
SHIBUYA?
HOW UNUSUAL...
...FOR YOU TO CALL ME.
DO YOU WANT A SOUVE-NIR?
SZZ-ZZ SZZ-ZZ SZZ-ZZ
SWING SWING SWING
HUH?
SOMEONE CON-FESSED THEIR LOVE TO YOU?
IS THAT THE ONLY REASON WHY YOU CALLED ME?
YOU PROBABLY TURNED HER DOWN, RIGHT?
HUH?
HOW DID YOU KNOW?
HOW DID I KNOW?

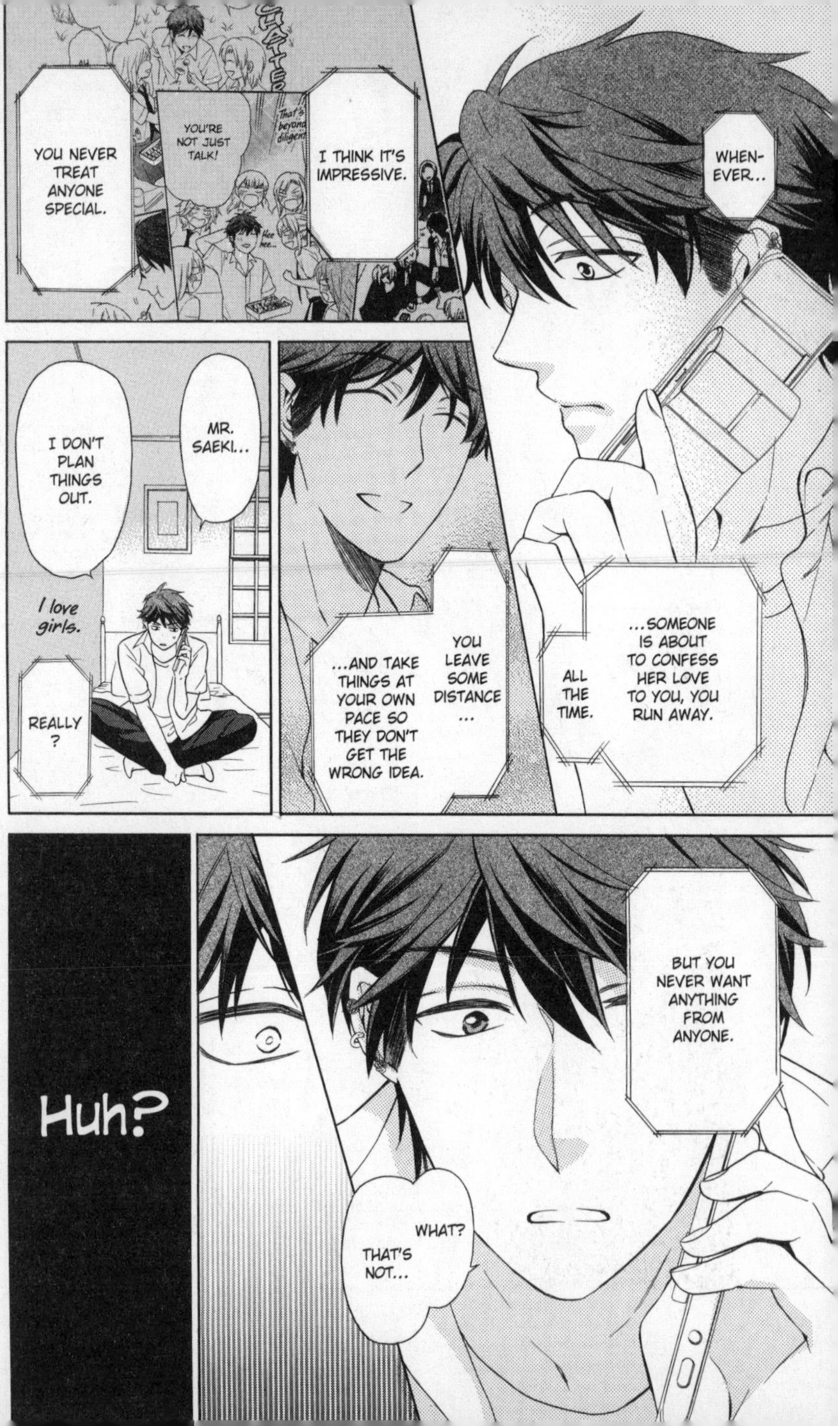
WHEN-EVER...
...SOMEONE IS ABOUT TO CONFESS HER LOVE TO YOU, YOU RUN AWAY.
ALL THE TIME.
I THINK IT'S IMPRESSIVE.
That's beyond diligent
YOU'RE NOT JUST TALK!
Hee hee...
YOU NEVER TREAT ANYONE SPECIAL.
YOU LEAVE SOME DISTANCE...
...AND TAKE THINGS AT YOUR OWN PACE SO THEY DON'T GET THE WRONG IDEA.
MR. SAEKI...
I DON'T PLAN THINGS OUT.
I love girls.
REALLY?
BUT YOU NEVER WANT ANYTHING FROM ANYONE.
WHAT? THAT'S NOT...
Huh?

Chapter 87

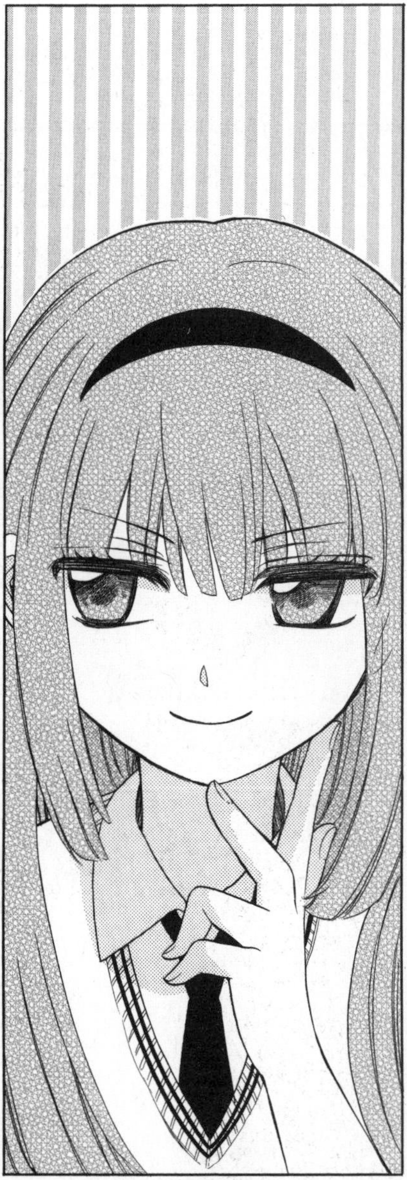
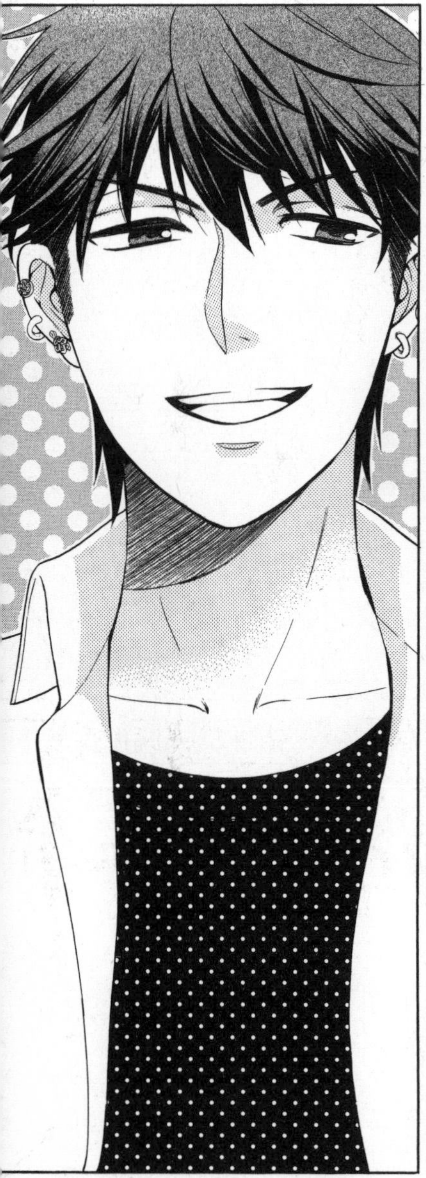

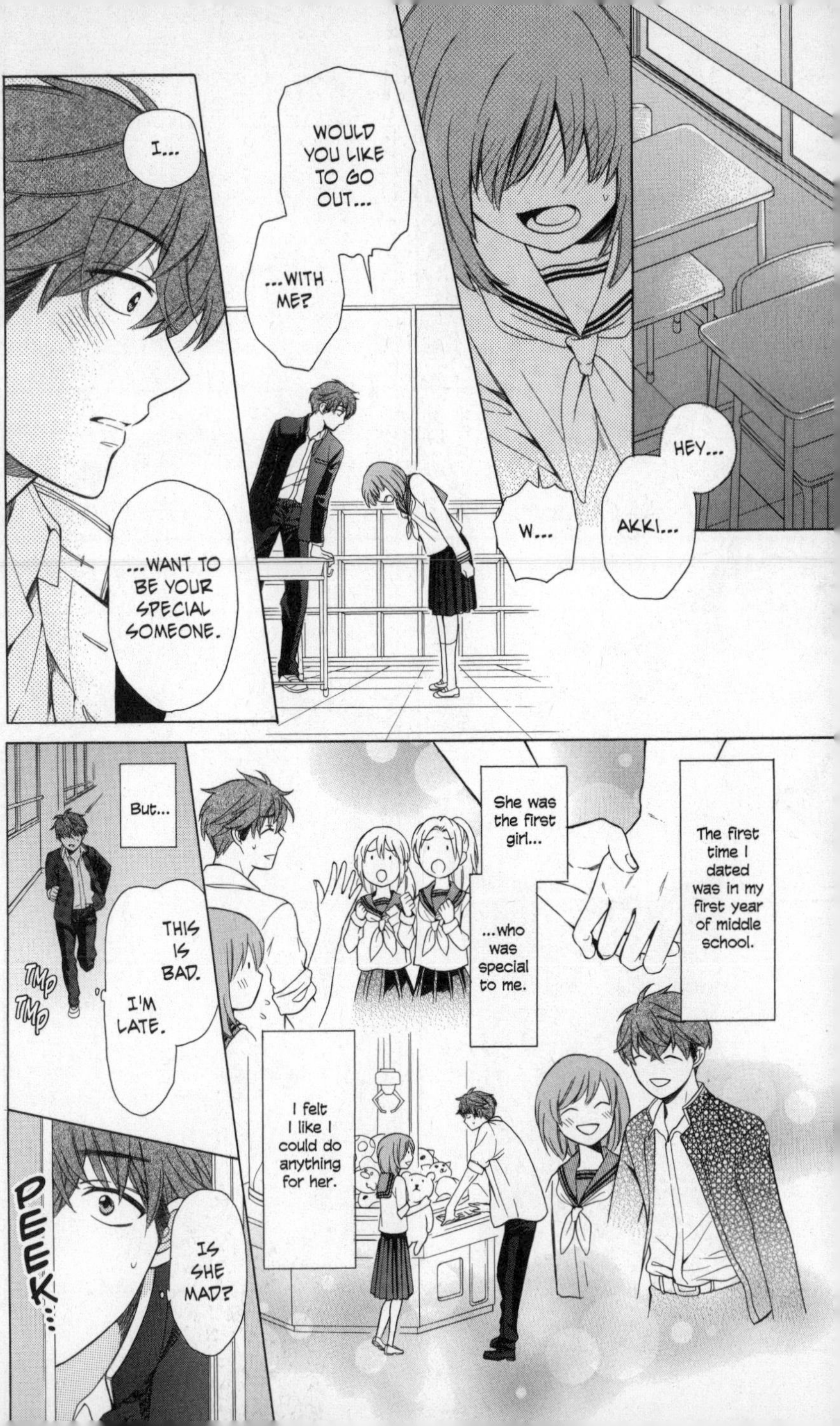
HEY...
AKKI...
W...
WOULD YOU LIKE TO GO OUT...
...WITH ME?
I...
...WANT TO BE YOUR SPECIAL SOMEONE.
The first time I dated was in my first year of middle school.
She was the first girl...
...who was special to me.
I felt I like I could do anything for her.
But...
THIS IS BAD.
I'M LATE.
TMP TMP
PEEK...
IS SHE MAD?

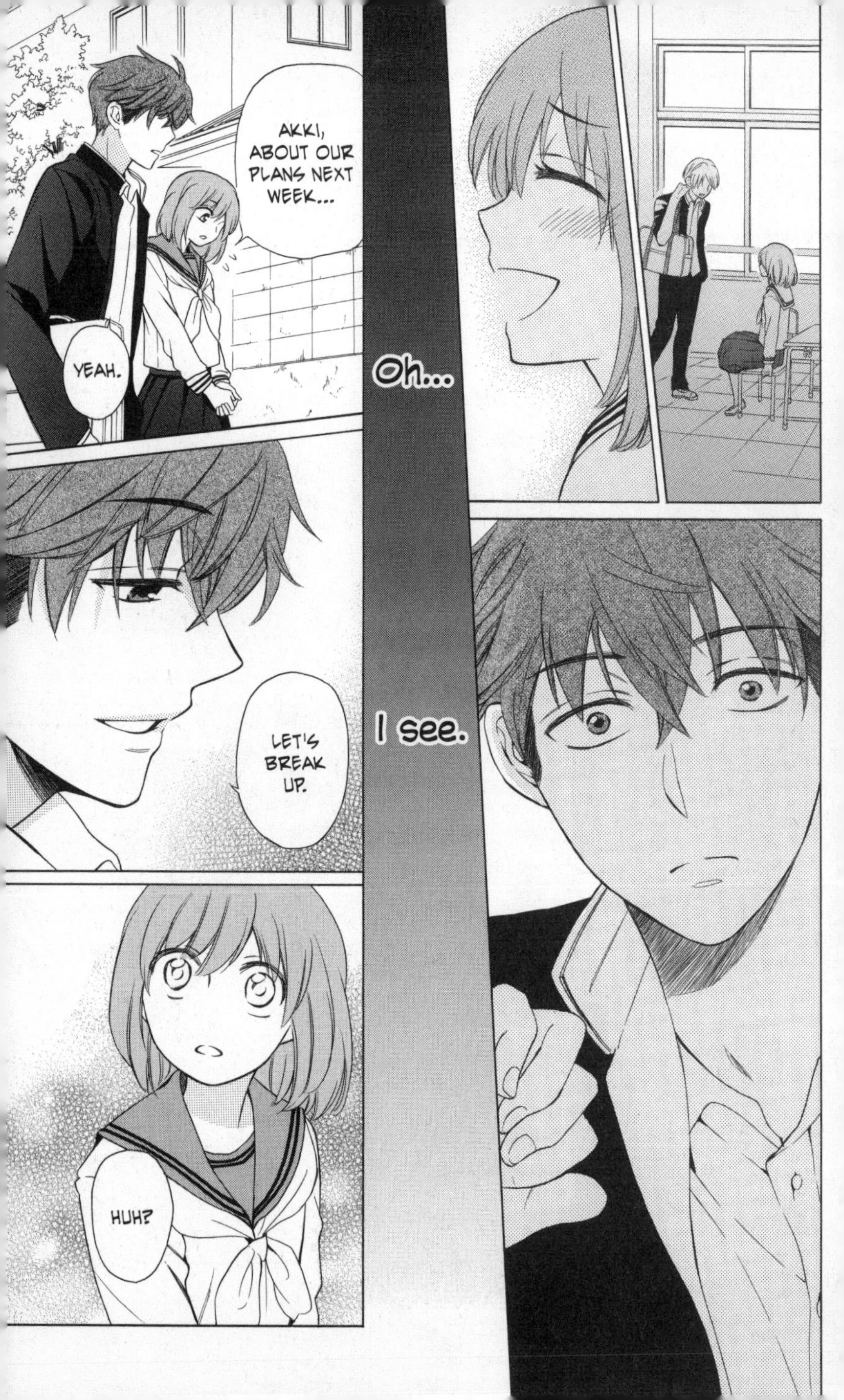
Oh...
I see.
AKKI, ABOUT OUR PLANS NEXT WEEK...
YEAH.
LET'S BREAK UP.
HUH?

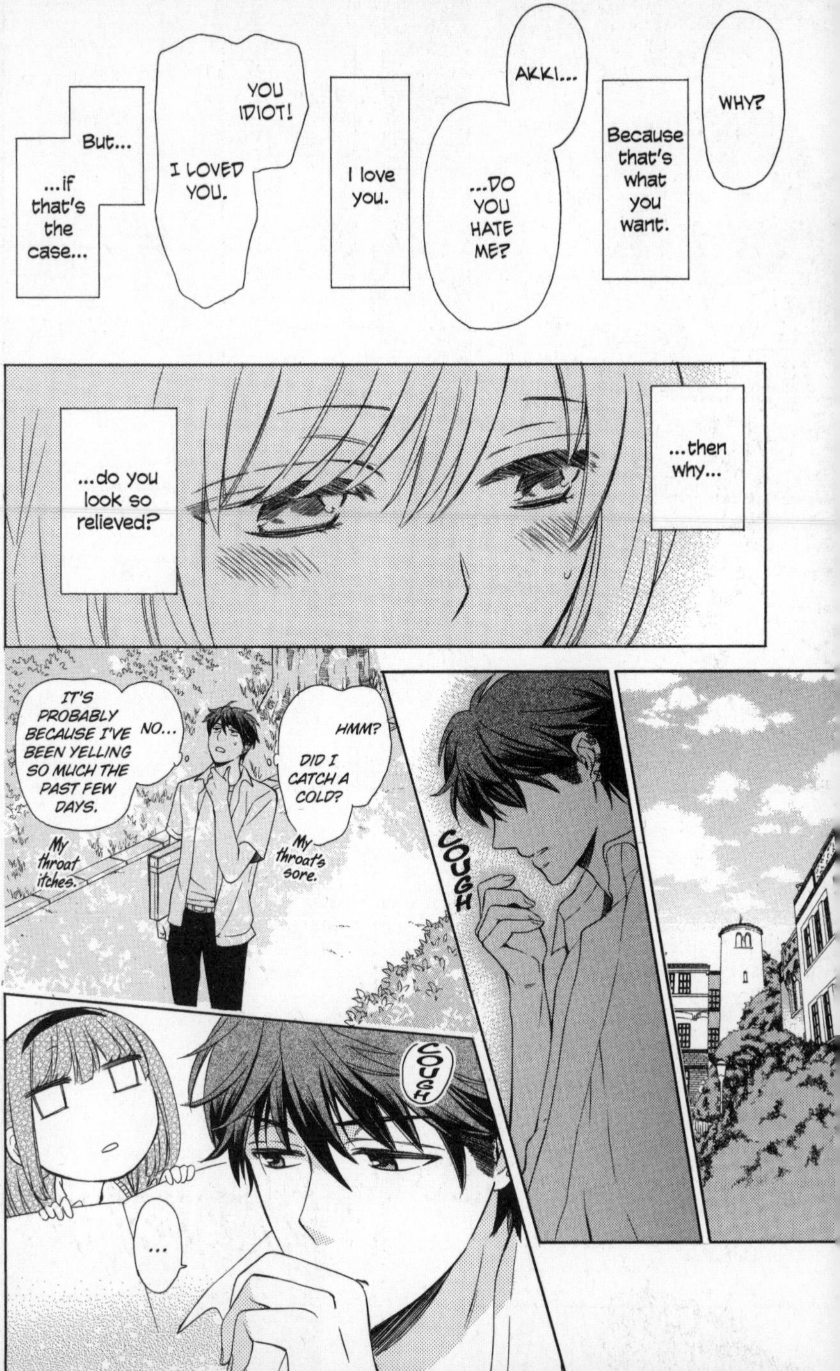
WHY?
Because that's what you want.
AKKI...
...DO YOU HATE ME?
I love you.
YOU IDIOT!
I LOVED YOU.
But...
...if that's the case...
...then why...
...do you look so relieved?
COUGH
HMM?
DID I CATCH A COLD?
My throat's sore.
NO...
IT'S PROBABLY BECAUSE I'VE BEEN YELLING SO MUCH THE PAST FEW DAYS.
My throat itches.
COUGH
...

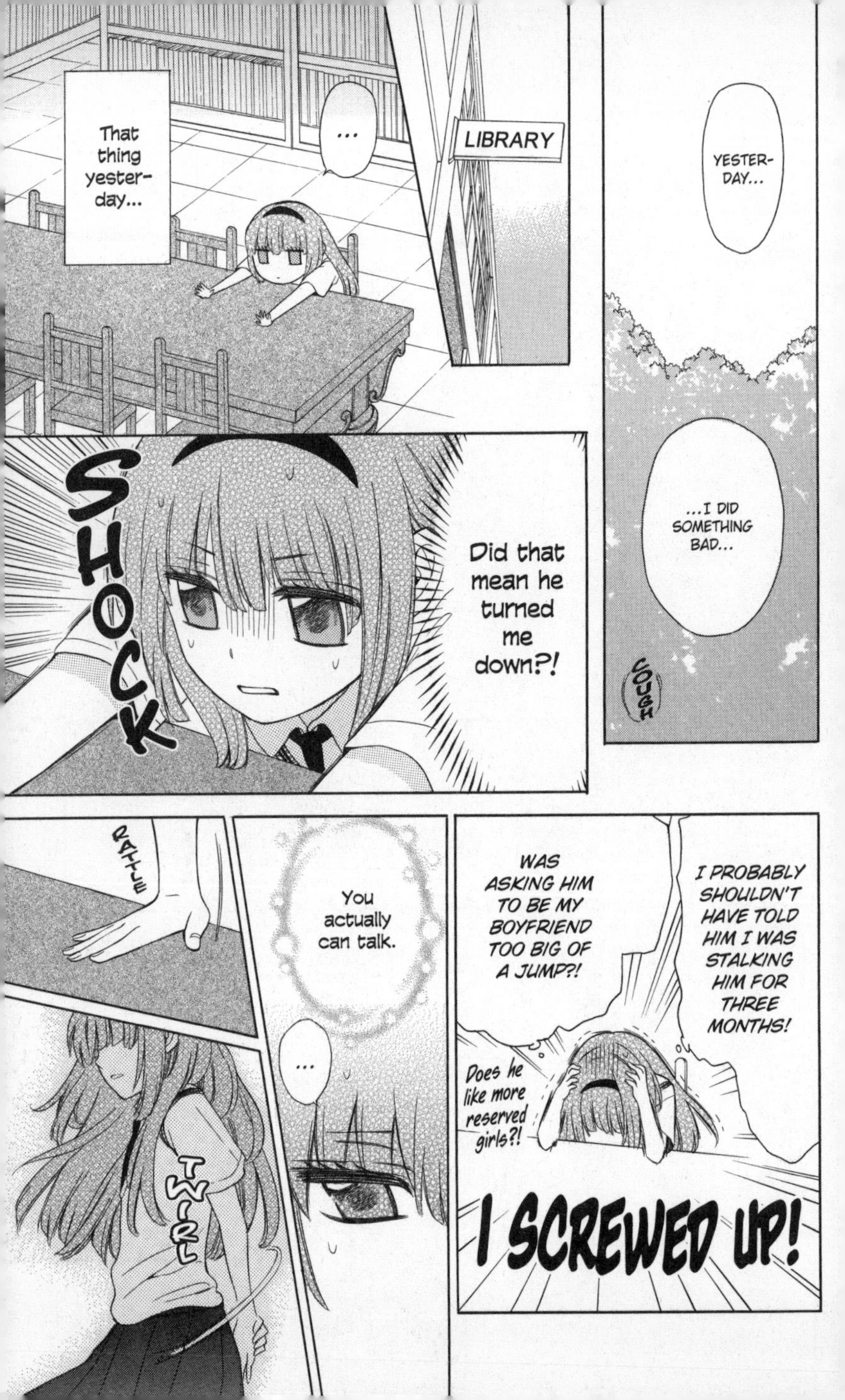
YESTER-DAY...
...I DID SOMETHING BAD...
COUGH
LIBRARY
...
That thing yester-day...
Did that mean he turned me down?!
SHOCK
I PROBABLY SHOULDN'T HAVE TOLD HIM I WAS STALKING HIM FOR THREE MONTHS!
WAS ASKING HIM TO BE MY BOYFRIEND TOO BIG OF A JUMP?!
Does he like more reserved girls?!
I SCREWED UP!
You actually can talk.
...
RATTLE
TWIRL

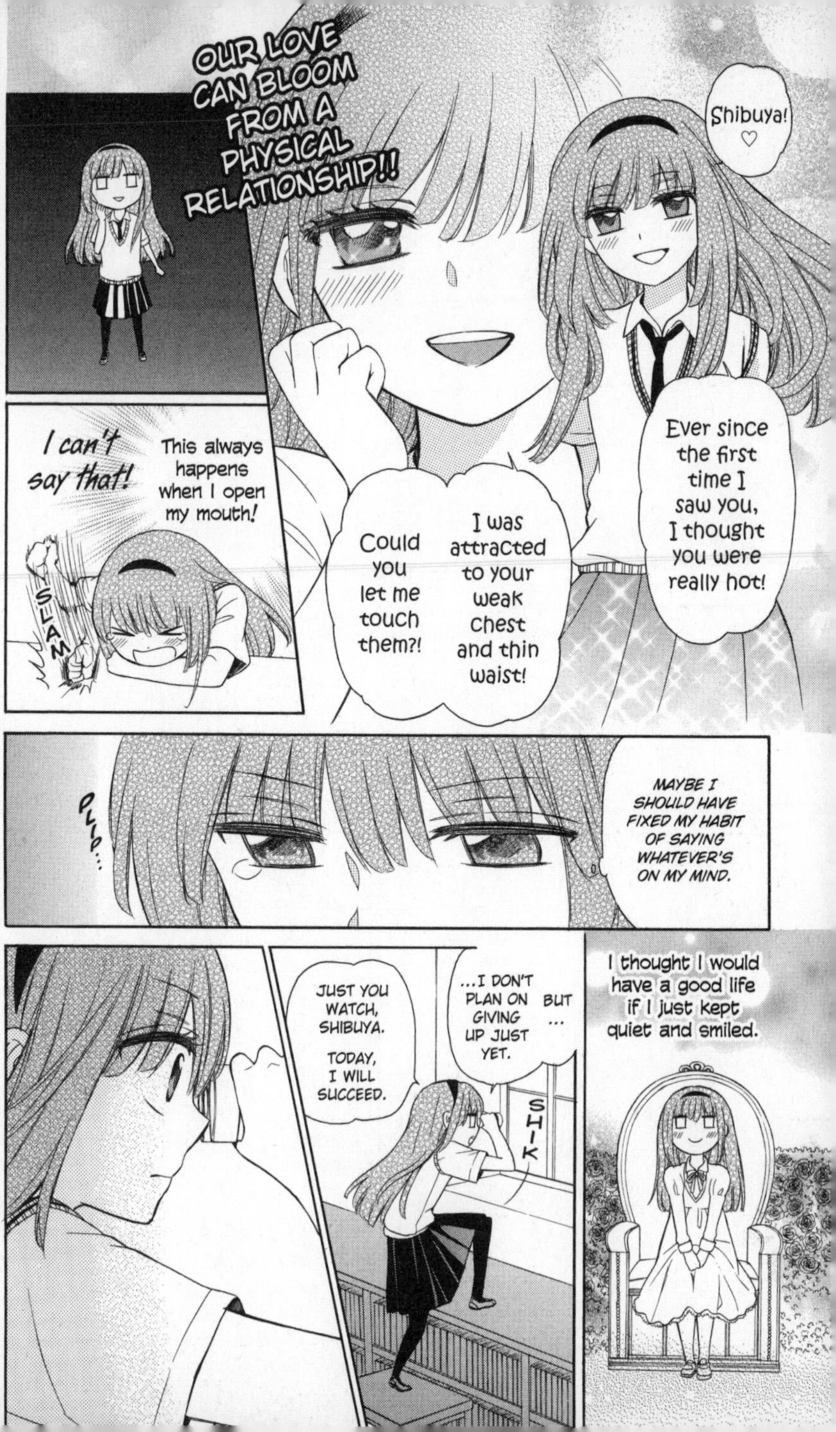
Shibuya! ♡
Ever since the first time I saw you, I thought you were really hot!
I was attracted to your weak chest and thin waist!
Could you let me touch them?!
OUR LOVE CAN BLOOM FROM A PHYSICAL RELATIONSHIP!!
This always happens when I open my mouth!
I can't say that!
SLAM
MAYBE I SHOULD HAVE FIXED MY HABIT OF SAYING WHATEVER'S ON MY MIND.
DRIP...
I thought I would have a good life if I just kept quiet and smiled.
BUT ...
...I DON'T PLAN ON GIVING UP JUST YET.
SHIK
JUST YOU WATCH, SHIBUYA.
TODAY, I WILL SUCCEED.

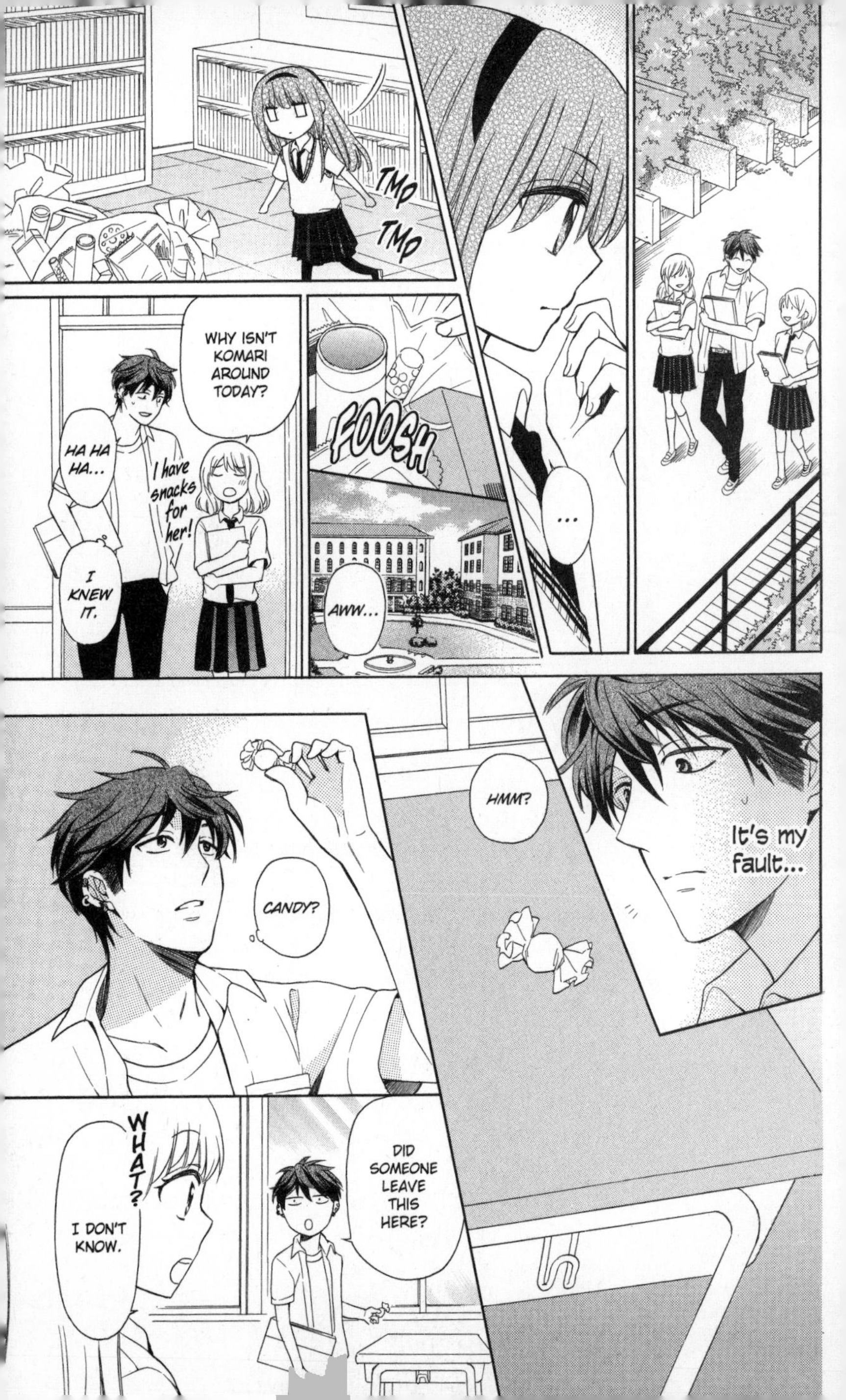
...
TMP TMP
FOOSH
AWW...
WHY ISN'T KOMARI AROUND TODAY?
I have snacks for her!
HA HA HA...
I KNEW IT.
HMM?
It's my fault...
CANDY?
DID SOMEONE LEAVE THIS HERE?
WHAT?
I DON'T KNOW.

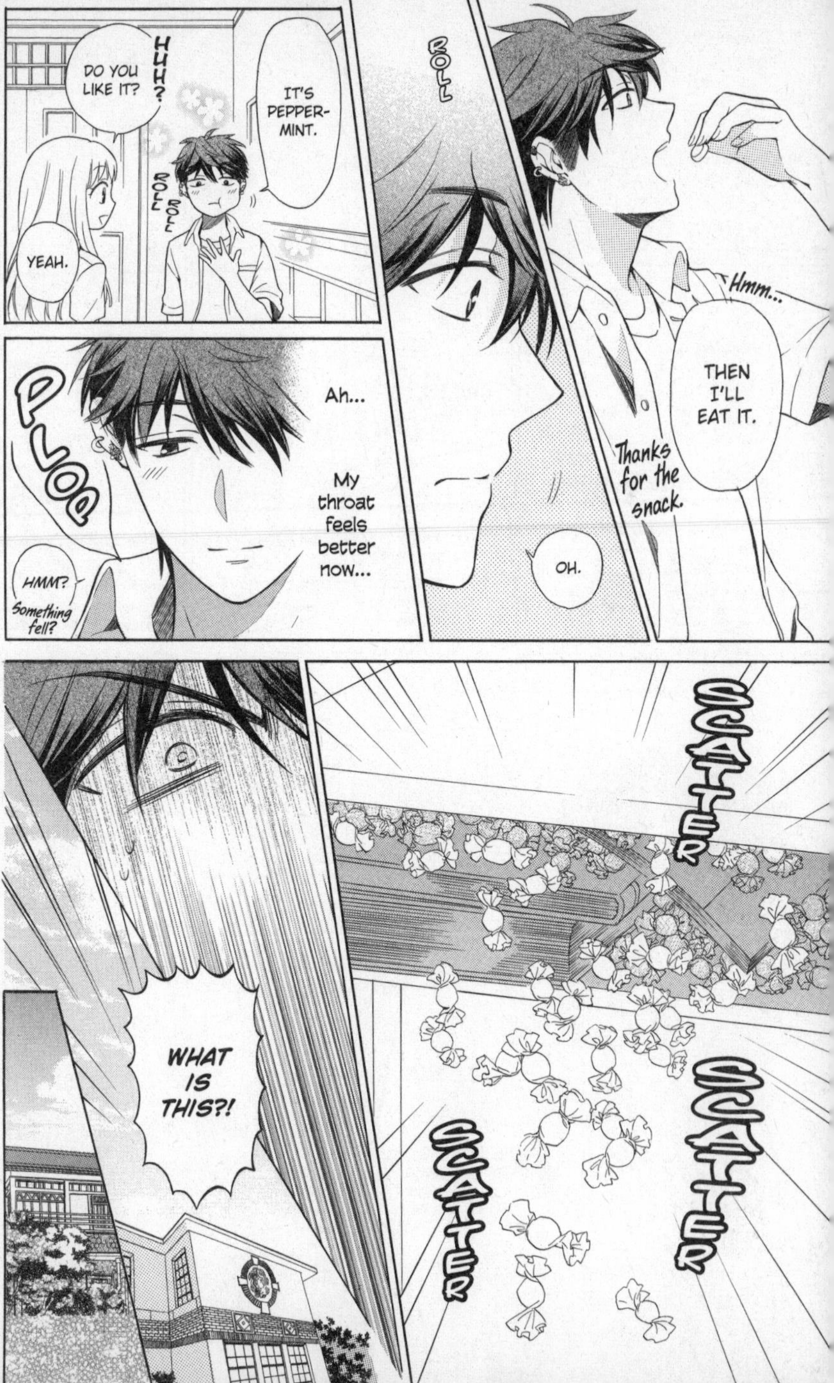
Hmm...
THEN I'LL EAT IT.
Thanks for the snack.
ROLL
OH.
IT'S PEPPERMINT.
HUHH?
DO YOU LIKE IT?
ROLL ROLL
YEAH.
PLOP
Ah...
My throat feels better now...
HMM?
Something fell?
SCATTER
SCATTER
SCATTER
WHAT IS THIS?!

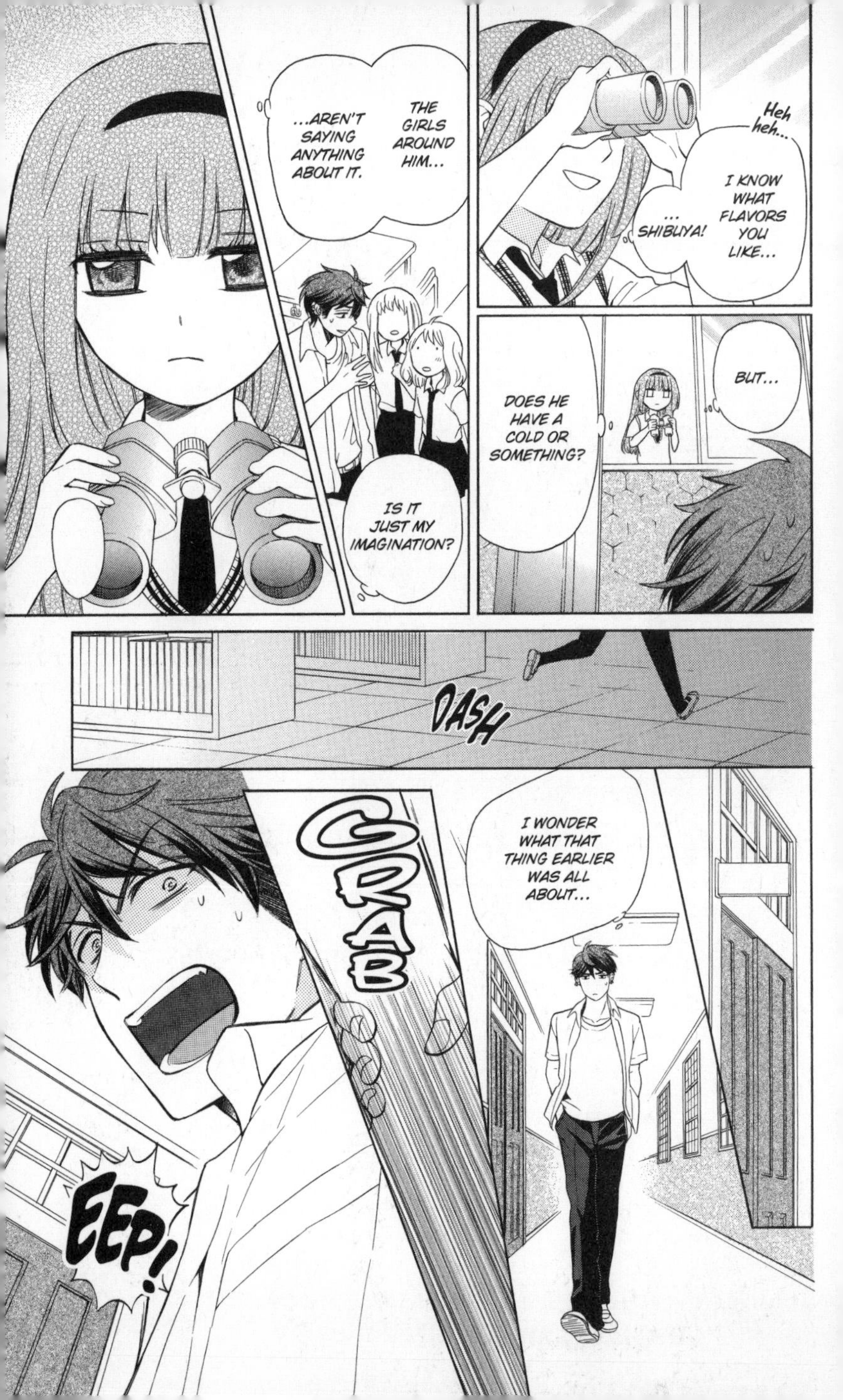
Heh heh...
I KNOW WHAT FLAVORS YOU LIKE...
...SHIBUYA!
BUT...
DOES HE HAVE A COLD OR SOMETHING?
THE GIRLS AROUND HIM...
...AREN'T SAYING ANYTHING ABOUT IT.
IS IT JUST MY IMAGINATION?
DASH
I WONDER WHAT THAT THING EARLIER WAS ALL ABOUT...
GRAB
EEP!

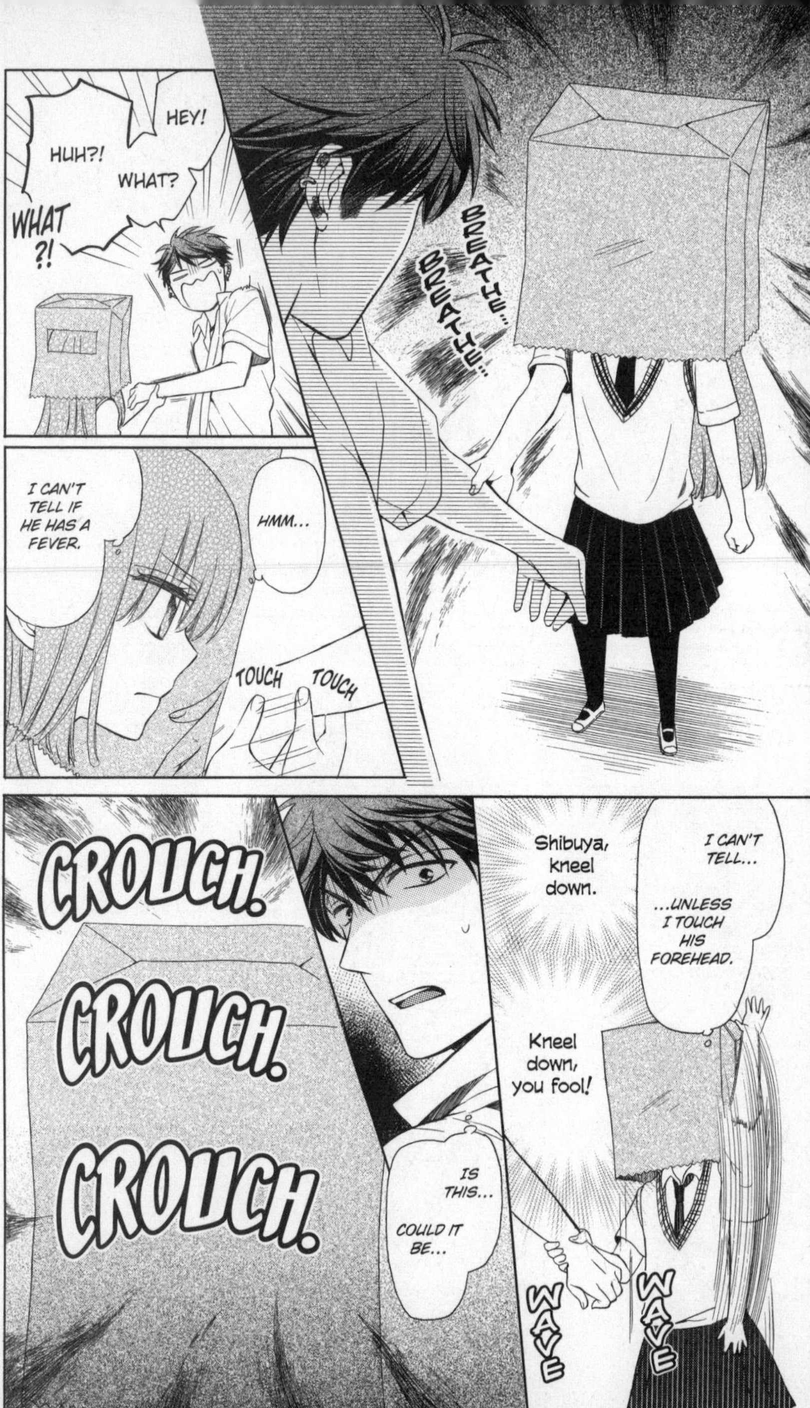
BREATHE...
BREATHE...
HEY!
HUH?!
WHAT?
WHAT ?!
I CAN'T TELL IF HE HAS A FEVER.
HMM...
TOUCH
TOUCH
I CAN'T TELL...
...UNLESS I TOUCH HIS FOREHEAD.
Shibuya, kneel down.
Kneel down, you fool!
WAVE
WAVE
IS THIS...
COULD IT BE...
CROUCH.
CROUCH.
CROUCH.

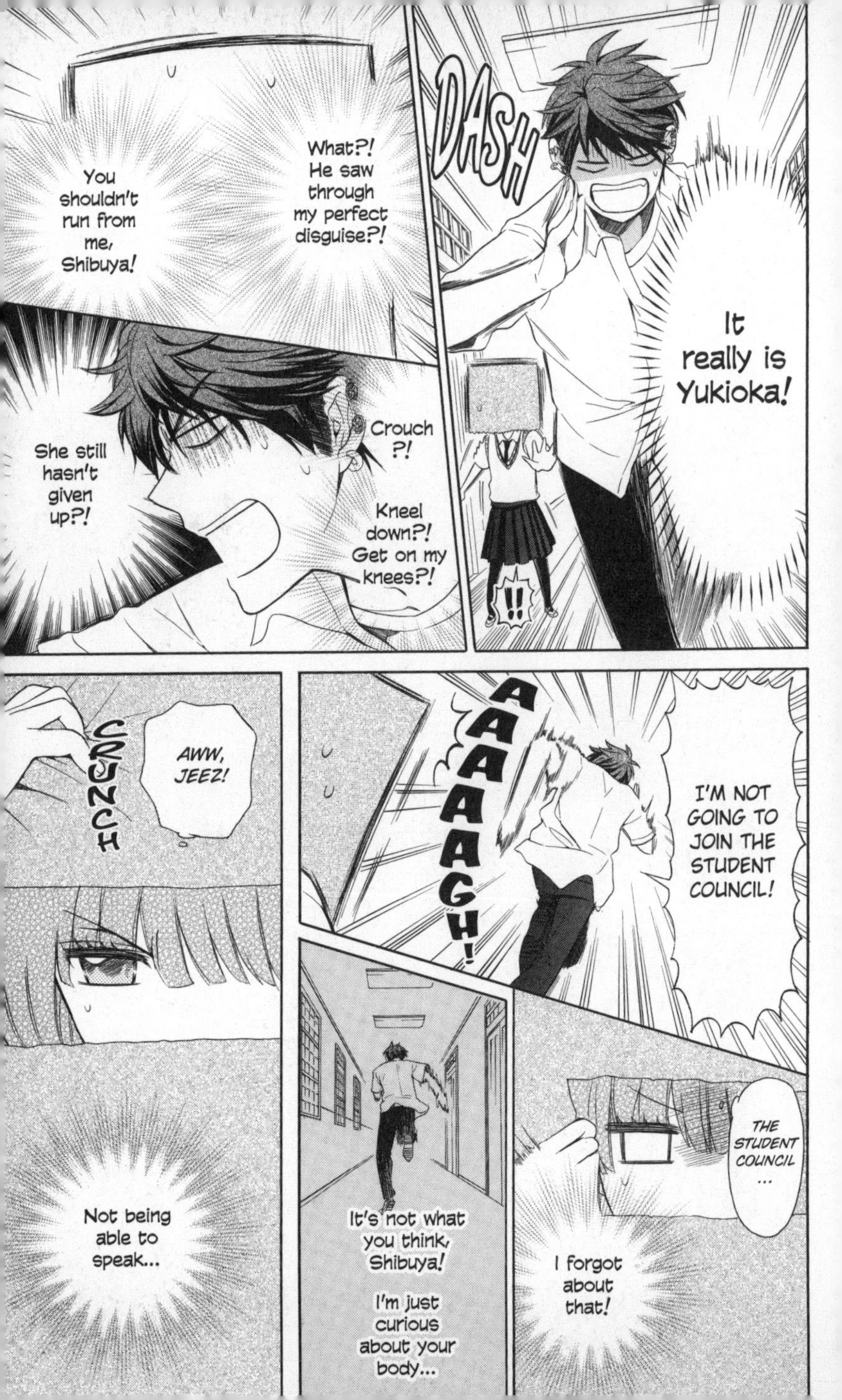
DASH
It really is Yukioka!
!!
What?! He saw through my perfect disguise?!
You shouldn't run from me, Shibuya!
Crouch?!
Kneel down?! Get on my knees?!
She still hasn't given up?!
I'M NOT GOING TO JOIN THE STUDENT COUNCIL!
AAAAAAGH!
AWW, JEEZ!
CRUNCH
THE STUDENT COUNCIL...
I forgot about that!
It's not what you think, Shibuya!
I'm just curious about your body...
Not being able to speak...

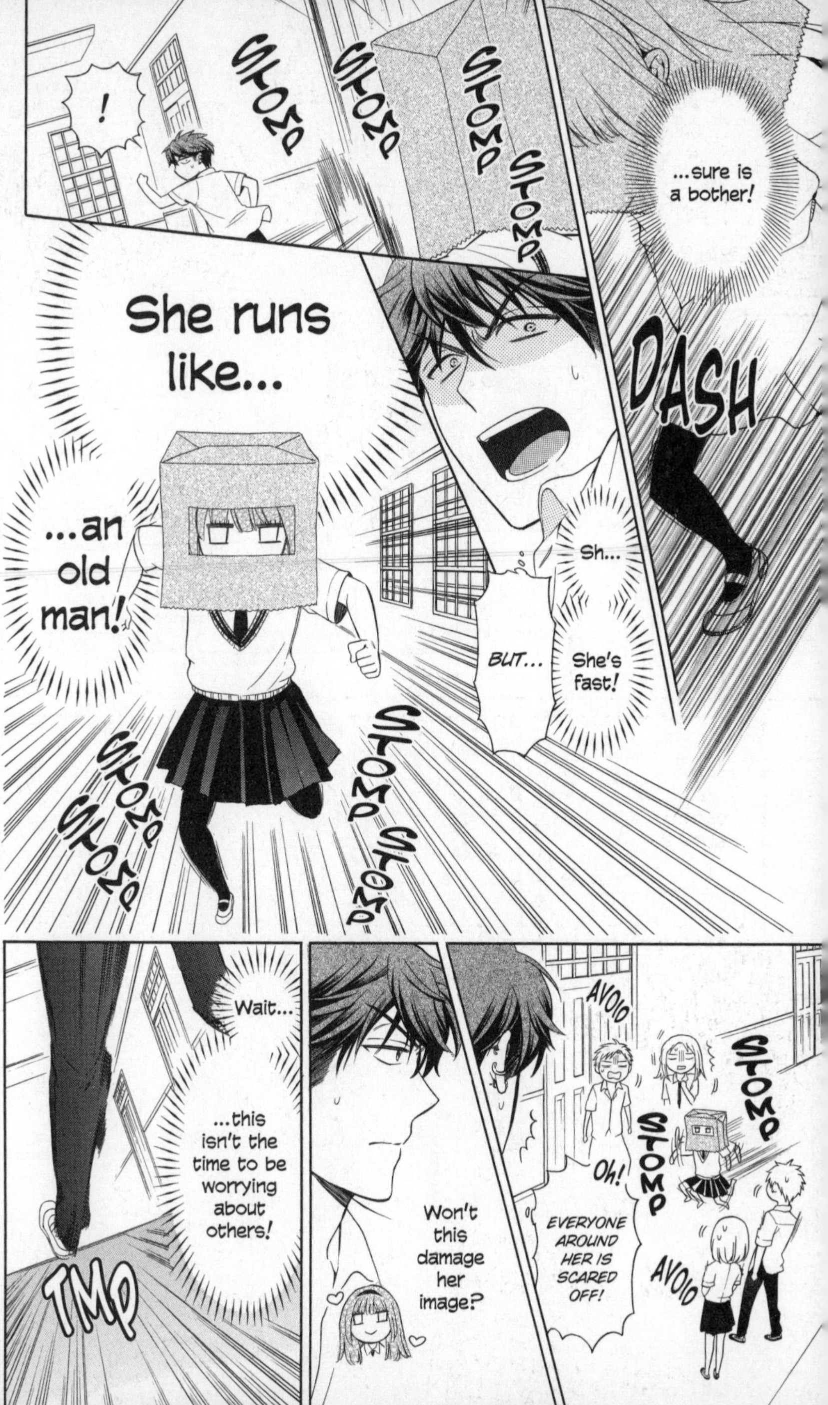
...sure is a bother!
DASH
STOMP
STOMP
STOMP
STOMP
!
Sh...
She's fast!
BUT...
She runs like...
...an old man!
STOMP STOMP
STOMP STOMP
STOMP
AVOID
EVERYONE AROUND HER IS SCARED OFF!
Oh!
STOMP
AVOID
Won't this damage her image?
Wait...
...this isn't the time to be worrying about others!
TMP

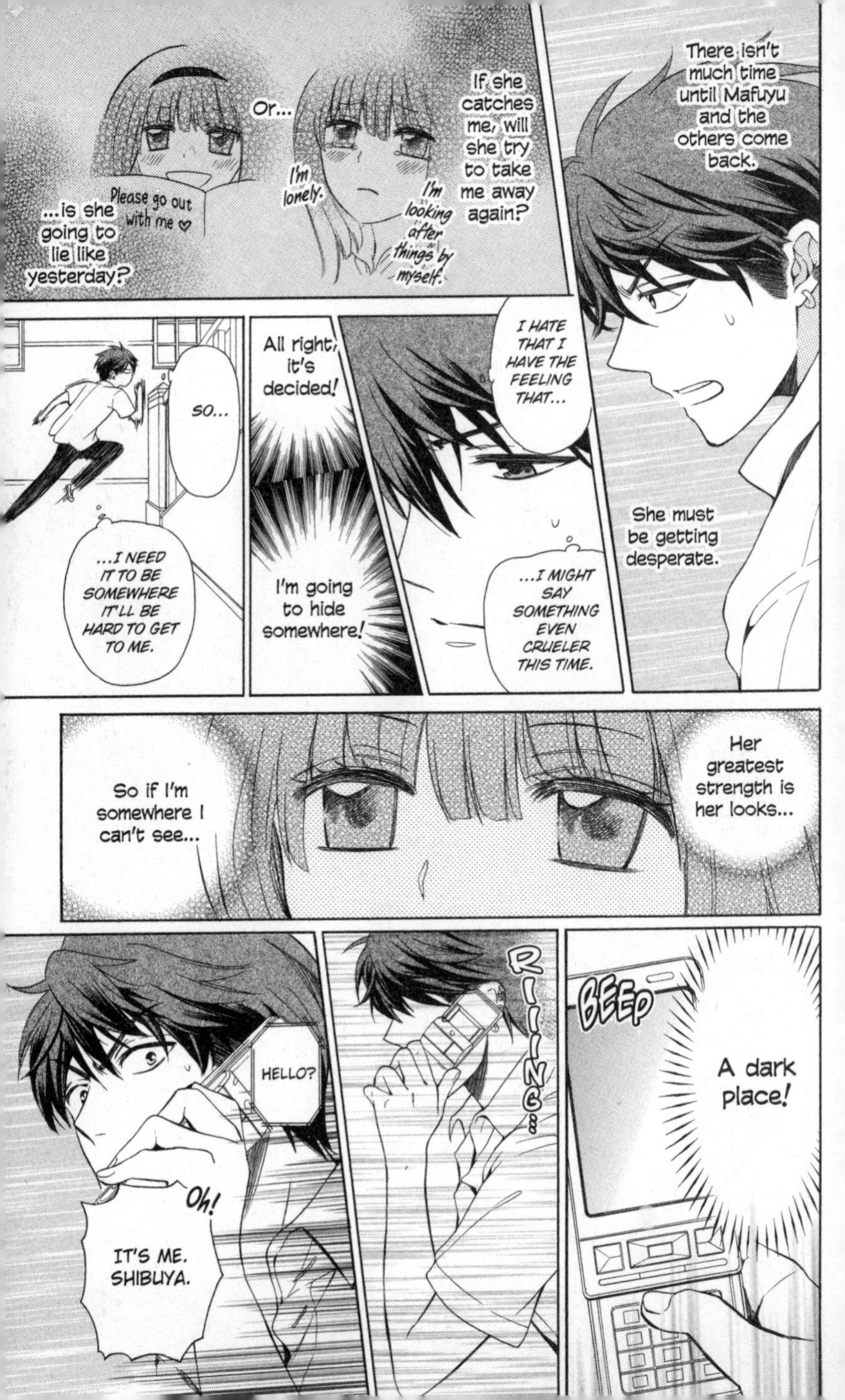
There isn't much time until Mafuyu and the others come back.
If she catches me, will she try to take me away again?
I'm looking after things by myself.
I'm lonely.
Or...
Please go out with me ♡
...is she going to lie like yesterday?
She must be getting desperate.
I HATE THAT I HAVE THE FEELING THAT...
...I MIGHT SAY SOMETHING EVEN CRUELER THIS TIME.
All right, it's decided!
I'm going to hide somewhere!
SO...
...I NEED IT TO BE SOMEWHERE IT'LL BE HARD TO GET TO ME.
Her greatest strength is her looks...
So if I'm somewhere I can't see...
BEEP
A dark place!
RIIING...
HELLO?
Oh!
IT'S ME. SHIBUYA.

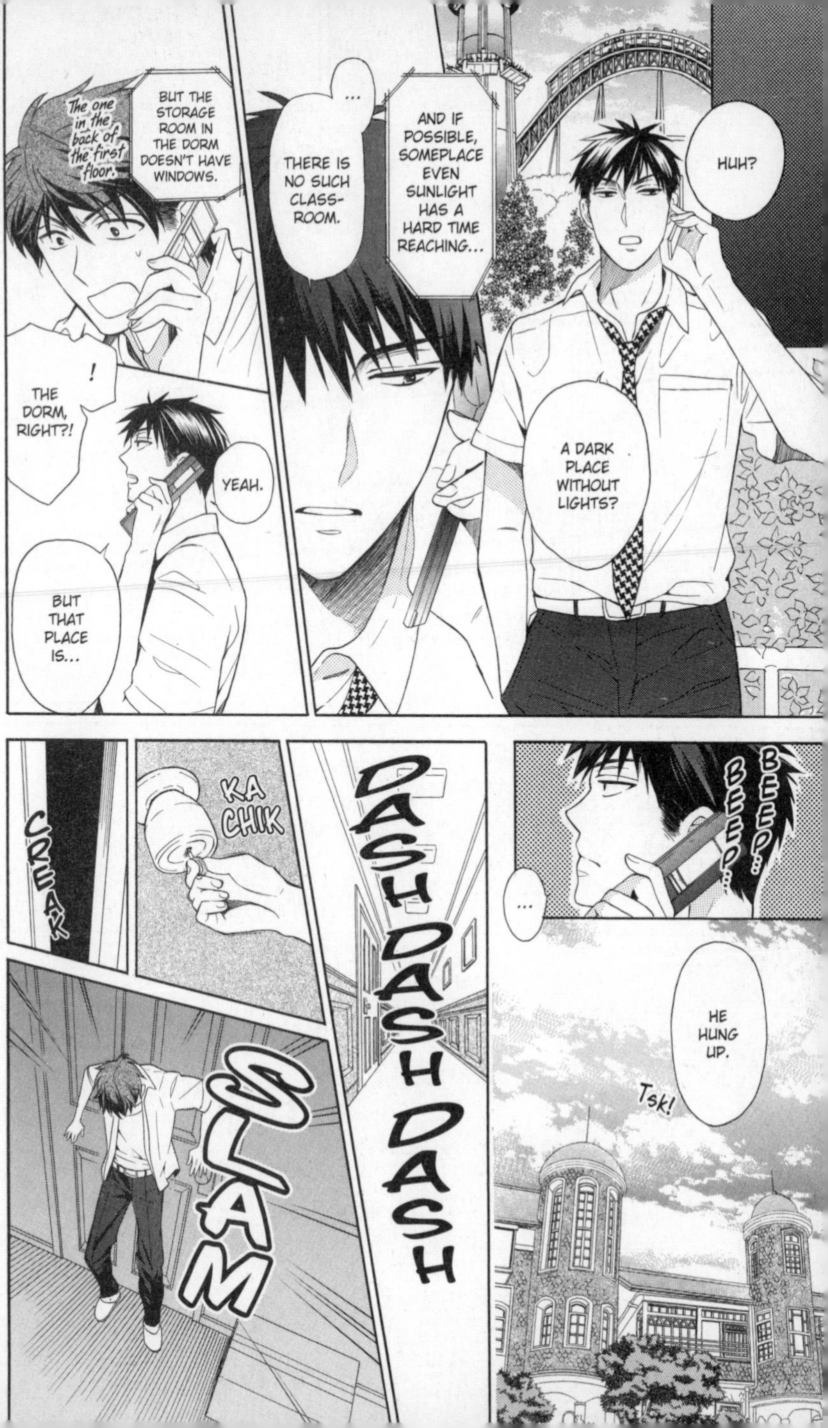

HUH?
A DARK PLACE WITHOUT LIGHTS?
AND IF POSSIBLE, SOMEPLACE EVEN SUNLIGHT HAS A HARD TIME REACHING...
THERE IS NO SUCH CLASSROOM.
...
BUT THE STORAGE ROOM IN THE DORM DOESN'T HAVE WINDOWS.
The one in the back of the first floor.
!
THE DORM, RIGHT?!
YEAH.
BUT THAT PLACE IS...
BEEP... BEEP...
...
HE HUNG UP.
Tsk!
DASH DASH DASH DASH
KA CHIK
CREAK
SLAM

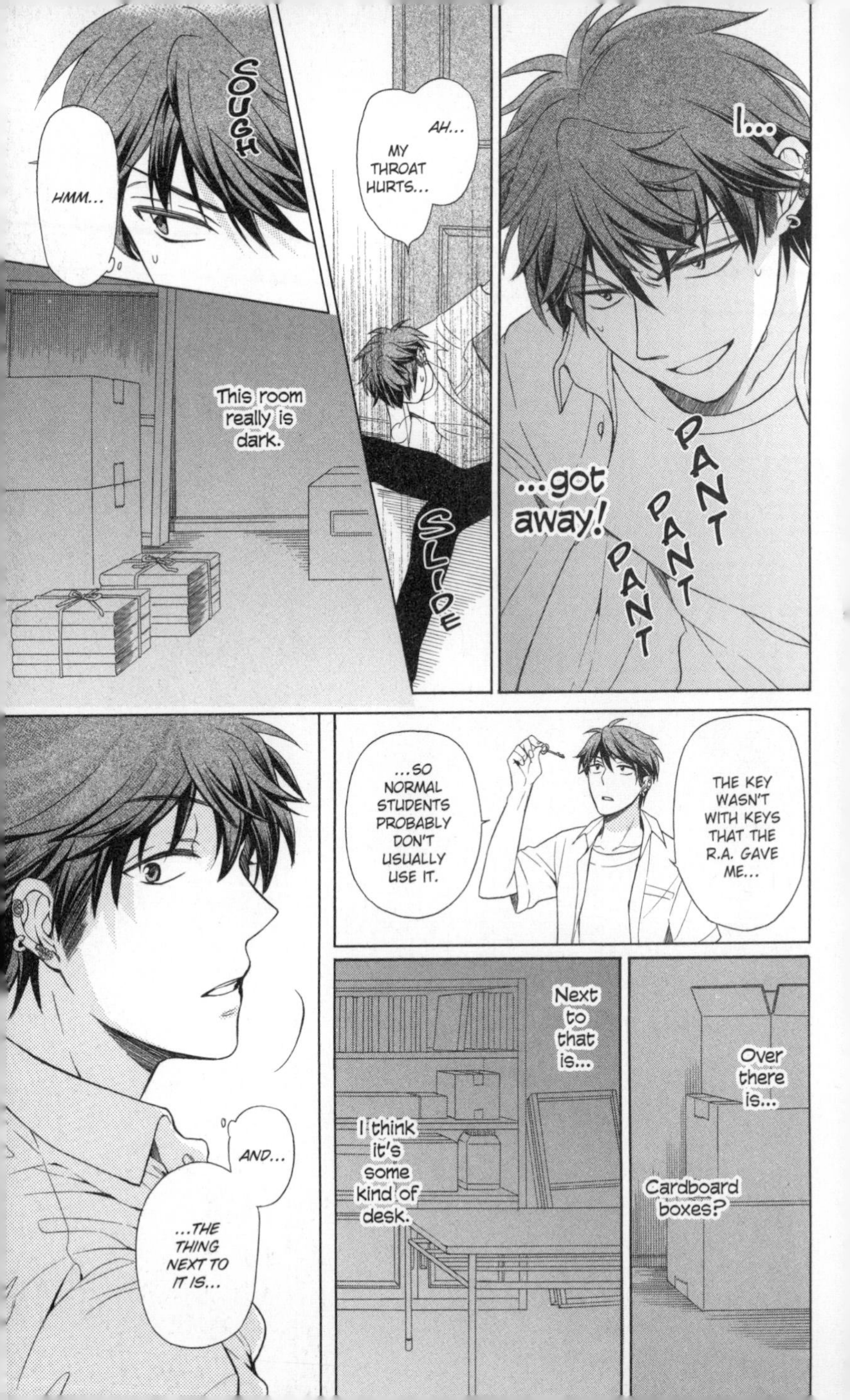
I...
...got away!
PANT PANT PANT
SLIDE
AH... MY THROAT HURTS...
COUGH
HMM...
This room really is dark.
THE KEY WASN'T WITH KEYS THAT THE R.A. GAVE ME...
...SO NORMAL STUDENTS PROBABLY DON'T USUALLY USE IT.
Over there is...
Cardboard boxes?
Next to that is...
I think it's some kind of desk.
AND...
...THE THING NEXT TO IT IS...

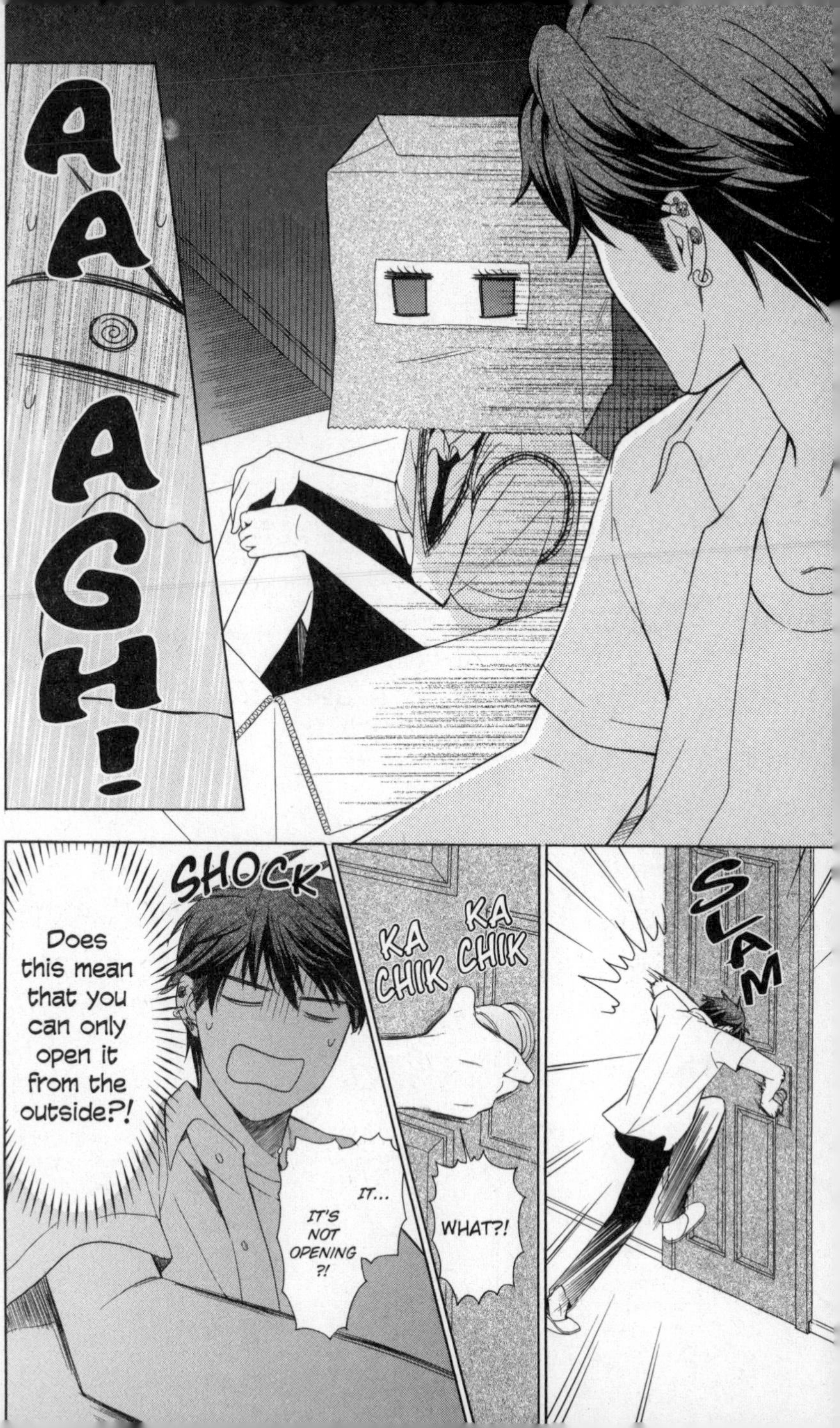
AAAGH!
SLAM
WHAT?!
KA CHIK KA CHIK
IT... IT'S NOT OPENING?!
SHOCK
Does this mean that you can only open it from the outside?!

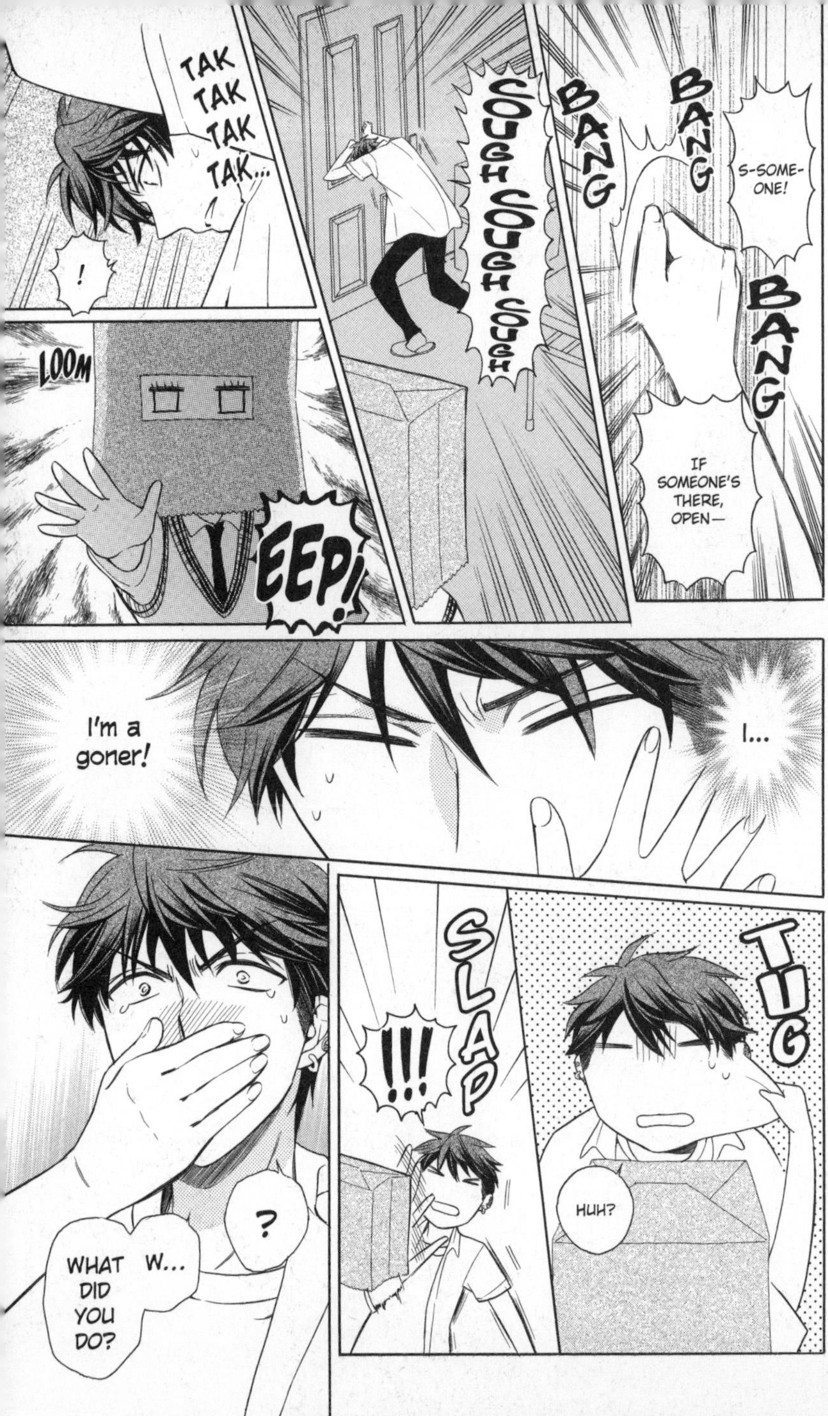
S-SOME-ONE!
BANG
BANG
BANG
IF SOMEONE'S THERE, OPEN—
COUGH COUGH COUGH
TAK TAK TAK TAK...
!
LOOM
EEP!
I...
I'm a goner!
TUG
HUH?
SLAP
!!!
?
W...
WHAT DID YOU DO?

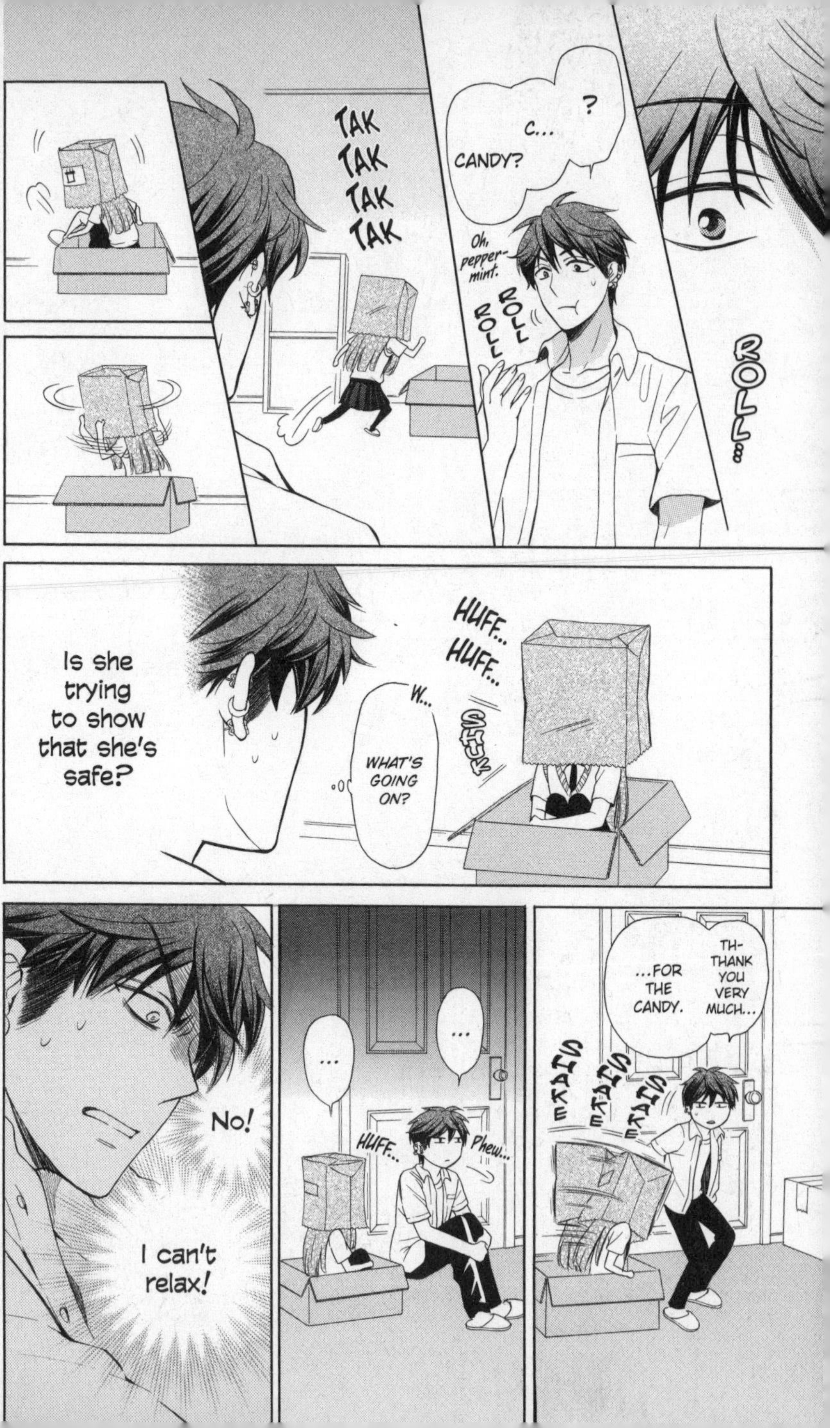
ROLL...
C...
CANDY?
?
Oh, pepper-mint.
ROLL ROLL
TAK TAK TAK TAK
HUFF... HUFF...
W...
WHAT'S GOING ON?
SHUK
Is she trying to show that she's safe?
TH-THANK YOU VERY MUCH...
...FOR THE CANDY.
SHAKE SHAKE SHAKE
...
...
HUFF...
Phew...
No!
I can't relax!

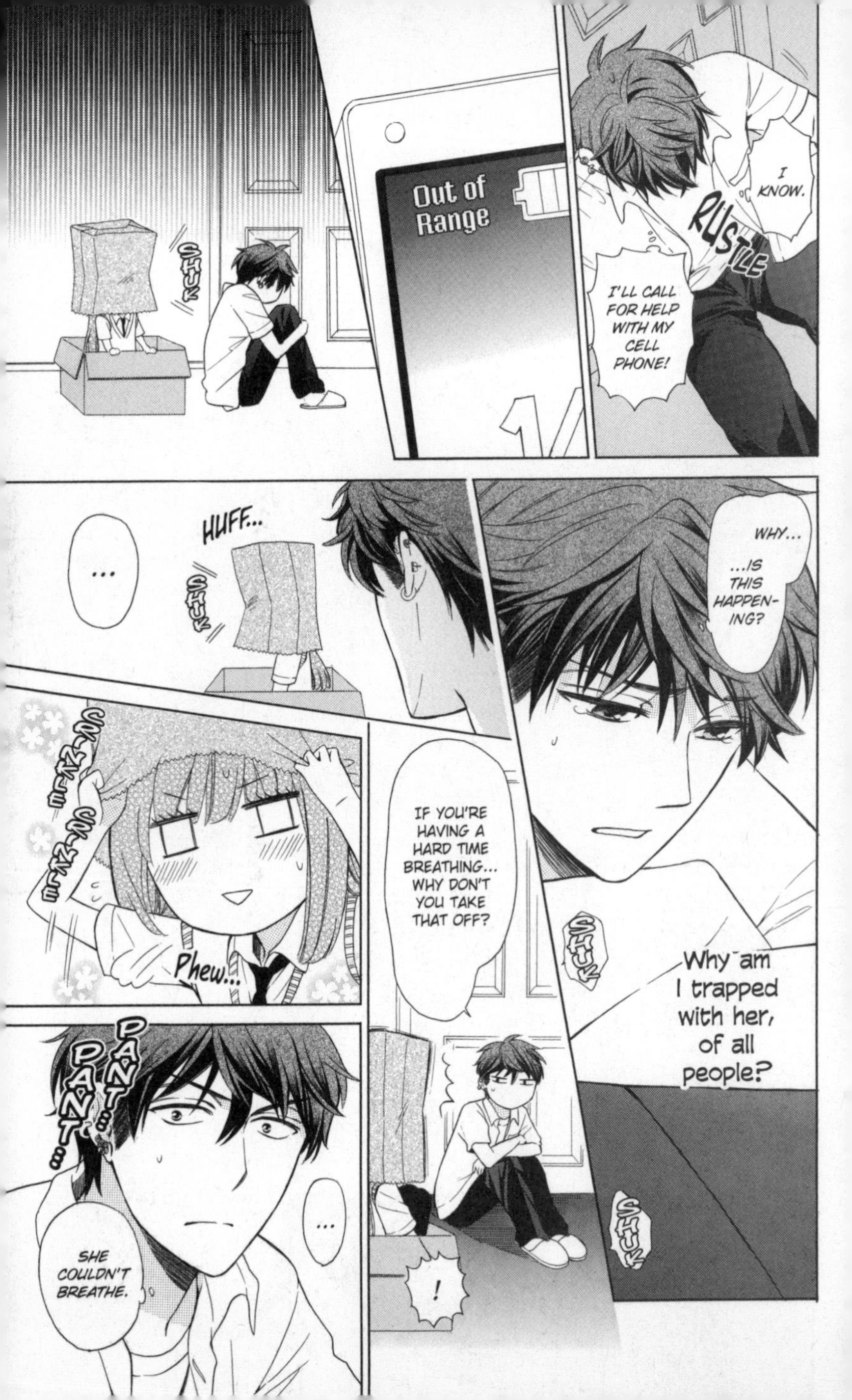
I KNOW.
RUSTLE
I'LL CALL FOR HELP WITH MY CELL PHONE!
Out of Range
SHUK
WHY...
...IS THIS HAPPEN-ING?
IF YOU'RE HAVING A HARD TIME BREATHING... WHY DON'T YOU TAKE THAT OFF?
SHUK
Why am I trapped with her, of all people?
SHUK
!
HUFF...
SHUK
...
Phew...
PANT... PANT...
...
SHE COULDN'T BREATHE.

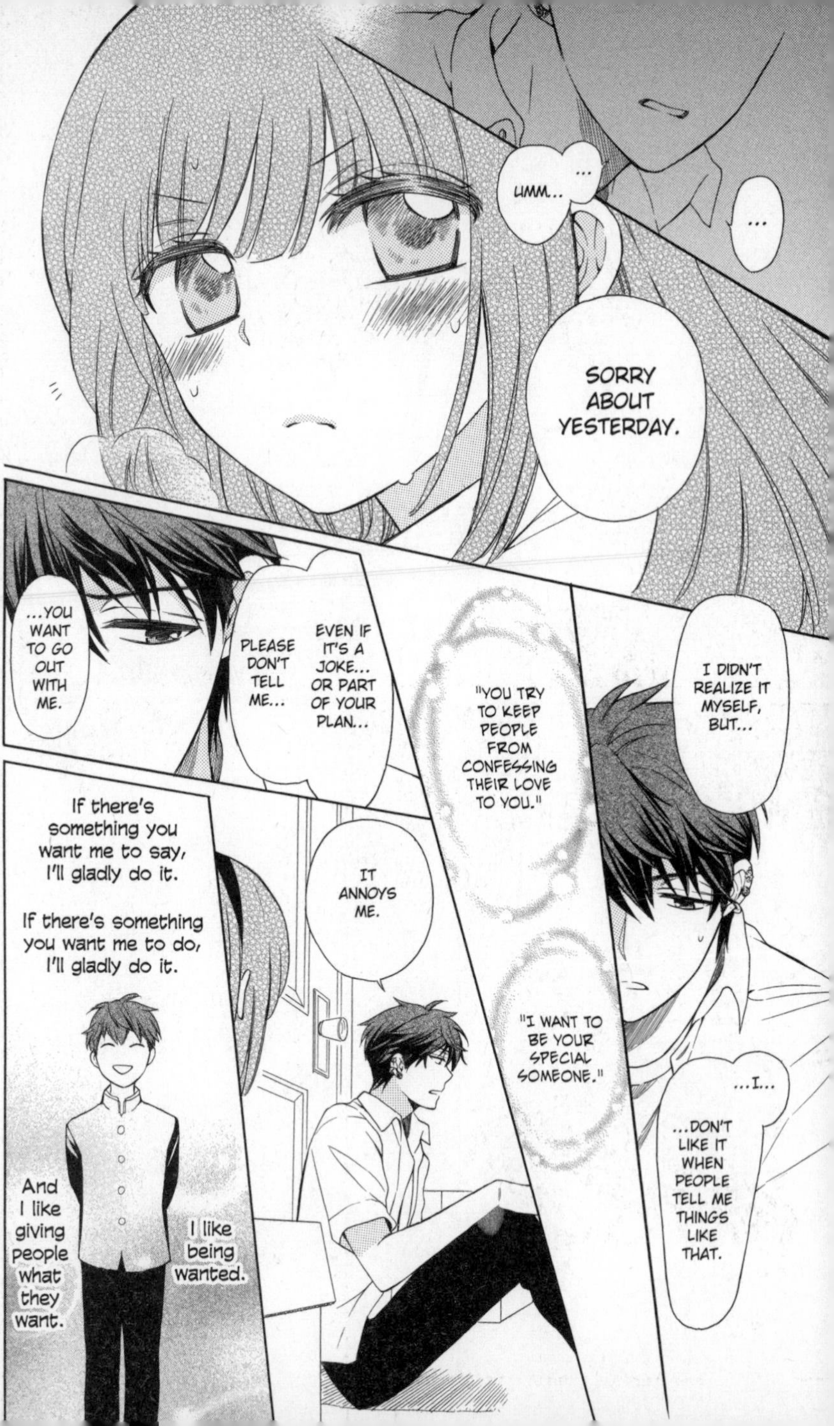
...
UMM... ...
SORRY ABOUT YESTERDAY.
I DIDN'T REALIZE IT MYSELF, BUT...
...I...
...DON'T LIKE IT WHEN PEOPLE TELL ME THINGS LIKE THAT.
"YOU TRY TO KEEP PEOPLE FROM CONFESSING THEIR LOVE TO YOU."
"I WANT TO BE YOUR SPECIAL SOMEONE."
IT ANNOYS ME.
EVEN IF IT'S A JOKE... OR PART OF YOUR PLAN...
PLEASE DON'T TELL ME...
...YOU WANT TO GO OUT WITH ME.
If there's something you want me to say, I'll gladly do it.
If there's something you want me to do, I'll gladly do it.
I like being wanted.
And I like giving people what they want.

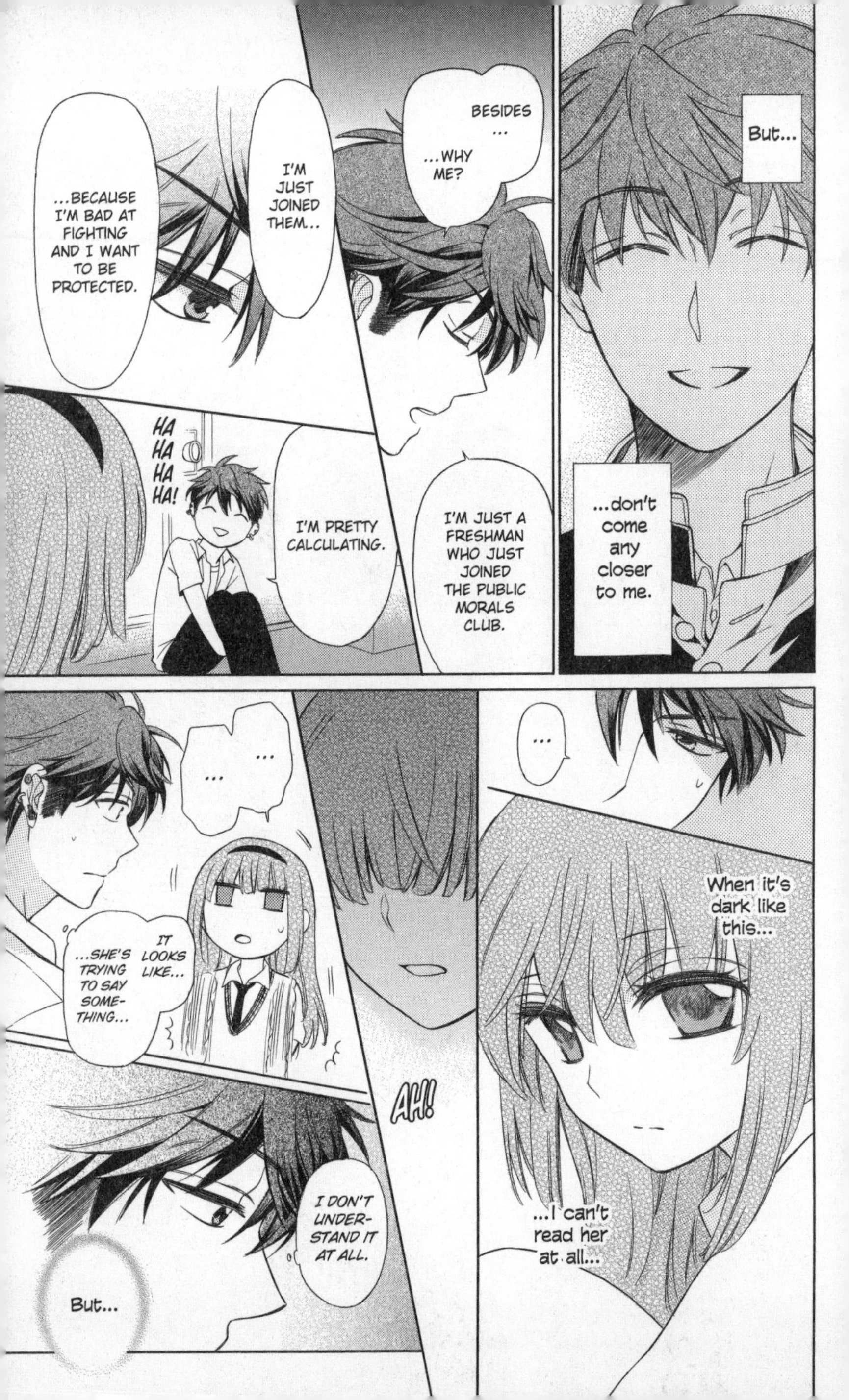
But...
...don't come any closer to me.
BESIDES ... ...WHY ME?
I'M JUST A FRESHMAN WHO JUST JOINED THE PUBLIC MORALS CLUB.
I'M JUST JOINED THEM...
...BECAUSE I'M BAD AT FIGHTING AND I WANT TO BE PROTECTED.
HA HA HA HA!
I'M PRETTY CALCULATING.
...
When it's dark like this...
...I can't read her at all...
AH!
... ...
IT LOOKS LIKE...
...SHE'S TRYING TO SAY SOME-THING...
I DON'T UNDER-STAND IT AT ALL.
But...

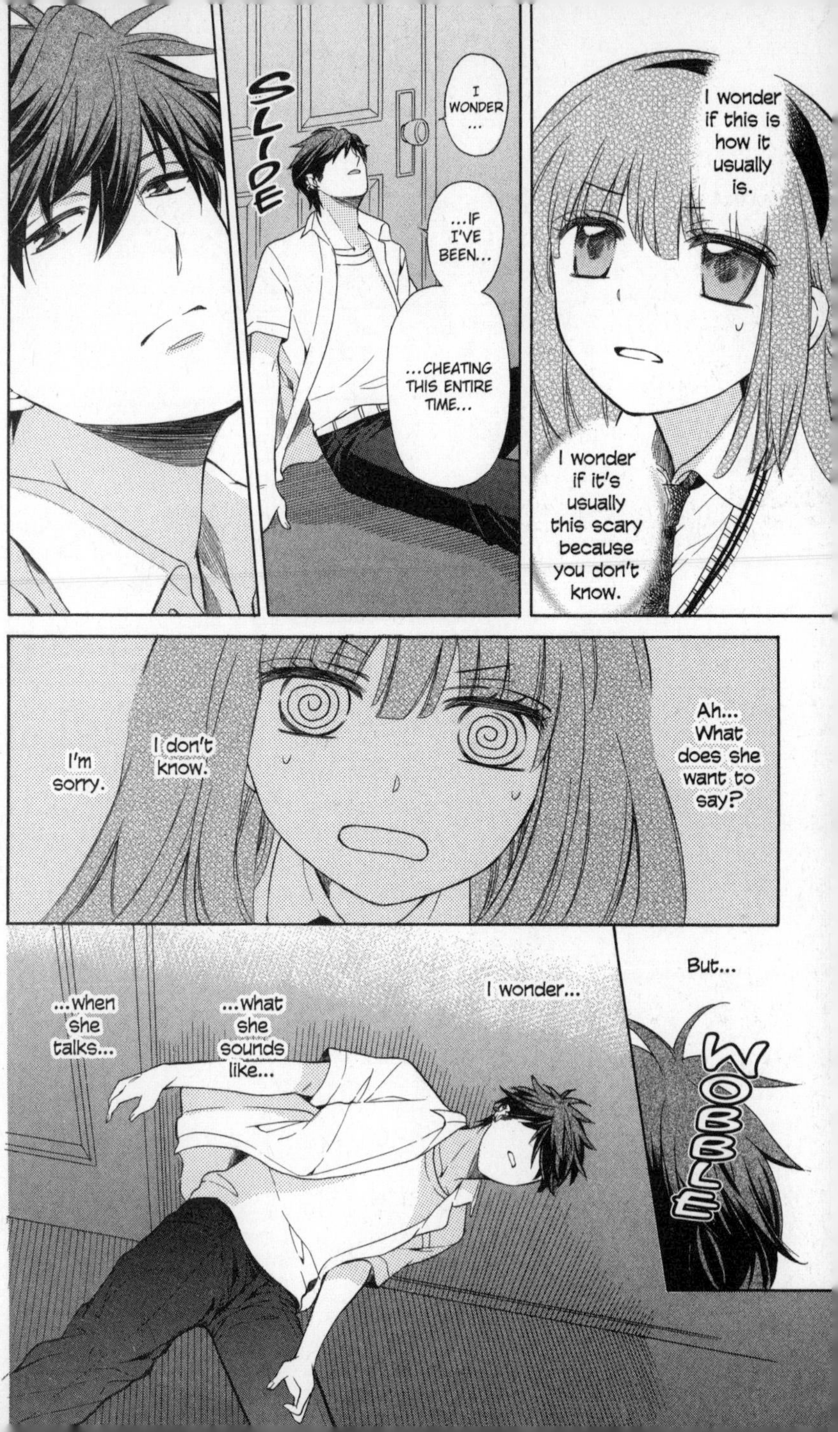
I wonder if this is how it usually is.
I wonder if it's usually this scary because you don't know.
I WONDER...
...IF I'VE BEEN...
...CHEATING THIS ENTIRE TIME...
SLIDE
Ah... What does she want to say?
I don't know.
I'm sorry.
But...
WOBBLE
I wonder...
...what she sounds like...
...when she talks...

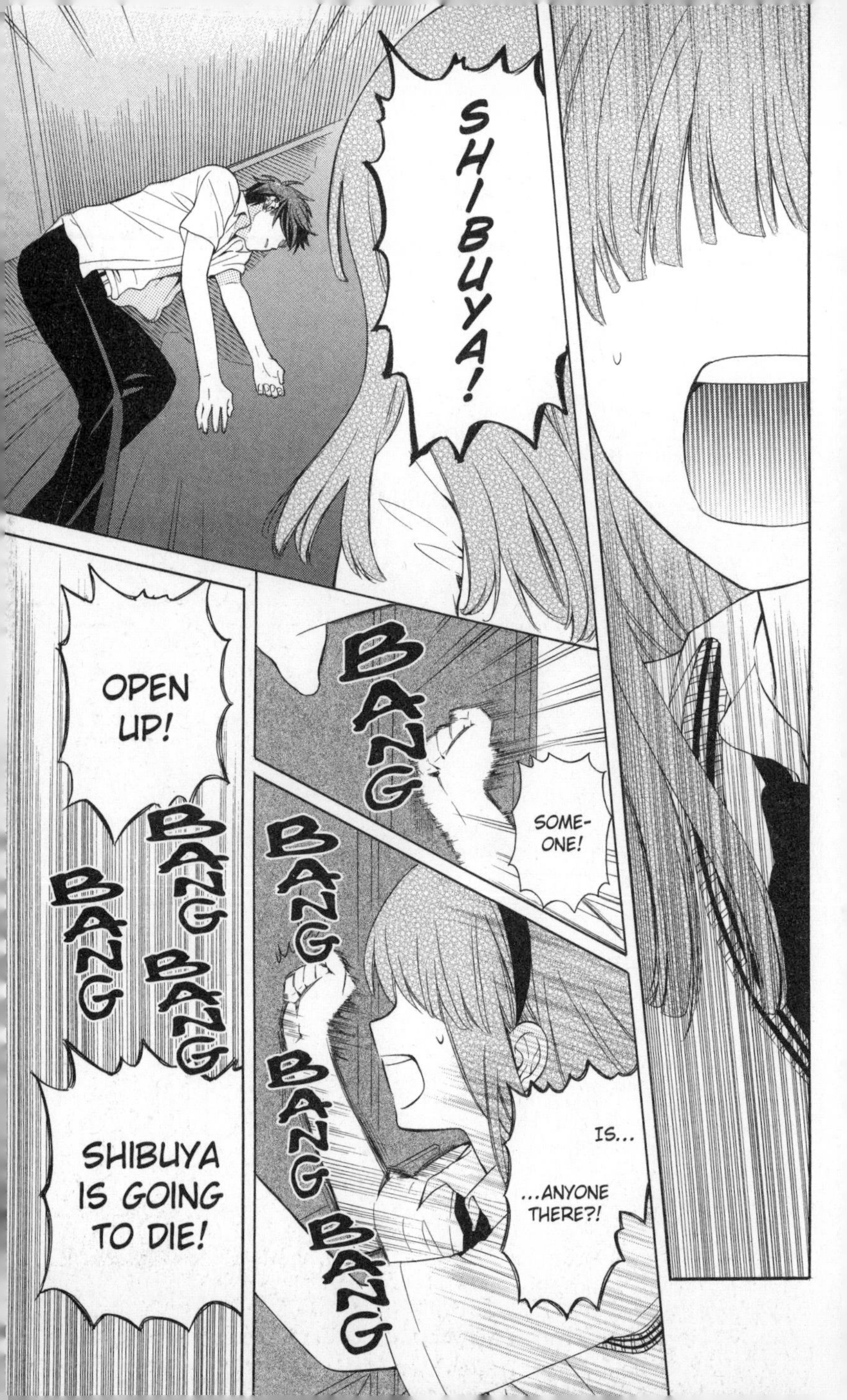
SHIBUYA!
IS...
...ANYONE THERE?!
BANG
SOME-ONE!
BANG BANG BANG
OPEN UP!
BANG BANG BANG
SHIBUYA IS GOING TO DIE!

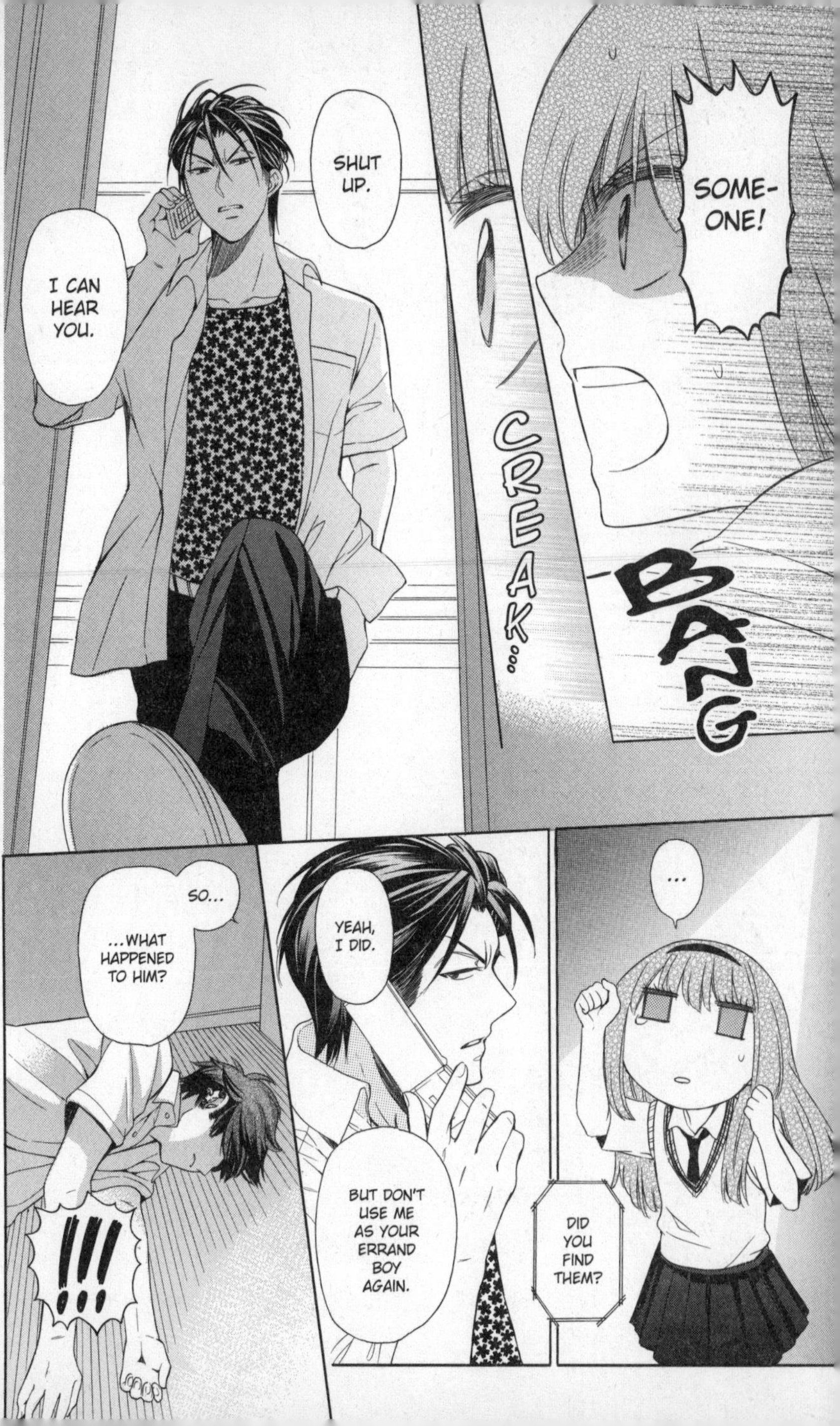
SOME-ONE!
BANG
CREAK...
SHUT UP.
I CAN HEAR YOU.
...
DID YOU FIND THEM?
YEAH, I DID.
BUT DON'T USE ME AS YOUR ERRAND BOY AGAIN.
SO...
...WHAT HAPPENED TO HIM?
!!!

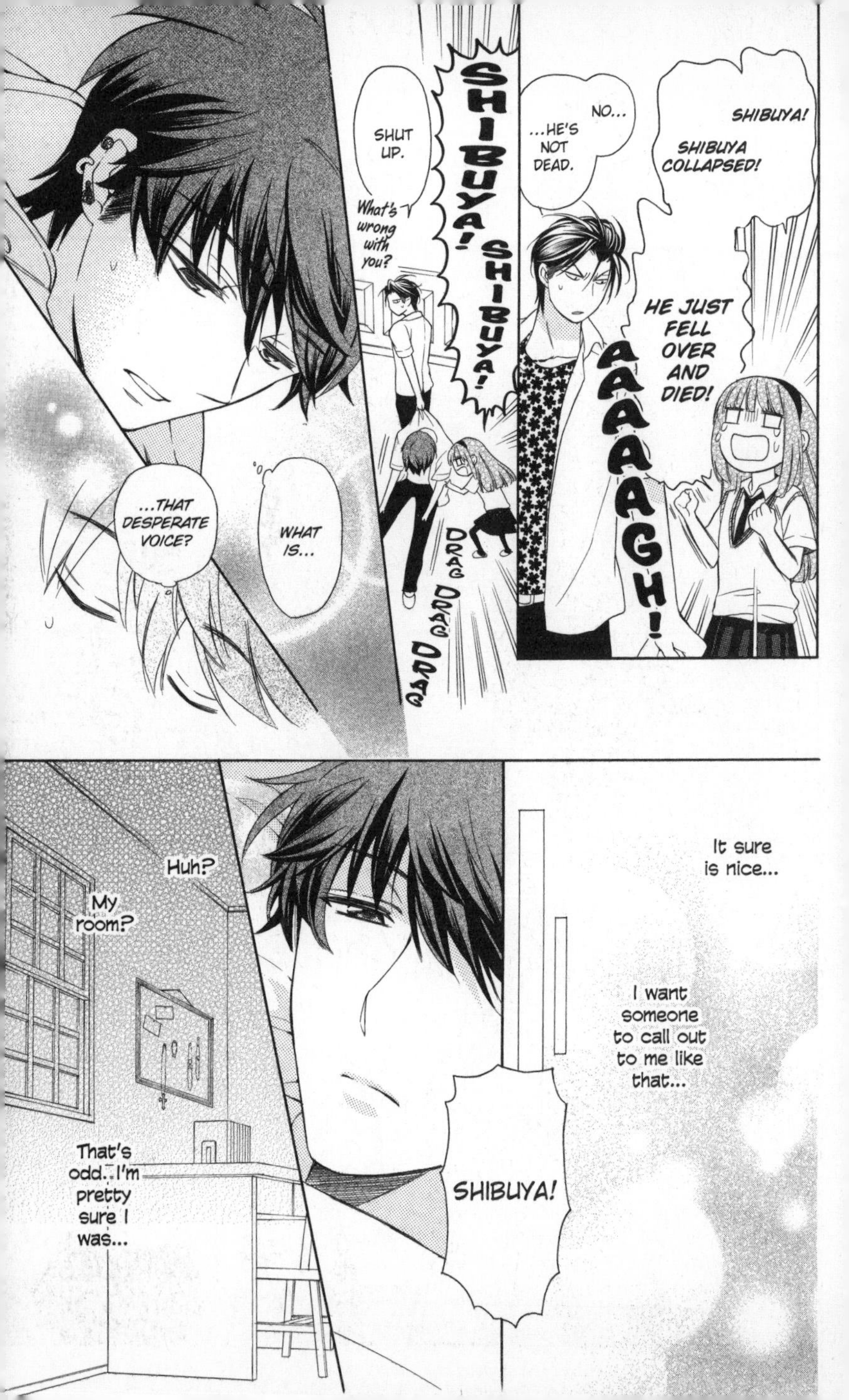
SHIBUYA!
SHIBUYA COLLAPSED!
HE JUST FELL OVER AND DIED!
AAAAAGH!
NO...
...HE'S NOT DEAD.
SHIBUYA! SHIBUYA!
SHUT UP.
What's wrong with you?
DRAG DRAG DRAG
WHAT IS...
...THAT DESPERATE VOICE?
It sure is nice...
I want someone to call out to me like that...
SHIBUYA!
Huh?
My room?
That's odd... I'm pretty sure I was...

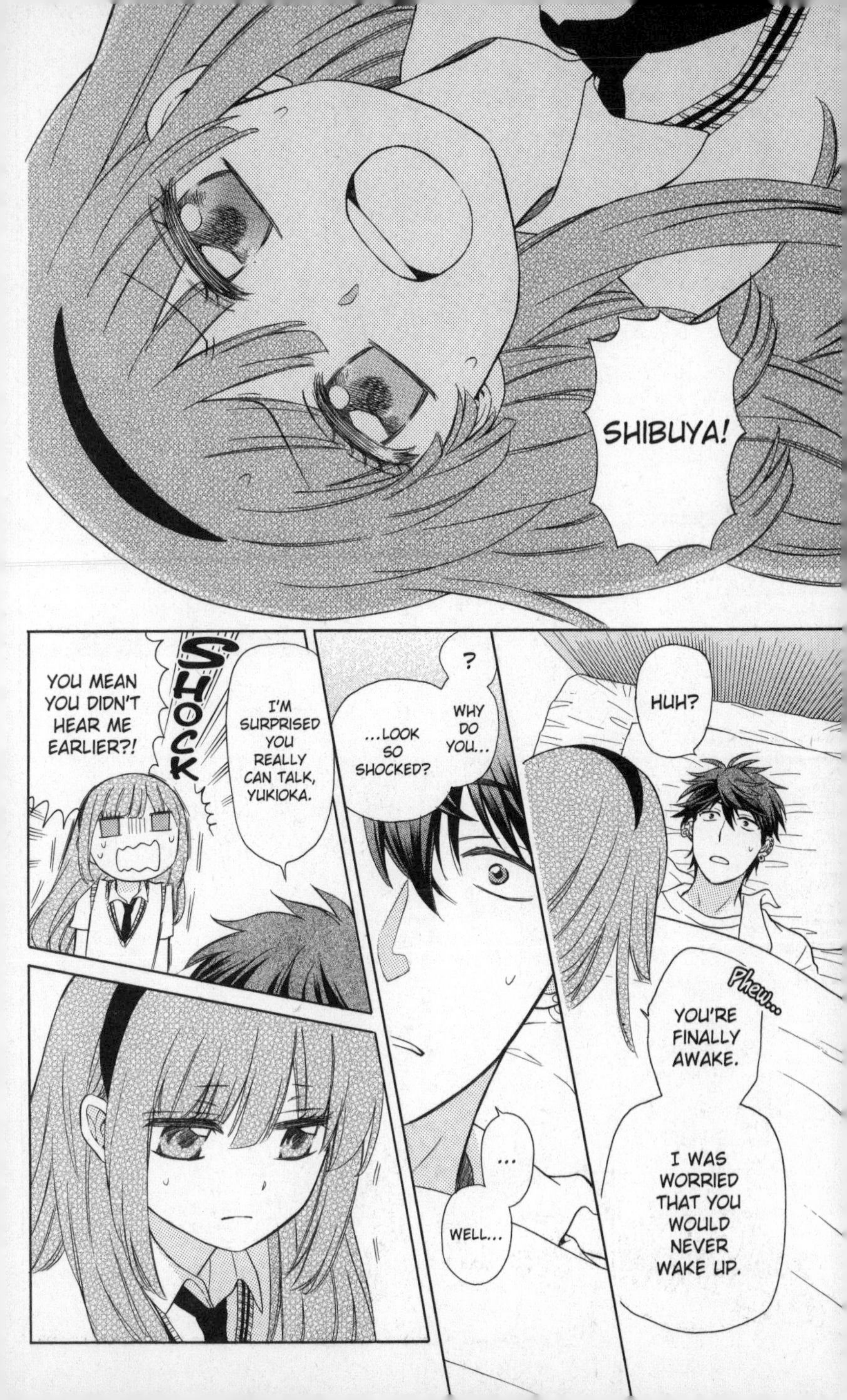
SHIBUYA!
HUH?
Phew...
YOU'RE FINALLY AWAKE.
I WAS WORRIED THAT YOU WOULD NEVER WAKE UP.
WHY DO YOU...
...LOOK SO SHOCKED?
?
...
WELL...
I'M SURPRISED YOU REALLY CAN TALK, YUKIOKA.
SHOCK
YOU MEAN YOU DIDN'T HEAR ME EARLIER?!

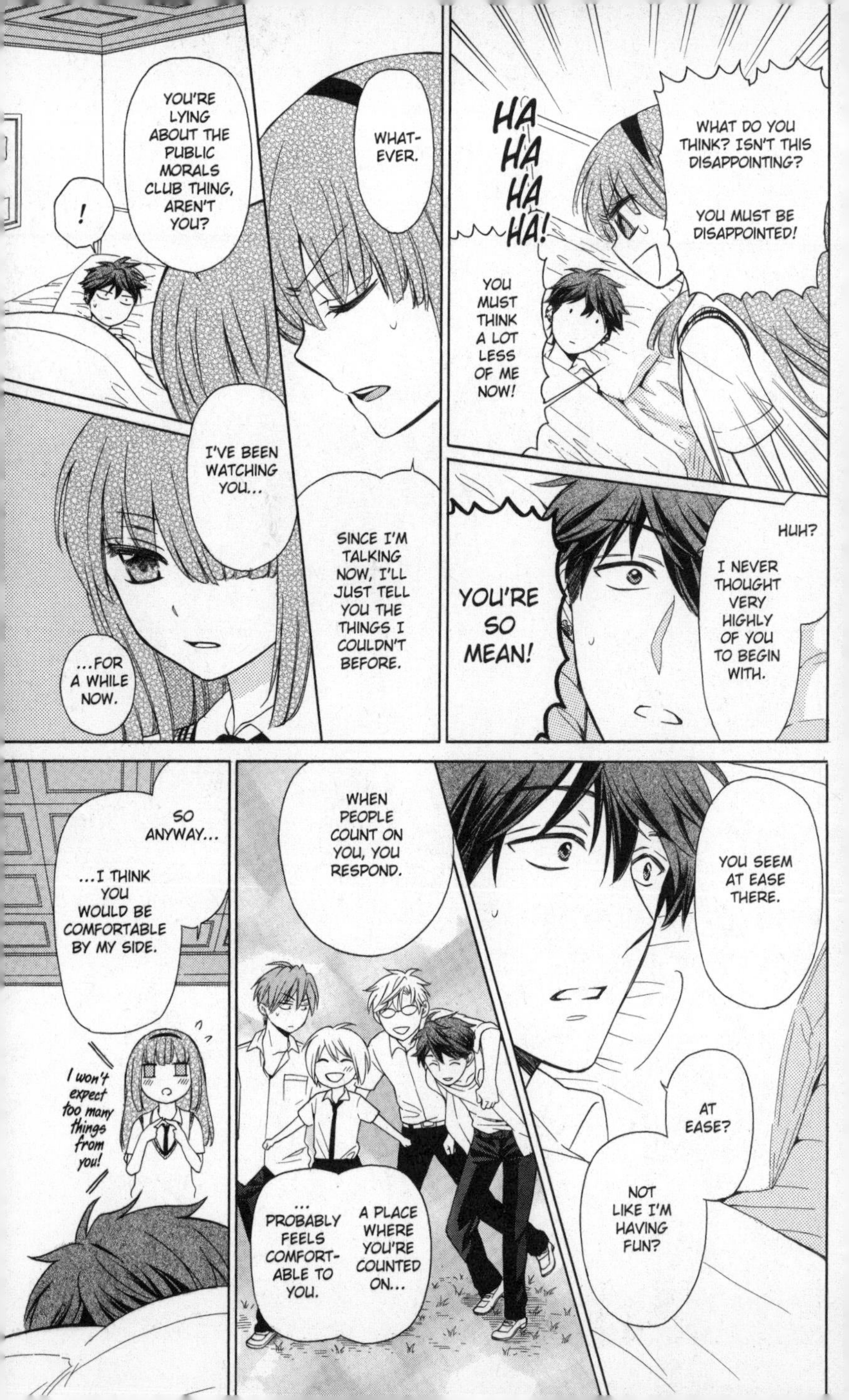
WHAT DO YOU THINK? ISN'T THIS DISAPPOINTING?
YOU MUST BE DISAPPOINTED!
HA HA HA HA!
YOU MUST THINK A LOT LESS OF ME NOW!
WHAT-EVER.
YOU'RE LYING ABOUT THE PUBLIC MORALS CLUB THING, AREN'T YOU?
!
HUH?
I NEVER THOUGHT VERY HIGHLY OF YOU TO BEGIN WITH.
YOU'RE SO MEAN!
I'VE BEEN WATCHING YOU...
...FOR A WHILE NOW.
SINCE I'M TALKING NOW, I'LL JUST TELL YOU THE THINGS I COULDN'T BEFORE.
YOU SEEM AT EASE THERE.
AT EASE?
NOT LIKE I'M HAVING FUN?
WHEN PEOPLE COUNT ON YOU, YOU RESPOND.
A PLACE WHERE YOU'RE COUNTED ON...
...PROBABLY FEELS COMFORT-ABLE TO YOU.
SO ANYWAY...
...I THINK YOU WOULD BE COMFORTABLE BY MY SIDE.
I won't expect too many things from you!

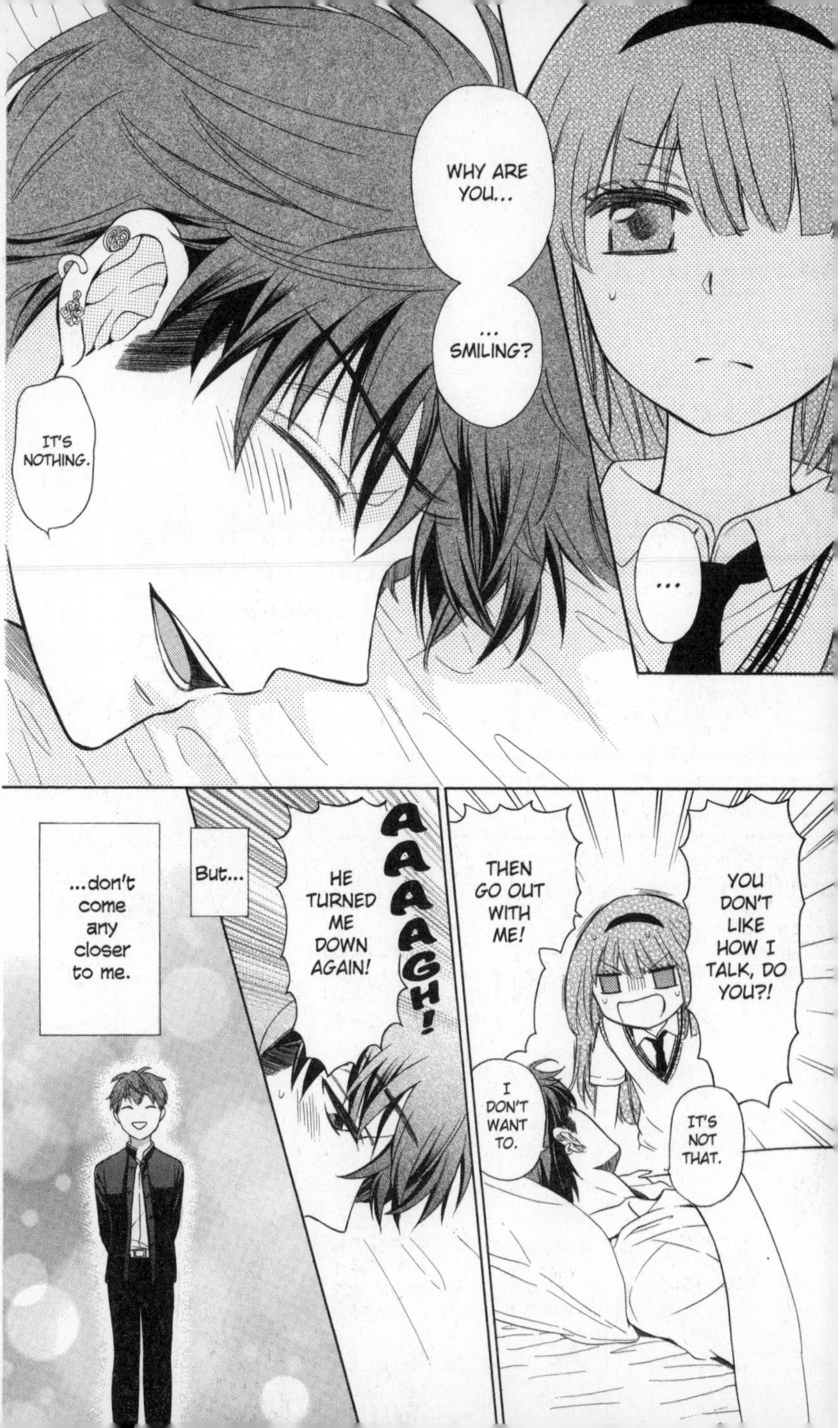
WHY ARE YOU...
... SMILING?
...
IT'S NOTHING.
YOU DON'T LIKE HOW I TALK, DO YOU?!
IT'S NOT THAT.
THEN GO OUT WITH ME!
I DON'T WANT TO.
HE TURNED ME DOWN AGAIN!
AAAAAGH!
But...
...don't come any closer to me.

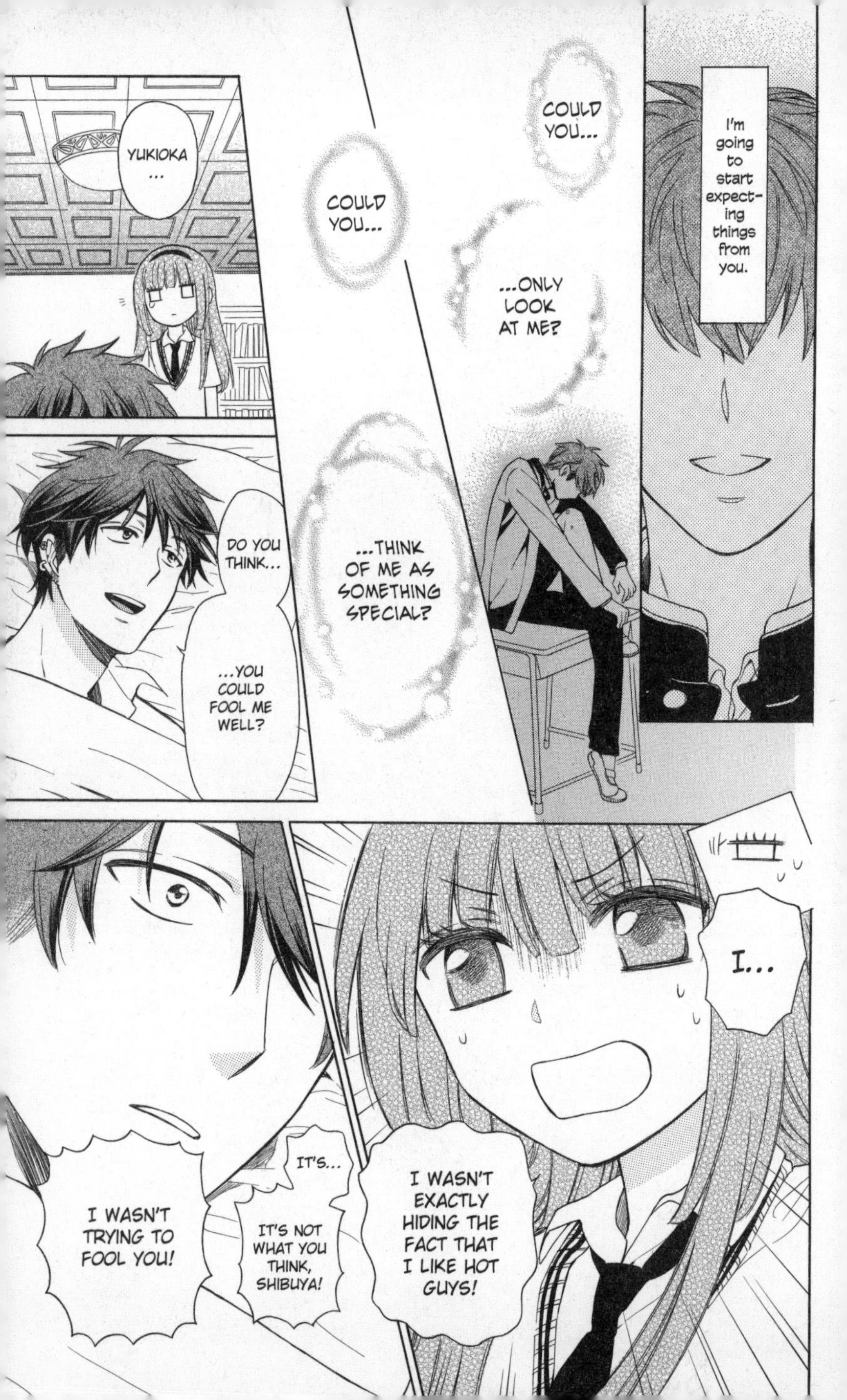
I'm going to start expecting things from you.
COULD YOU...
COULD YOU...
...ONLY LOOK AT ME?
...THINK OF ME AS SOMETHING SPECIAL?
YUKIOKA...
DO YOU THINK...
...YOU COULD FOOL ME WELL?
I...
I WASN'T EXACTLY HIDING THE FACT THAT I LIKE HOT GUYS!
IT'S...
IT'S NOT WHAT YOU THINK, SHIBUYA!
I WASN'T TRYING TO FOOL YOU!

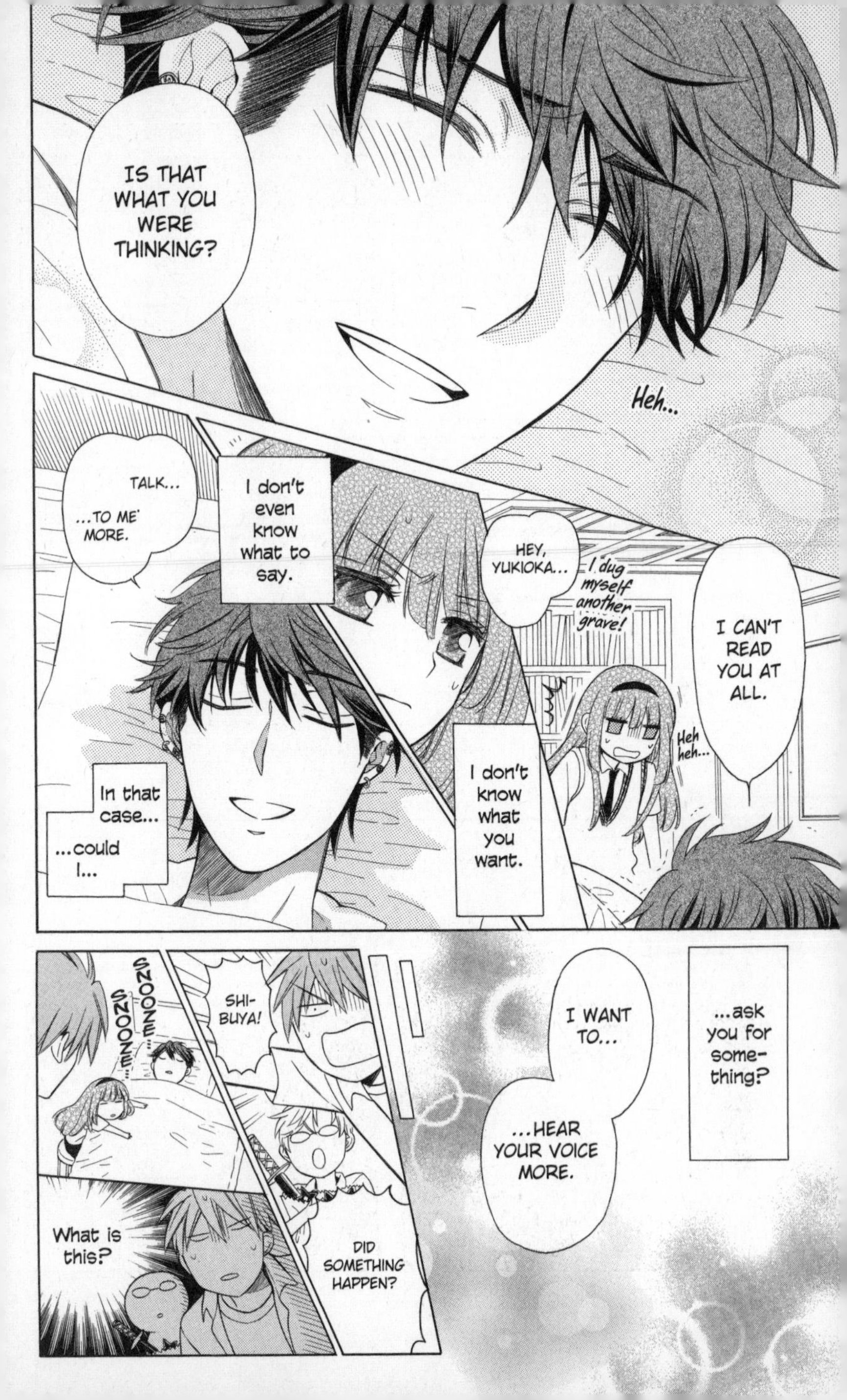
IS THAT WHAT YOU WERE THINKING?
Heh...
I CAN'T READ YOU AT ALL.
Heh heh...
HEY, YUKIOKA...
I dug myself another grave!
I don't even know what to say.
I don't know what you want.
TALK...
...TO ME MORE.
In that case...
...could I...
...ask you for some-thing?
I WANT TO...
...HEAR YOUR VOICE MORE.
SHI-BUYA!
SNOOZE...
SNOOZE...
DID SOMETHING HAPPEN?
What is this?

WHAT?! I'M SO JEALOUS!

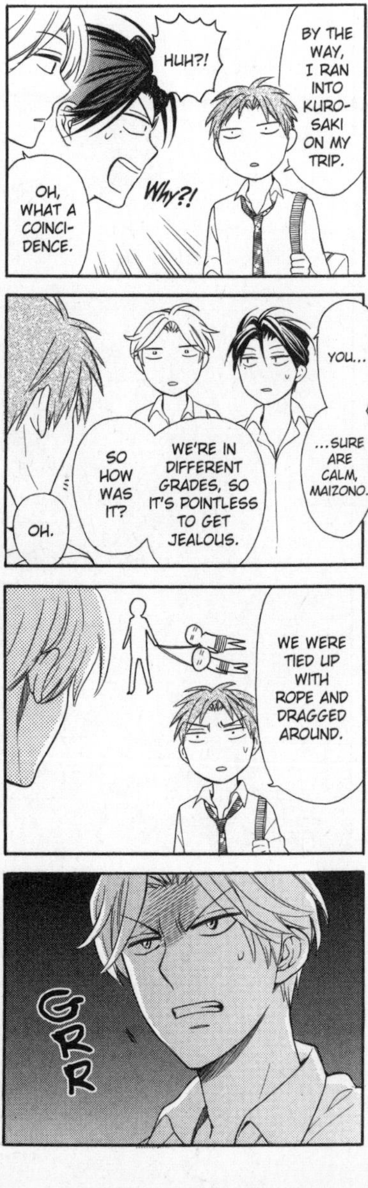
BY THE WAY, I RAN INTO KURO-SAKI ON MY TRIP.
HUH?!
Why?!
OH, WHAT A COINCI-DENCE.
YOU...
...SURE ARE CALM, MAIZONO.
WE'RE IN DIFFERENT GRADES, SO IT'S POINTLESS TO GET JEALOUS.
SO HOW WAS IT?
OH.
WE WERE TIED UP WITH ROPE AND DRAGGED AROUND.
GRR

BUT YOU HAVE ME!

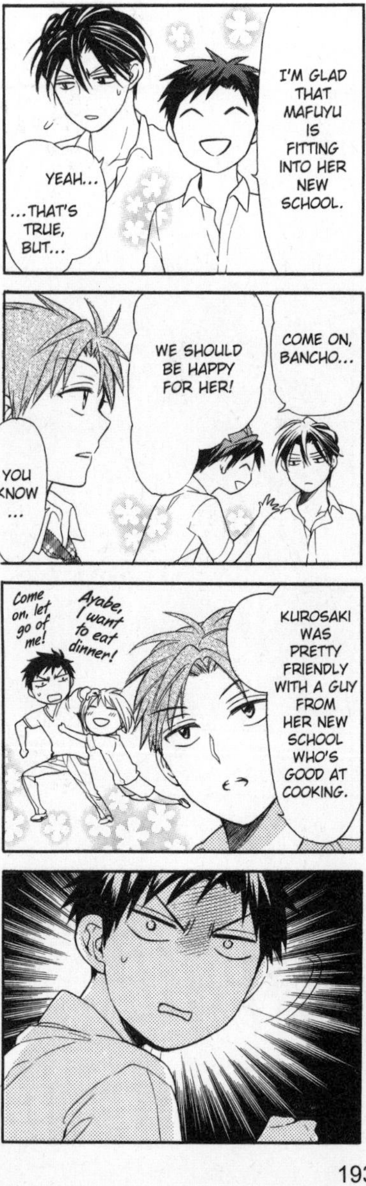
I'M GLAD THAT MAFUYU IS FITTING INTO HER NEW SCHOOL.
YEAH...
...THAT'S TRUE, BUT...
COME ON, BANCHO...
WE SHOULD BE HAPPY FOR HER!
YOU KNOW ...
KUROSAKI WAS PRETTY FRIENDLY WITH A GUY FROM HER NEW SCHOOL WHO'S GOOD AT COOKING.
Ayabe, I want to eat dinner!
Come on, let go of me!

KINDNESS OF AN UPPERCLASSMAN

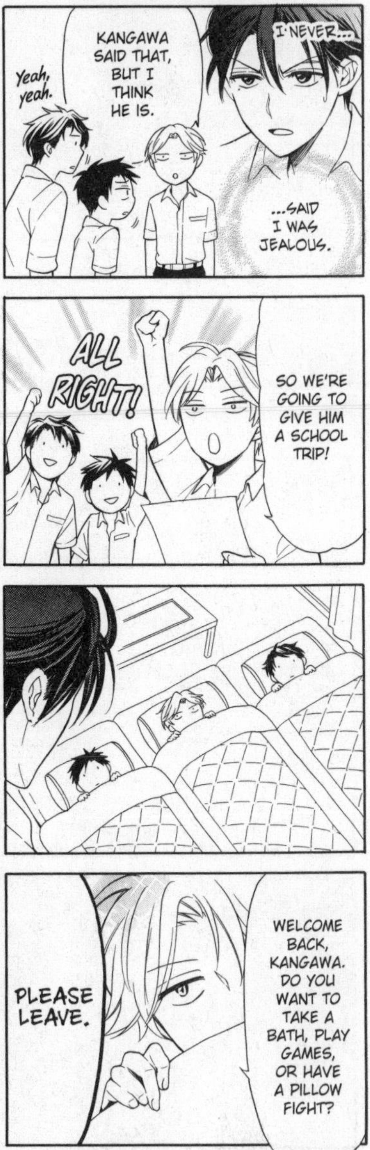
I NEVER...
KANGAWA SAID THAT, BUT I THINK HE IS.
Yeah, yeah.
...SAID I WAS JEALOUS.
SO WE'RE GOING TO GIVE HIM A SCHOOL TRIP!
ALL RIGHT!
WELCOME BACK, KANGAWA. DO YOU WANT TO TAKE A BATH, PLAY GAMES, OR HAVE A PILLOW FIGHT?
PLEASE LEAVE.

BIG BROTHER'S ROOM

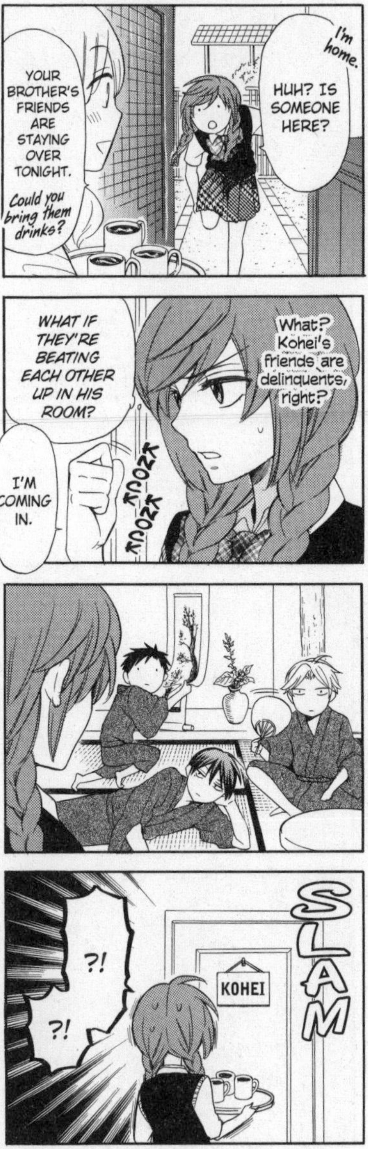
I'm home.
HUH? IS SOMEONE HERE?
YOUR BROTHER'S FRIENDS ARE STAYING OVER TONIGHT.
Could you bring them drinks?
What? Kohei's friends are delinquents, right?
WHAT IF THEY'RE BEATING EACH OTHER UP IN HIS ROOM?
KNOCK KNOCK
I'M COMING IN.
SLAM
KOHEI
?!
?!

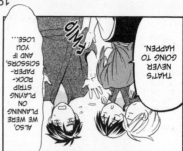

THE MOST SURPRISING THING

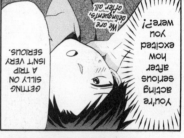

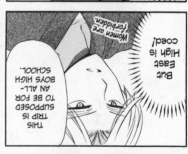

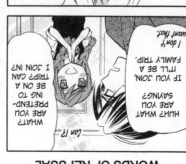

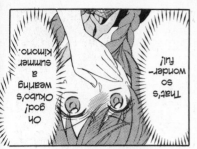

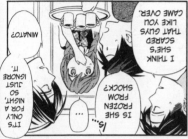

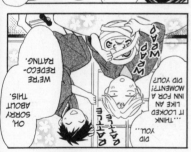

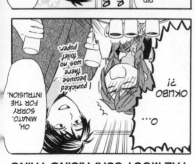

OH, MINATO. SORRY FOR THE INTRUSION.
I panicked because there was no toilet paper.
O...
OKUBO?!
OH, SORRY ABOUT THIS.
WE'RE REDECO-RATING.
RATTLE RATTLE
DID YOU...
...THINK IT LOOKED LIKE AN INN FOR A MOMENT?! DID YOU?
WRAP WRAP
IT'S ONLY FOR A NIGHT, SO JUST IGNORE IT.
MINATO?
...
Is...
IS SHE FROZEN FROM SHOCK?
I THINK SHE'S SCARED THAT GUYS LIKE YOU CAME OVER.
Oh god! Okubo's wearing a summer kimono.
That's so wonder-ful!

WORDS OF REFUSAL

WHAT? ARE YOU PRETEND-ING TO BE ON A TRIP? CAN I JOIN IN?
Can I?
HUH? WHAT ARE YOU SAYING?
IF YOU JOIN, IT'LL BE A FAMILY TRIP.
I don't want that.
THIS TRIP IS SUPPOSED TO BE FOR AN ALL-BOYS HIGH SCHOOL.
But East High is coed!
Women are forbidden.
GETTING SILLY ON A TRIP ISN'T VERY SERIOUS.
You're acting serious after how excited you were?!
We are delinquents, after all.
ALSO, WE WERE PLANNING ON PLAYING STRIP ROCK-PAPER-SCISSORS, AND IF YOU LOSE...
FWIP
THAT'S NEVER GOING TO HAPPEN.

MINATO: A GIRL WHO KNOWS WHAT TO DO

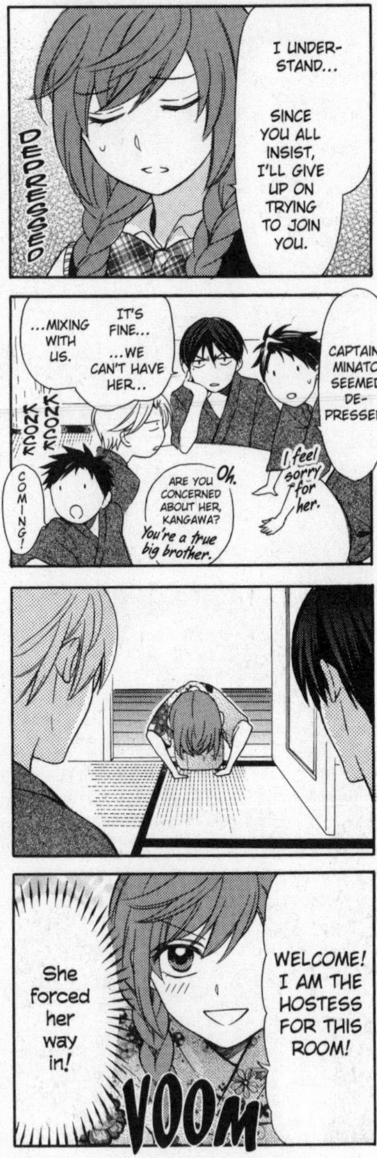
I UNDER-STAND...
SINCE YOU ALL INSIST, I'LL GIVE UP ON TRYING TO JOIN YOU.
DEPRESSED
CAPTAIN, MINATO SEEMED DE-PRESSED.
I feel sorry for her.
IT'S FINE... ...WE CAN'T HAVE HER...
...MIXING WITH US.
Oh.
ARE YOU CONCERNED ABOUT HER, KANGAWA?
You're a true big brother.
KNOCK KNOCK
COMING!
WELCOME! I AM THE HOSTESS FOR THIS ROOM!
She forced her way in!
VOOM

MINATO: A GIRL WHO STAYS FOCUSED

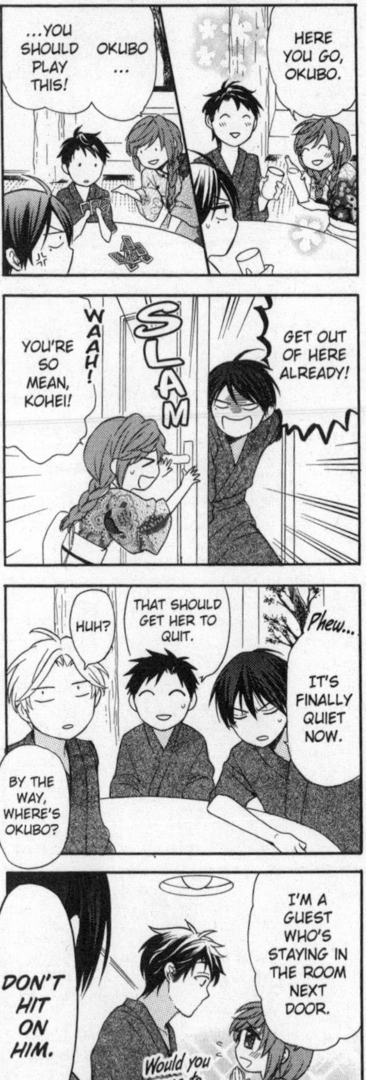
HERE YOU GO, OKUBO.
OKUBO...
...YOU SHOULD PLAY THIS!
GET OUT OF HERE ALREADY!
SLAM
WAAH!
YOU'RE SO MEAN, KOHEI!
Phew...
IT'S FINALLY QUIET NOW.
THAT SHOULD GET HER TO QUIT.
HUH?
BY THE WAY, WHERE'S OKUBO?
I'M A GUEST WHO'S STAYING IN THE ROOM NEXT DOOR.
Would you care to visit my room?
DON'T HIT ON HIM.

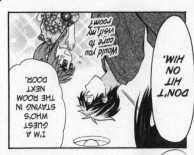

NOT GOING WELL 1

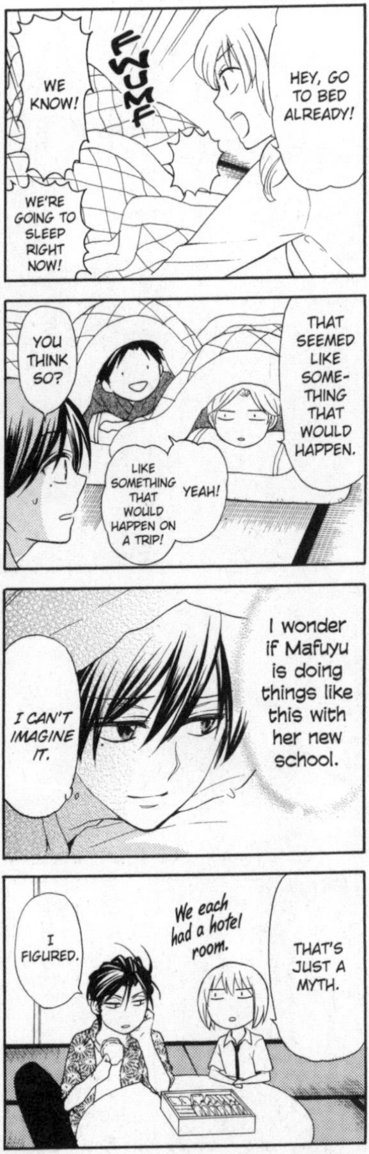
HEY, GO TO BED ALREADY!
FWUMF
WE KNOW!
WE'RE GOING TO SLEEP RIGHT NOW!
THAT SEEMED LIKE SOME-THING THAT WOULD HAPPEN.
YOU THINK SO?
YEAH!
LIKE SOMETHING THAT WOULD HAPPEN ON A TRIP!
I wonder if Mafuyu is doing things like this with her new school.
I CAN'T IMAGINE IT.
THAT'S JUST A MYTH.
We each had a hotel room.
I FIGURED.

NOT GOING WELL 2

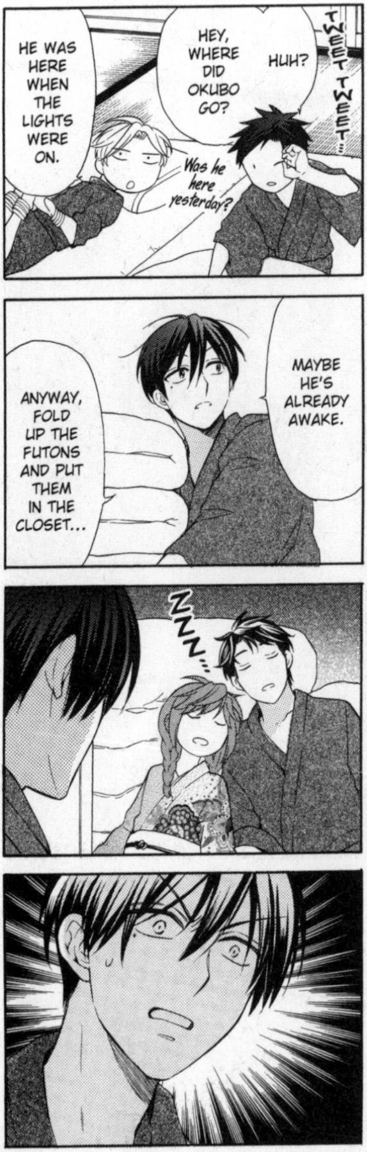
TWEET TWEET...
HUH?
HEY, WHERE DID OKUBO GO?
HE WAS HERE WHEN THE LIGHTS WERE ON.
Was he here yesterday?
MAYBE HE'S ALREADY AWAKE.
ANYWAY, FOLD UP THE FUTONS AND PUT THEM IN THE CLOSET...
ZZZ...

North South East West

SLEEP OVER ARC

THE END

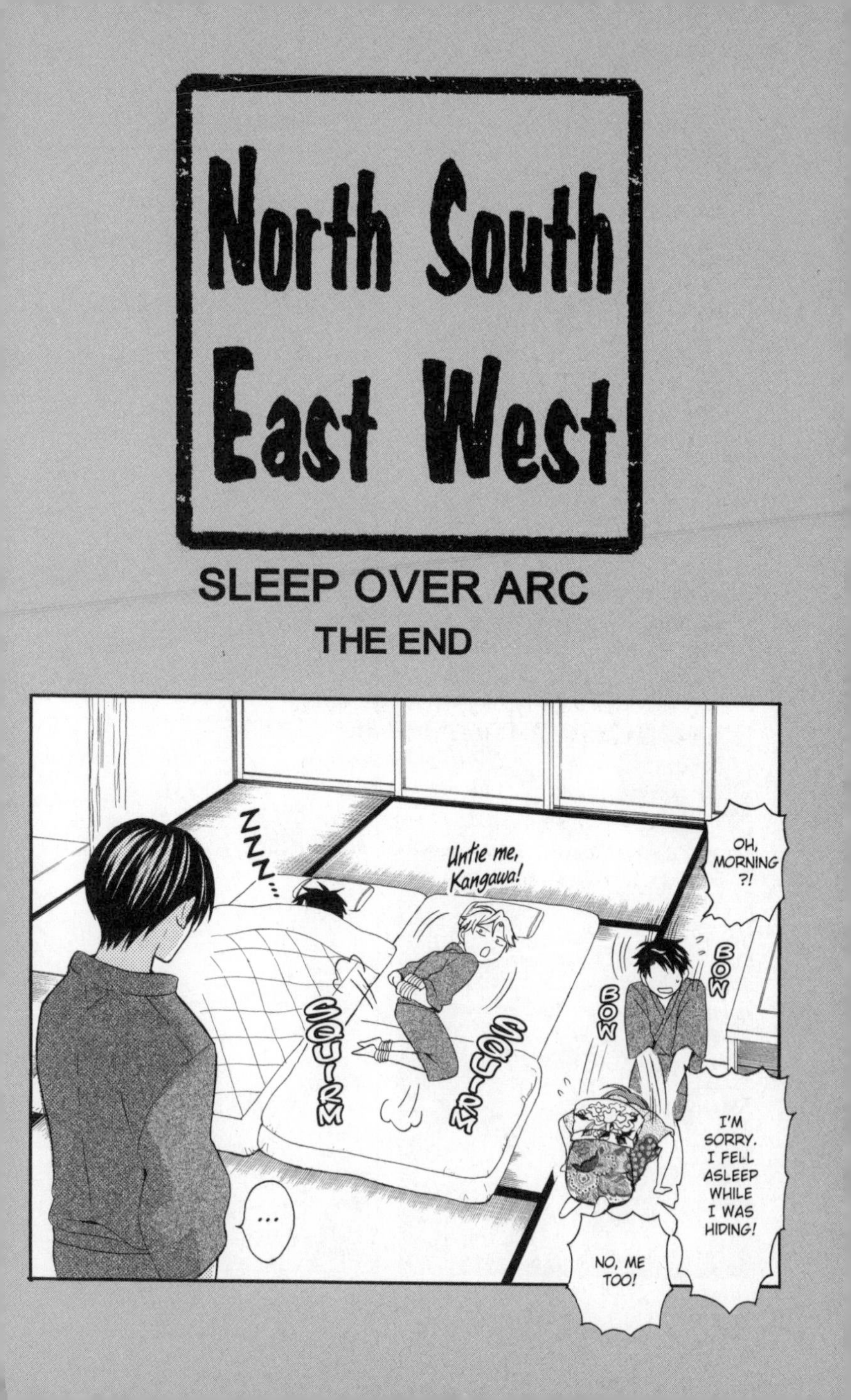
OH, MORNING ?!
BOW
BOW
I'M SORRY. I FELL ASLEEP WHILE I WAS HIDING!
NO, ME TOO!
Untie me, Kangawa!
SQUIRM
SQUIRM
ZZZ...
...

Izumi Tsubaki began drawing manga in her first year of high school. She was soon selected to be in the top ten of *Hana to Yume*'s HMC (*Hana to Yume* Mangaka Course), and subsequently won *Hana to Yume*'s Big Challenge contest. Her debut title, *Chijimete Distance* (Shrink the Distance), ran in 2002 in *Hana to Yume* magazine, issue 17. Her other works include *The Magic Touch* (*Oyayubi kara Romance*) and *Oresama Teacher*, which she is currently working on.

Oresama teacher. Vol. 15
33305233834740
6tgn   12/07/15

STORY AND ART BY
Izumi Tsubaki

English Translation & Adaptation/JN Productions
Touch-up Art & Lettering/Eric Erbes
Design/Yukiko Whitley
Editor/Pancha Diaz

ORESAMA TEACHER by Izumi Tsubaki © Izumi Tsubaki 2012
All rights reserved. First published in Japan in 2012 by HAKUSENSHA, Inc., Tokyo.
English language translation rights arranged with HAKUSENSHA, Inc., Tokyo.

The stories, characters and incidents mentioned in this publication are
entirely fictional.

Printed in Canada

Published by VIZ Media, LLC
P.O. Box 77010
San Francisco, CA 94107

10 9 8 7 6 5 4 3 2 1
First printing, November 2013

www.viz.com   www.shojobeat.com

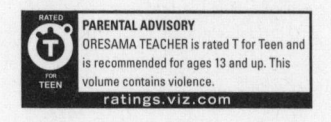